Macromedia®
Dreamweaver® 8
VISUAL™
ENCYCLOPEDIA

by Kim Cavanaugh and Sheri German

Macromedia® Dreamweaver® 8
VISUAL ENCYCLOPEDIA™

Published by
Wiley Publishing, Inc.
111 River Street
Hoboken, NJ 07030-5774

Published simultaneously in Canada

Library of Congress Control Number: 2005938271

ISBN-13: 978-0-471-75176-2

ISBN-10: 0-471-75176-6

Manufactured in the United States of America

10 9 8 7 6 5 4 3 2 1

Trademark Acknowledgments

Permissions

Permissions Granted

The following organizations and businesses have given
their permission to use their Web sites in this book:

Bergamot Books

Burke Veterinary Clinic

Clothesguy

Gemini Piano Trio

Maryland Council for Dance

Prince George's County Law Foundation

Potomac Thunder

Stein Opera

Steve Greenblat, attorney

TODcon

Umoja String Quartet

Contact Us

For general information on our other products and
services please contact our Customer Care
Department within the U.S. at (800) 762-2974,
outside the U.S. at (317) 572-3993, or fax (317)
572-4002.

For technical support please visit www.wiley.com/
techsupport.

Wiley Publishing, Inc.

Sales

Contact Wiley at
(800) 762-2974 or
fax (317) 572-4002.

CREDITS

Project Editor
Maureen Spears

Acquisitions Editor
Michael Roney

Product Development Manager
Courtney Allen

Copy Editor
Marylouise Wiack

Technical Editor
Dennis Short

Editorial Manager
Robyn Siesky

Manufacturing
Allan Conley
Linda Cook
Paul Gilchrist
Jennifer Guynn

Indexer
Kevin Broccoli

Special Help
Adrienne Porter

Book Design
Kathie Rickard

Production Coordinator
Maridee Ennis

Layout
Jennifer Heleine
Amanda Spagnuolo

Screen Artist
Elizabeth Cardenas-Nelson
Ronda David-Burroughs
Jill A. Proll

Illustrators
Ronda David-Burroughs
Cheryl Grubbs

Proofreader
Laura L. Bowman

Quality Control
Amanda Briggs

Vice President and Executive Group Publisher
Richard Swadley

Vice President and Publisher
Barry Pruett

Director of Composition Services
Debbie Stailey

ABOUT THE AUTHORS

Kim Cavanaugh has written 3 books about Dreamweaver and Fireworks, developed on-line courses, and written over 100 tutorials on the use of these and other programs. A partner in CommunityMX.com, Kim has been teaching others to develop Web sites for over 5 years. Currently employed as the instructional Webmaster for the School District of Palm Beach County, Kim also operates his own Web development company, Palm Beach Web Solutions, and writes frequently at his blog, www.brainfrieze.net. Kim lives in West Palm Beach Florida with his very patient wife and daughter who somehow put up with the number of hours he spends at the computer.

Sheri German has been teaching Dreamweaver since it was in version 2, to students in various venues such as Trinity University, the Institute for Federal Printing and Electronic Publishing at the Government Printing office, and the Washington Apple Pi user group. She is a partner in CommunityMX.com (www.communitymx.com), a Macromedia Education Leader, a Certified Dreamweaver MX 2004 developer, and a Web designer who specializes in creating Web sites for arts organizations. Her formal education includes a BA in literature, an MA in Music, and a Desktop Publishing certificate. She lives in the metropolitan Washington, D.C., area with her husband Andy, a lawyer for the USPS, two children, Jennifer and Joseph "Scotty," and three cats and a dog. When she is not developing sites or teaching, she is often taking a ballet class or listening to classical music.

DEDICATIONS

In memory of Freeman Cavanaugh. You are still the best craftsman I have ever known, Dad.
—Kim Cavanaugh

To my husband Andy who has supported me in all my endeavors over the years.
—Sheri German

ACKNOWLEDGMENTS

Kim Cavanaugh: No book gets written without a great deal of effort on the part of a huge number of people. While the thanks could go on and on, I want to be certain to thank my hard-working co-author Sheri German for all of her efforts in getting this book finished. To my wife Kayleen and daughter Katy, my thanks for your patience through the long months where I was absent from your lives as this book was being written. And finally, to all of those who helped me learn about the world of Web and graphic design through the years, my thanks for your time and efforts as well.

Sheri German: First thanks go to my husband Andy who brought home many carryout dinners to sustain us while I worked on the book, and to my children Jenn and Scotty who had to learn to operate more independently. I must also thank my cats for mitigating some of the solitude of writing. I thank all my wonderful Web clients — especially the musicians who entrusted me with their Web sites and who make Howard County the best place for music in the country. Finally, I wish to thank my co-author, Kim Cavanaugh, who has been my most important mentor over the last year.

PREFACE

Project Editor
Maureen Spears

Acquisitions Editor
Michael Roney

Product Development Manager
Courtney Allen

Copy Editor
Marylouise Wiack

Technical Editor
Dennis Short

Editorial Manager
Robyn Siesky

Manufacturing
Allan Conley
Linda Cook
Paul Gilchrist
Jennifer Guynn

Indexer
Kevin Broccoli

Special Help
Adrienne Porter

Book Design
Kathie Rickard

Production Coordinator
Maridee Ennis

Layout
Jennifer Heleine
Amanda Spagnuolo

Screen Artist
Elizabeth Cardenas-Nelson
Ronda David-Burroughs
Jill A. Proll

Illustrators
Ronda David-Burroughs
Cheryl Grubbs

Proofreader
Laura L. Bowman

Quality Control
Amanda Briggs

Vice President and Executive Group Publisher
Richard Swadley

Vice President and Publisher
Barry Pruett

Director of Composition Services
Debbie Stailey

Table of Contents

T

U

V

W

X

Z

Part II: Techniques 135

A

B

C

T

V

W

Appendix A

Appendix B

INTRODUCTION

When we were presented with the opportunity to write this book, we were both intrigued by the idea of a simple, easy to follow reference book that covers one of the most challenging software programs around. As long-time users of Dreamweaver ourselves, we have come to appreciate the power and complexity of both Dreamweaver and the world of web design.

Dreamweaver 8 is the world's leading Web development program for one simple reason. No other program allows the Web developer to have complete control over their Web site and the myriad ways that documents can be published on-line. That freedom comes with a price. Dreamweaver is not an easy program to learn, and with so many options for designing and publishing available, the program can be a bit overwhelming.

In this book we have attempted to simplify the learning process by breaking down the tools that you use and tasks you perform in Dreamweaver into short alphabetic listings that get right to the heart of the matter and show you exactly what you need to do to use the program. Rather than go into detailed explanations of both the how and the why of creating Web sites and Web pages, we focus on the tools and tasks you need to know to get your work done. Along the way we provide valuable tips about how the program is used and best practices for developing your sites.

Macromedia Dreamweaver 8 Visual Encyclopedia is divided into two parts and has two appendixes.

Part I is a comprehensive A to Z reference of the tools that you can use to build Web pages and manage your Web sites in Dreamweaver 8. Tools can be icons found in palettes, panels, or toolbars. Tools can also be specific commands accessed from the menu bar. A named dialog box, window, or panel that is used to accomplish a specific task can also be a tool.

In the Tools section you find short descriptions of the primary tools you use in Dreamweaver 8 to perform specific tasks. Each tool topic includes a visual representation of the tool, what its specific function is, and why you need to know how to use the tool. For those tools that perform multiple functions, such as the Properties inspector or Assets panel, you can find information about the most common ways to utilize the tools. This section also covers a number of automated commands that can be run to improve your workflow and make your use of Dreamweaver more efficient.

Because of the complexity of developing pages in a dynamic environment, the discussion of the tools and methods used for developing pages in PHP, ASP, ColdFusion, and other scripting environments is covered in Appendix A.

Part II is an alphabetical reference of techniques, including basic operations as well as advanced, solutions-based effects. Techniques represent final results from an operation that may involve the use of one or more tools.

The techniques covered in this book have a decided slant towards not only how to accomplish a task, but the best way to get the job done. In many cases there are multiple methods for accomplishing a task in Dreamweaver. In this book we have attempted to highlight those methods that produce the best results with the least amount of effort on the part of the developer, and those that take full advantage of the powerful features included in Dreamweaver.

Included with the coverage of how to perform tasks in Dreamweaver is a strong inclination towards developing with the latest Web standards in mind. You can find numerous references to Cascading Style Sheets and their essential use in the world of modern web design throughout the Techniques section. While all of the methods for page layout and styling in Dreamweaver are covered here, the emphasis is on design that separates page structure from page styling. Appendix B also discusses Web standards and CSS and expands on the coverage of these important concepts.

Appendix A

You will probably begin your Dreamweaver journey by creating basic HTML pages that include text, images, and media such as sound and Flash. Once you master these skills, you may want to investigate Dreamweaver's tools that help you create database-driven Web applications such as Web blogs, e-commerce pages, guestbooks, Content Management Systems (CMS), search engines, and login systems. This appendix explores the steps you need to take to configure your computer, connect to a database, and use Dreamweaver's visual dynamic page tools.

Appendix B

Cascading Style Sheets (CSS) is an exciting and deep technology that is the sole topic of many books. Because of its importance to the field of Web design, and consequently this software, no Dreamweaver book is complete without considerable attention to this subject. The book includes many topics that help you use Dreamweaver's sophisticated CSS tools. You may be new to CSS, and the purpose of this appendix is to provide you with guidance in approaching the topics in a logical sequence, as well as give you a road map for further study.

Kim Cavanaugh
West Palm Beach, FL, 2005

Sheri German
Elkridge, MD, 2005

Dreamweaver 8
Visual Encyclopedia

Part I: Tools

Dreamweaver 8 contains a wealth of tools, menu commands, panels, and inspectors that allow you to design and build Web pages as well as manage all the assets within a Web site. In this part of the book, you find a comprehensive A to Z listing of the tools you need to accomplish your work.

The working environment in Dreamweaver is unique in the world of computer software because it is so many things to so many different people. You may find that you use Dreamweaver as a place to write the HTML code that underlies each and every Web page. If this is the type of interface in which you work, you will find a complete coding environment and some terrific new tools in Dreamweaver 8 to make your work even more efficient.

If you prefer to work in a visual environment, Dreamweaver has your needs covered as well. You can work in Design view and never look at the underlying code in your page. Instead you can use the many tools that Dreamweaver provides to lay out and design pages. In addition to building pages, you can use the numerous Dreamweaver tools to manage and update your site as you make changes to it.

Regardless of your preferred method for building your Web pages, you can find the tools, commands, panels, and other interface objects to work in Dreamweaver in Part I of this book.

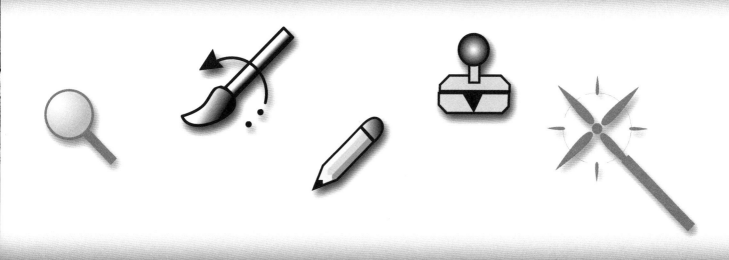

ACCESSIBILITY PREFERENCES:
Edit Accessibility Preferences

You can use Dreamweaver's Preferences panel to help you meet accessibility goals for your Web site. Some Web sites, such as for government or educational institutions, are legally required to make their Web pages accessible for individuals with disabilities.

When accessibility options are enabled, Dreamweaver displays a dialog box when you insert an object that requires additional information to meet accessibility guidelines. This may include a text description of the object or an indication of how users access it with the Tab key on the keyboard. This information allows disabled viewers to navigate through your documents or to use an assistive device that reads the page to them.

For images and media such as video or Flash movies, Dreamweaver prompts you for a description of the object in text format. Dreamweaver also prompts you for additional information when you create a frame and when you insert form objects into the page.

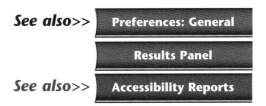

See also>> **Preferences: General**

Results Panel

See also>> **Accessibility Reports**

1 Click Edit.

2 Click Preferences.

The Preferences dialog box appears.

3 Click the Accessibility category.

4 Click the options appropriate to your situation (☐ changes to ☑).

● Click these options to determine which object insertions open an Accessibility window.

● You can click this to type your Accessibility settings immediately after the window opens.

● Deselect this option if you have trouble with dialog boxes in screen rendering mode.

5 Click OK to accept your changes.

ASSETS PANEL:
Organize and Manage Site Assets

Dreamweaver uses the Assets panel to put all of the files, documents, and references that belong to a particular Web site into one central location for easy access. You can use the Assets panel to insert images, select movies for use in a Web page, and even set colors using the color reference that Dreamweaver provides. In Dreamweaver, the term *assets* covers a variety of elements that you can include with your Web site, such as scripts, movies, links, and images.

The Assets panel is divided into nine categories: Images, Colors, URLs, Flash, Shockwave, Movies,

Scripts, Templates, and Library items. You can switch between categories by selecting the appropriate button in the Assets panel to see the objects in your Web site that are included in that particular group. You can also designate individual objects as Favorites, allowing you to more quickly find and insert those objects that you use frequently in your designs.

See also>> [Favorites]

See also>> [Assets Panel]

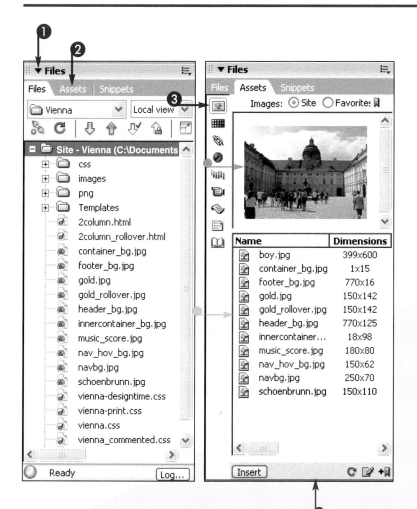

① Expand the Files panel.

② Click the Assets tab.

   The Assets panel appears.

③ Click an Asset category.

● Thumbnails of selected objects display in the preview area.

● Site assets are listed alphabetically here.

● You can click these buttons and icons to insert selected objects into a page, to refresh the assets listing ([C]), to edit a selected asset ([📝]) and to add items to Favorites ([+📄]).

ATTRIBUTES PANEL:
Modifying Objects with the Tag Inspector

You can use the Attributes panel of the Tag inspector to examine and edit the properties that you have applied to selected objects in a document.

The Attributes panel lists all of the attributes that you have previously applied to a selected HTML tag. For example, when you insert an image into a page, you must define both its height and width in the tag that creates the image. You can edit those types of attributes as well as others, such as background, borders, and identification, in this single panel. You can list attributes either alphabetically or by category.

The Attributes panel also allows you to change properties of selected objects. To change the attribute for a tag, you can select the attribute and type in the new value. Where the attribute points to a particular file, such as an image, you can use the Point to File or Browse to File icons to locate the file that you want to use in the tag.

See also>> **Properties Inspector**

See also>> **Tag Selector**

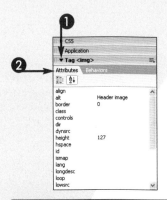

① Expand the Tag panel.

② Click the Attributes tab.

The Attributes panel appears.

③ Select the object that you want to examine or edit.

● You can click here to see a listing of the attributes for a selected object by category (⊞).

● You can click here to see an alphabetical listing of attributes (⊞).

● Attributes of the selected object display here; you can click inside an attribute listing to add new properties or edit an existing attribute.

BEHAVIORS PANEL:
Insert and Manage JavaScript Behaviors

You can use JavaScript to add functionality to a Web page. In Dreamweaver these functions are called *behaviors*, and you can manage them through the Behaviors panel.

You trigger a JavaScript behavior when you perform a particular event in a document. The browser detects the event and checks for an action that is associated with that event. For example, you can create a rollover image by using an event — a viewer's mouse moving over an image to trigger an action — the replacement of the image on the page.

To view, add, or edit a behavior, you first select the object to which the event is attached and then use the Behaviors panel to create or manage the JavaScript function. You can set behaviors to do many things that are helpful to users who view your pages, such as preloading the page images so that the document displays more quickly, or opening new windows when the user selects a link.

See also>>

Behaviors

Macromedia Exchange

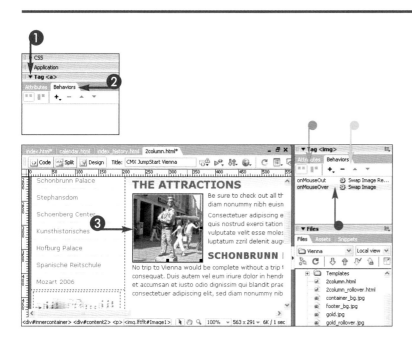

① Click here to expand the Files panel.

② Click the Behaviors tab.

The Behaviors panel opens.

③ Select an object in the page.

Existing behaviors appear in the panel.

● You can click these icons to see only existing behaviors ([==]) or all possible behaviors ([≡]).

● You can click these icons to add ([+]) or remove ([−]) a selected behavior, or to move a selected behavior up ([▲]) or down ([▼]) in the list.

● You can double-click an existing action to open a dialog box to edit behavior settings.

BROWSERS:
Preview Web Pages in a Browser

You can use different browsers to help you preview the pages that you design in Dreamweaver. Browsers use varying standards for how they apply the HTML and Cascading Style Sheet properties to objects in a page. This makes it critical that you preview your work in an actual browser to ensure that what you see in Dreamweaver is the same as what the end users see on their computer.

At minimum, most Web designers preview their work in Internet Explorer and a version of the Mozilla browser family, such as Firefox or Netscape. You may also want to preview your designs in the Safari browser on a Macintosh. Professional Web designers often go the extra step and have both Windows and Macintosh systems available so that they can test their designs in the widest possible combinations of browsers and operating systems.

You can select the browsers that you want to preview your work in and set the keyboard shortcuts in the Preferences panel.

See also>> **Preferences**

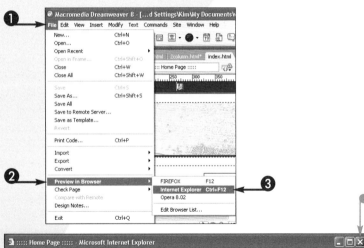

1 Click File.

2 Click Preview in Browser.

3 Click the browser in which you want to preview your design.

The selected browser window opens, allowing you to preview your page.

● You can click the Close icon (☒) to close the browser window when you are done.

CHECK SPELLING COMMAND: C
Using Check Spelling

You can check the spelling in a document using the built-in spell checker that comes with Dreamweaver. Unlike most word processors, Dreamweaver does not check spelling as you type. You must specifically check the spelling with the menu item in the menu bar or by using the keyboard shortcut Shift+F7. You can check spelling for an entire page or just for selected text in the document.

As Dreamweaver checks a document for spelling errors, a dialog box displays with each word that the program does not recognize. Dreamweaver provides you with options to add the word to your personal dictionary, to ignore the single instance or all instances of the word, or to change the word.

When Dreamweaver performs a spelling check, it ignores all HTML tags and other code, and only checks text for spelling errors in the page. By default, Dreamweaver uses the American Standard English dictionary to check spelling. You can change to a different dictionary by changing your preferences in the General category of the program preferences panel.

See also>> **Preferences: General**

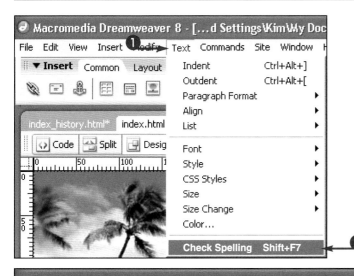

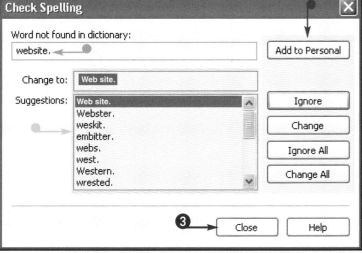

① Click Text.

② Click Check Spelling.

You can also press Shift+F7.

The Check Spelling dialog box appears.

● Words that do not appear in the dictionary display here.

● Dreamweaver suggests replacements and you can select additional replacements from the list of suggestions.

● You can use these buttons to add words to your personal dictionary, to ignore the word or all instances of it, to replace the word with the suggested replacement, or to replace all instances of the word.

③ Click Close when you have completed the spell check.

Dreamweaver either replaces or ignores words, based on your selections.

7

CLEAN UP HTML/XHTML:
Create Cleaner Code

You can produce cleaner HTML and XHTML documents by running the Clean Up HTML/XHTML command. This command combines font tags, and removes redundant tags as well as extra markup and comments in your documents.

When you run this command, Dreamweaver searches inside the code of your document and removes or replaces elements based on the settings that you specify in the initial Clean Up HTML/XHTML dialog box. Dreamweaver then presents you with a summary of the actions that it preformed to remove and combine your code.

Cleaning up your HTML or XHTML document makes it download faster, and makes it easier to read when

you edit it in Code view. Cleaning your code also meets current requirements for how you should format tags in both document types. XHTML formatted Documents get special handing because the specifications for that particular file type are stricter. As a result, Dreamweaver automatically looks at the document type declaration in the head of your page and determines the correct cleanup process to run.

See also>>

> **Preferences: Code Formatting**

> **Preferences: Code Rewriting**

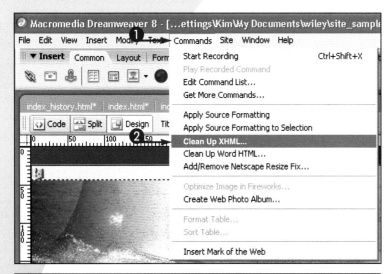

❶ Click Commands.

❷ Click Clean Up XHML.

Dreamweaver displays the name of the command based on the document type.

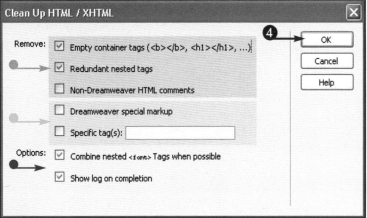

The Clean Up HTML/XHTML dialog box appears.

❸ Click the options that meet your needs (☐ changes to ☑).

● These options select empty, redundant, or third-party tags that you want to remove or combine.

● These options remove all special Dreamweaver markups, such as those used for template and library items, or let you enter specific tags that you want to remove.

● These options combine font tags and display a log of the corrections made after the process is complete.

❹ Click OK.

Dreamweaver cleans up the document based on the options that you select.

CLEAN UP WORD HTML:
Remove Proprietary Word Code

C

You can convert HTML created in Microsoft Word to standard HTML code by running the Clean Up Word HTML command.

When Microsoft Word saves a document as a Web page, it often inserts a lot of proprietary coding, including inline styles, nonstandard CSS, and unneeded font tags. While Word-created HTML often displays correctly in Internet Explorer on Windows computers, other operating systems and browsers may not display these pages properly, or may take too long to download. Word-created HTML can also be difficult to edit

in Dreamweaver due to the amount of code that Word creates.

The Clean Up Word HTML command has a number of options that determine how the code in a document converts; you have a choice of how you want Dreamweaver to handle the cleanup process. Because the process removes many of the required formatting for the file to display properly in Word, you should always retain the original Word document as a backup.

See also>> **Word Document**

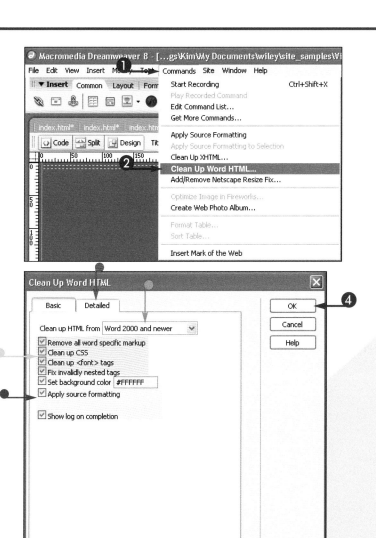

❶ Click Commands.

❷ Click Clean Up Word HTML.

The Clean Up Word HTML dialog box appears.

❸ Click the options you want to use (☐ changes to ☑).

● You can click here and select the version of Word used to create the document.

● These options let you remove and clean up tags and CSS styles specific to Word.

● These options change the page background color to white, run the standard Dreamweaver HTML cleanup process on the page, or perform the requested operations and present you with a summary of the changes.

● You can click the Detailed tab to set more specific options for tags and CSS.

❹ Click OK.

Dreamweaver performs the clean up.

9

CODE HINTING:
Get Help with Code Completion

You can access assistance while editing your code using Dreamweaver-provided hints. As you type your code directly in your page, Dreamweaver reads the characters and lists options to complete your entry. Code hints help you avoid errors in your code because they give you the correct syntax as you insert your tags and attributes. You can use code hints as a way to enter code, to revise code as you are editing, or to simply see available attributes that you can apply to an object.

As you begin typing in Code view, Dreamweaver lists the available tags or attributes that match

the first characters that you enter. For example, when you enter the opening bracket for an HTML tag, Dreamweaver displays all of the available HTML tags.

Code hinting is available for standard HTML tags, CSS properties, and attributes within your document.

See also>>

Preferences: General

Quick Tag Editor

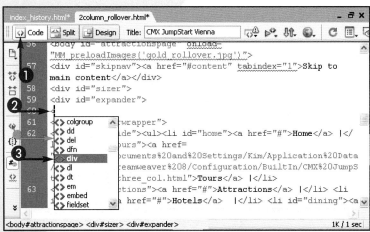

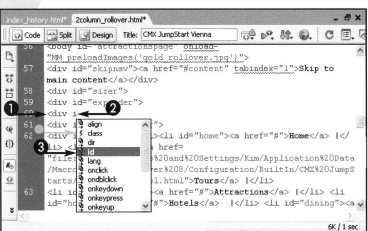

Display Code Hints for Tags

① Click inside a document in Code or Split view.

② Type an opening bracket for a tag.

● Dreamweaver displays code hints for available tags.

③ Select the desired tag.

④ Press Enter (Return).

Dreamweaver inserts the tag into your code.

Display Code Hints for Attributes

① Click inside an existing tag.

② Type the first letter of the attribute that you want to add.

● Code hints appear, beginning with the letter that you typed into your code.

③ Press Enter (Return) to accept the highlighted attribute. You can press the Up or Down arrow keys to move within the list.

Dreamweaver inserts the attribute with quotation marks for entering values.

CODE INSPECTOR:
Check Code While in Design View

You can use the Code inspector while working in Design view to quickly access the code for a particular object on the page. The Code inspector is a separate window that displays the HTML code for the selected object and it displays the same information that you see when in Code view.

Dreamweaver opens the Code inspector above Design view, with the insertion point matching the insertion point location in Design view. When you select objects in Design view, the accompanying code appears highlighted in the Code inspector.

The Code inspector contains its own toolbar for file management, browser checking, reference, and viewing options. It also contains the new Coding toolbar found in Dreamweaver 8.

See also>>

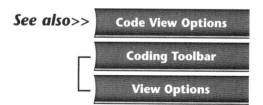

Code View Options

Coding Toolbar

View Options

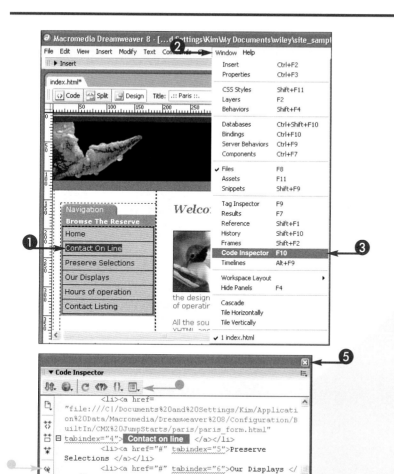

① Click or highlight an object that you want to inspect.

② Click Window.

③ Click Code Inspector.

You can also press F10.

The Code inspector displays the code for the selected object.

④ Click the appropriate button on the top or side toolbars.

● These buttons perform file operations (⊞), check the page in a browser (⊙), refresh the Design view after you change code (ℂ), open the Reference panel (◀▶), navigate inside your code (⊞), or help you modify Code view options (▦).

● The Coding toolbar contains the same options for code collapse and other coding view options as in the full-size Code view window.

⑤ Click the Close button (⊠).

Dreamweaver applies the changes to your code in Design view.

CODE VIEW OPTIONS:
Customize Your Coding Environment

You can change the way you view the code in a document by adjusting your Code view options. These options wrap the text in your code, display line numbers, set color-coding options for different kinds of code, set indenting properties, and show hidden characters.

Code view options allow you to work more quickly and efficiently with your code. Color-coding shows different code blocks using a variety of colors. For example, you can show all JavaScript code in one color, all code contained in a `<form>` tag in a second color, and the rest in a third color. You can also have

Dreamweaver highlight invalid code, which makes it easier to troubleshoot your code.

All Code view options are available via the View menu. You can find additional options in the Code Coloring category of Preferences.

See also>>

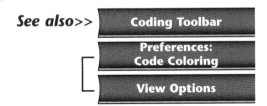

Coding Toolbar

Preferences:
Code Coloring

View Options

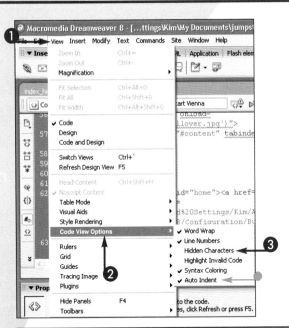

① Click View.

② Click Code View Options.

③ Click an unchecked item to enable its view option.

● You can click a checked item to disable its view option.

Dreamweaver displays your code with the view options that you select.

● Line numbers display on the left side of the code window.

● Code that may not be supported by browsers appears with a red underline.

● Dreamweaver performs code coloring based on your preferences.

● Long lines of code wrap within the code window when you enable the word wrap option.

● Invalid code is highlighted in yellow.

CODING TOOLBAR:
New Options for Working in Code View

You can use the Coding toolbar, a new feature in Dreamweaver 8, to perform many common coding operations efficiently in Code view such as inserting comments, highlighting invalid code, and inserting recently used code snippets. The Coding toolbar can also collapse your code in different ways so you can easily view the code that you want to edit without adjacent code distracting you.

The Coding toolbar is particularly helpful when you want to collapse the code in a document to make it easier to read. You can use the options in the Coding toolbar to expand or collapse your code, based on a tag or a selection. Once you apply code collapsing, you can work with the

markers that Dreamweaver inserts next to your code to quickly expand or collapse these selections.

You can use the Coding toolbar in any coding environment supported by Dreamweaver, including HTML, CSS, ColdFusion, and JavaScript.

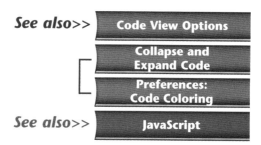

See also>> Code View Options

Collapse and Expand Code

Preferences: Code Coloring

See also>> JavaScript

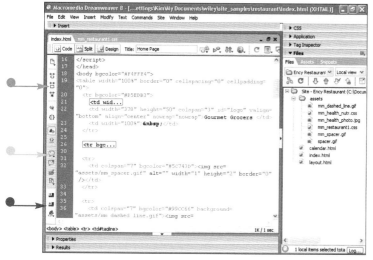

① Open a document in Code view.

② Click the button on the side toolbar that best meets your needs.

● You can collapse an entire tag (⧉), collapse a selection (⧉), expand collapsed code (⧉), select the parent tag of a code block (⧉), or select code within braces or parentheses (⧉).

● You can show or hide line numbers in your code (⧉), highlight invalid code (⧉), apply (⧉) or remove (⧉) a comment, turn on code wrapping (⧉), or insert recently used code snippets (⧉).

● You can indent (⧉) or outdent (⧉) code or apply source formatting to a selected code block (⧉).

● Code that has been collapsed is contained in a special wrapper.

● Collapsed code can be viewed in a fly-out box by hovering your mouse over the code block.

● You can click the plus sign that appears next to a collapsed code block (⊞) to expand your code.

13

COLLAPSE AND EXPAND CODE
Make Code Easier to Navigate

You can now collapse code fragments in a document while working in Code or Split view. This new feature allows you to view different sections of your code without having to scroll through long documents.

You can collapse code that is contained in a particular tag by selecting a section of code in the document. You can also collapse code inside braces or parentheses. Once you collapse the code, new buttons appear to the left of the code listing that allow you to either expand the collapsed code or expand to show all of the code.

These buttons appear as plus or minus signs in Windows, or as small triangles in Macintosh.

When you collapse code, you can still view the complete section of code by hovering your mouse over the collapsed selection. Dreamweaver displays all of the code that is hidden from view in a tooltip that appears as the mouse moves over the collapsed code.

See also>>

Code View Options

Coding Toolbar

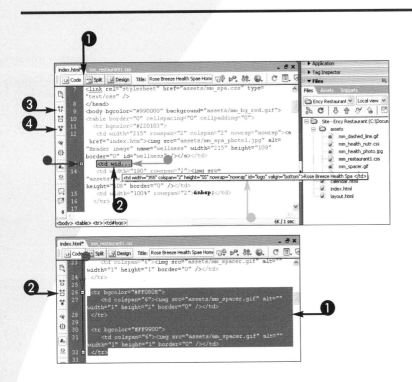

Collapsing and Expanding Tags

1 Click Code or Split view.

  The Coding toolbar appears to the left of your code.

2 Click next to a tag.

3 Click the Collapse Full Tag button (⌘).

● Dreamweaver collapses the entire tag and its contents.

● The contents of the collapsed tag appear in a tooltip when your mouse hovers over the collapsed code.

4 Click the Expand Collapsed Code button (⌘).

● You can also click the plus sign (⊞) (triangle ◢).

  The code expands.

Collapsing and Expanding Selected Code

1 Select a block of code.

2 Click ⊟ to collapse the selected code or ⌘ to expand all collapsed code.

● You can also click the minus sign (⊟) (triangle ◢) to collapse the selected code.

COLOR CUBES PALETTE:
Select Colors

You can select colors for elements in your design using Dreamweaver's predefined Color Palette. The Color Chooser button appears in the Properties inspector, the Preferences panel, the CSS Styles panel, and any panel where a color selection is possible. Selecting the Color Chooser button makes a small Eyedropper appear. You use the Eyedropper to select from the Color Palette or from other objects in your design. You can also enter a hexadecimal value in the provided text box.

In addition to the Web-safe colors that Dreamweaver provides in the Color Cubes, you can also select colors from your system color chooser via a second window. The

appearance of your system color chooser matches your operating system's palette of colors.

See also>>

Preferences:
Code Coloring

Properties Inspector:
Tables

Properties Inspector:
Text

View Options

See also>>

Background Colors

Color Palettes

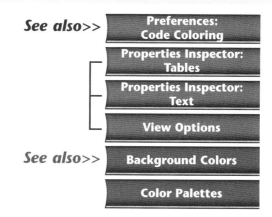

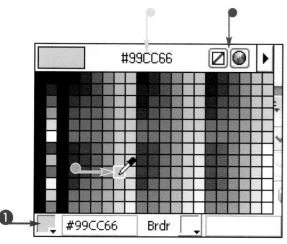

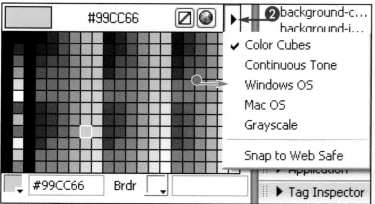

❶ Click the Color box (▣).

● You can use the Eyedropper tool to select from the Color Palette of Web-safe colors.

● The hexadecimal value of the color and a preview swatch of the color display at the top of the Color Palette.

● You can click these buttons to remove color attributes from the selected object (▨), or to open the system color chooser (◉).

Color values are applied to the selected object.

Setting Options

❶ Click Options (▶) to display the Options fly-out menu.

● You are presented with options that display the standard Color Cubes Palette, that change the appearance of the Color Palette, and that force selected colors to snap to the nearest Web-safe equivalent.

Dreamweaver modifies the appearance of the Color Cubes Palette based on your selection.

COLUMNS:
View and Assign Properties

You can use Dreamweaver's visual editing tools to quickly edit the layout of a table. You can clear column widths, set all column widths in a table to a consistent value, and insert new columns in a table.

When you select a table in Design view, Dreamweaver displays a set of markers above the table and above each column in the table. These markers indicate the width of the table and columns, and provide a drop-down menu where you can perform additional operations. These operations alter the basic properties of an entire table and all of its columns without you needing to edit each separate item. For example, you can clear all of the column widths in an entire table at one time, or set individual column properties without affecting the other columns.

See also>> Properties Inspector: Tables

See also>> CSS Styling: Tables and Cells

Tables: Examine and Set Properties

Tables: Using for Page Layouts

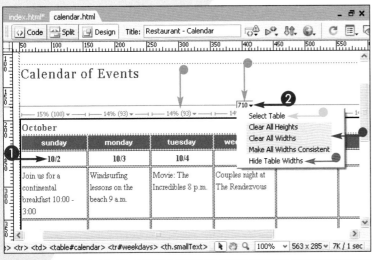

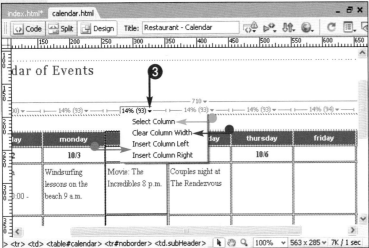

① Click inside a table in Design view.

● Dreamweaver displays information about the table and the table columns.

② Click here to access additional table options.

● You can use this option to select the entire table.

● You can use these options to remove previously entered height and width values or to make all column widths consistent.

● You can click here to hide the table and column values.

To re-enable the view of table and column widths, you can select the Table Widths option using the Visual Aids button ( ).

③ Click the column options arrow ( ).

● You can click here to select the entire column.

● You can click this option to clear the width of the selected column.

● You can click these options to insert a new column in the table.

16

CSS RULE DEFINITION WINDOW:
Create New Rules

You can set and edit the properties of CSS styling rules in the CSS Styles Definition dialog box. This integrated panel defines properties for a wide range of CSS styling rules and organizes them by category.

Using the list of categories, you can move through the different types of available styling rules for the elements in a design. You can create styling rules in the Type, Background, Block, Box, Border, List, Positioning, and Extensions categories. A rule may use one or several of these categories when you define or edit it.

Once you select a category, Dreamweaver provides you with text boxes, drop-down menus, color selectors, and buttons to define your CSS rules. As you select these properties, Dreamweaver

writes the necessary code for your CSS rules either in a separate CSS file or in the head of your document. The location for these styling rules is set when you create a new CSS rule.

See also>>
> **CSS Styles: Create a New Rule**

> **CSS Styles Panel: Edit Styling Rules**

See also>>
> **CSS: Create Embedded Style Sheet**

> **CSS: Create External Style Sheet**

> **CSS, Export Styles**

> **CSS Styling**

① Click the New CSS Rule button (🖉) in the CSS Styles panel.

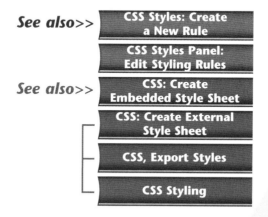

The CSS Rule Definition dialog box appears.

② Click a category.

You can use categories to set text, background properties, and spacing and alignment properties; to control the placement of elements on the page; to define borders and set properties of list items; to position layers and page divisions; and to set filters and pointer options.

③ Click OK.

Dreamweaver creates or modifies the CSS styling rules for the document.

CSS STYLES:
Create a New Rule

You can create new CSS rules for performing automated styling based on a tag or an identifier, or for applying styling information based on a defined class. First, you use the New CSS Rule dialog box, accessed via the New CSS Rule button in the CSS Styles panel, to determine where you should create the new rule, and how you should apply it. The dialog box describes the new rule's basic properties and allows you to determine if you should create the style only in the document that you are working on or in a separate CSS file.

Dreamweaver provides three basic options for creating a new CSS rule. You can create a rule that you can apply to any tag using a class definition,

redefine the default styling properties of an HTML tag, or use the Advanced setting to create a rule when a certain condition or identifier appears in your code.

See also>>

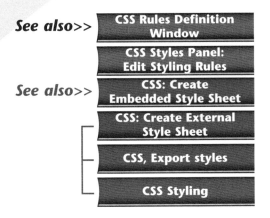

| CSS Rules Definition Window |
| CSS Styles Panel: Edit Styling Rules |

See also>> | CSS: Create Embedded Style Sheet |

| CSS: Create External Style Sheet |
| CSS, Export styles |
| CSS Styling |

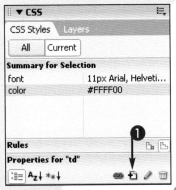

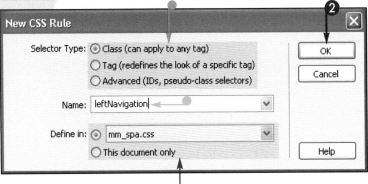

① Click the New CSS Style button (⊞) in the CSS Styles panel.

The New CSS Rule dialog box appears.

● You can click an option (○ changes to ⦿) to create a new class rule, a new tag rule, or a new rule based on IDs or selectors.

● You can type the name of a new class, tag, or selector for use in the new rule.

The options in the Name text box change, based on the type of rule that you have chosen to create.

● You can click an option to select where to create the new rule (○ changes to ⦿); if external style sheets exist for the site, you can select the file where the rule will be created.

② Click OK.

Dreamweaver opens the Rule Definition dialog box where the properties for the new rule are defined.

CSS STYLES PANEL:
Edit Styling Rules

You can use the CSS Styles panel to view, edit, create, and remove all of the styling rules defined by Cascading Style Sheets for a document. This integrated panel completely controls your CSS rules and allows you to view and edit rules applied to either an individual design element or to the entire document.

The new integrated CSS Styles panel in Dreamweaver 8 has numerous options for working with your CSS styles. You can view all of the rules that pertain to a document, or select an item in your design and see only those properties applied to it. You can also see the *inheritance,* or hierarchy of rules, in a tooltip.

In addition to viewing CSS rules, you can manually enter or edit the rules applied to an element in the properties area of the CSS Styles panel.

See also>> **CSS Rules Definition Window**

CSS Styles

CSS Styles Panel: Edit Styling Rules

See also>> **CSS: Create Embedded Style Sheet**

CSS: Create External Style Sheet

CSS, Export Styles

CSS Styling

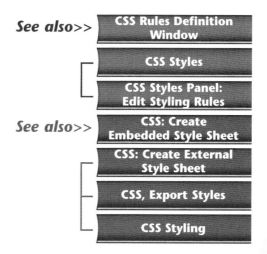

① Click Window.

② Click CSS Styles.

The CSS Styles panel opens.

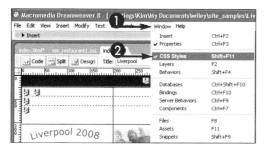

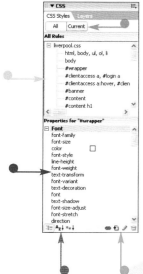

● You can switch between viewing all CSS styles and viewing rules for a currently selected item.

● You can view CSS styling rules, listed by name, for all or currently selected items here.

● You can view and enter new values for selected items in this area.

● These buttons switch the view of selected items from category (▤) to list (A↓) view, or show only those rules assigned to a selected item (**↓).

● Use these buttons to attach an external style sheet (◉), add a new rule (⊡), edit an existing rule (✎), or delete a rule (🗑).

19

CSS STYLES PANEL:
View Options

To better suit your needs, you can modify how Dreamweaver displays styling information in the CSS Styles panel. As Web design moves towards new design standards, many Web designers are using CSS exclusively for the styling and positioning of all page elements. Dreamweaver 8 supports this movement with an integrated panel, where you have freedom to display and edit your rules in a variety of ways.

Dreamweaver 8's new integrated CSS Styles panel displays rules applied to an entire document or to individual styling elements for selected items on the page. You can display all possible rules by category or list, or view only the rules applied to an individual object. The Options button in the panel allows you to perform additional operations such as duplicating existing rules, opening an external CSS editor, and

opening an external style sheet directly to a selected rule.

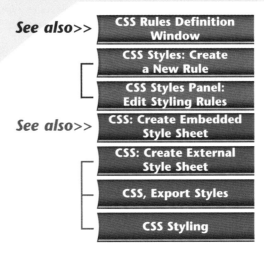

See also>> | CSS Rules Definition Window
See also>> | CSS Styles: Create a New Rule
| CSS Styles Panel: Edit Styling Rules
See also>> | CSS: Create Embedded Style Sheet
| CSS: Create External Style Sheet
| CSS, Export Styles
| CSS Styling

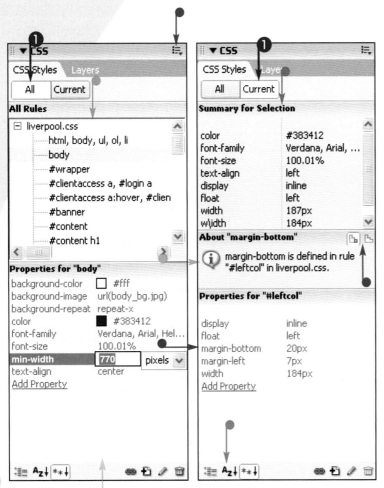

Viewing All Styles

① Click All.

● The names of external style sheets display here along with individual styling rules, shown by name in a tree structure.

● Properties for a selected styling rule display here; you can select a value in the Properties section to edit an existing rule.

● You can use the Options button (▤) to access additional operations and options.

Viewing Styles for a Selected Item

① Click Current.

● Defined rules display for the selected item in the page.

● Information about the rule and its location display here.

● These buttons switch between a view of the rule location (▤), and the rule's position and relationship in the cascade of styles (▤).

● You can edit properties for the selected item in this area.

● These buttons switch the view of selected items from Category view (▤) or List view (▤), or show only those rules assigned to a selected item (▤).

DATE:
Insert the Date into a Web Page

You can insert a date into a Web page using the Insert Date button in the Common category of the Insert toolbar.

When you insert a date into a Web page using the Insert toolbar, Dreamweaver reads the information from your computer and allows you to insert the day in one of six formats, and the date in one of 13 formats. You can also insert the time in one of two formats, and update the date and time settings automatically whenever you save the document.

You commonly use these date objects as a record of when you performed a revision to the document, such as when the page was last updated. For example, you may want a statement on your page that reads "Last updated: March 21, 2006." Using the Insert Date command allows you to do this quickly and with your preferred formatting.

See also>> **Insert Toolbar**

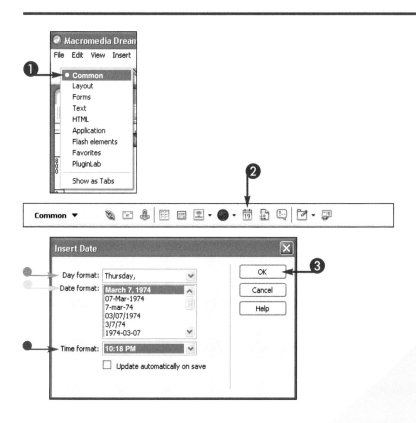

1 Click Common in the Insert toolbar.

2 Click the Insert Date icon (🗓).

The Insert Date dialog box appears.

● You can click here and select a day format.

● You can click here and select a date format.

● You can click here and select a time format.

3 Click OK.

Dreamweaver inserts the date in your document, based on your settings.

DESIGN NOTES:
Add Notes to a File

You can use design notes to include important information about any file or document in your Web site without actually inserting it into the document. For example, whenever you insert a Fireworks or Flash file into a Dreamweaver document, Dreamweaver automatically creates a design note that provides the filename of the source file. You can also create your own notes on procedures and other comments that you want to include with the file. For example, you may want to add notes about the process to design a particular page so that you have

a future reference. You can also share design notes with others who collaborate with you on a site to share information and processes in the design.

Before you can create design notes, you must first define and save the site or page. When you include a design note with a file, Dreamweaver creates a separate folder and document where it stores the design note information.

See also>> Manage Sites Window

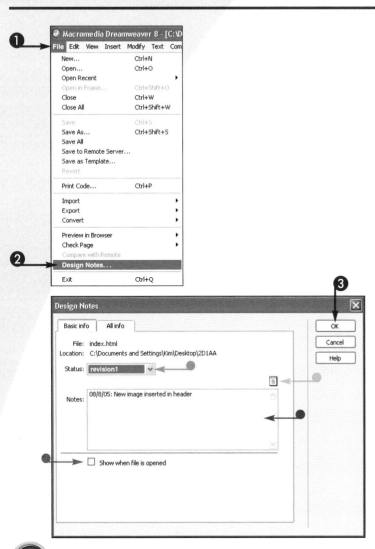

① Click File.

② Click Design Notes.

The Design Notes dialog box appears.

● You can click here and assign a status to the note.

● You can click the Insert Date icon (🗓) to insert a date.

● You can type your notes here.

● You can select this option if you want the design note to open when the file is opened.

③ Click OK.

Dreamweaver saves the design note.

DESIGN-TIME STYLE SHEETS: D
Using Alternate Style Sheets in a Document

You can use alternate CSS style sheets in a document by enabling special sets of styling rules that appear only when you are editing the document in Dreamweaver. You can also use this feature to hide style sheets while editing.

Design-time style sheets are useful when you want to create special rules that apply only while you design in Dreamweaver. For example, when designing with CSS-positioning, you can create a design-time style sheet that shows the position of the layout blocks on the page by using different-

colored backgrounds for the layout blocks.

Design-time style sheets are also helpful when you work with style sheets created for a particular browser or operating system. For example, if you need to support older browsers, such as Netscape version 4, then you can use a special style sheet with rules written for that browser. Hiding that style sheet with the design-time option allows you to work on your design without the confusion of conflicting style rules.

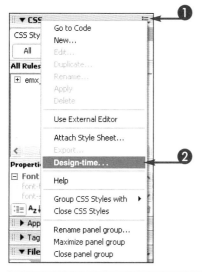

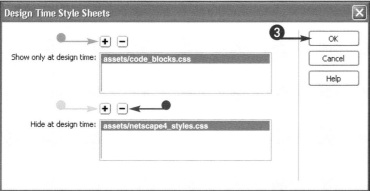

① Click the Options icon (▤) in the CSS Panel.

② Click Design-time.

The Design Time Style Sheets dialog box appears.

● You can click the plus sign (⊞) to browse to a CSS style sheet that you want to appear while editing your design.

● You can click ⊞ to browse to a CSS style sheet that you want to hide while you are editing.

● You can click the minus sign (⊟) in either area to remove a style sheet from the listing.

③ Click OK.

Dreamweaver shows or hides the styling rules that you have set for use during design time.

DESIGN VIEW:
Edit Visually in Dreamweaver

You can use the visual design environment in Dreamweaver to create and edit your pages.

Design view allows you to insert objects and text, apply styling rules, move page elements, and add new objects such as images and Flash movies, while immediately seeing the results of your work. Although the design you see in Dreamweaver is not an exact representation of what appears in a browser, it is a very close approximation, with major aspects such as colors, images, borders, and backgrounds faithfully represented.

Some elements of a design are not active while you are in Design view, such as JavaScript behaviors, Flash movies, and animated GIFs. In most cases you must preview your page in a browser to see those objects in action.

See also>>

Code View Options
Document Toolbar
Document Window
Split Code and Design View
Tags
View Options
Workspace: Macintosh
Workspace: Windows

1 Click Design.

Dreamweaver shows the current document in Design view, and tabs display for each open document.

- The Document toolbar contains common tasks for working with your document.

- The workspace shows the current design.

- The Status bar includes the Tag inspector and view tools.

- You can click here to expand the Design view and collapse the panel groups.

 TIP

Cross-Platform

Macintosh users will be pleased to note that Dreamweaver 8 finally provides them with document tabs. That simple little addition makes it much easier to work with multiple documents without having to resort to Exposé to reveal open windows or constantly move one window from behind another.

You can perform most of the common tasks that pertain to documents in Dreamweaver directly from the Document toolbar that appears at the top of each open document.

This toolset allows you to switch document views, edit the title of your document, check the document for browser support, validate the document against Web design standards, transfer the document to a server, preview the page in a browser, refresh the page, and modify your view settings and visual aids.

The Document toolbar contains a series of buttons that allow you to perform these functions. This section shows you their location and function. Many of the buttons include a menu that allows you to select from a series of options to perform a certain set of related tasks. For example, you can use the menu with the Preview in Browser button to preview a page in any browsers that you have set in your preferences. Where a menu provides additional options, Dreamweaver displays a small, downward-pointing arrow in the lower-right corner of the button.

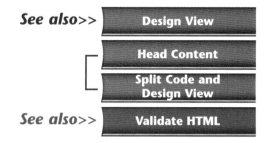

See also>> **Design View**

Head Content

Split Code and Design View

See also>> **Validate HTML**

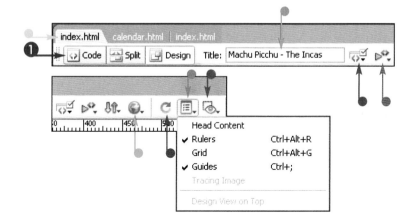

① Click either the Code, Split, or Design view button.

The view of the current file changes.

● The document title appears here.

● Tabs appear above the Document toolbar for each open document.

● This feature (⬚) checks browser compatibility.

● This feature (⬚) validates code to standards.

● You can click here (⬚) to preview your document in a browser.

● This button (⬚) refreshes the Design view when you edit the code.

● You can select View options with this menu (⬚).

● This button accesses visual aid options (⬚).

DOCUMENT TYPE DECLARATION:
Set and Modify Document Types

You can specify the format of your HTML document by modifying the properties for the page. This *document type declaration* passes information to the browser when a page is viewed so that the browser applies the correct styling and display properties for the page. Every Web page must contain a document type declaration. Dreamweaver automatically creates this tag when you create a new page.

Dreamweaver includes the most common document type declarations for Web pages, including HTML and XHTML formats. You select the type of document that you need, based on how you want your page to display and the browsers in which you expect it to be

viewed. For the widest possible compatibility, you can set the document type to HTML 4.01 Transitional. However, some pages do not display properly or cannot use advanced layout and design features when you publish them to this standard. The default document type for Dreamweaver 8 is XHTML 1.0 Transitional.

When you create a new document, Dreamweaver creates the document type using settings that you provide. You can modify the document type by modifying the page properties for the file.

See also>> New Document Window

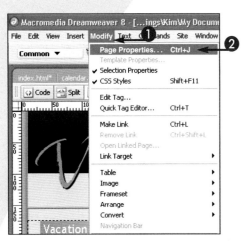

① Click Modify.

② Click Page Properties.

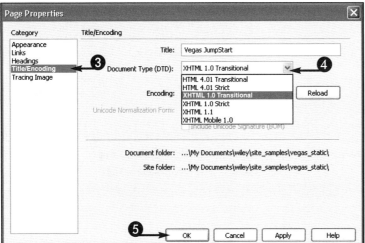

The Page Properties dialog box appears.

③ Click the Title/Encoding category.

④ Click here and select your document type.

⑤ Click OK.

Dreamweaver changes the document type declaration.

DOCUMENT WINDOW:
Explore the Dreamweaver Workspace

You can view your Dreamweaver documents in one of three ways — Code view, Split view, or Design view. Split view combines the other two views by displaying code next to the visual design of the page.

In the default layout, Dreamweaver provides four primary tools for each document: the Tabs toolbar where you can see the filenames of open documents; a Document toolbar for performing common operations with a document; the document workspace where you edit your code or visually edit your page; and a Status bar where you can find the Tag selector, as well as view options and other useful tools.

See also>>

Code View Options

Design View

Document Toolbar

Split Code and Design View

Status Bar

Tags

View Options

Workspace: Macintosh

Workspace: Windows

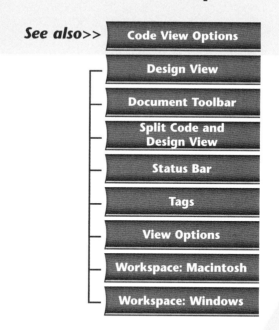

① Click the Code, Split, or Design view button.

The document view changes to the selected view, with tabs displaying for each open document.

● The Document toolbar contains common tasks for working with your document.

The workspace shows the current page in Code, Split, or Design view.

● The Status bar includes the Tag inspector and view tools.

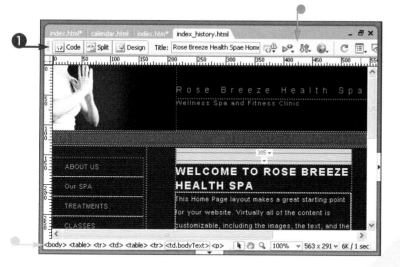

TIP

Did You Know?
Dreamweaver places an asterisk next to the filename in a document tab to let you know that the file has been modified since the last time it was saved. This is a useful visual clue that the file needs to be saved before it is copied to your Web server or closed.

DOWNLOAD TIME:
Estimate Page Size and Download Time

You can quickly determine how long a particular page will take to load in a viewer's browser with the estimated download time that displays in the Status bar. Dreamweaver displays the document size in kilobytes, and the download time for the file.

In order to estimate how long a page will take to load, you must determine the speed of the viewer's Internet connection. By default, Dreamweaver uses the average connection speed of 56 kilobits per second. If you know that your viewers have a faster connection, then you can change the connection speed in Preferences.

When estimating file sizes and download times, you must consider any external files that you intend to download when the document loads. These files, such as external style sheets or server-side includes, are not included when Dreamweaver reports the file size and download time.

See also>>

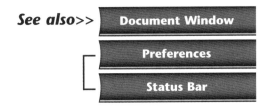

Document Window

Preferences

Status Bar

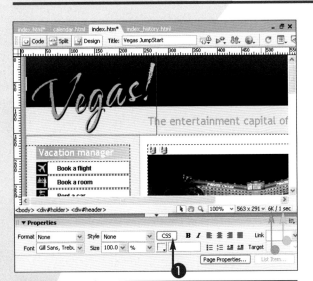

1 Click here to display the Preferences panel for the Status bar.

● The estimated file size appears here.

● The estimated download time appears here.

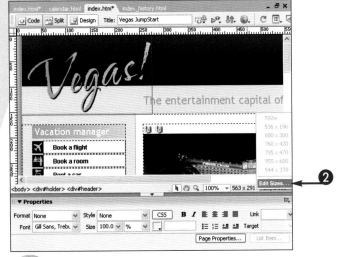

2 Click Edit Sizes.

The Preferences panel opens to the Status bar category where you can change your connection speed.

E-MAIL:
Insert a Link to an E-Mail Address

You can insert an e-mail link into a document using the button provided in the Insert toolbar. This button opens a small dialog box where you can insert the address to which you want to link.

When a link refers to an e-mail address, the viewer's computer opens their default e-mail application with the To field containing the address in the link. For example, if you want the link to create a new e-mail message to someone@somewhere.com, then you enter that exact address in the dialog box along with the text that you want to appear as a link.

You can also set e-mail addresses in the Properties inspector by selecting an image or text where you want the link to appear and typing the address preceded by "mailto:" in the Link field — for example, mailto:someone@somewhere.com. This method gives you more options because you can attach an image as well as text to the link.

See also>> **Insert Toolbar**

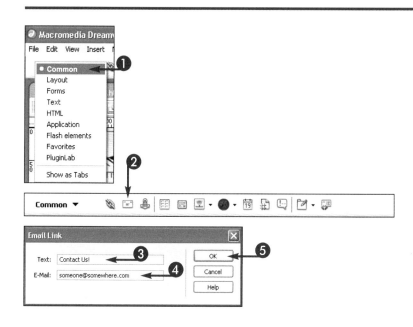

① Click Common in the Insert toolbar.

② Click the E-mail icon (⊡).

The Email Link dialog box appears.

③ Type the text for the link.

④ Type the e-mail address to which the message is to be sent.

⑤ Click OK.

Dreamweaver inserts the e-mail link at the cursor location on the page.

EXPANDED TABLES MODE:
Easier Editing with Tables

You can make the task of working with tables in Dreamweaver easier using the Expanded Tables mode. When Dreamweaver switches to this layout format, it adds extra padding to the insides of individual table cells, and the borders expand. This is purely a design-time device that allows you to more clearly see the contents of your tables and how the table is constructed.

A page that you design while in Expanded Tables mode appears the same as a standard Web page when you view it in a browser. Dreamweaver

removes the extra space that it provides during the design process in this mode before you save the page or publish it to a Web server.

Expanded Tables mode can be useful when you are designing complex tables or when tables are nested inside each other. This design mode is also helpful when you want to ensure that you have placed your cursor in the correct cell inside a table.

See also>> AutoStretch Tables

Tables

① Click View.

② Click Table Mode.

③ Click Expanded Tables Mode.

The page switches to Expanded Tables mode.

● A warning window and exit link appear at the top of the document window.

● Dreamweaver adds extra padding to the interior of table cells and expands the table borders.

● Column headers appear with a menu for editing a selected table.

④ Click the [exit] link.

EXPORT TABLES:
Convert an HTML Table to Tabular Data

You can export the contents of an HTML table from Dreamweaver into a format that you can use in other applications such as Microsoft Excel. For example, you may want to export a calendar of events that you maintain on your Web site and include the information in a printed document.

Dreamweaver allows you to export the data in a table in several formats based on settings that you enter in a dialog box. These options include the ability to export plain text or text with delimiters to separate the columns in the table. You can export the tabular data with delimiters

set to tabs, commas, colons, semicolons, or spaces. You can also select the file format for the tabular data based on the type of operating system in which you anticipate using the information — Windows, Macintosh, or Unix. Once you export the table and save the file, you can open it in a word processor or spreadsheet program for further editing.

See also>> **Excel Documents**

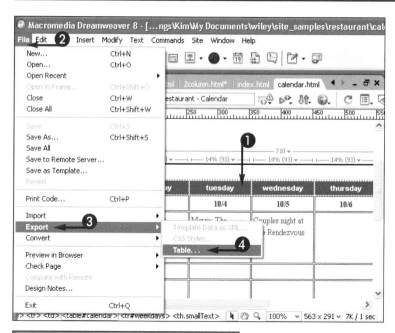

1. Select the table that you want to export.
2. Click File.
3. Click Export.
4. Click Table.

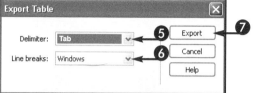

The Export Table dialog box appears.

5. Click here and select the delimiter that you want to use.
6. Click here and select the operating system line breaks.
7. Click Export.

Dreamweaver opens a Save As dialog box for you to choose the location where the exported file is to be saved.

EXTENSION MANAGER:
Extend and Enhance Dreamweaver

You can add new functions to Dreamweaver by downloading and installing software that modifies the program and adds new features. These programs — called *extensions* — are produced by Macromedia as well as third-party software developers. Once you download the file, you can use the Extension Manager to install and manage the extension. Dreamweaver extensions have their own file type and use the .mxp file extension.

Depending on the complexity of the extension, the developer may offer the program for free or it may cost hundreds of dollars. Macromedia maintains a

special area on their Web site where you can find many extensions. You can go directly to the Macromedia Exchange at macromedia.com/go/dreamweaver_exchange.

Double-clicking any file with the .mxp file extension automatically launches the Extension Manager. You can also find and open the Extension Manager in the programs listed with other Macromedia software in the Macromedia folder on your computer, or access it from the Help menu.

See also>> **Macromedia Exchange**

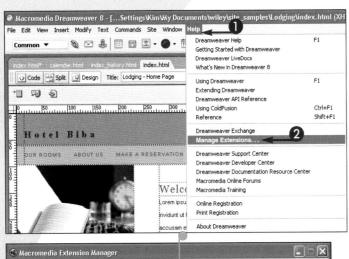

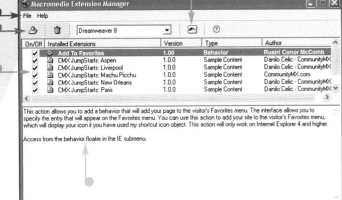

1 Click Help.

2 Click Manage Extensions.

The Extension Manager opens and lists the installed extensions.

● Active extensions are selected (☑) and disabled extensions are deselected (☐).

● Instructions for using the selected extension appear here.

● You can click File to install, package, and remove extensions, or go to the Macromedia Exchange.

● You can click the Install icon (⬚) to install an extension, or the Trash icon (🗑) to remove a selected extension.

● You can click the Macromedia icon (⬚) to visit the Macromedia Exchange.

FAVORITES:
In the Assets Panel

You can use the Favorites section of the Assets panel to store frequently used site assets. In Dreamweaver, *assets* are the variety of elements that you use on your pages, such as images, movies, and Flash files.

When you first define a site, Dreamweaver develops a database of site information that includes the assets that it finds in your local root folder. Because the Assets panel stores all recognized assets for a site, its lists can become large and unwieldy. By adding assets that you use often to the Favorites list, you make them easier to find and insert in pages.

You can create new folders for your favorites to group them by kind or function. You can also give Favorites nicknames. For example, if you have a hexadecimal color identified by the code #CC0000, you can give it a nickname of "red" to make it easier to recognize. The nickname does not change the original filename in the site.

See also>> **Assets Panel**

See also>> **Favorites**

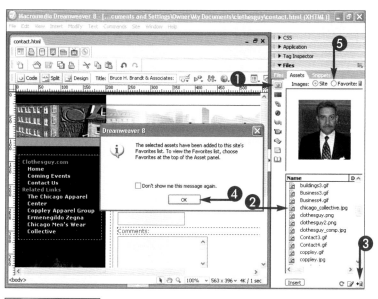

① Click an asset category.

② Click an asset name.

③ Click the Add to Favorites icon (⊞).

Dreamweaver displays an instructional message.

④ Click OK.

⑤ Click the Favorites option (○ changes to ⊙).

Dreamweaver displays your Favorites in the same set of categories as regular assets.

⑥ Click an asset icon.

You can click its name to type a nickname.

● You can click Insert to insert the asset in a page, click the Pencil icon (✎) to edit the selected asset, the Remove from Favorites icon (⊟) to delete the asset from the Favorites list, or the New Folder icon (▢) to create a new folder.

FILES PANEL:
Expand and Contract

You can view the Files panel as either one or two panes. Having two panes is helpful when you want to transfer files from the local computer to the remote server and you want to see both sides of the transaction simultaneously. Two panes also enable you to compare files for attributes such as size, type, and date modified.

When you launch Dreamweaver, it opens the Files panel in one pane that shows your local files. You can toggle to the remote or testing server view from a menu, but you can still only see one view at a time.

The expand/collapse button in the Files panel expands the view to two panes. One pane shows the local files, and the other pane shows either the remote server or the testing server. When you finish transferring or comparing files, you can click the expand/collapse button again to collapse the panel back to one pane.

See also>>

Files Panel: Using Files In

Preferences:
File Types and Editors

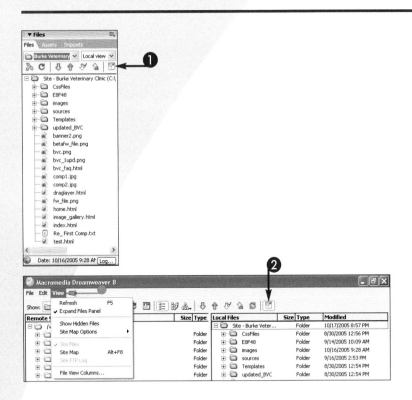

❶ Click the Expand/Collapse button (🔲) in the Files panel.

Dreamweaver expands the Files panel to show two panes.

❷ Click 🔲 again.

● You can also click View, and then click Expand Files panel to deselect the Panel.

Dreamweaver collapses the Files panel.

FILES PANEL:
Using Files In

You can use the Files panel to view, select, and manage the files in a site. The Files panel includes a menu that lists all of your defined Dreamweaver sites. It also includes a menu that lets you decide which of four views you want Dreamweaver to display: local, remote, testing server, or map view. You can also use the buttons to connect to the remote server, put or get files, refresh the file list, and check in or check out a file.

The Files panel includes an options button that displays menus for common site and file tasks. An expand/collapse button displays the local and

remote sites simultaneously or collapses the Files panel to only one view again.

See also>> **Files Panel: Expand and Contract**

Preferences: File Types and Editors

See also>> **Check In and Check Out**

Site Maps

Synchronizing

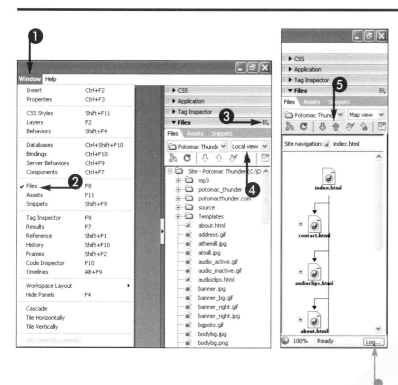

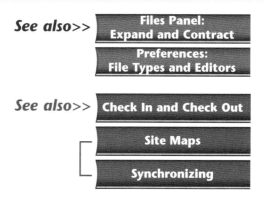

① Click Window.

② Click Files.

By default, Dreamweaver launches with the Files panel open.

③ Click the Files option button (⊞) to access file management menus.

④ Click a View option.

Dreamweaver opens the Files panel to the view that you select.

⑤ Click a File operations button.

You can use File operations buttons to connect to the remote server (🖧), put (⬆) or get (⬇) files, refresh the file list (C), check in (☑) or check out (🔒) a file, or expand or collapse your view (▣).

● You can click Log to save a log of a file transfer.

35

FIND AND REPLACE:
Using to Search Text and Code

You can use the Find and Replace dialog box to search for and replace text or code. You can search in selected text, a document or selected documents, all open documents, a folder, or an entire site. You can use the search menu to define a search in the source code or text of the document. You can also search for specific tags and attributes such as `<p>` tags with a certain class on them. An advanced text search enables you to find text within a specific tag. For example, you can find a word only when it appears within the strong tag.

Dreamweaver also includes options to refine your search. You can select Match Case to make searches case-sensitive, or Match Whole Word to match one or more complete words. You can let Dreamweaver ignore white space differences to reduce all tabs and multiple spaces to one space. You can also select Use Regular Expression to find patterns of text.

See also>> **Results Panel**

See also>> **Find and Replace**

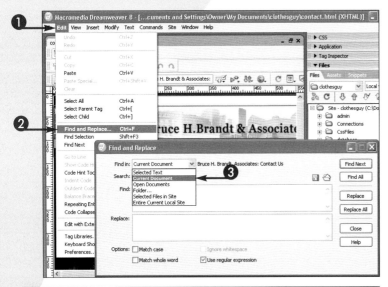

① Click Edit.

② Click Find and Replace.

The Find and Replace dialog box appears.

③ Click here and select a Find in option.

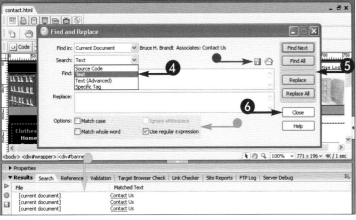

④ Click here and select a Search option.

● You can select extra options here (☐ changes to ☑).

⑤ Click one of the Find or Replace buttons.

● Dreamweaver displays the results in the Results panel.

● You can save a query before closing by clicking the Save button (🖫).

⑥ Click Close.

FILE TRANSFER:
Background FTP

You can perform non-server-related tasks while transferring files to or from the server. In past versions, Dreamweaver prevented you from using the program while you transferred files. However, the new Background File Activity feature lets you continue working on most common tasks.

While the Background File Activity dialog box is active, you can click the Hide button to minimize it, or move it behind other windows to get it out of the way. You can click the details triangle to expand the dialog box and watch a running list of the files and their status as Dreamweaver transfers them. You can save these details by

clicking the Save Log button. Dreamweaver saves the log as a plain-text file, and includes the start and end times of the transfer, the number of transferred files, and a list of each file and its operation status.

See also>>

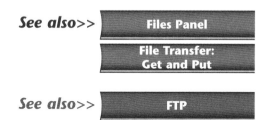

Transfer Files

① Select the files that you want to put or get.

② Click the Put (⬆) or Get (⬇) button.

The Background File Activity dialog box appears.

③ Click the Details arrow (▶).

Dreamweaver expands the dialog box to show transfer details.

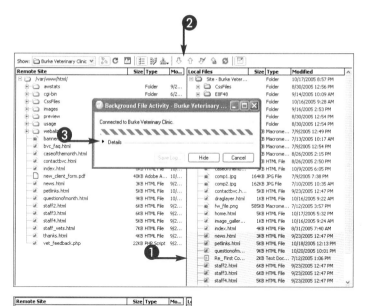

Minimize the dialog box

④ Click Hide.

Dreamweaver minimizes the Background File Activity dialog box.

● You can click the Details icon (▼) to display the Background File Activity dialog box again.

● You can click Save Log to save the transfer details.

● You can click Close to close the dialog box and cancel any file transfers.

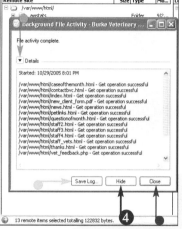

FILE TRANSFER:
Get and Put Files

You can use buttons and commands in the Files panel, the Document toolbar, or the Site menu to transfer your files to and from the remote host. Dreamweaver uses the standard File Transfer Protocol, or FTP, Get and Put commands. When you *put* a file, you upload it to the remote host, and when you *get* a file, you download it from the remote host.

The Files panel uses a green arrow that points downward to represent the Get command. It uses a blue arrow pointing upward to represent the Put command. It is easy to transfer files either way via

these arrows. When you open individual files, you can also use the Get and Put menus in the Document toolbar if you have the Document toolbar enabled from the View Toolbars menu.

See also>>

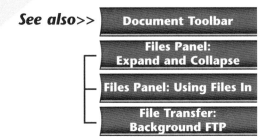

Document Toolbar

Files Panel:
Expand and Collapse

Files Panel: Using Files In

File Transfer:
Background FTP

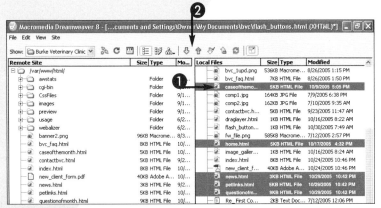

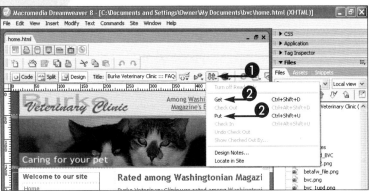

Transfer Files with Buttons

① Select a file or files in the Files panel.

You can Ctrl-click (⌘-click) to select multiple files.

You can transfer files while the Files panel is in either expanded or collapsed view.

② Click either the Put (⬆) or Get (⬇) button.

Dreamweaver uploads or downloads the files.

Transfer Files through the Menu

① Click the Get/Put menu icon (⬆⬇) in the Document toolbar.

② Click Get or Put.

Dreamweaver transfers the current document.

You can continue to work while Dreamweaver transfers files in the background.

FLASH BUTTONS:
Using the Insert Dialog Box

You can use the Insert Flash Button dialog box to insert a Flash button in your page with a variety of prebuilt buttons and button sets. You can set the dialog box options to customize the text, font, and button link. You can even match the button background to the background color of the page.

In the Insert Flash Button dialog box, you can either accept the options, or view what the button looks like on the page before you close the dialog box. You can also cancel the insertion of a Flash button. You can use the Get More Styles button to go to the Macromedia Exchange, where you can

download both free and commercial extensions that add more button styles. The Help button opens Help Viewer to a page that explains the insert options.

See also>>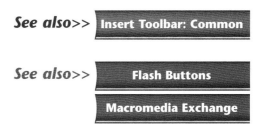

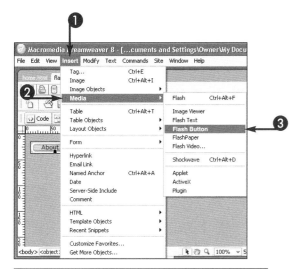

① Click Insert.

② Click Media.

③ Click Flash Button.

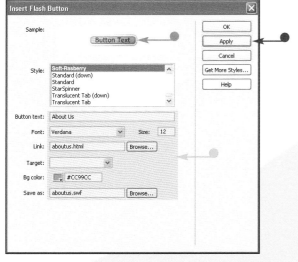

The Insert Flash Button dialog box appears.

You can also use the Media button (■) in the Common category of the Insert toolbar to insert Flash buttons.

④ Specify your Flash Button options.

● The Sample field previews the button Style.

● You can click in these fields and type or select these options to define the button text and font options, to link an optional target to the button, to match the button's background to the page background, or to save the Flash button file with a descriptive name.

● You can click OK to accept your changes, Apply to preview the Flash button, or Cancel to close the dialog box.

FLASH MOVIES:
Insert in Pages

You can use the Insert Flash command to add Flash movies at the insertion point in your page. You can also use the Flash button in the Media menu in the Common category of the Insert toolbar. Dreamweaver opens a dialog box so that you can navigate to your Flash movie, which you can recognize by its Shockwave Flash file, or .swf, extension.

The Properties inspector includes fields for modifying and setting movie attributes and parameters. It also includes an Edit button that launches the Flash authoring application. A dialog box asks you to locate the original Flash source, or FLA, file so that you can edit the movie. You can preview the movie in the browser or use the Play button in the Properties inspector to view the movie in Design view.

See also>>
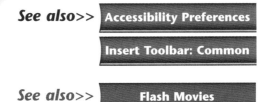

See also>> Flash Movies

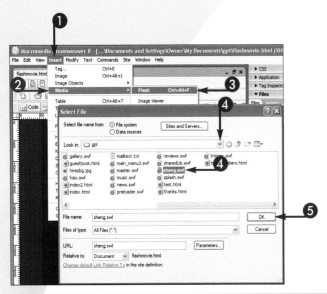

① Click Insert.

② Click Media.

③ Click Flash.

You can also use the Media button (🔘) in the Common category of the Insert toolbar to insert Flash movies.

The Select File dialog box appears.

④ Click here to navigate to a Flash movie file.

⑤ Click OK.

Your movie appears at the insertion point.

⑥ Select the movie.

● Dreamweaver displays movie parameters and controls in the Properties inspector.

FLASHPAPER:
Add to Dreamweaver Pages

You can add FlashPaper documents to your Web pages using the Insert Media menu or the FlashPaper button in the Media menu in the Common category of the Insert toolbar. When visitors load a page that includes a FlashPaper document, they can view all content without loading new pages. Each FlashPaper document includes a toolbar that allows you to zoom in, search, print, and pan around the document. FlashPaper documents have all of the advantages of small, well-compressed Flash movies. Most browsers now include the Flash Player by default, thus making FlashPaper documents almost universally available to all visitors.

FlashPaper can import documents that you create in Microsoft Office or almost any application and convert them to Shockwave Flash files, or SWF. The resulting Flash movie supports Copy and Paste commands, as well as text searching. It also includes the functioning links from the source document.

See also>>

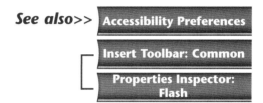

Accessibility Preferences

Insert Toolbar: Common

Properties Inspector: Flash

---

① Click Insert.

② Click Media.

③ Click FlashPaper.

You can also use the Media button (⬛) in the Common category of the Insert toolbar.

The Insert FlashPaper dialog box appears.

If the Accessibility preference for Media is enabled, then Dreamweaver displays its dialog box for you to fill out.

④ Click Browse to find your FlashPaper file.

● You can type a height and width or leave them blank.

⑤ Click OK.

● Dreamweaver inserts your FlashPaper document.

● When you select the FlashPaper, you can modify the document in the Properties inspector.

⑥ Click Play to view the document (Play changes to Stop).

FLASH TEXT:
Using in your Documents

You can create Flash movies that contain only text from within Dreamweaver by using the Flash Text command. You can also use the Flash Text button in the Media menu of the Common category of the Insert toolbar. Dreamweaver opens the Insert Flash Text dialog box to let you create movies with custom fonts and text, and inserts the Flash text at your insertion point.

The Insert Flash Text dialog box includes text options such as alignment, bold and italic style, color, font, and font-size. You can select a rollover color, assign a link and target, and set a background color for the

text so that it matches the page color. The dialog box also provides a field so that you can give your Flash text a descriptive name.

Flash text gives you a wider range of fonts in a format that usually contains less file size than a graphic. Because it uses vectors, you can resize it without losing file quality.

See also>> | **Insert Toolbar: Common**

See also>> | **Flash Text**

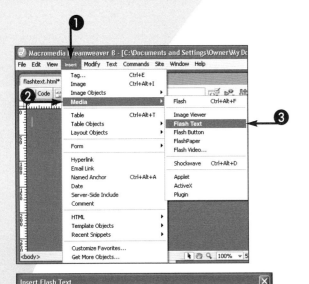

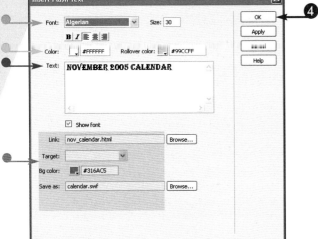

① Click Insert.

② Click Media.

③ Click Flash Text.

The Insert Flash Text dialog box appears.

● You can select a font and size.

● You can select a font style, color, rollover color, and alignment.

● You can type your text here.

● You can add a link and link target, as well as a background color and descriptive name.

④ Click OK.

Dreamweaver accepts your changes.

FLASH VIDEO:
Insert in Dreamweaver Pages

You can use the Flash Video command from the Insert menu to insert Flash Video, or FLV, files into your Dreamweaver pages without using the Flash authoring application. You can also use the Flash Video button in the Media menu in the Common category of the Insert toolbar. Flash video delivers well-compressed movies that include playback controls and only require visitors to have a browser with the Flash Player enabled. The dialog box even includes the default option to prompt visitors to download the Flash Player if they do not already have it installed in their browsers.

Dreamweaver opens a dialog box so that you can navigate to your FLV file and configure its options. You can select progressive download or streaming video. You can select a skin, or design, for your playback controls; Dreamweaver even provides a preview of each skin. You can manually type the width and height of the video if Dreamweaver cannot automatically detect its dimensions. You can also set options for auto play and auto rewind.

See also>> **Flash Video**

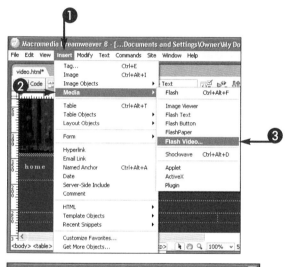

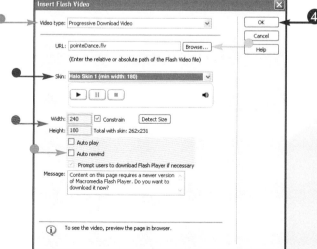

① Click Insert.

② Click Media.

③ Click Flash Video.

The Insert Flash Video dialog box appears.

● You can click here and set the Video type to progressive or streaming.

● You can click Browse to navigate to the FLV file.

● You can select Skin options.

● You can tell Dreamweaver to detect the video size, or manually type the width and height.

● You can select options to autoplay the video, rewind when it is done, and prompt users to download the Flash Player.

④ Click OK.

Dreamweaver accepts your changes.

FORMAT TABLE COMMAND:
Using to Format Data Tables

You can use the Format Table command to add colors, alignments, background colors, and other attributes to your tables. This is particularly useful for data tables or event calendars where visual formatting can increase legibility.

The Format Table command opens a dialog box that includes preset designs you can apply to a selected table. You can use the designs as they are, or you can modify individual options. Dreamweaver allows you to change row colors as well as how frequently rows alternate. You can customize the top row, which

may include column headings, and the left row, which may include row headings. You can set a border thickness, or eliminate the border altogether. You can also apply all attributes to each table cell, or `<td>`, instead of an entire table row, or `<tr>`.

See also>> Sort Table

See also>> Import Office Documents

Tables: Examine and Set Properties

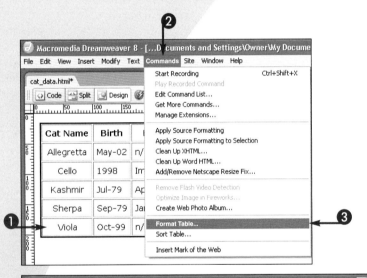

① Select the table that you want to format.

② Click Commands.

③ Click Format Table.

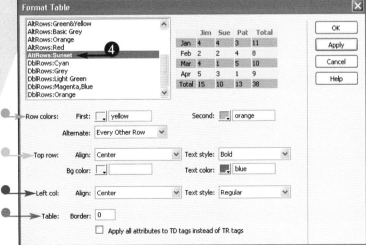

The Format Table dialog box appears.

④ Select a preset table design.

Dreamweaver previews the selected design.

● You can change row colors and how frequently they alternate.

● You can set text attributes and the background color for the top row.

● You can click here and set text attributes for the left column.

● You can type a table border, or type **0** if you do not want a border.

FORM ACCESSIBILITY:
Add Accessible Form Objects

You can ensure that your forms are accessible to visitors with disabilities. When you insert form objects into your page, Dreamweaver displays an Accessibility Attributes dialog box if you enabled forms in your Accessibility preferences. You can add labels, access keys, and tab index features to your form objects.

The Wrap with Label Tag option surrounds a form object with a label tag. The "Attach Label Tag using 'for' attribute" option adds an attribute to the form object tag. This is the best accessibility choice because the browser adds focus to the form object and associates the label and form object, even if they are separated in distant table cells.

You can also add a keyboard access key to let visitors select the form object in the browser. You can set a tab index so that visitors can tab through form objects in a specific order, even if there are intervening links.

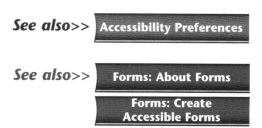

See also>> Accessibility Preferences

See also>> Forms: About Forms

Forms: Create Accessible Forms

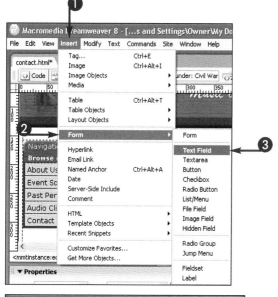

① Click Insert.

② Click Form.

③ Click a form object.

This example uses Text Field.

You can also use the Forms category of the Insert toolbar.

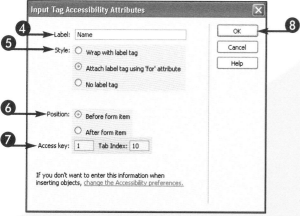

The Accessibility Attributes dialog box appears.

④ Type a Label name.

⑤ Click a Style option (○ changes to ⊙).

⑥ Click a Position option (○ changes to ⊙).

⑦ Type Access key and Tab Index numbers.

⑧ Click OK.

Dreamweaver adds the accessibility code to your form object.

GRIDS:
Work Within the Design Environment

You can use grids in Dreamweaver to help you visualize the layout of objects on the page. Grids are vertical and horizontal lines that Dreamweaver displays in the design environment to guide you in your design tasks. The lines only appear in Dreamweaver and are not visible in your published Web documents.

Grids are particularly useful when you design with absolutely positioned page divisions, known as *layers*. You can enable the Snap to Gridline setting so that when you draw layers on the page, they align at precise locations.

You can change the color and style of the lines in the Grid settings. Grids can display with either solid or dotted lines. You can also adjust the amount of space between the lines and how close an object must be to a grid line before it snaps into place.

See also>>

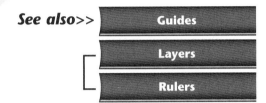

Guides

Layers

Rulers

① Click View.

② Click Grid.

③ Click Grid Settings.

● You can click Show Grid to toggle it on if you want to use the current settings, or click it again to toggle it off.

The Grid Settings dialog box appears.

④ Click to select options or type settings that you want to change.

● You can click Apply to see the settings before exiting the dialog box.

⑤ Click OK.

Dreamweaver applies the new settings.

GUIDES:
Using to Lay Out Pages

You can use Dreamweaver's new Guide feature to precisely place and align objects on the page. Guides are lines that you drag from the rulers onto the document. After you place a guide on the document, you can reposition it by dragging it again. You can remove it by dragging it off the page.

Guides use pixels as their unit of measurement and derive their coordinates from the top and left position of rulers. You can select a guide color that contrasts with your page, and you can also select a color for the guide that shows the distance between two guides. Guides have a Snap feature that works with absolutely positioned elements. You can let elements snap to guides as you insert them, or you can snap new guides to elements that are already on the page. You can also lock guides to keep from accidentally moving them.

See also>> Grids

Rulers

See also>> CSS, Positioning

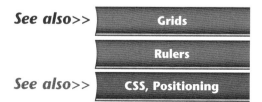

① Click View.

② Click Guides.

③ Click Edit Guides.

You can also click individual guide options to quickly apply them.

The Guides dialog box appears.

④ Click or select the guide options that you want to enable (☐ changes to ☑).

⑤ Click OK.

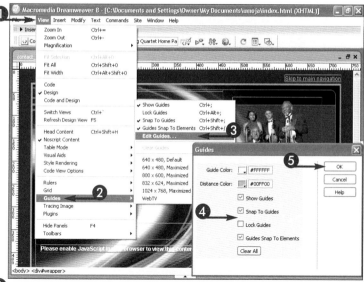

⑥ Position your mouse over a ruler.

⑦ Click and drag a guide into place.

You can click a horizontal ruler to drag out a horizontal guide, or click a vertical ruler to drag out a vertical guide.

● You can click while pressing and holding Ctrl (⌘) to see the numeric measurement of the distance guide between two guides.

To remove all guides, repeat steps **1** and **2**, and then click Clear Guides from the Guides submenu.

HEAD CONTENT:
View and Edit Tags in the Head of a Document

You can view the code that makes up the hidden part of a Web page by using the Head view option. When you select this option, a new toolbar appears below the Document toolbar with buttons that allow you to see the head content in the page.

Typical head content includes the page title, MetaTags such as keywords and page descriptions. It may also include links to CSS style sheets and JavaScript. Because this content is invisible in Design view, using this option allows you to select head content and view or edit its attributes in the Properties inspector.

You can also edit the head of the document by working in Code view.

When the Head Content toolbar is activated, you can select the button that corresponds to the content that you want to view or edit. The Properties inspector displays the content that is listed in the page when you select the button.

See also>>    Document Toolbar

See also>>   MetaTags

① Click View.

② Click Head Content.

The Head Content toolbar appears below the Document toolbar.

● Buttons appear for each instance of meta content, title, links, scripts, and comments.

③ Click the head tag that you want to view or edit.

● The tag properties appear in the Properties inspector, and you can enter or edit these properties.

Dreamweaver modifies the code in the head of your document as you make changes in the Properties inspector.

HISTORY PANEL:
Track Changes in a Document

You can use the History panel to track every change that you make to a document. This is a useful way to undo or redo edits that you make to a page. In addition, you can use the History panel to create custom commands that repeat a step or series of steps that you have taken in a document. These custom commands that you create are terrific timesavers when you need to perform repetitive operations in a series of documents.

Once you create a custom command, you can use that command in any Dreamweaver document.

For example, if you frequently insert a table with a certain number of rows and columns, then you can create a custom command that automatically inserts and formats the table.

While the History panel lists each step that you take to edit a document, some actions, such as moving an object with the mouse, cannot be automated. Dreamweaver lists those steps with a black line to separate them from adjacent steps.

See also>> **Preferences: General**

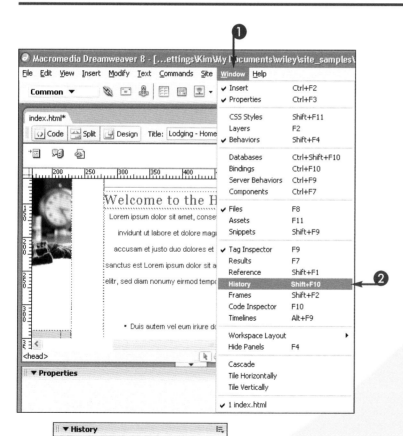

① Click Window.

② Click History.

The History panel opens and lists each change to the document.

● A separator bar appears between steps that you cannot combine to make a command.

● You can click and drag the slider to undo or redo steps.

● Buttons at the bottom of the panel allow you to replay steps, copy steps (🖹), or save selected steps (🖫) as a custom command.

INSERT TOOLBAR:
Application

You can use the Applications category of the Insert toolbar to place a variety of dynamic objects into your Web pages, such as dynamic data, recordsets, and user authentication.

The Insert toolbar contains a row of buttons that show the different types of dynamic objects that you can insert into a page. In some cases, you can insert additional objects through a drop-down menu. Buttons that contain multiple objects have a small triangle on their right side.

You can also insert Application objects into pages that are designed to work with dynamic data such as ASP, PHP, or ColdFusion. Pages that contain dynamic

objects must have the appropriate file extension that matches the server language that you are using. For example, a site using the ColdFusion server language has pages with the .cfm file extension. You can find out more about dynamic Web design in Appendix A.

See also>> Insert Toolbar: View Options

See also>> Appendix A

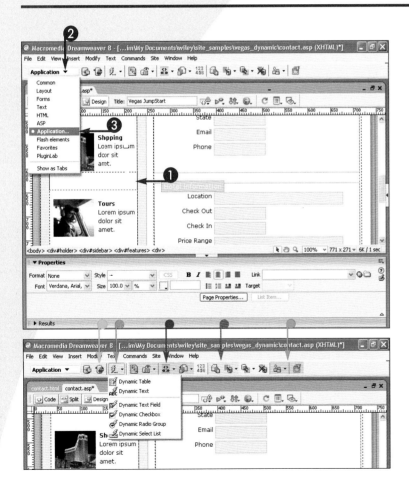

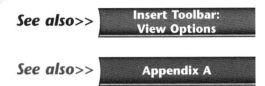

① Click inside the document where you want to insert the object.

② Click the Insert toolbar drop-down arrow (▼).

You can click the Applications tab if you are using the tabbed view of the Insert toolbar.

③ Click Application.

The Insert toolbar displays application objects.

● Buttons with multiple options display an arrow (▼) on the right.

● These buttons insert recordsets (⬚), commands (⬚), and dynamic data (⬚).

● These buttons insert dynamic regions (⬚), set region view properties (⬚), and insert recordset (⬚) and dynamic navigation (⬚).

● These buttons insert master page details (⬚) and records for database detail pages (⬚).

● These buttons are used to create user authentication (⬚) and to insert XSLT fragments into dynamic pages (⬚).

INSERT TOOLBAR:
Common

You can insert the most frequently used objects that appear in a Web page using the Common category of the Insert toolbar. These common objects include links, tables, images, Flash elements, and media. You can also insert HTML objects such as page divisions and comments, and access Dreamweaver template objects and the Tag chooser from the Common category.

Buttons in the Insert toolbar that contain multiple objects have a small arrow on their right, which means they have additional items. For example, when you select the Images button, you can insert items such as images, rollover images, Fireworks HTML, and a navigation bar.

Activating a button in the Insert toolbar displays a dialog box with additional information about the object that you are inserting. Depending what item you select, you may need to browse to the file that you are inserting, or provide formatting information for the selected object.

See also>>

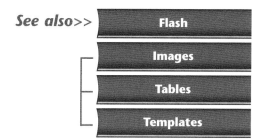

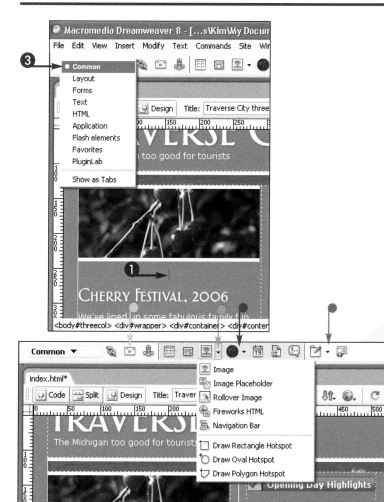

① Click inside the document where you want to insert the object.

② Click the Insert toolbar drop-down arrow (▼).

You can click the Common tab if you are using the tabbed view of the Insert toolbar.

③ Click Common.

The Insert toolbar displays common objects.

● Buttons with multiple options display an arrow on their right.

● You can use these buttons to insert links (🖫), e-mail links (🖻), and page anchors (🖾).

● You can use these buttons to insert tables (🖽), page divisions (🖾), image objects (🖾), Flash and media objects (●), dates (🖾), Server-Side Includes (🖾), and comments (🖾).

● You can use these buttons to insert template objects (🖾) and to access the Tag Selector (🖾).

INSERT TOOLBAR:
Favorites

You can designate certain items in the Insert toolbar as your personal favorites in order to provide quick access to those items that you most frequently insert into your documents. This feature allows you to build your own custom Insert toolbar that shows only those items that you want to appear.

Dreamweaver provides a dialog box where you can add, remove, or arrange the order of the objects that appear in the Favorites category of the Insert toolbar. To add an item to your favorites, you can choose from the available objects in the left pane of the dialog box. To remove an object from the Favorites

category of the Insert toolbar, you use the right pane in the dialog box. You can also change the order of items in the Favorites menu or add a separator bar between objects to further customize its appearance. Items are organized in the Favorites Insert toolbar from right to left.

Once you add items to the Favorites category, you can use them in the same manner as buttons in other Insert toolbars.

See also>> **Insert Toolbar:
View Options**

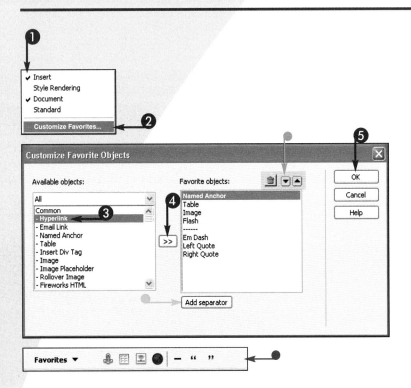

① Right-click (Ctrl-click) in the Insert toolbar.

② Click Customize Favorites.

The Customize Favorite Objects dialog box appears.

③ Click an item that you want to add as a favorite.

④ Click the arrow button ([>>]).

Dreamweaver adds the item to your favorites.

● You can click the Trash icon ([🗑]) to delete a selected item from the Favorites Insert toolbar, or you can move selected items up ([▲]) or down ([▼]) in the listing.

● You can use this button to add a separator line between items.

⑤ Click OK.

● The selected items appear in the Favorites Insert toolbar.

INSERT TOOLBAR:
Forms

You can insert a number of form objects with the Insert toolbar, including the form tag, text fields, hidden fields, text areas, check boxes, radio buttons, radio button groups, lists and menus, jump menus, image fields, file fields, buttons, labels, and fieldsets.

To insert form objects, you must first insert a form tag. If you do not, Dreamweaver prompts you to insert the necessary tag. If you enable accessibility attributes in your preferences, Dreamweaver also prompts you to create a label and provide access key and tab index properties for the form.

Once the form objects are in place, you must provide the required information in the Properties

inspector for the scripts and functions required to process the form and the included objects.

See also>> **Insert Toolbar: View Options**

See also>> **Forms: Insert Check Boxes and Radio Buttons**

Forms: Insert Fields

Forms: Insert Hidden Fields

Forms: Insert Text Fields

Jump Menus

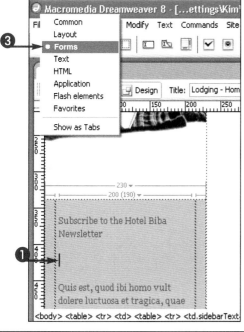

① Click inside the document where you want to insert the form object.

② Click the Insert toolbar drop-down arrow (▼).

You can click the Common tab if you are using the tabbed view of the Insert toolbar.

③ Click Forms.

The Insert toolbar displays form objects.

● Click this button (▢) to insert a form tag.

● Click these buttons to insert text fields (▣), hidden fields (▣), text areas (▢), check boxes (☑), radio buttons (▢), or radio groups (▤).

● Click these buttons to insert lists and menus (▣), jump menus (▨), image fields (▣), file fields (▣), and buttons (▢).

● You can use these buttons to insert a label tag (▣) or fieldsets (▢).

INSERT TOOLBAR:
HTML

You can insert a wide range of tags in both Design and Code view from the HTML category of the Insert toolbar.

In Design view, you can insert a horizontal rule as well as a MetaTag, keywords, a page description, a Refresh command, a base tag, and a link. You can also insert a script tag, a no-script tag, and a Server-Side Include.

While in Code or Split view, you can add table objects directly into your code, including table tags, table rows, table header cells, table data cells, and a table caption. You can also insert frame objects in Code view, such as a frame, frameset, or a floating

frame. After you insert the basic tag, you must add attributes to the tag in Code view or through the Properties inspector.

In the Insert toolbar, a button with multiple objects has a small arrow on its right. This arrow opens additional items for insertion.

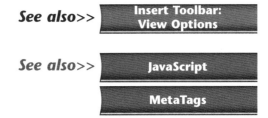

See also>> **Insert Toolbar: View Options**

See also>> **JavaScript**

MetaTags

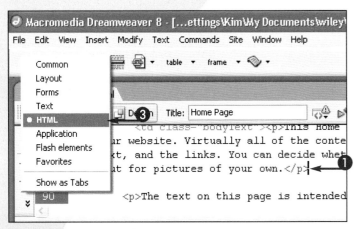

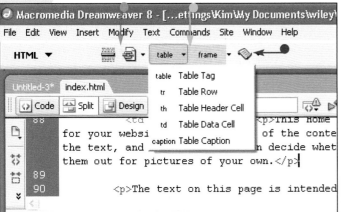

① Click inside the document where you want to insert the form object.

For table and frame objects, your cursor must be in the Code view window.

② Click the Insert toolbar drop-down arrow (▼).

You can click the HTML tab if you are using the tabbed view of the Insert toolbar.

③ Click HTML.

The Insert toolbar displays HTML objects.

Buttons with multiple options display an arrow on the right.

● You can click these buttons to insert a horizontal rule (▦), or to insert MetaTags, keywords, descriptions, a page refresh tag, a base tag, or a link tag (▣).

● You can use these buttons to add table and frame tags.

● You can click this button (▨) to insert a script or no-script tag.

INSERT TOOLBAR:
Layout

You can use the Layout category of the Insert toolbar to switch the Design view of Dreamweaver into a more visual editing mode where you can draw tables and table objects on the screen. This allows you to create a complete page design with the separate areas of your page in the positions that you want, with freedom to move the layout blocks around the page. Once you complete your layout design, you can add content to the page.

Layout mode uses tables and table cells to create the containers that you use for your page content. From the Insert toolbar, you can add new layout

tables, insert page divisions or DIV tags, draw layers, and modify existing layout tables. You can also create frameset and frame objects, as well as insert tabular data from a data file such as an Excel document. You can also use the buttons in the Insert toolbar to switch between Standard view, Expanded Tables view, and Layout view in the Design Window.

See also>> **Tables:
Using for Page Layout**

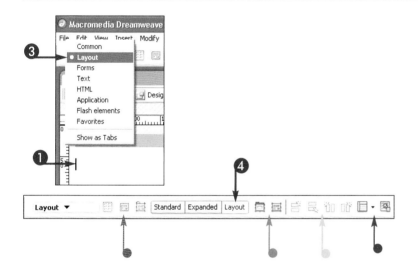

① Click inside the document where you want to insert a layout object.

② Click the Insert toolbar drop-down arrow (▼).

You can click the Layout tab if you are using the tabbed view of the Insert toolbar.

③ Click Layout.

The Insert toolbar displays layout objects.

④ Click Layout.

● These buttons add a new layout table (▦) or let you draw a layout cell inside a layout table (▦).

● These buttons add new rows above (▦) or below (▦) a selected row, or to the left (▦) or right (▦) of a selected column.

● These buttons add frame objects (▦) or tabular data (▦).

● These buttons are active only when in Standard or Expanded Tables mode, and are used to insert tables (▦), page divisions (▦), or layers (▦).

INSERT TOOLBAR:
Text

You can use the Insert toolbar to insert text, format existing text, and insert special characters and symbols when you select the Text category.

Dreamweaver provides a wide range of text options in the Insert toolbar for working with your text. You can open the Font Tag editor to style existing text, or use the buttons to apply bold or italic styling. You can also insert formatting instructions to change a text block to paragraph, block quote, or preformatted text, and apply a heading style and create lists directly from the Insert toolbar. In addition, you can insert special characters such as line breaks, currency symbols, and trademark and copyright symbols.

To style or format text using the Insert toolbar, you must first select the text you want to modify in your document. To insert special characters, you simply place the insertion point in your document where you want the character to appear, and use the Insert toolbar to add the object.

See also>> **Insert Toolbar: View Options**

See also>> **Special Characters**

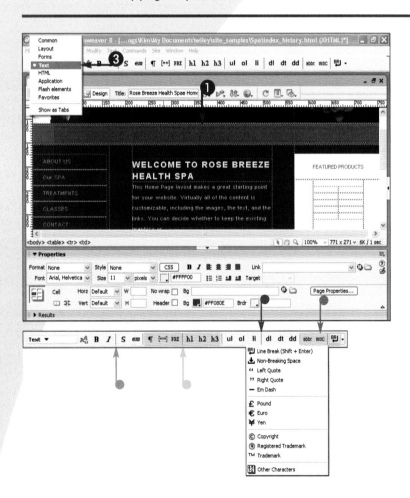

① Click inside the document where you want to insert a text object.

To format or style text, you must first select the existing text to be modified.

② Click the Insert toolbar drop-down arrow (▼).

③ Click Text.

The Insert toolbar displays text objects.

● These buttons open the Font Tag Editor (🖳) or apply bold (**B**), italic (*I*), strong (**S**), or emphasis style (*em*) to selected text.

● These buttons format selected text as a paragraph (¶), block quote ("'"), preformatted text (PRE), or heading sizes one to three (h1 h2 h3).

● These buttons create unordered or ordered lists (ul, ol), a new list item (li), or a definition list (dl), term (dt), or description (dd).

● These buttons create an abbreviation (abbr) or acronym tag (🗂) with the drop-down menu having options for specially formatted text objects, currency, and other nonstandard text items.

INSERT TOOLBAR:
View Options

You can modify the appearance of the Insert toolbar to change its basic layout. This allows you to access the different categories of the Insert toolbar through either a drop-down menu or a tabbed interface.

You can bypass the dialog boxes that appear when you insert objects in a page and have Dreamweaver insert an empty placeholder object without the full set of attributes. Doing this means you must either set the properties of the inserted object directly in the code or through the Properties inspector.

Using the tabbed view option in Windows, you can collapse, expand, or undock the Insert toolbar. Undocking creates a floating toolbar, which you position according to your own preferences. The Insert toolbar in the Macintosh version always floats, but you can dock it at the top or bottom of the Design Window.

See also>>

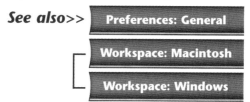

Preferences: General

Workspace: Macintosh

Workspace: Windows

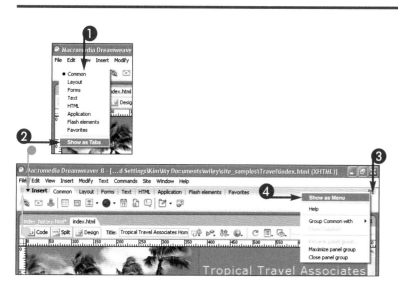

Switch from Menu View to Tabbed View

1 Click the Insert toolbar drop-down arrow (▼).

2 Click Show as Tabs.

The Insert toolbar switches to Tabbed view.

Switch from Tabbed View to Menu View

3 Click the File Options button (▤).

4 Click Show as Menu.

● You can click here (▼) to expand or collapse the Insert toolbar.

● You can click and drag the Grabber button (▥) to undock the Insert toolbar.

The Insert toolbar switches to Menu view.

INVISIBLE ELEMENTS:
Show, Hide, and Edit

You can view, edit, delete, and move invisible elements in a Web page using the special markers that Dreamweaver places in your document. These markers visually mark HTML elements that do not appear in a browser window.

Dreamweaver inserts a small icon into the Design Window to show the presence of invisible elements such as JavaScript, page anchors, comments, hidden form fields, and other code that does not otherwise appear in the browser window. You can control which items display as well as toggle them on or off to make them visible or invisible.

You can select the icon representing an invisible element in the same way that you do any other object in the page, and then set its attributes in the Properties inspector. You can also drag the object to a new location, open the object for editing, or delete the object.

See also>> Preferences: Invisible Elements

See also>> Comments

JavaScript

Link Within a Page

Visual Aids

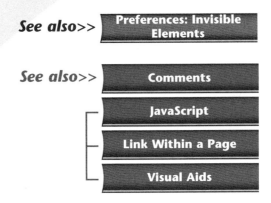

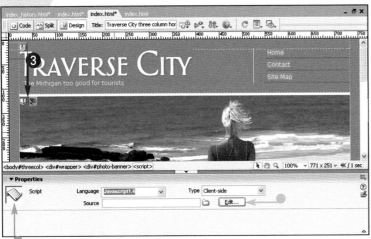

① Click the Visual Aids button (🖾).

② Click Invisible Elements.

Dreamweaver displays the invisible elements in the page when this option is checked.

③ Click an invisible element icon.

● You can use the Properties inspector to edit the item.

● Some invisible elements, such as JavaScript, display an Edit button in the Properties inspector when selected; you can click this button to open a separate editor.

Dreamweaver edits the code in the document to reflect any changes to the invisible element.

JAVASCRIPT:
Insert Scripts into a Page

You can add functions, such as scrolling text messages and interactive objects, to your Web page by inserting JavaScript. You can find many free JavaScript resources online to add functions that Dreamweaver does not include in the behaviors tool set. Although you can copy and paste JavaScript directly in Code view, Dreamweaver also allows you to insert scripts while in Design view.

Normally, you use the Behaviors panel to add interactivity to a page based on Dreamweaver's list of preset behaviors. However, if you create your own JavaScript functions or want to use a script downloaded from the Web, then you must

insert the JavaScript into your page manually. In Design view, you can use the Script dialog box to paste a copied script in place, or link to an external JavaScript file. You can also use the Script dialog box to make edits to your JavaScript code.

See also>>   **Behaviors Panel**

See also>>   **JavaScript**

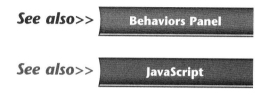

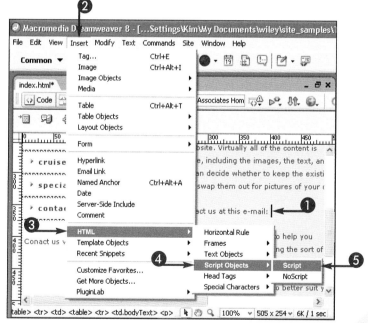

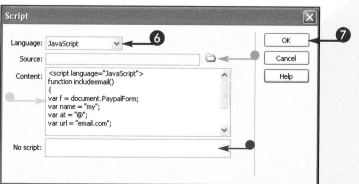

① Place your cursor where you want to add the script.

② Click Insert.

③ Click HTML.

④ Click Script Objects.

⑤ Click Script.

The Script dialog box appears.

⑥ Click here to select the type of script you want.

● You can click the Browse icon (🗀) to find a file if you are using external JavaScript.

● You can type or paste script into this field.

● You can insert HTML here for browsers that do not support JavaScript.

⑦ Click OK.

Dreamweaver inserts the script into the page.

KEYBOARD SHORTCUT SETS:
Create and Modify

You can use keyboard shortcuts to perform common operations in Dreamweaver. In addition to the common keyboard shortcuts such as copy and paste, Dreamweaver contains many shortcuts that are specific to the program. For example, to preview a Web page in your default Web browser, you press F12 in Windows or Option+F12 on a Macintosh.

You can modify the standard keyboard shortcuts set that comes with Dreamweaver by adding new shortcuts, removing existing shortcuts, or changing the key combinations used for operations. You can

even assign keyboard shortcuts along with custom commands to perform a series of steps that you may frequently use, such as inserting a table with a set number of rows and columns.

To create your own set of keyboard shortcuts, you must first save your own copy of the shortcut set that comes with Dreamweaver. You can then add to and modify the shortcuts to suit your needs.

See also>> **History Panel**

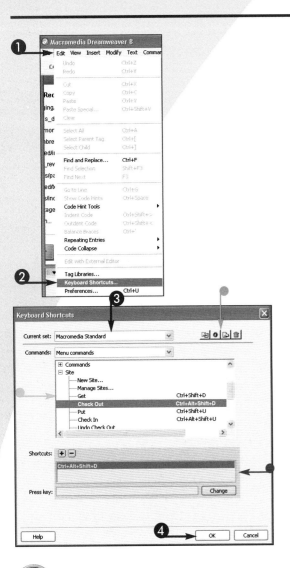

① Click Edit.

② Click Keyboard Shortcuts.

The Keyboard Shortcuts dialog box appears.

③ Click here and select an active keyboard shortcut set.

● You can click these buttons to duplicate (🔲), rename (⊙), export as HTML (🔲), and delete keyboard shortcut sets (🗑).

● You can view information about possible commands and assigned keyboard shortcuts here.

● You can add, edit, or remove key combinations for selected shortcuts in this area.

④ Click OK.

Dreamweaver activates the edited keyboard shortcuts set.

LAYERS:
Drawing

You can use Layout mode in the Insert toolbar to draw layers on your page. The Insert toolbar provides a Draw Layer icon when you are in either Standard or Expanded mode.

After you draw your layer, you can select it and then modify it in the Properties inspector. You can change its position, dimensions, Z-index, visibility, and background color, assign it a name that your document uses for scripting and CSS styling purposes, and assign a class or overflow property.

You can also position a layer visually by using its selection handle at the top-left corner. You can resize a layer by dragging inward or outward from

a corner square. You can resize it horizontally by dragging a middle square on the right or left side, or vertically by dragging a middle square on the top or bottom side.

See also>>
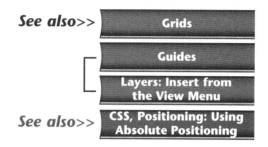

Grids

Guides

Layers: Insert from the View Menu

See also>> CSS, Positioning: Using Absolute Positioning

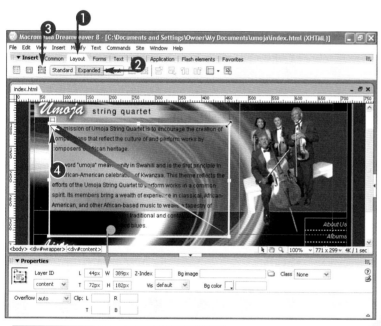

① Click the Layout tab in the Insert toolbar.

② Click the Standard or Expanded mode button.

③ Click the Draw Layer icon (🖹).

④ Click and drag diagonally to create a rectangle for your layer.

Dreamweaver places a layer on the page.

● You can type values in the Properties inspector for precise layouts.

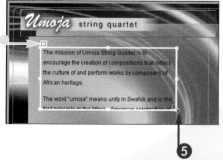

⑤ Click and drag the selection handle to move the layer to where you want it.

The layer moves to the new position.

● You can modify the layer size by dragging a square icon.

You can drag a corner square to resize the entire layer, change the width by dragging a side square, and change the height by dragging a top or bottom square.

61

LAYERS:
Insert from the View menu

You can use Dreamweaver's View menu to insert layers where you place the cursor on your page. Layers are actually DIVs that Dreamweaver uses to lay out as absolutely positioned elements. This means that they are at fixed coordinates on the page and are not affected by the flow of other page elements.

Dreamweaver inserts the layer with the default dimensions of 200 x 115 pixels. After you select the new layer using its selection handle, you can change its properties in the Properties inspector.

Dreamweaver names your layers in numerical order, for example, Layer1 and Layer2. You can rename

them with descriptive names that make it easier for you to manage multiple layers. Dreamweaver writes the layer name as an ID in the code of your page.

See also>>

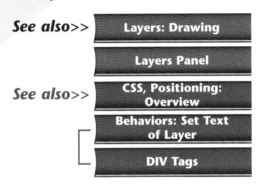

- Layers: Drawing
- Layers Panel

See also>>

- CSS, Positioning: Overview
- Behaviors: Set Text of Layer
- DIV Tags

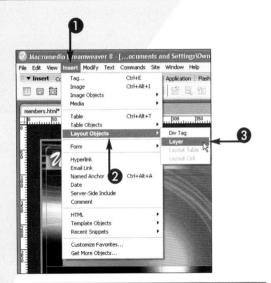

① Click Insert.

② Click Layout Objects.

③ Click Layer.

Dreamweaver inserts a layer with the default dimensions of 200 x 115 pixels at your insertion point.

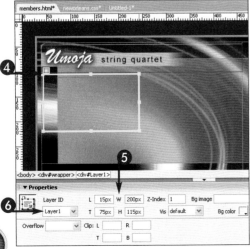

④ Select the layer by clicking its selection handle.

⑤ Type new values in the Properties inspector.

Dreamweaver changes your layer to reflect the new values.

⑥ Type a new name for the layer.

You can also drag the layer by its selection handle to move it.

LAYERS PANEL:
Using to Manage Layers

You can use Dreamweaver's Layers panel to manage the layers on your page. You can rename a layer, change its visibility, and change its Z-index value.

The eye column determines the visibility of a selected layer. An open eye indicates a visible layer, while a closed eye means the layer is hidden. If you see no icon, this indicates that the layer is set to Dreamweaver's default setting when you insert it, which is with visibility turned on.

You can select the Prevent Overlaps option to keep layers from invading each other's space. When you prefer the effect of overlapping layers, the Z-index manages their stacking order. Higher-numbered layers sit on top of lower-numbered ones.

See also>>

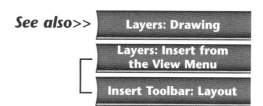

Layers: Drawing

Layers: Insert from the View Menu

Insert Toolbar: Layout

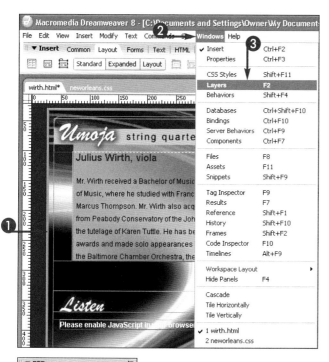

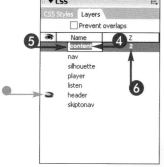

1 Open a page that contains layers.

2 Click Windows.

3 Click Layers.

The Layers panel opens.

4 Click a layer name in the Layers panel.

Dreamweaver selects the layer on the page.

5 Double-click the layer name to highlight it, and type a new name for the layer.

6 Click here and type a Z-index number for the layer.

● You can click the eye icon column to turn visibility on (👁) and off (👁).

LAYOUT MODE:
Using to Visually Lay Out Pages

You can use Layout mode in the Insert toolbar to lay out your pages with visual tools. You can use icons to draw tables and table cells, import tabular data, and create common frameset layouts. Dreamweaver places a bar at the top of your document that is labeled Layout mode. The bar also includes a link to exit from Layout mode into Standard mode.

Dreamweaver displays icons to draw tables and table cells within them. Tables display with a green outline, and table cells display with a blue outline. You can

also use icons to add rows above and below a cell, or to add columns to the right and left of a cell.

See also>> Insert Toolbar: Layout

See also>> AutoStretch Tables

Frames

Import Office Documents

Layout Tables

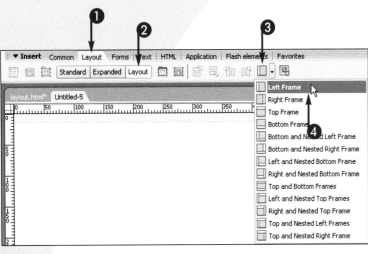

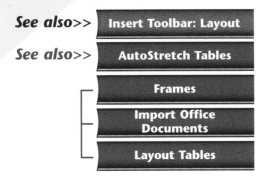

❶ Click the Layout tab in the Insert toolbar.

❷ Click the Layout mode button.

Dreamweaver displays icons for visual layout.

❸ Click the Frames menu icon (▣).

❹ Click a Frameset option.

Dreamweaver allows you to select a common frameset option.

● You can click the Layout Table icon (▣) to draw a table on the page, or the Draw Layout Cell icon (▣) to draw cells in the table.

● You can click the Row (▤▤) and Column (▥▥) icon to add rows and columns.

● You can click the Tabular Data icon (▦) to import data as a table.

64

LIBRARY ITEMS:
In the Assets Panel

You can use the Library category in the Assets panel to create and manage library items, which are reusable bits of code. Library items are appropriate for individual page elements such as logos or copyright notices that you may use on many pages of a site. Library items can be Flash files, sounds, tables, and just about any other page element that you may want to insert throughout the site. Dreamweaver stores library items in a Library folder in the local root folder for your site.

The Library section of the Assets panel lists the name, file size, and location of each item in the current site. It also displays a preview of a

selected library item. Library items are linked assets. This means that when you edit and save a library item, Dreamweaver updates every document that uses it.

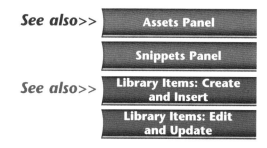

See also>>   Assets Panel

Snippets Panel

See also>>   Library Items: Create and Insert

Library Items: Edit and Update

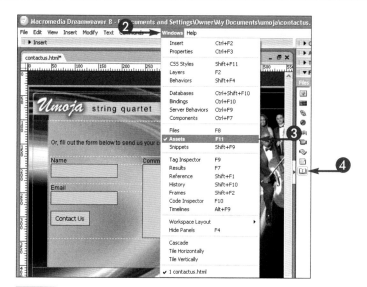

① Open a page in the current site to which you want to add a library item.

② Click Windows.

③ Click Assets.

The Assets panel opens.

④ Click the Library icon (⊞).

Dreamweaver displays all of the library items for the current local site.

⑤ Select the name of a library item.

● The Preview pane displays the asset.

● You can click these buttons to refresh the list (©), and add (⊞), edit (✎), and delete (🗑) library items.

● You can click Insert to add the item where you have placed your cursor in the page.

You can also drag library items to the page.

LINK CHECKER:
Using to Check a Page

You can use Dreamweaver's Check Links command from the Files menu to quickly run the Link Checker and check the status of various kinds of links on your page. Dreamweaver opens the Results panel with a summary of the links status at the bottom; it lists a tally for orphaned files, external links, and broken links. By default, running the Check Links command displays a list of broken links. You can use the green arrow to access and run the options for orphan files and external links.

Over time, you may need to update your links. For example, if you link to external Web pages, their

location may move or no longer be available. You should perform regular checks on both the *relative* and *absolute* links on your site. Broken links frustrate visitors, possibly leading them to leave your site.

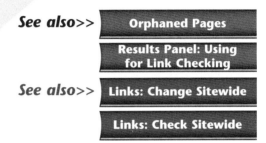

See also>> Orphaned Pages

Results Panel: Using for Link Checking

See also>> Links: Change Sitewide

Links: Check Sitewide

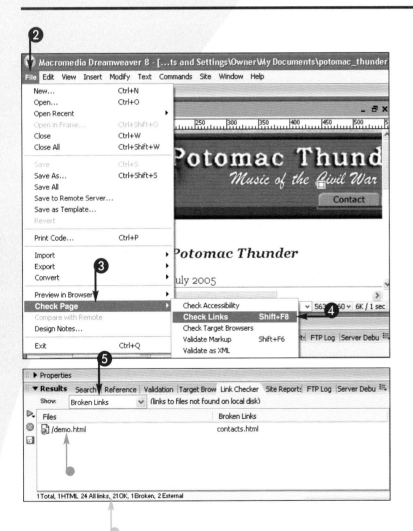

① Open the page for which you want to do a link check.

② Click File.

③ Click Check Page.

④ Click Check Links.

The Results panel opens and displays the Link Checker tab.

● Dreamweaver lists the broken links that it encounters here.

● Dreamweaver displays a tally for the links that it checks.

⑤ Click here to run the external links or orphaned files options.

MAGNIFICATION:
In Document Window

You can use the magnification option in the View menu to zoom in or out of your document. Dreamweaver gives you magnification values that go from 6 percent to 6400 percent. With this and Dreamweaver's other new visual tools, you can lay out your documents with the control that you used to achieve only with desktop publishing programs.

You can also use magnification keyboard shortcuts. Ctrl+Alt+plus the appropriate number (⌘+Option+number) gives you keyboard shortcuts for seven magnification levels. For example, Ctrl+Alt+8 lets

you zoom in at 800 percent and Ctrl+Alt+5 lets you zoom out to 50 percent.

Another way to use magnification is for zooming in on a specific color in an image. You can then sample it with the eyedropper tool to match exact colors in other elements such as paragraph text.

See also>>

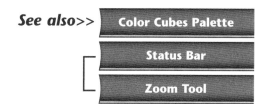

Color Cubes Palette

Status Bar

Zoom Tool

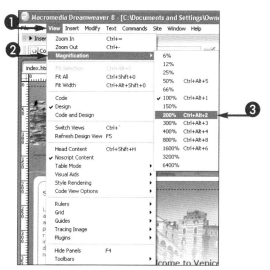

① Click View.

② Click Magnification.

③ Click a magnification value.

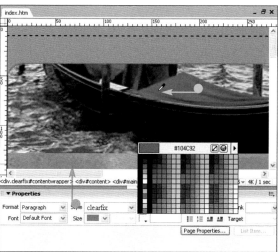

● Dreamweaver displays the document at the magnification value.

● You can examine the document or sample exact colors.

MANAGE SITES WINDOW:
Using the Manage Sites Dialog Box

You can manage all of your Web sites in Dreamweaver using a single dialog box. The Manage Sites dialog box allows you to create new sites, edit, remove, or duplicate sites, as well as export and import site settings.

To use the features that Dreamweaver provides for site management, you must first *define* the site by giving it a project name and pointing Dreamweaver to the folder where you store all your site files. You can define a new site from the Manage Sites dialog window or from the Start window that displays when no document is open.

Once a site is defined, its name displays in the Manage Site window. To manage a site, you select it from the list and use the buttons on the right side of the window to perform site management functions.

See also>> **Site Definition**

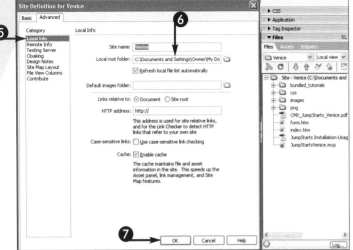

① Click Site.

② Click Manage Sites.

The Manage Sites dialog box opens.

③ Click a site name.

④ Click Edit.

Dreamweaver opens the Site Definition For dialog box.

⑤ Click a Category.

⑥ Edit its information.

⑦ Click OK.

The Manage Sites dialog box returns.

⑧ Click Done.

Dreamweaver updates the information and returns you to the application window.

MONITOR RESOLUTION
Set and Create

You can specify the way that Dreamweaver displays the document window so that it conforms to standard monitor resolutions; you can also create your own custom window sizes. By switching these settings in the Status bar, you can preview how a page looks to a person visiting your site with different monitor settings.

It is important for Web designers to consider the different conditions under which visitors view their Web pages. For example, if you design a page that is 1000 pixels wide and the person viewing the page has his or her monitor set to display 800

pixels in width, your design will be cut off horizontally.

You can switch among the most common monitor resolutions such as 800X600 or 1024X768 or use custom settings that you provide. In order to use this feature, your document window cannot be maximized. Dreamweaver resizes the window based on the settings you apply.

See also>>

Preferences
Status Bar

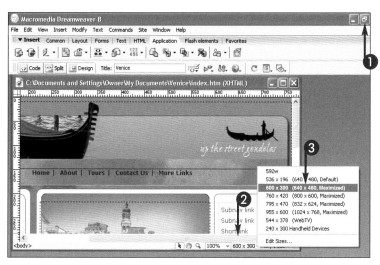

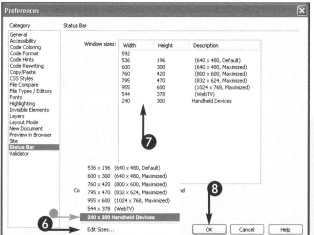

① Click the Minimize button (□) (Windows only).

Dreamweaver resizes the design window.

② Click the Window Size menu on the Status bar.

Dreamweaver displays available window sizes.

③ Click the resolution in which you want to preview the page.

Dreamweaver resizes the document window.

⑤ Repeat Step 2.

⑥ Click Edit Sizes.

Dreamweaver opens the Status Bar preference dialog box.

You can press your tab and arrow keys to size the window to move through the settings so that you can type in a new size.

⑦ Type the attributes for the new size.

⑧ Click OK.

● Dreamweaver adds the new dimensions to the Window Size menu.

NEW DOCUMENT WINDOW:
Using to Create New Documents

You can use the New Document window in Dreamweaver to create new files of many different types and formats. Dreamweaver provides a full range of options for creating new documents.

When you open the New Document window, Dreamweaver presents you with two tabs that organize the choices for new pages. You can choose from pages in the General category if you want to use common file types, or in the Templates category if you want to create a document from an existing template.

The General tab includes categories for creating basic and dynamic pages; CSS, JavaScript, and XML documents; and page designs with much of the page structure already in place. The Templates tab displays all your defined sites and lists any templates that you created for them.

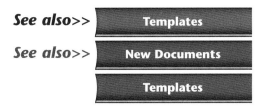

See also>> Templates

See also>> New Documents

Templates

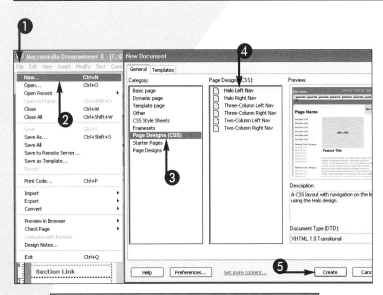

① Click File.

② Click New.

   Alternatively, you can press Control+N (⌘+N)

   The New Document dialog window opens.

③ Select a Category.

④ Select a page design.

⑤ Click Create.

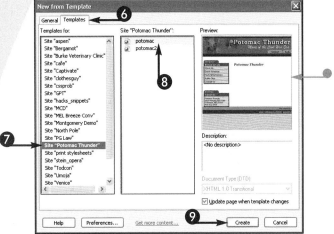

Dreamweaver creates and displays the document.

⑥ Click the Templates tab.

⑦ Click a Site name.

⑧ Click a Template name.

● Dreamweaver gives a preview of the page.

⑨ Click Create.

   Dreamweaver creates and displays a page based on the template that you can edit and save.

OPEN LINKED PAGES:
In Design View

You can open linked pages from a document that is currently open in Design view. Though links are not active until you preview your page in a browser, you can open local files from your Dreamweaver document. This convenience prevents you from having to rummage around in the Files panel or a site folder to find a linked document in a page. You can use a menu command or a keyboard shortcut to quickly open the linked file.

You can also use this command in conjunction with Preview in the browser. Sometimes when you

check a page in the browser and click a link to another page in the site, you will see an error you want to fix or a modification you want to make on the linked page. You can return to Design view and use the Open Linked Page command to quickly retrieve the page.

See also>> **Browsers**

See also>> **Links: Change Sitewide**

Links: Check Sitewide

① Place your cursor inside a link to a page that resides on your computer.

You can also select an image that links to another page.

② Click Modify.

③ Click Open Linked Page.

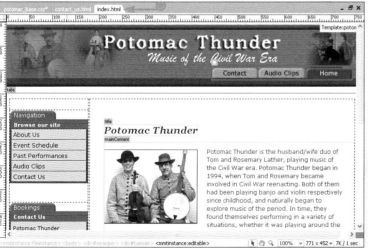

Dreamweaver opens the linked page in a new tab in Design view.

ORPHANED PAGES:
Identify and Delete

You can use the Check Links Sitewide feature to find orphaned files. These are files in your site folder that no longer link to any other files in your site. Maybe you have different images you were trying out on a page, or have unlinked pages you no longer intend to publish to the Web. These files can quickly accumulate and litter up your site, making it difficult to wade through working files.

After you run the Check Links Sitewide command, Dreamweaver checks all the files in your site. It generates several lists from which you can choose in

the Results panel, and one of these is a list of orphaned files. You can examine the list and delete the files you no longer need. You can delete files one at a time, or you can select multiple files to delete a group at one time.

See also>>  Results Panel

See also>> Links

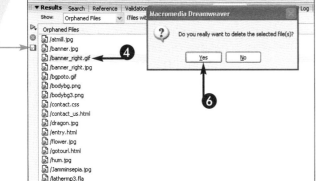

① Click Site.

② Click Check Links Sitewide.

Dreamweaver checks all the links in your site and displays broken ones in the Results panel.

③ Click here and select Orphaned Files.

Dreamweaver displays files that have no other files that link to them.

④ Click an orphaned file that you want to delete.

⑤ Press the Delete key (⌘ and Delete on the Macintosh).

Dreamweaver asks you if you really want to delete the selected files.

⑥ Click Yes.

● You can click the Save icon (▣) in the Results panel if you want to save a report to your computer.

PAGE PROPERTIES:
Modify Basic Page Attributes

You can set attributes that govern a Web page's font, background, link styles, and other properties using the Page Properties dialog box. In this single location, you can set basic formatting properties that control your page's appearance.

By default, Dreamweaver uses CSS styles that are inserted into the head of the document to control the appearance of the page. For example, when you set a document's font style, Dreamweaver writes a rule that modifies the body tag to apply the styling that specifies the font. Dreamweaver uses CSS styling for all properties for the appearance of the page, links, and headings. You can modify the settings to use HTML styling

instead of CSS by changing the Preferences settings.

In addition to appearance settings, you can modify the page title, encoding, document type, and Unicode settings, and select a tracing image for your page design.

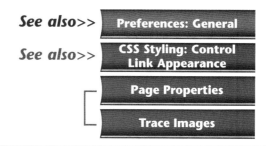

See also>> **Preferences: General**

See also>> **CSS Styling: Control Link Appearance**

Page Properties

Trace Images

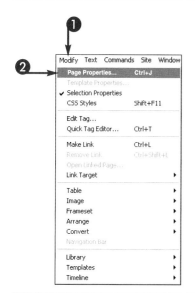

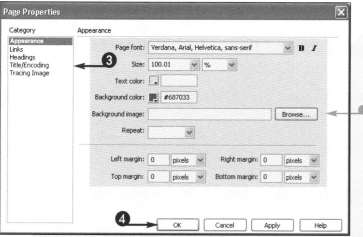

① Click Modify.

② Click Page Properties.

The Page Properties dialog box appears.

③ Click the category of the property that you want to change; available settings display for each selected category.

● You can use the Appearance category to specify fonts and font colors, the page background, and margins.

You can use the additional categories to edit link styles, headings, the page title, and tracing image.

④ Click OK.

The selected properties are applied to the page.

PANELS:
Manage Panels and Panel Layouts

Panels in Dreamweaver are the interface objects where you access important information about files, your site, your style sheets, and many other workflow and editing functions. By integrating all of these panels together into one area of the Dreamweaver workspace, the clutter in the working environment is seriously reduced. You can customize the behaviors of these panels in Dreamweaver to make the workspace more effective and easier to use.

Panel groups consist of different panels that are placed together. You can access the individual panels

by using the tab that appears when a panel group is expanded. You can also remove an individual panel from a group, combine panels into groups that are more suitable to your needs, and expand and collapse groups of panels. All of these customization features are intended to allow you to work on your documents and site more efficiently.

See also>> | **Workspace: Macintosh**

Workspace: Windows

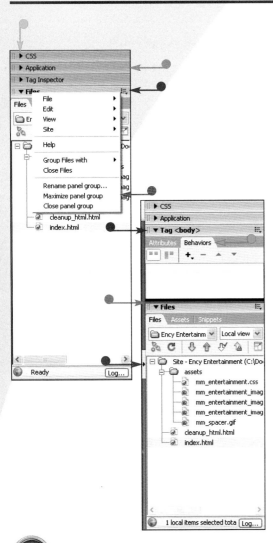

- Panels are grouped by function on the right side of the Dreamweaver workspace.

- You can click the arrow to expand or collapse a panel.

- You can click the File Options button (📧) to access additional functions for an open panel.

- You can use these options for renaming, expanding, and closing a panel.

- You can click the tab in a panel group to open a panel.

- To undock a panel, you can place your mouse over the Gripper button (📊) and drag away from the panel group.

- To redock a panel, you can place the panel on top of the panel group, and then release your mouse button to dock the panel.

- You can click here to collapse all panels to the right, and then click again to expand them.

PREFERENCES:
Accessibility

You can use the Preferences panel to determine how Dreamweaver assists you in meeting accessibility requirements when you insert certain objects into a Web page. If you want to be prompted when form objects, framed Web pages, media, and images are inserted into your page, Dreamweaver will display a dialog box where you type in text descriptions and set other properties related to accessibility. To stop the dialog boxes from appearing for some or all objects, you can deselect the option in the Preferences panel.

Accessibility guidelines specify that objects that may not be usable by people with certain physical disabilities must have additional information provided so that the assistive devices that they use can function properly. For example, a person who is blind may use a screen reader to read aloud the text description of an image found in the page.

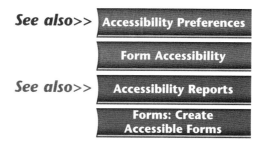

See also>> **Accessibility Preferences**

Form Accessibility

See also>> **Accessibility Reports**

Forms: Create Accessible Forms

① Click Edit (Dreamweaver 8).

② Click Preferences.

The Preferences dialog box appears.

③ Click the Accessibility category.

● You can select items (☐ changes to ☑) for which you want an Accessibility dialog box to appear when you insert them into a page.

● You can select this option (☐ changes to ☑) when testing pages with screen reader software.

● You can deselect this option (☑ changes to ☐) if your screen reader software does not render the page properly.

④ Click OK.

PREFERENCES:
Code Coloring

You can use code coloring and styling preferences to set the way that Dreamweaver applies different colors to the text in your code. Using code coloring allows you to more quickly see different types of code and even lets you set your own color schemes for different coding environments. You can modify the code coloring for a wide variety of document types and scripts, including ASP, ColdFusion, JavaScript, HTML, and CSS.

Dreamweaver 8 significantly expands the different ways that you can color and highlight your code. For example, you can set code coloring for individual

tags in HTML, for rules in CSS, and by designated functions and arguments in JavaScript.

To set code coloring preferences, you begin by selecting the document type. You can set your own color scheme for each document type by specifying different colors from the default colors that Dreamweaver provides. You can also set the text in your code to bold, italic, or underlined.

See also>>

> **Code View Options**
>
> **Coding Toolbar**

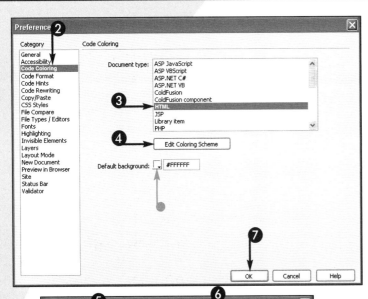

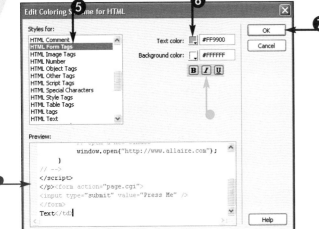

① Open the Preferences dialog box.

Note: See the section "Preferences: Accessibility" to open the Preferences dialog box.

② Click the Code Coloring category.

③ Click a document type.

④ Click Edit Coloring Scheme.

● You can use the Color box (■) to change the background of each document type.

The Edit Coloring Scheme dialog box appears.

⑤ Select the code object to color code.

⑥ Click ■ to change the text and background colors.

● You can also click these options to make text bold (**B**), italic (*I*), or underlined (U).

● Dreamweaver displays a preview of the code color and style.

⑦ Click OK in both open dialog boxes.

Dreamweaver accepts the changes.

PREFERENCES:
Code Formatting

You can use the code formatting preferences in Dreamweaver to specify how your code displays when working in Code view.

You can specify settings for indenting and wrapping code, line breaks, the case of tags, and the method that Dreamweaver uses for setting attribute case. These settings customize the coding environment in Dreamweaver to match your preferred method of working with code.

You can also set preferences here that ensure that an external code editor works properly with the code that Dreamweaver creates. For example, if you use Notepad in Windows to edit your code, you can set the line break to CR LF. Macintosh

users who want to edit in SimpleText can set their line breaks to CR.

In most cases, changes to code formatting are not applied until you create a new document or type new code in Code view. You can force your code formatting to apply to existing documents by running the Apply Source Formatting option from the Commands menu.

See also>> **Code View Options**

Coding Toolbar

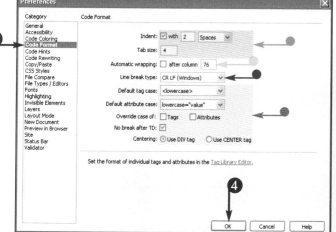

① Click Edit (Dreamweaver 8).

② Click Preferences.

The Preferences dialog box appears.

③ Click Code Format.

● You can use these settings to determine how far new code indents.

● You can use this setting to control where Dreamweaver begins to wrap your code.

● You can set the Line Break option to match your server environment or external code editor.

● You can set preferences for code capitalization and attributes.

④ Click OK.

Dreamweaver applies these preferences to all new documents.

PREFERENCES:
Code Hints

You can get assistance while editing your code by using the hints that Dreamweaver provides as you type. Code hinting works by reading the characters that you type, and then providing a list of options to complete your entry. Code hinting is available for standard HTML tags, CSS properties, and attributes found within your document.

As you begin typing in Code view, Dreamweaver provides a list of available tags or attributes that match the first characters that you enter. For example, if you type the opening bracket for an HTML tag, then Dreamweaver displays all of the

available tags. To accept one of the hints, you can select the suggestion in the list.

Code hinting preferences allow you to specify when code hints appear based on what you type, and how long Dreamweaver waits before providing a hint. It also allows you to determine the kinds of hints that you want to appear.

See also>>

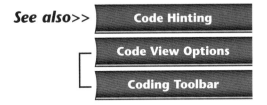

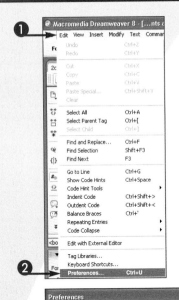

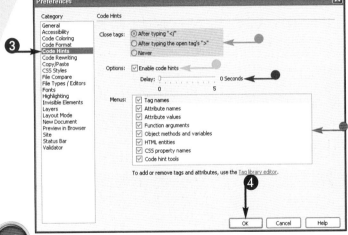

① Click Edit (Dreamweaver 8).

② Click Preferences.

The Preferences dialog box appears.

③ Click Code Hints.

● These settings (○ changes to ◉) determine how closing tags are created.

● Deselecting this box (☑ changes to ☐) disables all code hinting.

● The timeline slider sets how long Dreamweaver waits before displaying a code hint.

● You can select the types of code objects (☐ changes to ☑) for which Dreamweaver provides a menu of code hints.

④ Click OK to accept your preferences.

PREFERENCES:
Code Rewriting

You can control the way that Dreamweaver modifies code when documents are opened, when code is copied and pasted from one document to another, and when code is rewritten as properties of objects are edited. These preferences allow you to determine when and if Dreamweaver should rewrite your code, and for which items.

By default, Dreamweaver tries to repair invalid and incorrect code whenever possible. For example, if tags are improperly nested when inserted into the page in Code view, then Dreamweaver can automatically adjust your code. Dreamweaver also performs helpful operations

such as renaming form tags when you paste them from another document to prevent the duplication of the form tag identifiers. You can specify that Dreamweaver precede these changes with a warning that you are about to rewrite the code.

You can also specify which types of code should never be rewritten. This is helpful if you work in a coding environment where third-party code may be present.

See also>>
Code View Options

Coding Toolbar

---

① Click Edit (Dreamweaver 8).

② Click Preferences.

The Preferences dialog box appears.

③ Click Code Rewriting.

● Click these options (☐ changes to ☑) to specify which types of coding errors are automatically repaired, to specify the file extensions of file types that should not be rewritten, or to automatically maintain the validity of attribute values by forcing legal characters to be used.

● You can click an option (○ changes to ◉) to specify the method that Dreamweaver uses to force valid characters for page URLs.

④ Click OK.

Dreamweaver accepts your preferences.

PREFERENCES:
Copy and Paste

You can use the Copy/Paste Preferences dialog box to control how Dreamweaver handles text that you copy from another application and paste into Dreamweaver. These preferences apply only to text that you paste into Dreamweaver in Design view.

When you copy text from an application, it often contains extra tags and control characters that cause the code to display improperly in an HTML document. For example, text that you type into a Microsoft Word document contains in-line styles and other information inappropriate for Web pages.

You can tell Dreamweaver to paste only unformatted text with no formatting information, allow text with

structure such as paragraphs and tables, retain basic formatting such as bold and italic styles when pasting, or retain all text formatting. By default, Dreamweaver uses the structure and basic formatting method for pasting text.

You can also specify how to handle line breaks, and allow Dreamweaver to remove extra paragraphs from the text in pasted Word documents.

See also>>   **Copy and Paste**

Word Document

① Click Edit (Dreamweaver 8).

② Click Preferences.

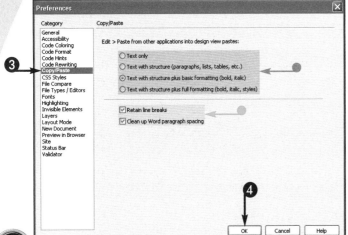

The Preferences dialog box appears.

③ Click Copy/Paste.

● These settings determine how copied text is pasted into a Dreamweaver document (○ changes to ◉).

● You can select these options (☐ changes to ☑) to retain line breaks in pasted text, and to remove extra paragraphs when you paste text from a Word document.

④ Click OK.

Dreamweaver applies your preferences for all documents.

PREFERENCES: CSS Styles

P

You can control the way that Dreamweaver writes your CSS code by modifying the CSS Styles preferences. These options allow you to use CSS shorthand for common styling rules such as fonts, backgrounds, margins, and padding, as well as borders and lists. You can also determine how shorthand code annotation for CSS is handled for existing CSS files and whether you want Dreamweaver to open the original CSS file when you perform edits on your CSS rules.

You can also modify the way that Dreamweaver opens CSS files when using the CSS panel by specifying which action should take place when you select a listed property.

You should only use shorthand CSS annotation when you create new styles in the CSS Rule Definition box. If you create rules using the Properties area of the CSS panel or the Properties inspector, Dreamweaver uses longhand annotation, regardless of how you have set your preferences.

See also>> **CSS Styles Panel**

See also>> **CSS Styling: Control Text Appearance**

CSS Styling: Style List Objects

---

① Click Edit (Dreamweaver 8).

② Click Preferences.

The Preferences dialog box appears.

③ Click CSS Styles.

④ Click the preferences that you want (☐ changes to ☑ or ○ changes to ◉).

● These settings (☐ changes to ☑) determine how rules are written with shorthand annotation when you create new rules.

● These options (○ changes to ◉ and ☐ changes to ☑) set how existing CSS rules are handled when edited.

● These settings (○ changes to ◉) determine where the editing of CSS rules occur.

⑤ Click OK.

Dreamweaver applies your preferences for all documents.

81

PREFERENCES: File Types and Editors

You can determine how Dreamweaver handles files other than standard Web pages by setting the rules for file types in the Preferences dialog box. These settings allow you to decide which files automatically open in Code view and which programs open files such as images and Flash movies. By applying these settings, you decide which program edits a particular file type when you open the file from the Dreamweaver Files panel.

The File Types/Editors panel lists the most common file types that you encounter when developing your Web pages, but it also allows you to add new file types. The default image editor for Dreamweaver is Fireworks. If you prefer to use Adobe Photoshop or another image editor, you must specify it in this panel. In addition, if you prefer to use an external code editor, such as Notepad, when writing code manually, you must also specify it in this panel.

See also>> Editors

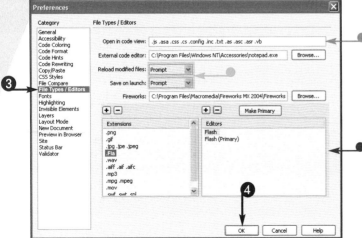

① Click Edit (Dreamweaver 8).

② Click Preferences.

The Preferences dialog box appears.

③ Click File Types/Editors.

● You can type the file extension of files that should automatically open in Code view.

● You can select an external file editor, as well as how Dreamweaver handles externally edited files.

● You can match file editors to the appropriate file types.

④ Click OK.

Dreamweaver applies your preferences.

PREFERENCES:
Fonts

You can modify the fonts that Dreamweaver uses in your documents with the Font category of the Preferences panel. Font settings determine the type style you use in Dreamweaver. If you plan to develop documents in multiple languages, these settings control the font for each available language.

To determine the type of font to use, you must first select the language based on the document encoding of your page. For example, to develop pages in Japanese, you must select that category before applying changes to the font settings. For English and Western European languages, use the Western European font settings.

To set font preferences, you first select the document encoding and then choose from the three available settings that Dreamweaver provides — proportional, fixed, and code. Proportional fonts determine the default text style that Dreamweaver uses in your documents, while Code view sets the default text for working with your code. You use fixed fonts in special circumstances such as when text is wrapped by the `<pre>` tag.

See also>> Preferences: New Document

See also>> Languages

---

① Click Edit (Dreamweaver 8).

② Click Preferences.

The Preferences dialog box appears.

③ Click Fonts.

④ Select the language encoding of the document.

● You can set your proportional font type and size, the font and size of your fixed fonts, and the font and size that you use when you work in Code view.

⑤ Click OK.

Dreamweaver applies your font preferences.

PREFERENCES:
General

You can change many of the basic document and editing options in Dreamweaver in the General category in order to modify the program's basic working environment. Dreamweaver separates the general preference settings into two basic categories: document options and editing options.

The document options area contains preferences for how Dreamweaver updates links when you move files in the Files panel. It also contains options regarding the appearance of the Start page, and whether files should automatically open the next time you restart Dreamweaver.

The editing options area includes options for showing a dialog box when you insert such objects as images and tables. Other options relate to using CSS instead of HTML for styling information that you set, and the use of `<strong>` and `<em>` tags in place of the deprecated `<b>` and `<i>` tags for bold and italic text. You can also set the number of steps that Dreamweaver records in the History panel, and the spelling dictionary that you want to use.

See also>>

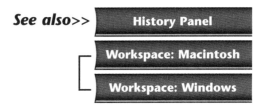

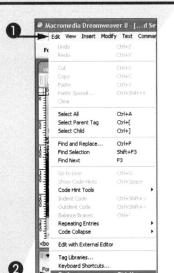

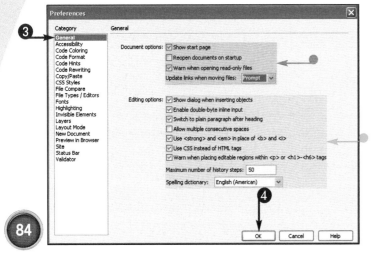

① Click Edit (Dreamweaver 8).

② Click Preferences.

The Preferences dialog box appears.

③ Click General.

● You can specify options (☐ changes to ☑) for the Start page, opening documents at startup, opening read-only files, and how Dreamweaver handles links when you move files in the Files panel.

● You can set general editing options (☐ changes to ☑), specify the number of history steps and undo steps, and specify the dictionary to be used to check spelling.

④ Click OK.

Dreamweaver applies your preferences.

PREFERENCES:
Highlighting

You can change the color of the visual cues that Dreamweaver uses to highlight special regions of a document. These special regions include template regions, library items, third-party tags, layout elements, and certain code blocks.

In Design view, Dreamweaver highlights special elements on the page. For example, when you create an editable region in a Dreamweaver template, a small tab appears with the region name highlighted by the color indicated in your preferences. By default, Dreamweaver highlights the border of a page division, or DIV tag, when your mouse moves over the border. It also highlights editable, nested, and locked regions in

a template file, library items, and certain live data in a dynamic page.

If the highlighting that Dreamweaver uses is hard to see against the colors of your page elements, you can change the color to make your elements more visible.

See also>>

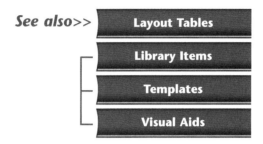

Layout Tables

Library Items

Templates

Visual Aids

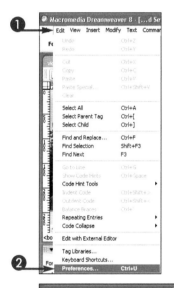

① Click Edit (Dreamweaver 8).

② Click Preferences.

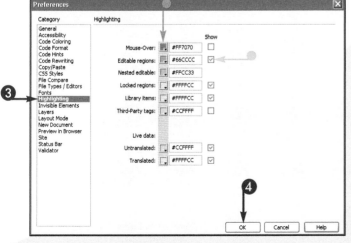

The Preferences dialog box appears.

③ Click Highlighting.

● You can use the Color boxes (▣) to select a color for each category of highlighted elements.

● You can select the Show option (☐ changes to ☑) to highlight a selected object in Design view.

④ Click OK.

Dreamweaver applies your highlighting preferences for all documents.

85

PREFERENCES:
Invisible Elements

You can modify the way that Dreamweaver displays invisible elements in your designs by changing the settings in the Preferences panel.

When you insert an object into a page that cannot be seen, such as JavaScript or page anchors, Dreamweaver places a marker on the page to indicate their presence. These markers appear as a yellow shield with icons representing their function. You can select the icon while editing a page in order to modify, move, or delete the item. When you select an invisible element using its icon, the properties for the object display in the Properties inspector.

You can specify which invisible elements display in your design through the Preferences panel. When you select the check box for a particular invisible element, the icon appears in Design view when you insert one of these objects into the page. This allows you to see, select, and modify these objects as needed. You can also turn the visibility of all invisible elements off or on through the View menu.

See also>> Invisible Elements

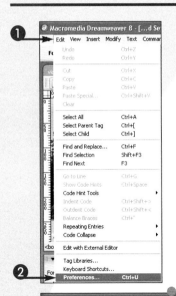

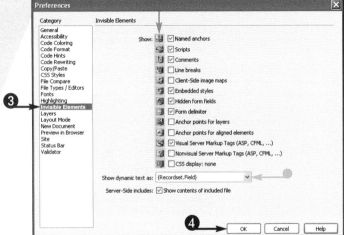

① Click Edit (Dreamweaver 8).

② Click Preferences.

The Preferences dialog box appears.

③ Click Invisible Elements.

● When selected (☐ changes to ☑), these icons display when you insert an invisible element; deselected items do not display when you insert an invisible element.

● You can click here to change how dynamic text displays.

④ Click OK.

Dreamweaver applies your invisible element preferences.

PREFERENCES:
Layers

You can use the Preferences panel to change the default properties that Dreamweaver applies to layers that you insert into a document.

Dreamweaver considers any absolutely positioned page division, or DIV tag, to be a layer. When you insert a layer into a document, certain properties are automatically assigned to it, including its visibility, width, height, and background. You can change these default values and assign a different property. For example, you can set a layer to be visible or hidden, or to inherit the visibility properties of a parent layer.

You can also set a background color or background image to appear by default each time you insert a layer. By setting these values ahead of time in Preferences, you can control how your layers appear each time you insert them into a page.

Dreamweaver also automatically applies a JavaScript function to your document that allows Netscape version 4 to display the layer in its proper location. If you are not designing for Netscape 4 browsers, you can turn this option off.

See also>> **Layers Panel**

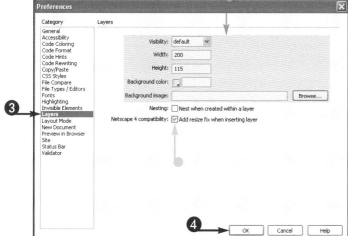

① Click Edit (Dreamweaver 8).

② Click Preferences.

The Preferences dialog box appears.

③ Click Layers.

● You can specify the visibility properties and the default width and height of inserted layers, as well as a background color or an image that you want to appear in inserted layers.

● You can select the Netscape 4 compatibility option (☐ changes to ☑) to automatically apply the Netscape 4 resize fix to inserted layers.

④ Click OK.

Dreamweaver applies your layer preferences.

PREFERENCES:
Layout Mode

You can change how Dreamweaver creates layout tables as well as color-coding for layout objects in the Layout Mode category of the Preferences panel.

When you use a layout table in a design, you often need *spacer images*, a tiny, invisible GIF, to maintain table integrity by constraining the table to a certain width and height, or to prevent it from becoming too small if a user reduces the browser window.

You can choose to automatically have spacers inserted in the tables that you create or to never use them. You can also select a spacer image for each

defined Web site, or have Dreamweaver create one for you. You can then use the same image for all pages in a site that you build with layout tables.

This panel also allows you to set the default colors for cell and table outlines, and the background of layout tables.

See also>>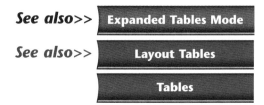

See also>>

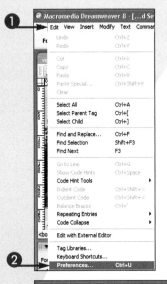

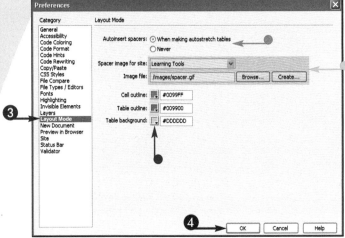

① Click Edit (Dreamweaver 8).

② Click Preferences.

The Preferences dialog box appears.

③ Click Layout Mode.

● You can click an option (○ changes to ⦿) to specify whether a spacer image is automatically inserted when you create a layout table.

● You can select a defined site and the location of the spacer image for the site, browse for an existing spacer GIF file, or have Dreamweaver create one for you.

● You can use the Color box (▣) to select outlines and background colors for layout cells and tables.

④ Click OK.

Dreamweaver applies your layout table preferences.

PREFERENCES:
New Document

P

You can specify the type of new documents and file extensions that Dreamweaver creates through the New Documents category of the Preferences panel.

You can specify the default file type when you create a new file in the Files panel. You can use the contextual menu generated from a folder in the Files panel to select the New File command and create a new file based on the preferences that you set. By default, the new file is an HTML file, but you can also select different file types such as ASP and XSLT instead. These settings do not affect new files that you create through the New Document dialog box.

You can also specify either the three-letter .htm extension or the longer .html extension for HTML files.

This panel also allows you to determine the document type declaration (DTD) that is used for new files, and choose whether Unicode normalization is followed in new documents.

See also>> Files Panel

See also>> New Documents: Create from Starter Pages

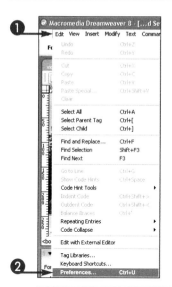

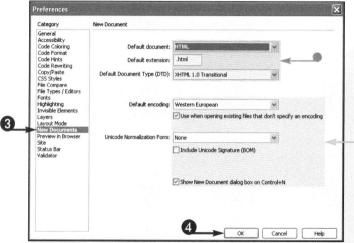

1 Click Edit (Dreamweaver 8).

2 Click Preferences.

The Preferences dialog box appears.

3 Click New Documents.

● You can select a default file type for new documents generated from the Files panel, the default file extension for HTML files, and the default DTD for new HTML pages.

● You can choose document encoding and Unicode settings for new documents, and specify whether the New Document dialog box appears when you create a new file through the File menu or by keyboard shortcuts.

4 Click OK.

Dreamweaver applies your new document preferences.

89

PREFERENCES:
Preview in Browser

You can select the browsers with which you preview your designs through the Preview in Browser category of the Preferences panel.

While the Design view is fairly accurate, it is not exactly what you will see in a Web browser. Because each browser translates HTML and CSS code in different ways, it is essential that you preview your Web pages in the most popular browsers as you work. Most Web designers preview their work in Internet Explorer, Netscape, and Firefox on the Windows platform. On the Macintosh, the Safari

browser is also popular, and many professional Web developers test their designs in both platforms.

Dreamweaver allows you to specify both a primary and secondary browser in the Preferences panel. By establishing which browser opens your files, you gain quick access to a preview of your pages. Browsers that you specify also appear in the File menu.

See also>> Preferences: Preview in Browser

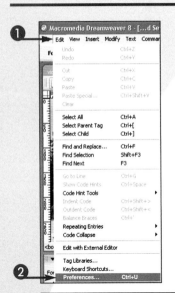

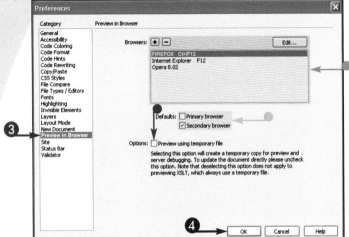

1 Click Edit (Dreamweaver 8).

2 Click Preferences.

The Preferences dialog box appears.

3 Click Preview in Browser.

● You can add (**+**) or remove (**−**) a browser from the list of browsers that are available for previewing.

● You can select a default browser (☐ changes to ☑).

● This option (☐ changes to ☑) creates a temporary file each time you preview a document.

4 Click OK.

Dreamweaver applies your browser preview preferences.

You can preview your page by pressing the F12 key (Opt+F12); the secondary browser opens your page when you press Ctrl+F12 (⌘+F12).

PREFERENCES:
Site

You can specify how Dreamweaver displays your local and remote files, as well as set options for putting and getting files to and from your remote server, in the Site category of the Preferences panel.

Dreamweaver's full-size Files panel displays both your local and remote files in a two-column view. By default, your local files appear in the right-hand column, with the remote files on the left. You can also reverse this arrangement.

You can specify whether you want to be prompted to get or put dependent files such as images when uploading a Web page. With these options

selected, Dreamweaver prompts you each time you transfer a page to the server.

You can also use this panel to specify how long you should remain connected to your server, your firewall settings, and options for saving or moving files on your server.

See also>>

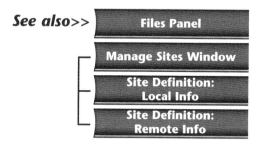

Files Panel

Manage Sites Window

Site Definition:
Local Info

Site Definition:
Remote Info

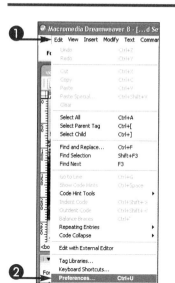

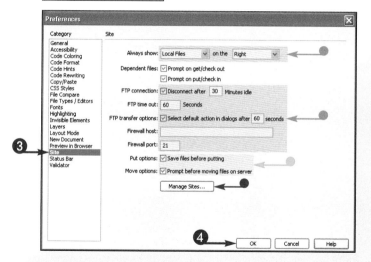

1 Click Edit (Dreamweaver 8).

2 Click Preferences.

The Preferences dialog box appears.

3 Click Site.

● You can specify the position of your Local and Remote file listings, as well as how Dreamweaver connects to your remote server.

● You can have Dreamweaver automatically save files when a Put action is performed, and display a prompt when you move files (☐ changes to ☑).

● You can click Manage Sites to provide additional information for individual sites.

4 Click OK.

Dreamweaver applies your site preferences.

91

PREFERENCES:
Status Bar

You can change the default page sizes and estimated download times that Dreamweaver displays in the Status bar through the Status Bar category of the Preferences panel.

Dreamweaver displays seven possible Web page sizes in the Status bar so that you can check your page design against different monitor resolution settings. In order to avoid scroll bars due to pages that are too wide, you can check your pages for monitor settings ranging from 544 x 378 to 1024 x 780 pixels. When you choose one of these settings from the Status bar, the Design window resizes to match the selected resolution.

You can modify these settings by changing the width, height, and description values in the Preferences panel.

You can also modify the connection speed that Dreamweaver uses to estimate the download time for documents. By default, the connection speed is set to 56 Kb per second. You can specify connection settings as slow as 14.4 Kb or as fast as 1500 Kb per second.

See also>> | Status Bar

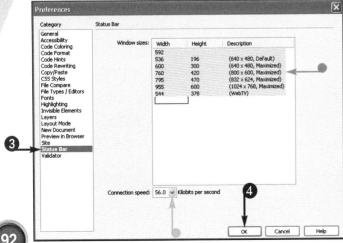

① Click Edit (Dreamweaver 8).

② Click Preferences.

The Preferences dialog box appears.

③ Click Status Bar.

● You can click an existing width, height, or description value to type a new value, or you can click below the last listed value to enter a new width, height, or description.

● You can click here and select a new connection speed.

④ Click OK.

Dreamweaver applies your Status bar preferences.

PREFERENCES:
Validator

You can use the built-in validator in Dreamweaver to check your documents for errors in the code or syntax. By validating your documents, you can correct the errors and prevent your Web viewers from experiencing problems. The Preferences panel also allows you to select the coding environment in which you publish.

The Validator category of the Preferences panel contains options for the languages that Dreamweaver should check, the types of errors that it should check for, and how it should report those errors.

Dreamweaver provides two types of code validation. For XML and XHTML files, Dreamweaver checks for errors in the languages that you have specified. For other file types, such as ColdFusion, Dreamweaver checks the markup of your code and reports any errors that it encounters. You can access these reports from the File menu or with the Validate Markup button in the Document toolbar. You can check an open document, selected files, or an entire Web site.

See also>> **Validate Forms**

Validate HTML

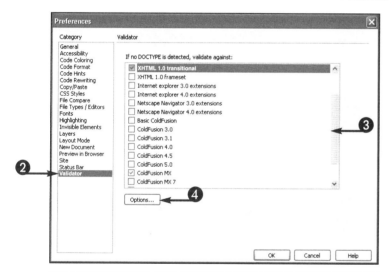

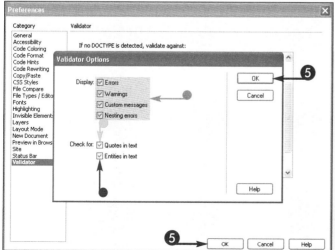

① Open the Preferences dialog box.

Note: For more on opening the Preferences dialog box, see the section "Preferences: Status Bar."

② Click Validator.

③ Select the coding language that you want to validate
(☐ changes to ☑).

Note: You may only select one version of each language. For example, if you select XHTML Transitional, then you cannot also select HTML 3.2.

④ Click Options.

The Validator Options dialog box appears.

● You can select the error types that Dreamweaver reports (☐ changes to ☑).

● This setting (☐ changes to ☑) checks the use of quotation marks, and prompts you to replace them with the &quot tag.

● This setting (☐ changes to ☑) prompts you to use alternate characters for certain text values such as the ampersand, less-than, or greater-than characters.

⑤ Click OK in the open dialog boxes.

Dreamweaver applies your validator preferences.

PROPERTIES INSPECTOR:
Flash

You can use the Properties inspector to view, edit, and modify the values that pertain to your Flash movies. When you select a Flash movie, Dreamweaver displays the Properties inspector for the Flash file and provides text boxes, menus, and buttons for changing the properties of the movie.

When you select a movie, Dreamweaver displays the path and name of the file, the movie's width and height, and default settings for quality, scale, and alignment. You can also use the Properties inspector to assign the movie an ID, set pixel values for

spacing around the file, designate the location of the source Flash file, and assign a background color.

You can use the Play button to see a live preview of the movie in your document, and the Parameters button to assign additional properties through scripting embedded into the page. If you have Flash installed on your computer, then the Edit button allows you to open and edit the source file in Flash.

See also>> **Flash Movies**

Flash Video

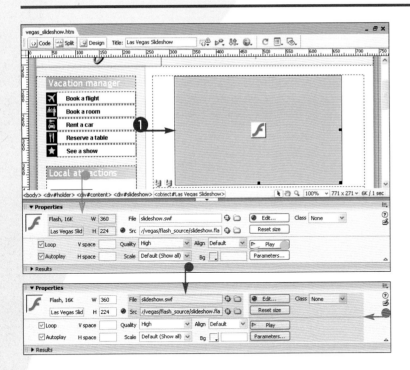

① Click a Flash movie in your document.

The Properties inspector displays the selected movie's properties.

② Change the properties in the inspector.

● You can type an ID for the movie, and modify the width and height.

Dreamweaver automatically sets the width and height based on the inserted file's properties.

● You can set movie playback properties, create vertical and horizontal space around the movie, adjust movie quality, scale the movie, align the movie within its container on the page, and assign a background color.

● The path and filename of the SWF and the source Flash file display here; you can click the Point to File (⊙) or Browse (📁) button to locate the file in your site.

● You can click these buttons to edit the source file in Flash, reset the file to its original size, play the movie in the Design window, and assign additional parameters and a CSS class to the movie.

Dreamweaver modifies the properties of the Flash movie based on the values entered in the Properties inspector.

PROPERTIES INSPECTOR: Forms

You can use the Properties inspector to ensure that the form objects inserted into your Web pages function correctly.

When you select a form tag, the Properties inspector displays the form name, the method used to process the form, and the location of the script that handles the form data and passes information to a database. It also allows you to specify a MIME encoding format and whether the form results should open in a new browser window. When you select a specific form object such as a check box, the Properties inspector displays information particular to that type of form object.

Almost every form that you insert into a page requires that you enter specific properties to allow the form to function.

See also>>

Forms: Create and Insert
Forms: Insert Buttons
Forms: Insert Check Boxes and Radio Buttons
Forms: Insert Fields
Forms: Insert Hidden Fields
Forms: Insert List and Menu Items
Forms: Insert Text Fields

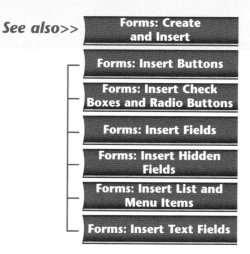

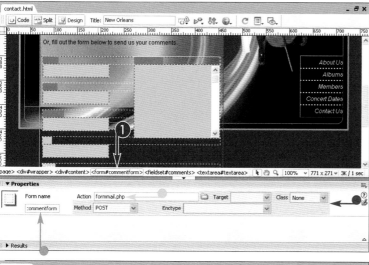

① **Click the form tag in the Tag selector, or click the form.**

Dreamweaver displays the properties for the form tag.

② **Change properties in the inspector.**

● You can type a unique name for the tag.

● You can type the name and path of the file that processes the form.

● You can click ☑ and select either the GET or POST method; open the page results in a new window; type an encoding format; or assign a CSS class to the form.

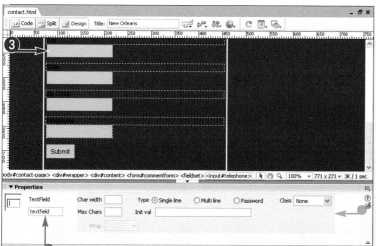

③ **Click a form object in your Web page.**

Dreamweaver displays the properties for the object.

● You can type a unique name for the form object.

● You can modify the properties for the form object, and click ☑ to select a CSS class to the object.

Dreamweaver modifies the properties of the form or form object based on the values you entered.

95

PROPERTIES INSPECTOR: Images

You can use the Properties inspector to view, edit, and modify the values for images that you insert into a document. When you select an image, Dreamweaver displays the properties for the image and provides text boxes, menus, and buttons that allow you to change its properties and edit the image.

When you insert an image into a page, Dreamweaver displays the width and height of the image, as well as the path to the image. You can also modify the image by assigning it a name to be used with JavaScript behaviors, adding a link from the image,

creating a hotspot, aligning the image, and assigning it a CSS class. You can perform basic editing operations to the image, such as cropping it and adjusting its brightness and contrast. If you have Fireworks installed, then you can also perform more advanced editing operations by opening the image in that program.

See also>>

Align Images: To Text with CSS

Fireworks: Edit Images

Hotspots

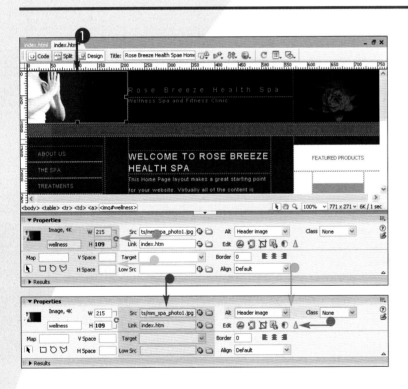

① Click an image in your document.

Dreamweaver displays the properties for the image.

● You can name the image, set its width and height or click the Reset Size button (⟳) to reset the image to its original dimensions.

● You can draw a hotspot map on top of an image, and create vertical or horizontal space, in pixels, around the image.

● You can use these settings to display the name and path to the image file and any link that you have assigned to the image; to assign a target to open the link in a new window; and to assign a low-contrast alternate image for faster loading.

● These buttons open the image in Fireworks (⬚), optimize the image in Fireworks (⬚), crop the image (⬚), refresh the view of the image in the document (⬚), adjust brightness and contrast (⬚), and adjust the sharpness (⬚).

● You can provide an alternate text description of the image and assign a CSS class.

Dreamweaver modifies the properties of the image based on the values that you enter.

PROPERTIES INSPECTOR:
Tables

You can use the Properties inspector to view, edit, and modify the values for tables that you insert into a document. When you select a table, Dreamweaver displays the attributes of the table, including the number of rows and columns, its width and height, padding and spacing properties, and background colors or images that you have applied.

When you insert a table into a page, Dreamweaver displays the table attributes through the Insert Table dialog box. Once the table is in place, you can modify its properties by

changing values in the Properties inspector or by entering new properties. For example, you can change the number of rows or columns, modify the table width, or add padding and spacing to the table. You can also use the buttons that Dreamweaver provides to clear width properties or convert the widths to pixel or percentage values.

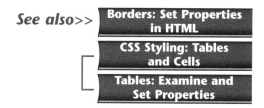

See also>>

Borders: Set Properties in HTML
CSS Styling: Tables and Cells
Tables: Examine and Set Properties

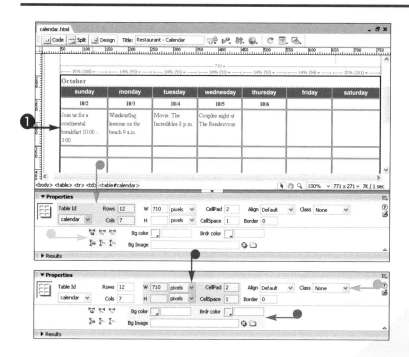

① Click a table in your document.

Dreamweaver displays the properties for the table in the Properties inspector.

● You can name the table and set the number of rows and columns in the table.

● These buttons allow you to clear width and height values from the selected table and change the unit of measurement from pixels to a percentage.

● You can modify the width and height of the table, assign padding, spacing, and border values, and set the alignment of the table within a containing element.

● You can assign a background color or image, as well as the border color.

● You can click here and assign a CSS class to the table.

Dreamweaver modifies the selected table based on the values that you enter.

PROPERTIES INSPECTOR: Text

You can format text in a document by using the Properties inspector to change either the HTML or CSS attributes of the text.

Dreamweaver allows you to change the HTML properties of selected text to modify the font, size, and color of the text, as well as set bold or italic styles. You can also create a new CSS style for formatting your text, or assign an existing CSS class.

You can also use the Properties inspector to perform operations with selected text such as creating links and lists, formatting lists, and aligning text.

See also>>

CSS Styling: Control Text Appearance

Fonts

Headings

Link to a Document Inside Your Site

Link to a Document Outside Your Site

Link within a Page

Text: Create Lists

Text: Formatting Options

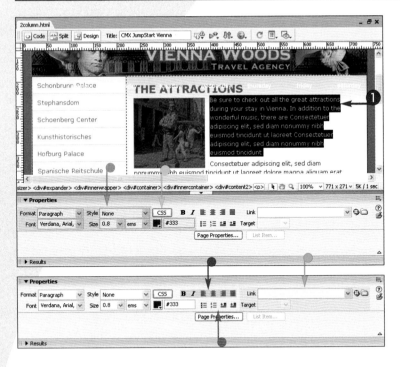

① Click and drag to select text in a document.

Dreamweaver displays the properties for the selected text in the Properties inspector.

● You can change the text font and format, assign a CSS style, set the text color, and modify the size and unit of measurement.

● You can click CSS to open the CSS panel, where you can view and edit styling information for selected text.

● These buttons apply bold ([**B**]) and italic ([*I*]) styling and set alignment properties to selected text.

● These buttons create unordered ([≣]) and ordered ([≣]) lists from selected text, and indent ([≣]) or outdent ([≣]) text.

● You can assign a link to selected text.

Dreamweaver modifies the selected text, based on the values that you enter, and displays the results in the Design window.

QUICK TAG EDITOR:
Insert HTML in Design View

Q

You can use the Quick Tag Editor to insert HTML tags directly into your document while in Design view. This allows you to remain in a visual design environment while still working directly with your code. The Quick Tag Editor can also modify an existing object or the object's attributes. You can make these changes in a small window that appears when you open the editor. Your changes take effect immediately after you close the editor.

The Quick Tag Editor is available through a keyboard shortcut or from a contextual menu. In both cases, a small window appears, where you

can enter tags directly, choose from a menu of available tags, or use the editor to modify attributes for an object that you have selected. You can also open the Quick Tag Editor from the Tag Selector, located in the document Status bar.

See also>>

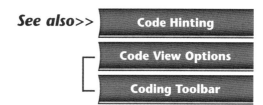

Code Hinting

Code View Options

Coding Toolbar

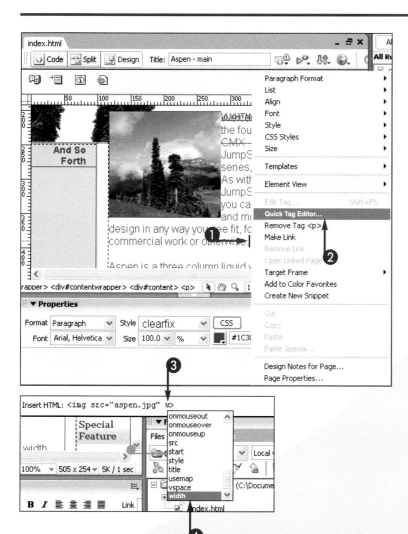

1 Right-click (⌘-click) at the position in the page where you want to insert the tag.

2 Click Quick Tag Editor.

Alternatively, you can press Ctrl+T (⌘+T) to open the editor.

The Quick Tag Editor appears.

3 Type the first letter of your tag.

● The editor displays a list of tags.

4 Click the tag that you want to insert.

5 Press Enter to accept the selected tag.

You can also double-click a tag in the list, or press Esc to exit the Quick Tag Editor without applying the tag.

Dreamweaver returns to Document view with the new tag inserted.

RECORD COMMANDS:
For Temporary Use

You can use Dreamweaver's Recording commands to create a sequence of actions that you can apply repeatedly to page elements. This feature is particularly helpful for setting attributes for images in a photo gallery. You can select your image on the page, record the formatting options that you type in the Properties inspector, and replay the command with your other images.

Dreamweaver saves your set of actions in memory, letting you use it until you record a different set of actions or you quit Dreamweaver. The Start Recording, Stop Recording, and Play Recorded

Command features provide a way to create temporary commands for short-term use.

The cursor turns into a cassette-like tape icon until you stop recording. Dreamweaver does not allow you to use the mouse during recording; your actions are confined to keyboard combinations and arrow keys, as well as what you can type into panels such as the Properties inspector.

See also>> **History Panel**

1. Open a page for which you want to record a command.

2. Click Commands.

3. Click Start Recording.

4. Perform the actions that you want to record.

5. Click Commands.

6. Click Stop Recording.

   Dreamweaver stores a temporary command that you can use to automatically add elements to your page.

7. Select the object or click the cursor at the place where you want to begin playing back the command.

8. Click Commands.

9. Click Play Recorded Command.

   Dreamweaver performs the recorded actions.

REFERENCE PANEL:
Using for More Information

You can use the Reference panel to look up information about the technologies that Dreamweaver offers. Dreamweaver includes three sources for its reference material. For example, the UsableNet Accessibility Reference explains how to make your pages accessible to all users. There are also two Macromedia ColdFusion references — a CF Function Reference and a CFML Reference. In addition, there are ten references that include "books" for CSS, HTML, XML, and the popular server model technologies.

Because new Web technologies are continuously emerging and evolving, it is hard to keep up with

them. Although Dreamweaver is primarily a visual tool, it can make your workflow easier if you understand what you are doing. Dreamweaver's online Reference panel supplies authoritative resources to which you can quickly turn whenever you have a question. For example, you can use the CSS reference in combination with the CSS panel when you need to understand how a property or attribute works with a selector.

See also>> Results Panel

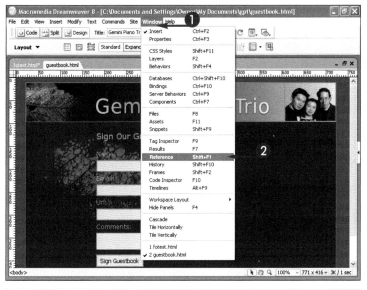

① Click Window.

② Click Reference.

The Reference panel opens.

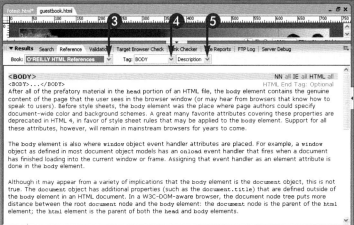

③ Click here and select a book.

Dreamweaver displays another menu whose options depend on which book you select.

④ Click here and select an option.

Dreamweaver displays a third menu based on the first two menus.

⑤ Click here and select an option.

Dreamweaver displays the appropriate information.

RESULTS PANEL:
Using for FTP Logs

You can use the FTP log in the Results panel to troubleshoot connection problems with a remote host. If you have ever used another FTP application, you may have noticed that it reveals line-by-line details of the transfer process. By default, Dreamweaver hides these details from the user. You can see them by opening the FTP log. Dreamweaver explains the transactions with standard code and commands.

Macromedia provides a table of FTP code and commands when you type the following into your browser: **www.macromedia.com/cfusion/knowledgebase/index.cfm?id=tn_14536**. You can find both a list of the 100 through 500 series

codes — such as 331, username OK, need password — and a list of the common FTP commands, such as PASS for sending the user password and SIZE to return the size of a file. By reading your FTP log and interpreting the results, you can analyze connection problems.

See also>>

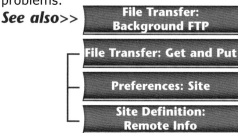

File Transfer: Background FTP

File Transfer: Get and Put

Preferences: Site

Site Definition: Remote Info

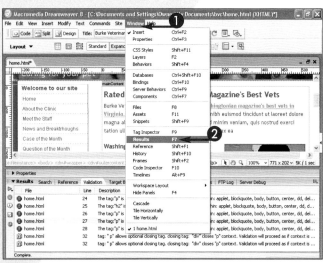

❶ Click Window.

❷ Click Results.

The Results panel opens.

❸ Transfer a file to the server.

❹ Click the FTP Log tab.

Dreamweaver displays the FTP log.

❺ Read the log to find clues about your FTP problems.

RESULTS PANEL:
Using Link Checking

You can use the Results panel to check the links in your site. The panel allows you to check for broken links, external links, and orphan files. When you run the Link Checker, Dreamweaver verifies links within the local site and generates lists of broken links and orphaned, or unreferenced, files. It also compiles a list of links to external sites, although you must verify these links yourself.

The report that you see in the Results panel is only a temporary file. If you want to save the report, then you can use the Save Report icon in the Results panel. Dreamweaver displays a dialog

box to allow you to choose where you want to save the report. It then saves the report as a plain text document with a list for each of the three categories of links that it checks.

See also>> **Link Checker**

Orphaned Pages

See also>> **Links: Change Sitewide**

Links: Check Sitewide

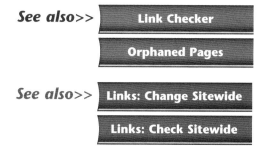

① Click Window.

② Click Results.

   The Results panel opens.

③ Click the Link Checker tab.

④ Click here and select an option.

⑤ Click the Run icon ([▶]).

⑥ Click an option.

   Dreamweaver checks for broken links and lists them in the Results panel.

⑦ Double-click a broken link in the list.

   Dreamweaver opens the page to the broken link.

⑧ Click the Save Report icon ([▣]) to save the report.

RESULTS PANEL:
Using for Target Browser Check

You can use the Target Browser Check in the Results panel to check your page for compatibility with target browsers that you configure in Dreamweaver's Browser Check settings.

When you build a site, you should determine who your target audience is and which browsers they are most likely to use. A large percentage of users prefer Internet Explorer, but there are others, such as those in education or government, who may still use Netscape 4. Many Web-savvy people use Firefox, and Mac users often use Safari. Once you identify your audience, you can adjust your browser settings

so that Dreamweaver warns you when you use code that does not work in those browsers.

There are many browsers, and they often implement code in their own ways. Although the Web Standards movement is guiding browsers towards some uniformity, there are still browser anomalies for which you may need to adjust your pages.

See also>>

Document Toolbar

Target Browser Check

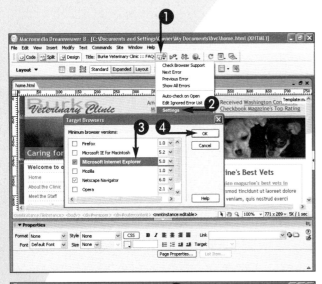

① Click the Browser Check icon (🔲) in the Document toolbar.

② Click Settings.

The Target Browsers dialog box appears.

③ Click to select the browsers that you want to support.

④ Click OK.

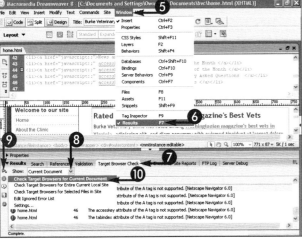

⑤ Click Window.

⑥ Click Results.

Dreamweaver opens the Results panel.

⑦ Click the Target Browser Check tab.

⑧ Click here and select a Show option.

⑨ Click ▶.

Dreamweaver checks your page against the target browser settings.

⑩ Double-click a file in the errors list.

Dreamweaver opens the page to the problem area.

RESULTS PANEL:
Using for Validation

You can use the Validation feature in the Results panel to validate the code for your site. Validation is the process whereby you check the syntax of your code to see if it has errors that break the rules of a particular language. Dreamweaver can validate your document for HTML; XHTML; ColdFusion Markup Language, or CFML; JavaServer Pages, or JSP; Wireless Markup Language, or WML; and Extensible Markup Language, or XML. Dreamweaver uses the settings that you provide in the Validator category of the Preferences dialog box as the basis of its results.

Validation errors can cause elements on the page to display improperly or even keep your page from displaying at all in some browsers. Search engines also need to interpret your pages, and clean, error-free code can improve your site's search engine rankings. If you manually code pages, validation catches typos, and even if you do not manually code pages, you can learn more about a language through validation.

See also>> **Preferences: Validator**

See also>> **Validate HTML**

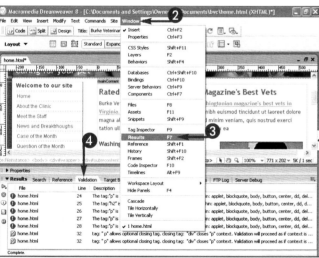

① Open a page or site that you want to validate.

② Click Window.

③ Click Results.

The Results panel opens.

④ Click the Validation tab.

⑤ Click ⊳.

⑥ Select a Run option.

Dreamweaver checks the page or site against your Validation settings in Dreamweaver's Preferences.

⑦ Double-click a browser-check error.

Dreamweaver opens the page to the error.

● You can click the Browse Report icon (🔲) to read an expanded Validation report in the default browser.

RULERS:
Using to Lay Out Pages

You can use the rulers in Dreamweaver's document window to precisely align elements in your layout. You can select from pixels, inches, or centimeters as the ruler's unit of measurement.

You can toggle rulers on and off in your document window from the View menu. By default, when you show rulers, Dreamweaver sets the point of origin at the top left of the page. You can change the origin to make it easier to align objects within your layout. Dreamweaver also allows you to reset the origin back to the top left.

When you use rulers in combination with guides and grids, you have powerful visual tools to help you position, measure, and resize elements in Design view. These tools are especially useful when you use CSS instead of tables to lay out pages.

See also>>

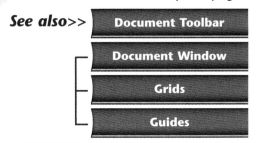

Document Toolbar

Document Window

Grids

Guides

1 Click View.

2 Click Rulers.

3 Click Show to toggle rulers on and off.

● Rulers display on the top and left of the Document Window.

4 Repeat steps **1** and **2** to display the Rulers submenu, and select a unit of measurement.

The default unit of measurement is pixels.

5 Click the Ruler Cross-hairs icon (⌖).

6 Drag the point of origin to a new location.

● Dreamweaver changes the 0, 0 coordinates to your new location.

To reset the 0, 0 coordinates to the top and left of the Document Window, you can click View, then click Rulers, and then click Reset Origin.

SITE DEFINITION:
Cloaking

You can use cloaking to exclude selected folders and file types from Dreamweaver operations. These operations include getting or putting, Check in and Check out, generating reports, synchronizing, finding newer local or remote files, checking and changing links, working with the Assets panel, and updating templates and library items. This feature is useful when you have archived material, parts of a site under construction, or source files that you do not want to include in these day-to-day tasks.

You can cloak folders, but not individual files. However, you can cloak any file that is of a certain

type. For example, you may have large Photoshop images with the .psd file extension that would take up a lot of space on the server. You can add this extension to the Cloaking settings in the Site Definition dialog box to prevent Dreamweaver from transferring them to the remote server.

See also>> Files Panel: Using Files In

See also>> Cloak Files and Folders

FTP

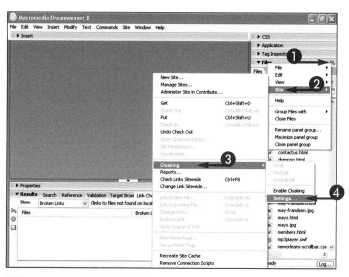

① Click the File Options button (📑) in the Files panel.

② Click Site.

③ Click Cloaking.

④ Click a cloaking option.

This example uses the Settings option.

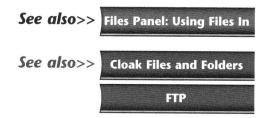

The Site Definition dialog box appears, with the Cloaking category selected.

⑤ Click the "Cloak files ending with" option (☐ changes to ☑) to cloak files by type.

Dreamweaver turns this feature on by default.

⑥ Type extensions for file types, preceded by a period.

⑦ Click the Enable cloaking option (☐ changes to ☑) to enable cloaking.

SITE DEFINITION:
Local Info

You can set up the Local Info category of the Site Definition dialog box to tell Dreamweaver the location of the folder where you are storing your site files, as well as the location of the default images folder within this root folder. You can also type the HTTP address if you are using site-relative links, and tell the Link Checker whether to distinguish between links by case. By default, Dreamweaver also enables cache, the database that it maintains for site information.

Dreamweaver needs a site definition for each site in order to perform all of its management functions,

such as link checking, template- and library-based updates, and file and folder tracking. Local Info is the most critical category, and is the only category that you absolutely must define in order to begin. You can always tweak the other categories later.

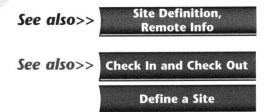

See also>> Site Definition, Remote Info

See also>> Check In and Check Out

Define a Site

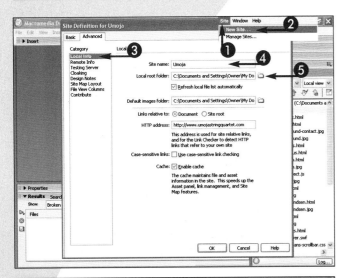

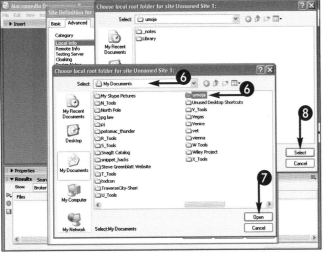

1 Click Site.

2 Click New Site.

3 In the Advanced tab of the Site Definition dialog box, click the Local Info category.

4 Type a descriptive name for the site in the Local Info section.

5 Click the folder icon (📁) next to the Local root folder field.

The Choose local root folder for site dialog box appears.

6 Click here and navigate to the folder that contains your site files.

7 Click Open.

Dreamweaver opens the folder and displays its contents.

8 Click Select.

On the Macintosh, you simply navigate to the file and click Choose.

You can now add information to other categories in the Site Definition dialog box.

SITE DEFINITION:
Remote Info

You can use the Remote Info category of the Site Definition dialog box to configure settings for transferring files to and from the remote server with Dreamweaver's native FTP features. Dreamweaver provides a menu of options, including: None, if you do not plan to upload the site; FTP, or File Transfer Protocol, which you can use to transfer your files from your computer to a Web host; Local/Network, if you are hosting the files from a local or networked computer; Remote Development Services, or RDS, in conjunction with a ColdFusion server; Microsoft Visual SourceSafe, a Windows technology; and Web-based Distributed Authoring and Versioning, or WebDAV, with an appropriately configured server.

Dreamweaver also offers other site management options. Maintain Synchronization Information is a default option that allows Dreamweaver to maintain the information it needs to synchronize local and remote files. You can also enable the Check In and Check Out options, and have Dreamweaver automatically upload files whenever you save them.

See also>> **Manage Sites Window**

Site Definition: Local Info

See also>> **Check-In and Check-Out**

Define a Site

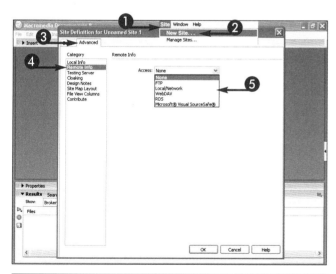

① Click Site.

② Click New Site.

You can also click Manage Sites if you want to select a site for which you have already entered Local Info.

③ In the Site Definition dialog box, click the Advanced tab.

If you have not already done so, you must first configure Local Info options.

④ Click Remote Info.

⑤ Click here and select an Access option.

Dreamweaver displays a series of fields based on your Access option.

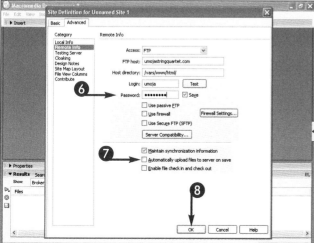

⑥ Type your remote information.

⑦ Click to select your site management options (☐ changes to ☑).

⑧ Click OK.

Dreamweaver accepts your remote info settings.

SNIPPETS PANEL:
Using to Store Reusable Code

You can use the Snippets panel to store reusable bits of code that you use frequently in your sites, thus saving you development time. You can use Dreamweaver's predefined snippets or create your own. Snippets can be HTML, JavaScript, or any programming language that you may use in your pages.

Dreamweaver stores its predefined snippets in folders according to their category. You can create new folders for your own snippets. You can also add new snippets, or edit, rearrange, and delete snippets using the icons in the Snippets panel.

Dreamweaver provides a preview pane so that you can see a snippet before you insert it. When you edit a snippet, Dreamweaver does not update instances of it in your pages. You can either insert snippets as solid blocks or wrap them around selections. You can also use them in all sites.

See also>> Library Items

See also>> Snippets: Create New

Snippets: Using Predefined

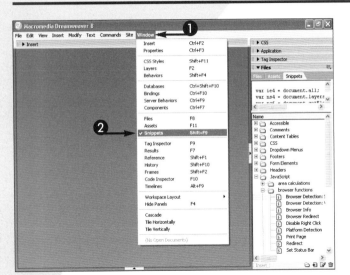

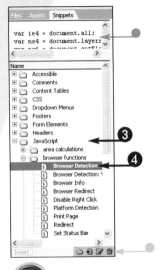

① Click Window.

② Click Snippets.

The Snippets panel opens.

③ Double-click to open a folder of predefined snippets.

④ Click a snippet.

● The Preview pane displays a preview of the code.

● You can click the New Folder icon (⬜) to create new folders for categories of snippets, the New Snippet icon (⬜) to create a new snippet, the Edit Snippets icon (⬜) to edit selected snippets, and the Trash icon (⬜) to delete selected snippets.

SORT TABLE:
Using to Sort Data in Tables

You can use the Sort Table command to sort columns of data in a table. You can decide which column to sort, and even sort by a second column for more complex tables. You can sort either alphabetically or numerically, and you can sort in ascending or descending order.

Dreamweaver offers you additional sorting options. For example, you can include the first row of the table in your sort if you are not using it as a header row. If you have thead and tfoot rows in your table, you can sort them by the same criteria as the rest of the table, although these

rows do so within their own section of the table. If you have row colors associated with your data, then you can keep these color associations after Dreamweaver sorts the data. You should save your document before you sort in case you get unexpected results.

See also>> **Format Table Command**

See also>> **Import Office Documents**

Tables: Examine and Set Properties

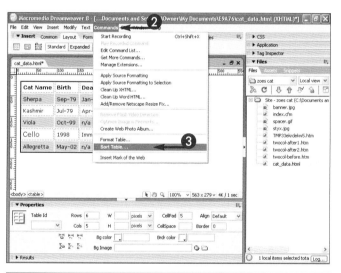

① Open a page with a data table.

② Click Commands.

③ Click Sort Table.

The Sort Table dialog box appears.

④ Click in these fields to select a column and select a sort order.

To sort by a second column, you can repeat steps **4** and **5** in the Then by fields.

⑤ Click any options that you want to use (☐ changes to ☑).

⑥ Click Apply to see the sort operation, or OK to apply and close the dialog box.

● Dreamweaver sorts the table in the order that you selected.

SPLIT CODE AND DESIGN VIEW:
View Documents With

You can use Split view to see both the code and the design of your document simultaneously. You may find it helpful to see HTML, even if you usually work only with Dreamweaver's visual tools. You may sometimes see odd behavior in Design view that you cannot fix visually, but can quickly correct by examining the code. Many developers even use Dreamweaver's Split view to learn HTML because they can watch the code that Dreamweaver writes as they insert elements in the page. Conversely, you can type in Code view and watch the effect in Design view.

You can access this option either via Code and Design under the View menu or the Split button in

the Document toolbar. Dreamweaver splits your page so that the code is on top and the design is on the bottom.

See also>>

| Code View Options |
| CSS Styles Panel: View Options |
| Design View |
| Document Toolbar |

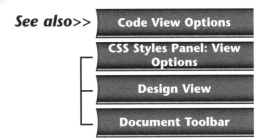

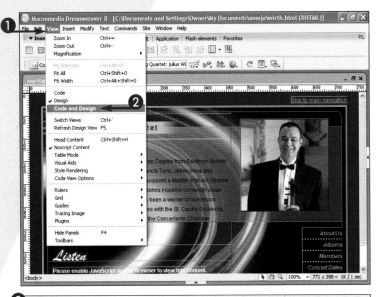

① **Click View.**

② **Click Code and Design.**

Dreamweaver switches to Split view.

③ **Click Split in the Document toolbar.**

Dreamweaver opens the page with the code on top and the design on the bottom.

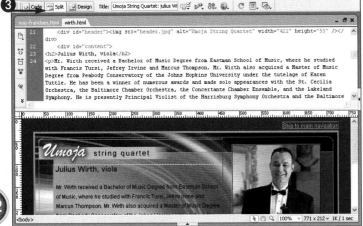

STANDARD TOOLBAR:
Use to Perform Common Tasks

You can use the Standard toolbar to quickly perform common file and editing tasks. The toolbar has familiar buttons like those you find in Microsoft Office applications. The first two icons allow you to create new documents and open existing ones. The New icon opens the New Document window. The third and fourth icons allow you to save the current document or save all open documents. The fifth icon allows you to print the Code view of your document. The last five icons allow you to edit documents with standard tasks; you can cut, copy, paste, undo, and redo.

Dreamweaver does not turn on the Standard toolbar by default. You must turn it on from the Toolbar menu in the View menu. After you turn it on, it appears on top of your document below its filename.

See also>>

New Document Window

Workspace: Macintosh

Workspace: Windows

1 Click View.

2 Click Toolbars.

3 Click Standard.

Dreamweaver displays the Standard toolbar.

The last five icons allow you to edit documents with standard tasks; you can cut, copy, paste, undo, and redo.

● You can click to create new files (🗋) or open existing ones (📂).

● You can click these buttons to save current (💾) or all open (🗐) documents.

● You can click this button to print code (🖨).

● You edit documents using the Cut (✂), Copy (📄), Paste (📋), Undo (↶) and Redo (↷) buttons.

START PAGE:
Using to Initiate Tasks

You can use the Start page as your starting point when you launch Dreamweaver. When no page is open, Dreamweaver displays a Start page by default. It is a type of command central for performing common tasks. You can use it to go to the Macromedia Dreamweaver exchange so that you can download new extensions. You can also use it to open existing documents or to create new documents of many different file types. When you select a category in the Create from Samples list, Dreamweaver opens the New Document window to the design category that you select.

The Start page also provides links to learning tools such as a Dreamweaver quick tour, documentation resources, the Developer Center, and authorized training resources.

See also>> **New Document Window**

Preferences: General

Preferences: New Document

See also>> **New Documents**

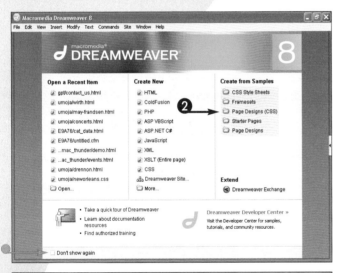

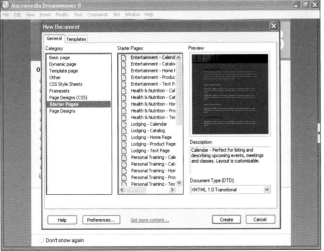

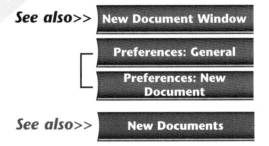

① Launch Dreamweaver without opening a document.

Dreamweaver displays the Start page.

You can click an option to open an existing document, create a new document, or go to the Dreamweaver Exchange or a learning resource.

● You can click the Don't show again option to turn off this feature (☐ changes to ☑).

② Click an option in the Create from Samples list.

Dreamweaver opens the New Document dialog box to the category that you selected.

STATUS BAR:
Get Information From

You can use the Status bar at the bottom of the Document Window to quickly glean information about the current document. For example, when you select an element on the page, the Status bar's Tag Selector shows the hierarchy of tags for that element. You can also keep track of the document's size and the amount of time that it takes a visitor to access it at the default connection speed that you set in the Status Bar preferences. You can also select a window-size option to view your page boundaries for different screen resolutions.

The Status bar also includes some new tools for viewing your document. There are the Select, Hand, and Zoom tools, and a Set Magnification menu to help you focus on page elements.

See also>>

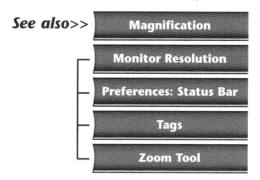

Magnification

Monitor Resolution

Preferences: Status Bar

Tags

Zoom Tool

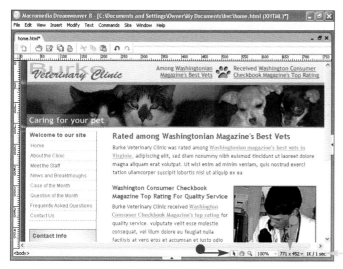

① Open a document.

Dreamweaver displays the Status bar at the bottom of the window.

● You can click here to select a window size.

● You can view document size and download time.

● You can use the new visual tools.

② Select an element on the page.

● The Tag Selector shows the tag hierarchy of the selected element.

STYLE RENDERING TOOLBAR:
Use with Style Sheets

You can use the new Style Rendering toolbar to see how your design looks in different media types. By default, Dreamweaver displays your design for the screen media type, which shows how your design looks on a monitor. Dreamweaver's Style Rendering toolbar also includes buttons to show how your page looks in print, on a handheld device such as a Blackberry, on a projection screen, on a Teletype machine, or on a TV screen. You can also toggle style sheets on and off to see your unformatted page.

You must create and attach a media-specific style sheet to your document in order for its media button to work. Dreamweaver simulates the document's display on the device for which it is intended when you activate the appropriate media type button.

See also>>   CSS Styles Panel

See also>>   CSS, Media Type Style

Style Rendering Toolbar

1 Click View.

2 Click Toolbars.

3 Click Style Rendering.

● Dreamweaver displays the Style Rendering toolbar in your Document Window.

4 Click a media type button to display the document with a device-dependent style sheet.

5 Click the Toggle Displaying of CSS Style button (⬚) to toggle the style sheets on and off.

SYNCHRONIZE FILES COMMAND:
Select Synchronize Options

You can synchronize files between your computer and the remote server to ensure that both have the newest versions. When you select the synchronize option, Dreamweaver first displays a Synchronize Files dialog box for setting options. You can either synchronize the entire site or selected files only.

You can select the direction in which you want to transfer the newest files. The Put Newer Files to Remote command uploads newer local files to the remote server. The Get Newer Files from Remote command downloads newer files from the remote server to the local computer. The Get and Put

Newer Files command transfers the newest versions of the files in either direction.

After you set your options, you can preview the list of files that Dreamweaver is set to synchronize. If you want, you can select individual files and click an action button. For example, you can put, get, or delete a file, or have Dreamweaver ignore a file during the synchronization process.

See also>> | **Files Panel: Using Files in**

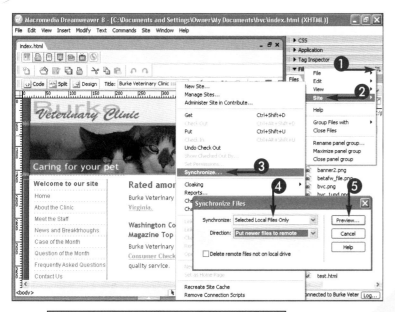

① Click the File Options button (▤) in the Files panel.

② Click Site.

③ Click Synchronize.

The Synchronize Files dialog box appears.

④ Click here to select synchronize options.

⑤ Click Preview.

The Synchronize dialog box appears.

● Dreamweaver lists the files that it is set to update.

● You can click to select actions for each file.

● You can click the Show all files option (☐ changes to ☑) to show all files.

TAGS:
Insert Using the Tag Chooser

You can use the Tag Chooser to insert tags into your page when you are in Code view. You can locate and insert a tag, and even select attributes and CSS styles for it at the same time. Dreamweaver inserts the tag at the insertion point in your document.

Some Web developers prefer to manually code their documents. Dreamweaver includes many robust tools for expediting this workflow, of which the Tag Chooser is one. You can insert any tag included in Dreamweaver's Tag libraries. Dreamweaver offers libraries for the common languages that developers use, including ColdFusion, ASP.NET, ASP, PHP, HTML, JSP, Jrun, and WML.

When using this feature in combination with the new Coding toolbar and Code Collapse feature, experienced developers can manually code their documents as quickly as they can design them visually.

See also>>

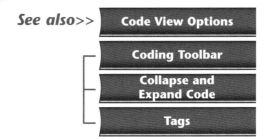

Code View Options

Coding Toolbar

Collapse and Expand Code

Tags

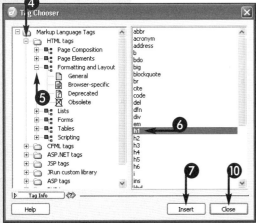

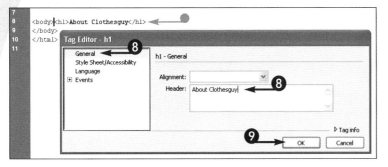

① Open a page in Code view.

② Right-click (Ctrl-click) in the page where you want to insert the tag.

A menu appears with different options.

③ Click Insert Tag.

The Tag Chooser dialog box appears.

④ Click a plus sign (⊞) to open a Tag library.

The Tag library expands, and ⊞ turns to a minus sign (⊟).

⑤ Click a (⊞) to expand a category.

⑥ Click a tag.

⑦ Click Insert.

The Tag Editor opens for your element.

⑧ Fill in the fields for each category that you want to use.

⑨ Click OK.

The Tag Chooser reappears onscreen.

⑩ Click Close in the Tag Chooser.

● Dreamweaver inserts the tag at the insertion point that you selected.

TAG LIBRARIES:
Manage and Create

You can use the Tag Library Editor to manage and create Tag libraries. Dreamweaver includes libraries for many of the common languages that developers use, including ColdFusion, ASP.NET, ASP, PHP, HTML, JSP, Jrun, and WML.

A Tag library is a collection of tags in a particular language, along with information about how Dreamweaver should format these tags. Dreamweaver needs Tag library information for use with code hints, target browser checks, the Tag Chooser, and other coding features.

You can edit tags in existing libraries, or you can use the Tag Library Editor to delete libraries and

add new ones. You can name your new libraries and add tags and attributes to them. You can also set library properties and decide in which document types you want to use them.

See also>>

| Code View Options |
| Coding Toolbar |
| Collapse and Expand Code |
| Tags |

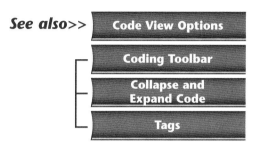

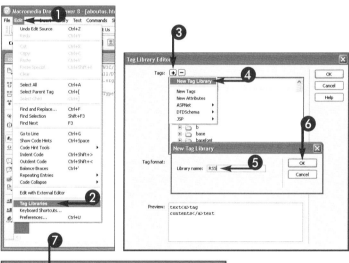

1 Click Edit.
2 Click Tag Libraries.
   The Tag Library Editor appears.
3 Click the Tags ⊞.
4 Click New Tag Library.
   The New Tag Library dialog box appears.
5 Type a name for the new library.
6 Click OK.
   The Tag Library Editor opens and selects your new library.

7 Click the Tags ⊞.
8 Click New Tags.
   The New Tags dialog box appears.
9 Type a tag name.
10 Click OK.
   Dreamweaver adds the tags to the new library.
11 Click OK.

TEMPLATES:
Using the Category in the Insert Panel

You can use the Template category in the Insert toolbar to create templates or to add template objects to a template page. Templates ensure design consistency in each page of your site. When visitors know where repeating elements such as headers, footers, and navigation buttons are located on each page, they can concentrate on the content. Templates also protect locked regions of the page so that you do not inadvertently delete or modify them.

The Common category of Dreamweaver's Insert toolbar provides a menu of template objects that you can use with a single mouse-click.

Basing each page of the site on a template saves a lot of time both during the development of the site and when you need to update the site.

See also>> Insert Toolbar: Common

New Document Window

See also>> New Documents: Create from Templates

Templates: Create a Template

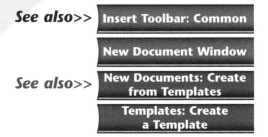

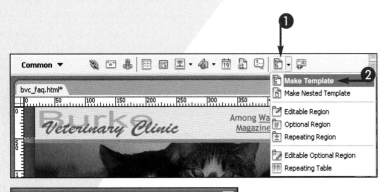

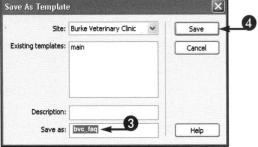

1. Click the Template icon (🗐) in the Common category of the Insert toolbar.

2. Click an option.

A dialog box appears for the option.

3. Type the text that you want in the fields of the dialog box.

4. Click Save to accept your changes.

Dreamweaver executes your template option.

120

TIMELINES:
Using the Panel

You can animate layers by using the Timeline panel, a visual interface that includes rewind, play, and playback frame controls as well as a play head. When you manipulate a layer with the Timeline, Dreamweaver writes JavaScript into your HTML code. This creates Dynamic HTML, or DHTML, for pages that have movement and include the possibility of user-driven interactions.

Timelines consist of a series of still frames that combine to create the illusion of motion. Each frame shows how the object looks and where it is located at a particular moment in time. You can use timelines to change a layer's size, visibility,

location, and Z-index. You can also use the Behaviors Channel to add a Dreamweaver behavior to a specific frame. You can even use multiple timelines to animate different layers simultaneously.

See also>>

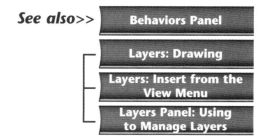

Behaviors Panel

Layers: Drawing

Layers: Insert from the View Menu

Layers Panel: Using to Manage Layers

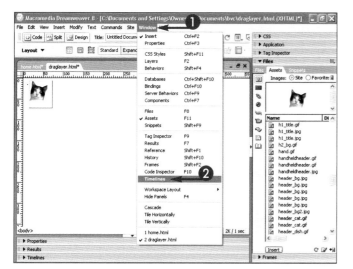

① Click Window.

② Click Timelines.

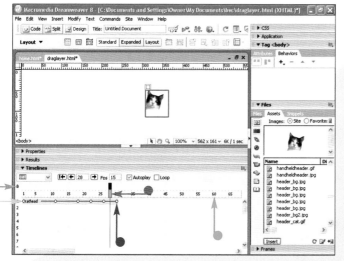

The Timelines panel opens.

● The Behavior Channel is where you add behaviors to a specific frame on the timeline.

● The Animation bar shows the duration of the timeline's animation.

● Keyframes let you control the objects position in the timeline at key points during the animation.

● You can drag the Play back head to go back and forth in the animation

● Frame numbers show the number of frames in the timeline and show where you are in the sequence.

UNTITLED DOCUMENT REPORTS:
Create a Listing for All

You can create a report that lists the untitled documents in your site, a specific folder, or the current document. You can then add the missing titles to pages before uploading them to your Web host.

Adding titles to documents is important for a variety of reasons. When a visitor bookmarks or adds your page as one of their favorites, the browser uses your document title as the bookmark or favorites name. If you do not enter a title for the page, then the browser lists your page with Dreamweaver's default

"Untitled Document." This makes it difficult for the visitor to later remember what the page is about.

Page titles are also important for accessibility. Your page title is the first thing that the screen reader reads to the visually impaired visitor. Because these visitors cannot scan a page to see if it includes the information that they need, a descriptive page title is very helpful.

See also>> **Results Panel**

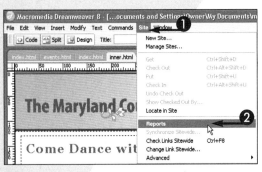

① Click Site.

② Click Reports.

The Reports dialog box appears.

③ Click here and select an option.

④ Click Untitled Documents under HTML Reports (☐ changes to ☑).

⑤ Click Run.

● Dreamweaver lists all untitled documents in the Results panel.

⑥ Double-click a document in the Results list.

● Dreamweaver opens the document so that you can enter a new title.

UPDATE TEMPLATE PAGES:
Current Page or Entire Site

You can use the Update Pages command to manually update pages based on templates. When you update an entire site, Dreamweaver reapplies the appropriate templates to individual files. However, you can also allow Dreamweaver to update only files that are based on one particular template within the site.

When you make a change to a template and then save it, Dreamweaver displays a dialog box asking if you want to update all child pages that are based on the template. Most of the time, this is exactly what you want to do. However, you may sometimes make changes to a template and choose not to immediately update the child pages.

You can also use the Update Current Page command to update only the open document. In this case, Dreamweaver does not display a dialog box, and automatically updates the page.

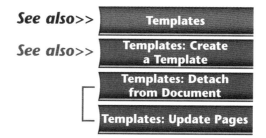

See also>> Templates

See also>> Templates: Create a Template

Templates: Detach from Document

Templates: Update Pages

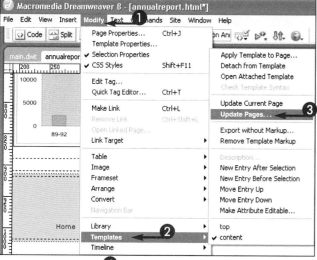

1 Click Modify.

2 Click Templates.

3 Click Update Pages.

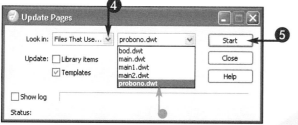

The Update Pages dialog box appears.

4 Click here and select either Entire Site or Files That Use.

● If you select Files That Use, you can click here and select a target template.

5 Click Start.

● When Dreamweaver finishes updating pages, the Start button changes to a Done button.

6 Click Close.

VIEW OPTIONS: In Document Window

You can use the View Options menu in the Document toolbar of the Document Window to display and hide various design and code options on your page. If you are in Design view, then the menu shows design options such as grids, guides, and rulers. If you are in Code view, then it shows options such as line numbers, word wrap, and syntax coloring. If you are in Split view, then all of the options display.

Design and Split views both allow you to enable the Head Content toolbar. This toolbar displays icons that represent each head element on your page, such as a link to a CSS document or a script. Split view also

allows you to display Design view on the top and Code view on the bottom.

See also>> | Code View Options |

See also>>
| Document Toolbar |
| Document Window |
| Split Code and Design View |
| Trace Images |

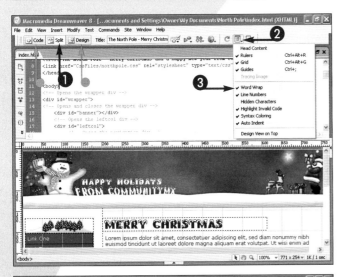

1 Click Split in the Document toolbar.

● If you want only code or design options, you can click either Code or Design.

2 Click the View Options icon (▣) to display a menu.

3 Click all of the options that you want to display on your page.

Dreamweaver displays the selected options.

4 Click ▣.

5 Click the Head Content option to display the Head Content toolbar.

6 Repeat steps **4** and **5**, selecting Design View on Top in step **5**.

Design view displays on the top and Code view displays on the bottom.

7 Click an option on the Head Content toolbar.

● The code displays the selected head content.

VISUAL AIDS:
CSS Layout Backgrounds

You can use the Visual Aids icon in the Document toolbar to enable and disable CSS visual aids. Dreamweaver provides tools to help you visualize and troubleshoot your CSS layout blocks in Design view. A CSS layout block is an HTML element that you can position anywhere on your page. Examples of CSS layout blocks include DIV tags, an image or other element with an absolute or relative position assigned to it, or a tag with display:block assigned to it.

CSS layout backgrounds show each CSS block with a temporarily assigned background color. This background color hides the other background colors and images that appear when the page is in normal view. Dreamweaver assigns each CSS layout block a distinctive background color that clearly differentiates it from the surrounding elements, thus making it easier to troubleshoot layout problems.

See also>>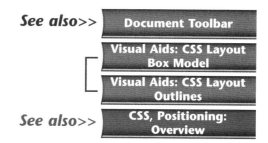

See also>>

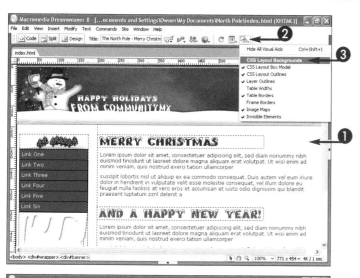

① Open a page that includes CSS layout blocks.

② Click the Visual Aids icon (🖼) in the Document toolbar.

③ Click CSS Layout Backgrounds.

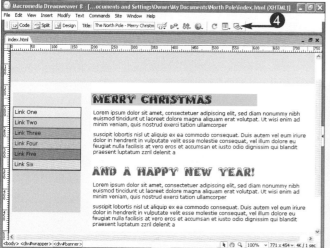

Dreamweaver applies color backgrounds to the CSS blocks on your page.

④ Repeat steps **2** and **3**.

Dreamweaver turns off the background colors.

125

VISUAL AIDS:
CSS Layout Box Model

You can use the Visual Aids icon in the Document toolbar to enable and disable the CSS Layout Box Model visualization tool. When turned on, this tool adds crosshatching around a selected element to represent its margins and padding. When you move your mouse over the areas of crosshatching, Dreamweaver displays a tooltip with values for the margin, padding, and border properties of the element.

Box model problems are a common source of CSS layout discrepancies in different browsers. Some versions of Internet Explorer render boxes in an unorthodox way, causing padding and borders to skew layouts that need to have precise dimensions.

The Layout Box Model visualization feature of Dreamweaver 8 can help you troubleshoot and fix your layouts.

See also>>

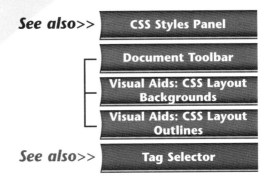

CSS Styles Panel

Document Toolbar

Visual Aids: CSS Layout Backgrounds

Visual Aids: CSS Layout Outlines

See also>> **Tag Selector**

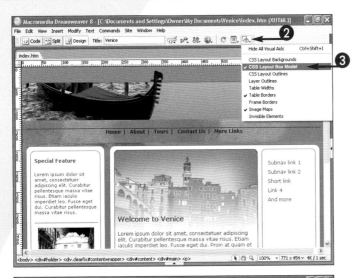

① Open a page that includes CSS layout blocks.

② Click 🔊 in the Document toolbar.

③ Click CSS Layout Box Model.

Dreamweaver applies the box model visualization to the current page.

④ Select a block element in the Tag Selector.

● Dreamweaver displays margins and padding for the element.

These are updated.

● You can view and change properties in the CSS panel.

● You can view tooltips when your mouse points at the crosshatching.

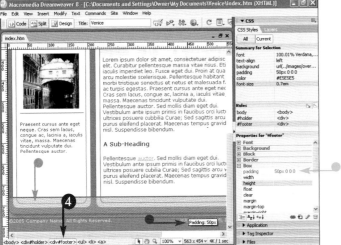

VISUAL AIDS:
CSS Layout Outlines

You can quickly see where DIVs and other elements with the display:block property are located on the page with the CSS Layout Outlines visualization tool.

The DIV tag defines divisions or sections on an HTML page. Unless you give them background colors or borders, their boundaries can be hard to see. The DIV is a critical element in laying out pages with CSS positioning rather than tables. Although these elements are tricky to manage and troubleshoot, CSS Layout Outlines helps you see the exact location of each DIV on the page.

Dreamweaver outlines DIVs and objects that have the display:block property with a dashed line, and

activates these outlines by default. When you move your mouse over the side of a DIV, the outline turns into a solid, colored line. You can change the color of this line in the highlighting preferences.

See also>>

| Preferences: Highlighting |
| Visual Aids: CSS Layout Backgrounds |
| Visual Aids: CSS Layout Box Model |

See also>>

| CSS, Positioning: Overview |
| DIV Tags |

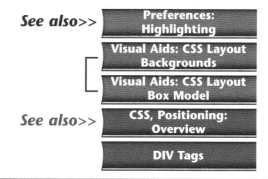

① Click 🖳 in the Document toolbar.

② Click CSS Layout Outlines.

Dreamweaver selects this option by default.

● Dreamweaver adds dashed lines around the divs on the page.

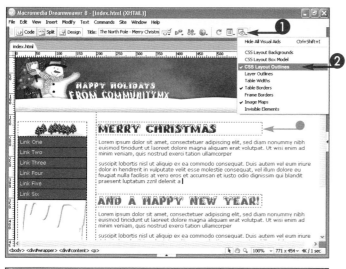

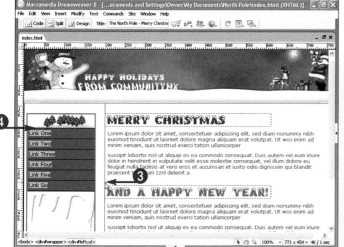

③ Position your mouse over a dashed line around a DIV.

The dashed line changes to a solid colored line.

④ Click a dashed line.

Dreamweaver selects the DIV and surrounds it with a thick, solid blue line.

⚠ WARNINGS:
Reset Dependent File Prompts

After you have chosen to hide dependent file prompt dialog boxes, you can display them again by resetting this option in Site preferences.

Dreamweaver displays a dialog box for such server tasks as putting and getting dependent files, putting and getting files in sites enabled for check in and check out, and moving files on the server. Dependent files are referenced files such as style sheets, media, and images that load when your page loads. After you upload these dependent files, you often do not need to upload them again when you update a page. Having to select "No" to dismiss the prompts can become annoying, and so Dreamweaver allows you to turn the prompts off.

You may sometimes want to see the dialog boxes again. For example, you may want to reset the prompts before you upload the files and their dependent files for a new site.

See also>> **File Transfer: Get and Put**

Preferences: Site

See also>> **Check In and Check Out**

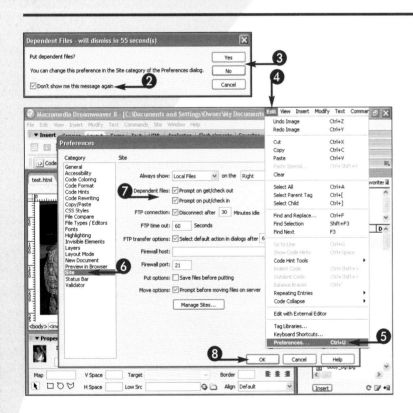

① Put or get a file.

A dialog box displays, asking you to confirm the action.

② Click the "Don't show me this message again" option (☐ changes to ☑).

The dialog box does not display the next time you put or get files.

③ Click Yes or No to confirm or reject the action.

④ Click Edit.

Macintosh users click the Dreamweaver menu.

⑤ Click Preferences.

The Preferences dialog box appears.

⑥ Click Site from the Category list.

⑦ Click to select the Dependent Files options (☐ changes to ☑).

⑧ Click OK.

Dreamweaver resets the warning dialog boxes.

WORKSPACE LAYOUTS:
Customize Your Workspace

You can create and manage customized workspace layouts for different page development needs. For example, you can set up the groups of panels that you use most often when creating CSS documents or when coding database-driven Web pages. Dreamweaver saves layout options and attributes such as collapsed or expanded states, the size and position of the panels, and the size and position of the application window.

After you save a custom layout, its name displays in the Workspace Layout menu along with Dreamweaver's default layouts. You can then select it from the list whenever you want to use it.

You can also manage layouts. Dreamweaver lists all of your custom layouts in the Manage Workspace Layouts dialog box. You can easily rename or delete a name in the list.

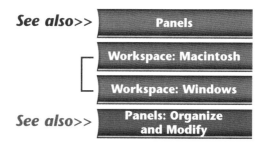

See also>> Panels

Workspace: Macintosh

Workspace: Windows

See also>> Panels: Organize and Modify

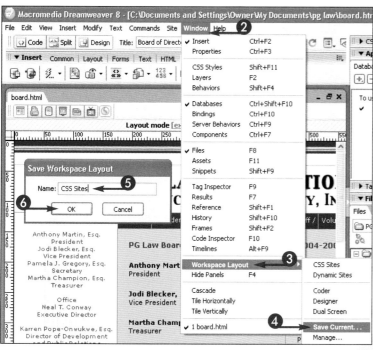

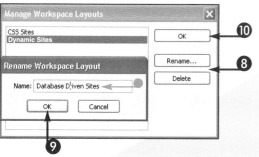

1. Arrange panels and the document window on the screen.
2. Click Window.
3. Click Workspace Layout.
4. Click Save Current.
5. In the Save Workspace Layout dialog box, type a name for the layout.
6. Click OK.

7. Repeat steps **2** to **4**, clicking Manage in the Workspace Layout submenu in step **4**.

   The Manage Workspace Layouts dialog box appears.
8. Click Rename or Delete.
   - You can type a new name here.
9. Click OK.
10. Click OK.

WORKSPACE: Macintosh

You can open multiple documents in a single window with the Macintosh Workspace Layout command. Each document has a tab that identifies it, and the tab brings its document to the front so that you can view and edit it. You can also display a menu with document options using the tab. One of these options allows you to open the tabbed window as a separate floating window.

The menu also allows you to create documents, save documents, revert to the last saved version of a document, and save all currently open tabbed documents. The menu also displays various options

for closing documents: You can close the current document, close all documents except for the current document, or close all documents.

If you have a file comparison utility on your computer, then you can also use the menu to use the Compare with Remote option to compare the local document to the equivalent document on the remote server.

See also>>

Document Window

Workspace Layouts

---

① Click Window.

② Click Workspace Layout.

③ Click an option.

The Default option arranges the panels, document window, and Properties inspector in an integrated layout that works best for many users.

④ Open several documents.

Dreamweaver displays the documents in one window.

⑤ Click a document's tab.

The document moves to the front of the document window.

⑥ Ctrl-click a tab.

A menu displays with document options.

WORKSPACE:
Windows

If you use a Windows computer, then you can choose between a Coder and a Designer workspace layout. The Designer workspace layout is a Multiple Document Interface, or MDI, with all panels and document windows integrated into one large application window. If you select this layout, then Dreamweaver arranges the panels on the right, and displays the Properties inspector by default. Documents open in Design view.

Dreamweaver offers a Coder workspace layout that looks similar to those that Macromedia Homesite and Macromedia ColdFusion Studio use. It is also an integrated workspace, but the panels appear on the left, and documents open in Code

view. This workspace does not display the Properties inspector.

The first time you launch Dreamweaver, a dialog box allows you to choose between the Coder and designer workspaces. You can switch workspaces at any time by accessing the Workspace Layout menu option.

See also>>

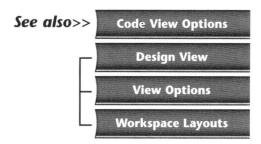

Code View Options

Design View

View Options

Workspace Layouts

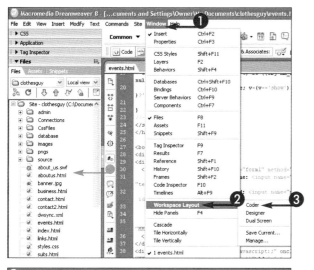

① Click Window.

② Click Workspace Layout.

③ Click Coder.

● Dreamweaver arranges an integrated set of panels and a document window for coders.

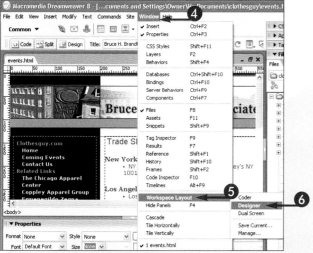

④ Click Window.

⑤ Click Workspace Layout.

⑥ Click Designer.

Dreamweaver arranges an integrated set of panels and a document window for designers.

XML:
Attach XSL Page To

You can use the Attach an XSLT Stylesheet command to link an XSLT page to an XML document.

Extensible Markup Language, or XML, is a language that allows you to structure information. Although XML uses tags similar to HTML, XML tags are not predefined as they are in HTML. Instead, XML lets you create tags that most accurately describe your data. For example, you can create tags called title, author, description, and price to describe the data for a book. Just like HTML tags, your new XML tags include an opening and closing tag.

Dreamweaver 8 includes new visual authoring tools that can help you to integrate XML-based data into your Web pages. After you create an XSLT document, attach an XML source to it, and bind and format the XML data in the XSLT document, you must attach the XSLT document to the XML document. You can then preview the results in a modern browser directly from Dreamweaver's Design view.

See also>>   **XSLT**

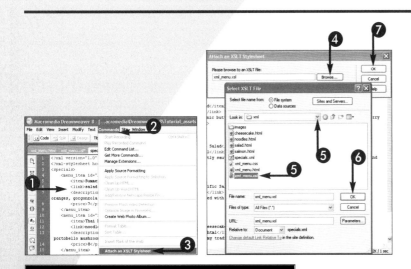

1. Open an XML document.
2. Click Commands.
3. Click Attach an XSLT Stylesheet.

   The Attach an XSLT Stylesheet dialog box appears.
4. Click Browse.

   The Select XSLT File dialog box appears.

5. Navigate to your XML file.
6. Click OK to close the dialog box.
7. Click OK.

   Dreamweaver attaches the XSLT style sheet.

   You can preview the page in a modern browser.

   Note: A Tutorial assets folder in the Dreamweaver application folder includes files for an imaginary Web site called Cafe Townsend within which are XML files. These files help you follow along with the Dreamweaver Help XML/XSLT tutorial.

XSLT:
Convert HTML Page To

You can use the Convert to XSLT 1.0 command to convert a regular HTML page into an XSLT document.

Dreamweaver 8 includes new visual authoring tools that can help you to integrate XML-based data such as RSS feeds into your Web pages. The core workflow involves creating an XSLT document or converting an existing HTML page to an XSLT document, attaching an XML source to the XSLT document, binding and formatting the XML data in the XSLT document, and finally, attaching the XSLT document to the XML document. You can preview the result in a modern browser directly from Dreamweaver's Design view.

XSL is an acronym for Extensible Stylesheet Language. XSL is the language for specifying style sheets for documents that are created with Extensible Markup Language, or XML. XSL Transformation, or XSLT, is used with XSL to describe how an XML document is transformed into another document, such as an HTML page, that a modern browser can read.

See also>> **New Document Window**

XML

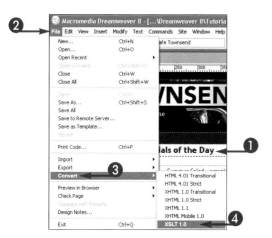

① Open the HTML page that you want to convert to XSLT 1.0.

② Click File.

③ Click Convert.

④ Click XSLT 1.0.

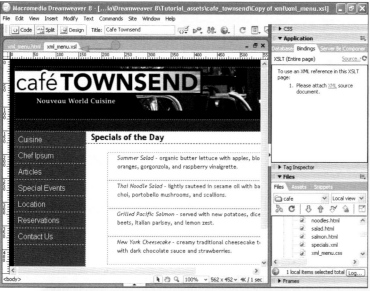

● Dreamweaver converts the page to XSLT 1.0 and changes the file extension to .xsl.

The page is now ready for you to attach an XML source document.

ZOOM TOOL:
Zoom In and Out of Documents

You can use the Zoom tool to increase or decrease the magnification of design elements on the page in Design view. This is particularly useful when you are designing layouts that need pixel-perfect alignments. It is also useful when you need to decipher small text, zoom in on an image to match a specific color, or select small objects.

The Zoom tool and its related tools, the Hand tool and the Select tool, are in the Status bar of the Document Window. After you zoom in or out of your document, you can use the Select tool to select elements that you want to edit. You can also use the

Hand tool if you need to pan around a large document.

Dreamweaver offers several zooming options. You can enter a value in the magnification field, select a value from the magnification menu, use keyboard shortcuts, or use the Zoom tool magnifying glass icon.

See also>>

Magnification

Status Bar

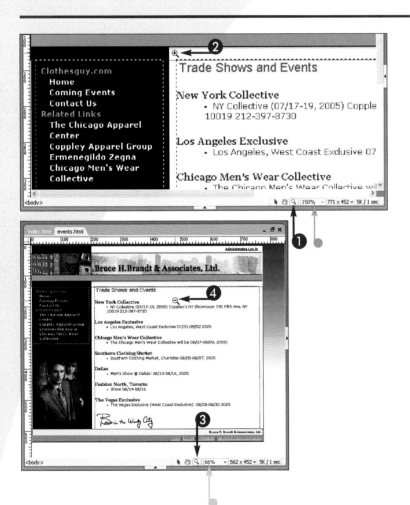

Zoom In

1. Click the Zoom tool (🔍) in the Status bar.

2. Click the page to zoom in.

   The Magnifying Glass icon displays a plus sign (🔍).

   • The Status bar displays the percent at which you magnified the document.

   You can also type a magnification value in this field or select an option from the menu.

Zoom Out

3. Click 🔍 in the Status bar.

4. Press and hold the Alt (Option) key and click the page to zoom out.

   The Magnifiying Glass icon displays a minus sign (🔍).

   • The Status bar displays the percent at which you magnified the document.

Dreamweaver 8
Visual Encyclopedia

Part II: Techniques

Working in the Dreamweaver environment can be a challenging task. With so many options for completing your work, you may feel overwhelmed by the many choices the software presents to you. Part II demystifies the process of working in Dreamweaver by giving examples of the common day-to-day tasks that every Web developer faces. You can find real-world examples of how to get your work done in a manner that is efficient for you while utilizing modern design techniques centered on Web standards.

Building Web sites with Dreamweaver requires the use of multiple interface tools, dialog boxes, and even different workspace layouts. You may find, for example, that for some design tasks you prefer to work directly in your code in Code view, while in other cases you prefer a more visual approach using the Design view. Or perhaps you want to work in a visual environment but have quick access to the underlying code to make small changes as needed. Dreamweaver makes all of this possible through the multiple inspectors and editors within the program.

No matter how you work in Dreamweaver, the techniques in this section get you started in the right direction by showing the most efficient and timesaving methods available for accomplishing common tasks.

ACCESSIBILITY REPORTS:
Create and Save

You can ensure that your pages follow accessibility guidelines by running an accessibility report on a page, selected pages, a folder, or even an entire site. You can check against all available accessibility guidelines, or check against those from the World Wide Web Consortium Web Accessibility Initiative — W3C/WCAG P.1 and P.2 accessibility — or from Section 508 of the Federal Rehabilitation Act, or 508 accessibility.

A disability can be visual, auditory, cognitive, or related to motor impairment. Government agencies require that Web authors follow Section 508

accessibility laws to accommodate disabled visitors, and many states require schools to make Web pages accessible to disabled students. You may also want to develop pages with accessibility in mind to ensure that people with disabilities can access the content of your site.

The accessibility report identifies potential problems, allows you to open the page with the problem area selected, and makes a reference panel available if you need to understand more about the problem.

See also>> Accessibility Preferences

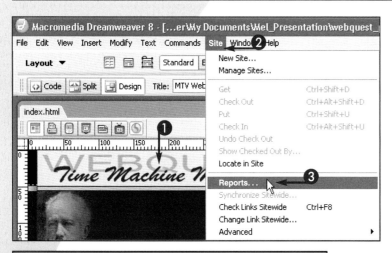

① Open the page that you want to check against accessibility guidelines.

② Click Site.

③ Click Reports.

The Reports dialog box appears.

④ Click here and select the option that you want to test.

⑤ Select the Accessibility option (☐ changes to ☑) in the HTML Reports list.

⑥ Click Report Settings.

The Accessibility dialog box appears.

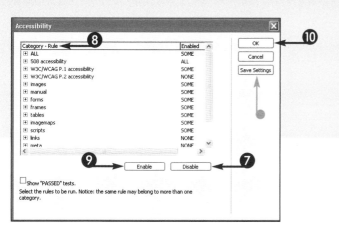

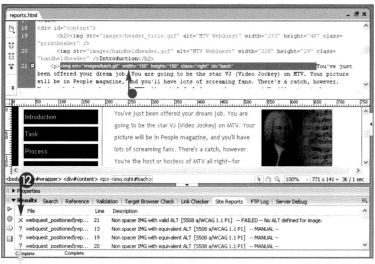

You can click OK to accept the default setting, which selects all categories.

⑦ To select only one category, click Disable to turn off all categories.

⑧ Click a category.

⑨ Click Enable.

● You can click Save Settings if you want to use these settings for all reports.

⑩ Click OK to close the Accessibility dialog box.

⑪ Click Run in the Reports dialog box.

Dreamweaver displays an accessibility report based on your settings.

● A question mark (?) indicates that you should check for a possible problem, and a red X (X) indicates that there is a definite problem.

⑫ Double-click X.

● Dreamweaver opens the page to the selected problem object.

TIPS

More Options!

If you do not understand the problem that the report displays, then select it in the Results panel and click the Info button (🖼️) on the left side. Dreamweaver opens the Reference panel with the UsableNet Accessibility Reference book. The book displays the problem rule and description, as well as how to fix it.

Check It Out!

You can get more information about accessibility initiatives at the following sites: the Web sites of the World Wide Web Consortium Web Accessibility Initiative, at www.w3.org/wai; Section 508 of the Federal Rehabilitation Act, at www.section508.gov; and Macromedia at www.macromedia.com/resources/accessibility.

ALIGN IMAGES:
To Text with CSS

You can use the CSS float property to align images to the right or left of text. When you add an image to your Web page, by default, the image's bottom aligns with the baseline of the surrounding text. Sometimes you may prefer to wrap your text around the image, achieving a magazine-like effect.

You can set up two classes in your style sheet, one to float images to the left of text, and the other to float images to the right. You can also include margins so that there is space between the image and the text. Once you create your classes, you can add them to as many images as you like.

See also>>

CSS Rule Definition Window

CSS Styles

See also>>

CSS: Create Embedded Style Sheet

CSS: Create External Style Sheet

Images: Insert in Documents

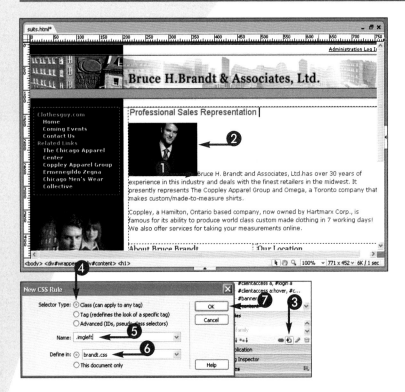

Align Image Left or Right

① Click to the left of the text that you want to align with an image.

② Insert an image at your cursor.

③ Click the New Rule button (⬚) in the Unified CSS panel.

The New CSS Rule dialog box appears.

④ Click the "Class (can apply to any tag)" option (○ changes to ⦿).

⑤ Click here and type a period followed by a descriptive name.

⑥ Select a Define in option for either an external CSS document or the document only (○ changes to ⦿).

⑦ Click OK.

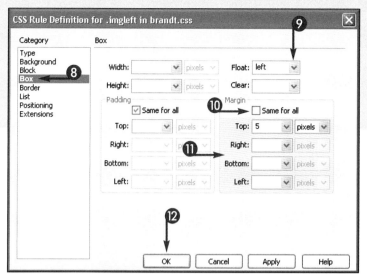

The CSS Rule Definition dialog box appears.

⑧ Click Box.

⑨ Click here and select either right or left.

The left option places the image to the left of the text, and the right option places the image to the right of the text.

⑩ Deselect the Same for all option (☑ changes to ☐).

⑪ Type the margin space to appear between your image and the text.

⑫ Click OK.

The CSS Rule Definition dialog box closes.

⑬ Select the image on the page.

⑭ Right-click (Ctrl-click) the img tag in the Tag Selector at the bottom of the Document Window.

⑮ Click Set Class.

⑯ Select a new class name.

Your image aligns to the surrounding text.

TIPS

Try This!

You can give your images more emphasis by adding borders. The Dreamweaver CSS panel allows you to add borders of various styles to one or all sides of the image, in the width and color of your choice. If you want all of your images to have the same border, then you can add the property directly to your image float classes.

Check It Out!

Some tasks seem simpler with the old HTML Properties inspector methods, than with CSS. If you want to align one image on the right and one image on the left, then read this article from Community MX for detailed directions on how to do this: www.communitymx.com/abstract.cfm?cid=529B0.

ALIGN IMAGES:
To Text with CSS (Continued)

You can use CSS to center images in a container. Images are inline elements that remain within the document flow, as opposed to block elements that appear on their own lines. As a result, you cannot use the `text align` property to center images. Instead, you must wrap images in block elements that center them, such as paragraphs or divs. You can also change the image to a `block` element with the `display` property.

When there is not enough text next to a floated image, objects beneath the text creep up next to the image. To prevent this, you can create a class that includes a Clear: both rule from Dreamweaver's Box

category, and apply the class to the element that follows the floated image and text.

See also>>
CSS Styles: Create a New Rule

CSS Rule Definition Window

See also>>
CSS: Create Embedded Style Sheet

CSS: Create External Style Sheet

Images: Insert in Documents

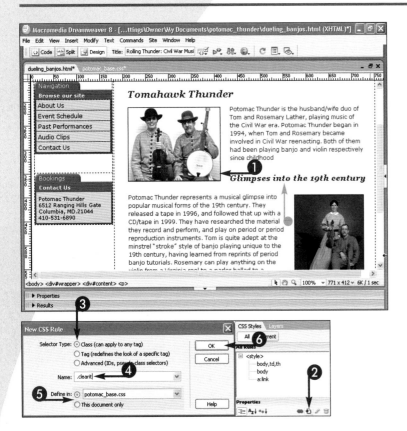

Clear Floated Images

① Insert a floated image in your page that has a height that exceeds the adjacent text.

● The text that follows creeps up next to the floated image.

② Click the New Rule button (⊞) in the Unified CSS panel.

The New CSS Rule dialog box appears.

③ Click the "Class (can apply to any tag)" option (○ changes to ◉).

④ Click here and type a period followed by a descriptive name.

⑤ Select a Define in option (○ changes to ◉) for either an external CSS document or the document only.

⑥ Click OK.

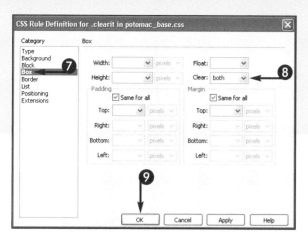

The CSS Rule Definition dialog box appears.

⑦ Select Box.

⑧ Click here and select either right, left, or both.

If your image floats to the left, then select left; if your image floats to the right, then select right.

If you have some images that float to left, and some that float to the right, then use both so that you can use the same class for either float direction.

⑨ Click OK.

The CSS Rule Definition dialog box closes.

⑩ Select the text on the page that you want to clear from the image's float.

⑪ Right-click (Ctrl-click) the HTML tag in the Tag Selector.

⑫ Click Set Class.

⑬ Select a new class name.

Your text appears below the image.

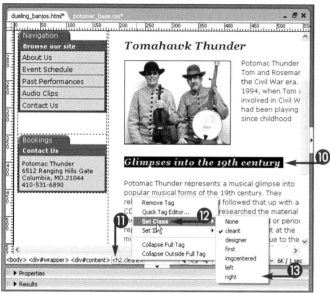

Try This!

Because many users visit your site with Internet Explorer 6, you may want to add some MetaTags in the head of your document to prevent Microsoft from meddling with your images by resizing them or adding its Image toolbar to the browser window:

```
<meta name="mssmarttagspreventparsing"
content="true" />
<meta http-equiv="imagetoolbar" content="no" />
<meta http-equiv="MSThemeCompatible"
content="no" />
```

For more, visit: www.microsoft.com/windows/ie/using/howto/customizing/imgtoolbar.mspx.

Did You Know?

Although HTML assigns an inline or block default to elements, you can often use the CSS display property to reverse this effect. For example, a popular accessibility technique is to format groups of links as unordered lists. If you want your link lists to appear horizontally rather than vertically, then you can set their display property to inline in your CSS document.

ALIGN IMAGES:
To Text with HTML

You can use the Align menu in the Properties inspector to align a selected image to the text on your Web page. When you add an image to the page, by default the bottom of the image lines up with the baseline of the surrounding text. Sometimes you may prefer to wrap your text around the image, achieving a magazine-like effect.

The Align menu includes a variety of alignment choices, such as Left, Right, Middle, and TextTop. The Properties inspector also includes H Space and V

Space attributes so that you can add horizontal and vertical space between the image and text.

When there is not enough text to reach the bottom of the image, headings below the image creep up into the empty space beneath the text. In these cases, you can use the `clear` attribute of the `break` element to correct the problem.

See also>> **Images: Insert in Documents**

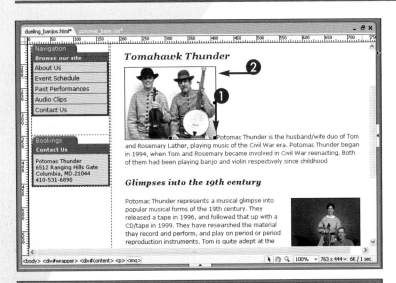

① Click your cursor to the left of the text that you want to align with an image.

② Insert your image.

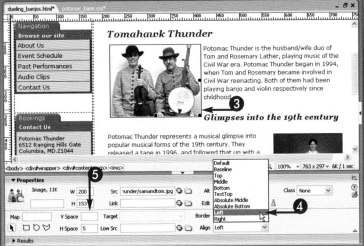

Your image aligns with the baseline of the text.

③ Select the image.

④ Click here and select an alignment option.

⑤ Type an H Space or V Space value to add space between the text and image.

In this example, the image aligns to the left of the text and has margin space around it.

If there are headings and text that follow a short paragraph next to the image, then they also wrap around the image.

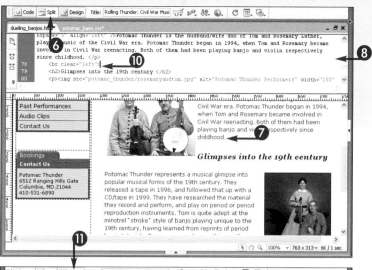

⑥ Click Split.

⑦ In the Design view, click your cursor after the text that you want to clear.

The cursor blinks in the same place in the Split view.

⑧ Switch to Split view.

⑨ Press Return.

⑩ Type **<br clear="*left*">**, with an alignment — either *left*, *right*, or *all*; all clears images on both the left and right side of the image.

⑪ Click the Design view button.

● The text following the image does not wrap around the image, nor does the surrounding text.

Try This!
In addition to text, you can also align an image with another image, a Flash object, a plug-in, or any other element that appears on the same line.

Did You Know?
Traditionally, designers have used tables to align their images in image galleries. This technique involves creating a table with multiple columns and rows, and adding a thumbnail image to each cell. When the visitor clicks a thumbnail image, it links to a full-sized version of the image, usually in a separate window. Many designers now prefer to use CSS to create image galleries. You can learn how to do this by reading the Floatutorial at css.maxdesign. com.au/floatutorial/tutorial0401.htm

ALIGN TEXT:
Within Documents (HTML)

You can select from four possible alignments for your text: Left, Center, Right, and Justify. By default, when you insert text on the page, it aligns left. You can use the Properties inspector to either select or remove an alignment option. You can also indent text by using the Indent and Outdent buttons. Dreamweaver uses the blockquote tag to indent text. Indenting text again adds a second `blockquote` tag, and outdenting removes `blockquote` tags.

Alignment is one of the core principles of good design. You should think about how your text and objects align and form a cohesive design that allows the reader's eye to flow easily around the page.

Beginners tend to overuse center alignments, which create a more formal appearance in the page, but which create large blocks of text that are harder to read. Web designers should also be careful about using justified text, which creates a sharp, straight edge to each side of the text. When readers view your page, their browsers may produce varying line widths, which can create unsightly spacing in justified text.

See also>>  **Properties Inspector: Text**

See also>> **CSS Styling: Control Text Appearance**

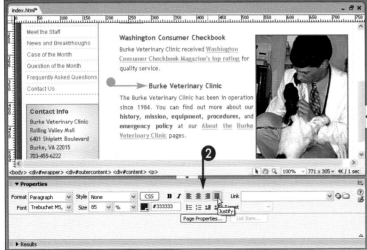

Using the Align Buttons

① Click in a heading or select the text that you want to align.

You can align any text, including paragraphs, headings, and link text; you can also align images.

② Click an alignment button, either Left (⬛), Center (⬛), Right (⬛), or Justify (⬛), in the Properties inspector.

● The text alignment changes.

③ Repeat steps **1** and **2** for any other text or headings that you want to align.

To remove an alignment, you can click the same alignment button that you clicked when you applied the alignment.

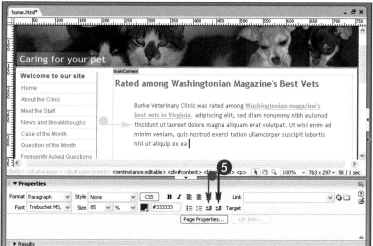

④ Select the text that you want to indent.

⑤ Click the Indent button (▤) in the Properties inspector.

● The text indents according to your selection.

You can repeat step **5** if you want to indent the text more.

● To remove an indent, you can click the Outdent button (▤) once for each indent that you want to remove.

Dreamweaver uses the `blockquote` tag to indent text. Indenting text again adds a second `blockquote` tag, and outdenting removes `blockquote` **tags.**

Did You Know?

The World Wide Web Consortium, or W3C, which is the governing body that oversees the development of Web technologies, has *deprecated* the code that writes HTML alignments into your document. Instead, it suggests that you keep all design elements out of your markup and put them into Cascading Style Sheets, or CSS.

Did You Know?

The W3C suggests that you use *semantic markup.* This means that you use each HTML tag only for its original purpose. For example, the `blockquote` tag is meant for presenting quotations and not for indenting text. As a result, purists instead use the `margin` property in CSS to indent text in their documents. Using alignments and indents in the Properties inspector is still useful for quickly testing different layouts.

ASSETS PANEL:
Insert Objects With

You can drag objects and other site resources from the Assets panel to your page while in either Design or Code view. You can do this with objects from any Assets panel category except for Templates, which you can only apply to an entire document. In addition to Flash, Shockwave, movie, and image objects, you can add library items, add colors to selected text, add links to text or images, and link external script files in the head of your document.

Because the Assets panel stores all of your site assets in one place, it makes your workflow easier and more organized. It allows you to bypass a dialog box where you must navigate to an image or object, and thus helps to prevent broken links. It also permits you to see what you are adding; for example, you can select an image and preview it first in the Assets panel preview pane.

See also>> **Assets Panel**

See also>> **Assets Panel: Manage Assets**

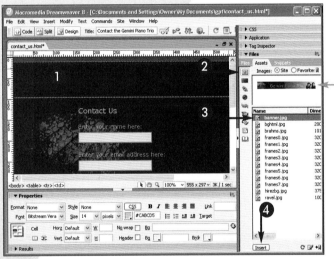

Insert Objects

1 Click the page location where you want to add an asset.

2 Click the category of the asset that you want to use.

3 Click the name of the asset that you want to insert.

4 Click Insert.

● You can view your asset in the preview pane of the Assets panel.

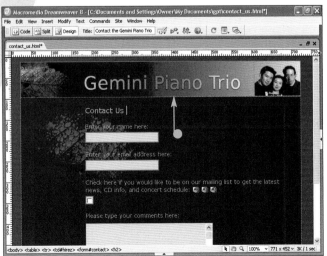

● Your asset appears on the page at the insertion point that you specified.

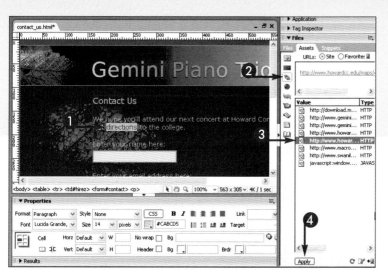

Wrap Assets around Selections

① Select text to which you want to apply a URL or color.

② Click the category of the asset that you want to use.

③ Select the URL or color that you want to apply.

④ Click Apply.

● The link or color applies to the selected text.

TIPS

Important!

When you first define your site, all images and other assets are automatically added to the Assets panel. This is because the Site Definition dialog box defaults to enable the cache, which is the method by which Dreamweaver maintains file and asset information. However, if you add assets and files to your site later, then Dreamweaver sometimes does not recognize them until you click the Refresh icon (⟳) in these panels.

ASSETS PANEL:
Manage Assets

You can add, remove, and edit site resources, also known as assets, in the Assets panel. As you accumulate more images and other assets, you can add the ones that you use most frequently to a favorites category and avoid tedious scrolling through long lists.

Dreamweaver places favorites into appropriate categories such as images and scripts, just like regular site assets. However, converting your assets to favorites allows you more sophisticated ways to organize them. For example, you can create folders and subfolders for your favorites. You can also give

them meaningful nicknames to make them more easily recognizable, such as changing a hexadecimal color code to a common color name.

The Assets panel also has other powerful management tools. For example, you can quickly copy assets to other sites and share them with teams. You can also use the Assets panel to locate the original instance of the asset within the Files panel.

See also>> **Assets Panel**

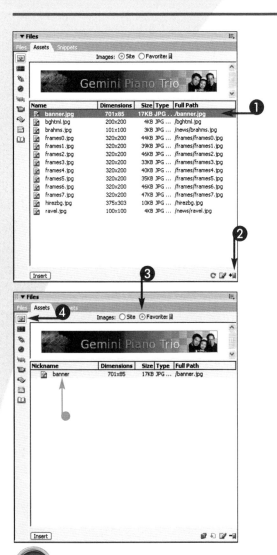

Add to Favorites

① Select the asset that you want to add to Favorites.

② Click the Add to Favorites button (⊞).

Dreamweaver adds the asset to favorites.

③ Click the Favorites option (○ changes to ◉).

④ Click the category button for your asset.

● The asset appears in the Favorites list.

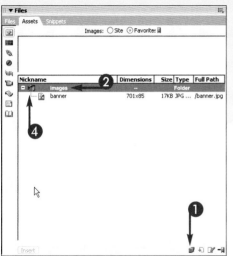

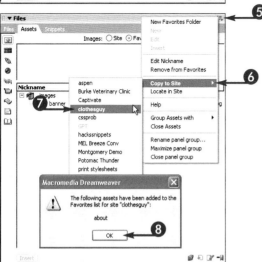

Manage Assets

1 Click the New Favorites Folder button ().

2 Click here and type a new name for the folder.

3 Press Enter to accept the name.

4 Drag assets to the folder to organize them.

The assets move to the folder and appear indented in the list.

5 Click the File Options button ().

6 Click Copy to Site.

7 Select a site name.

Dreamweaver displays a confirmation dialog box to indicate that the asset is now in the selected site's Favorites list.

8 Click OK.

TIPS

Find It!

The Assets panel makes it easy to drag assets to a page, but sometimes you need to know where an asset is actually stored in the site. To do this, select the asset and click the Assets panel's File Options button () to select Locate in Site. Dreamweaver opens the Files panel and highlights the object so that you can see exactly where it is in the site hierarchy.

More Options!

Many designers initially embed their styles in the document while developing a page layout, rather than creating an external style sheet. This gives them the opportunity to test and troubleshoot the design. After they complete the design, they export styles to an external style sheet by clicking File, then clicking Export, and then clicking the Refresh icon ().

ATTACH AND DETACH:
Cascading Style Sheets

After you create an external Cascading Style Sheet, you can use the CSS panel to attach it to as many documents as you like. Whenever you update the style sheet, every page that is linked to it updates as well. An external style sheet makes your pages consistent, cuts down on file size, and saves many hours of work.

The Attach External Style Sheet dialog box allows you to link or import style sheets. It displays a menu for selecting a media type for your style sheet, such as for printing or handheld devices. It also offers a link to sample style sheets that you can click to open

a Sample Style Sheets dialog box. These samples include full-page designs and accessible form layouts.

You can also use the CSS panel to easily detach style sheets from pages.

See also>>

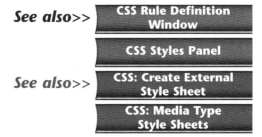

CSS Rule Definition Window

CSS Styles Panel

See also>>

CSS: Create External Style Sheet

CSS: Media Type Style Sheets

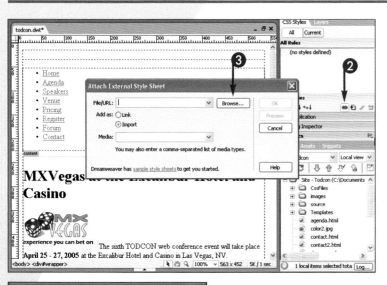

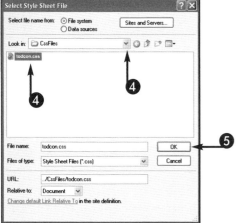

Attach a Style Sheet

① Open a page to which you want to attach a style sheet.

② Click the Attach Style Sheet button (▣).

The Attach External Style Sheet dialog box appears.

③ Click Browse.

The Select Style Sheet File dialog box appears.

④ Navigate to your external style sheet from the drop-down menu.

⑤ Click OK.

The Select Style Sheet File dialog box closes.

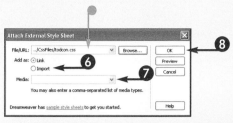

- In the Attach External Style Sheet dialog box, the name and path to your style sheet appear in the File/URL field.

6 Click an Add as option (○ changes to ⦿).

7 Click here and select a media type if your style sheet is for alternative devices.

You can leave the Media field blank if you want your style sheet to default to all media types.

8 Click OK.

The page appears with the style sheet attached.

Detach a Style Sheet

9 Select the style sheet name in the CSS panel.

10 Click the Trash button (🗑).

Dreamweaver removes the style sheet from the page.

More Options!

The Attach External Style Sheet dialog box allows you to either link or import style sheets. Although either choice works, there are two special uses for the import method. First, older browsers, such as Netscape 4, can crash when they encounter styles that they do not support. These browsers do not understand the import method, and so designers exploit this deficiency by linking a style sheet for Netscape 4 and importing a second style sheet for standards-compliant browsers. Read more at www.communitymx.com/content/article.cfm?cid=1EAB6.

More Options!

The second use of the import method is to create a modular system. You can organize your rules into separate style sheets and import each style sheet. Some designers modularize hacks, which are unique ways of overcoming browser anomalies in applying styles.

AUTOSTRETCH TABLES:
Lay Out Pages With

You can mix fluid and fixed-width columns in tables by using the autostretch feature in Layout mode. The standard way of creating tables is to either specify a width that is a fixed number of pixels, or assign them a width that is a numerical percentage of the browser window.

However, you may want to combine a fixed-left navigation column that is 200 pixels wide with a stretchy content column that takes up the rest of the available space in the browser window. In this case, you can use Column Header menus to create hybrid tables.

Dreamweaver performs this trick by giving the fluid column a width of 100 percent. This would ordinarily collapse the other column's width to zero. However, Dreamweaver inserts a small, transparent placeholder image, called a spacer gif, into the fixed-width column to keep the column open. You can set the spacer gif to any height or width.

See also>> **Layout Mode**

Rulers

See also>> **Layout Tables**

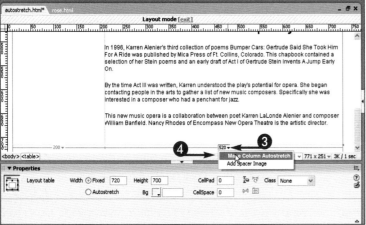

① Create a table with columns in Layout mode.

② Draw the fixed-width columns at the width you want them to have when the table combines them with an autostretch column.

You can only have one autostretch column per table.

● You can use the rulers as guides.

③ Right-click (Ctrl-click) the column header menu of the column that you want to autostretch.

④ Select Make Column Autostretch.

The Choose Spacer Image dialog box appears.

5 Click OK.

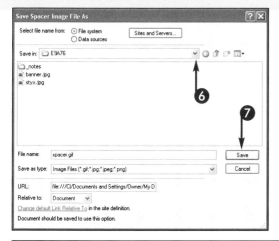

The Save Spacer Image File As dialog box appears.

6 Click here and navigate to the site location where you want to save the spacer.gif file.

7 Click Save.

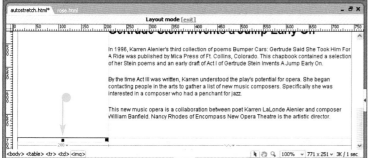

Dreamweaver saves the spacer.gif image to your site and places it in the fixed-width columns of your layout table.

● Dreamweaver props open the fixed-width columns by setting the width of the spacer.gif to the desired column width.

Apply It!

There are advocates on both sides of the fixed-width versus fluid-layout debate. Fluid layouts can result in very long lines of text. However, it is difficult to determine a good width for a fixed-width layout because visitors to your site have different screen resolutions, monitor sizes, and browser window widths. Many designers try to compromise by applying a minimum or maximum width property in their CSS documents. Internet Explorer does not recognize this property, but there is a JavaScript that corrects this problem.

Did You Know?

You can read more about minimum and maximum widths and find a JavaScript for Internet Explorer at the Project Seven Web site: www.projectseven. com/extensions/info/minwidth/.

BACKGROUND COLORS:
Apply to Page Elements with HTML

You can apply background colors to your page elements by using the Color boxes in the Properties inspector. These boxes offer a number of options for displaying their colors, such as with color cubes or continuous tones. You can also type in the hexadecimal code that Web documents use to express colors. You can even use the Eyedropper tool to match colors with those of other elements on the page, such as the colors within images.

Color is an important tool for enhancing communication. The intelligent use of color can unify your page design as well as help guide the reader's eye around

the page. Color also creates psychological effects. By understanding the mood that each color evokes, you can design your site with a color scheme appropriate to its purpose.

Accessibility is another issue that you should consider when selecting colors. For example, you should ensure that there is good contrast between backgrounds and text so that the visually impaired can read your content.

See also>> Properties Inspector: Tables

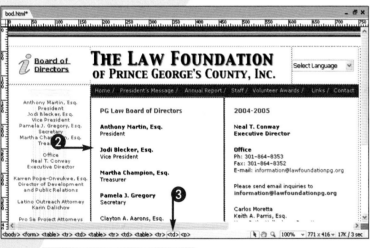

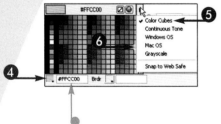

Apply Background Colors

1 Open the page to which you want to add background colors.

2 Click in a page element.

3 Click the tag for the page element in the Tag Selector.

4 Click the Color box (▦).

5 Click here and select a color palette option.

6 Select a color.

● If you know the hexadecimal code of your color, then you can also type it in the Color field.

Dreamweaver applies the background color.

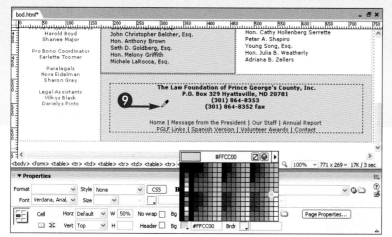

7 Click ▣.

8 Move your mouse over the color that you want to match.

The cursor turns into an Eyedropper (🖉).

9 Click the color.

Dreamweaver adds the hexadecimal code for the color to the Color field.

● Dreamweaver adds the background color to your element.

TIPS

Caution!

Older versions of Netscape do not display color in a table cell if the cell is empty. You can get around this by adding a nonbreaking space to the cell. Select the cell and click Split in the Document toolbar. Find the opening and closing table cell elements: `<td>` and `</td>`. Type this code between them: ` `

Try This!

There are many color tools on the Web that enable you to create color schemes for your pages. You can select your first color, and then have the tool generate color schemes based on the selected color model, such as complementary or analogous. The tool then gives you the hexadecimal code for each color. Try this color scheme tool: http://createafreewebsite.net/html-color-tool.html.

BACKGROUND IMAGES:
Insert into Cells and Tables

You can insert background images in tables and table cells by using the CSS background property. These backgrounds can add pizzazz to your pages as long as you take care to avoid busy, distracting images that do not contrast well with the text and other content in the cells.

With HTML, background images always repeat until they fill the available space. With CSS, you have more control; for example, you can set your image to repeat, not repeat, or to repeat only on the X-axis or Y-axis. CSS also allows you to select an attachment style, where background images can either scroll with the page or stay fixed in place while the rest of the page scrolls.

The CSS background property also allows you to set the positioning of your background image, either by entering values for the horizontal and vertical positions, or by selecting position keywords from a menu.

See also>> **CSS Rule Definition Window**

See also>> **CSS: Create Embedded Style Sheet**

CSS: Create External Style Sheet

Descendent Selectors

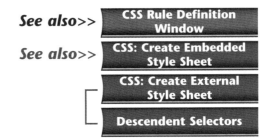

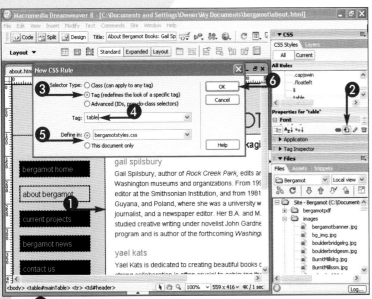

① Open the page to which you want to add background colors.

② Click the New CSS Rule button (⊞) in the CSS panel.

③ In the New CSS Rule dialog box that appears, click the Tag option (○ changes to ◉).

④ Type **table** or **td** next to the Tag Selector Type option.

⑤ Click to select a Define in option (○ changes to ◉).

⑥ Click OK.

The CSS Rule Definition dialog box appears.

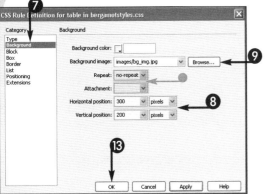

⑦ Click Background.

● You can click here and select a Repeat and an Attachment option.

If you leave the Repeat field blank, your image repeats; if you leave the Attachment field blank, your image scrolls.

⑧ Click here to select the Horizontal and Vertical positions as well as a unit of measurement.

⑨ Click Browse.

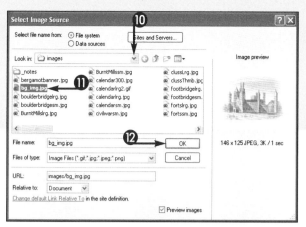

The Select Image Source dialog box appears.

10 Click here and navigate to your image folder.

11 Select the image.

12 Click OK to close the dialog box.

13 In the CSS Rule Definition dialog box, click OK.

● Dreamweaver inserts the image in the table or cell according to the attributes that you specify.

Check It Out!

Adding a background image to an element such as a table or table cell is a global action; Dreamweaver places the image in every cell or every table on the page. If you want an image as a background in only one cell or table, then you should use the power of the descendant selector. Learn how to create descendant selectors at Macromedia's DevNet: www.macromedia.com/devnet/dreamweaver/articles/css_concepts_mx2004_print.html.

Caution!

Not all browsers support the fixed value that you specify, or they may only support it on the body element. You should always test the pages that you design with CSS in as many browsers as possible. You can also check CSS properties in browser support charts on the Web, such as the one at www.westciv.com/style_master/academy/browser_support/.

B

BACKGROUND IMAGES:
Using CSS to Insert in a Page

You can add background images to your page with the CSS background property. Background images are popular because they add visual interest to the page or provide a framework for laying out other page elements. Common background image techniques include the use of gradients, patterns, and soft, faded images.

When an image's width and height are less than those of the page, by default, the image repeats until it fills the available space. However, with CSS, you can set your image to repeat, not repeat, or repeat only on the X-axis or Y-axis. You can also allow the image to scroll with the rest of the page or remain in a fixed position while the rest of the page scrolls. In addition, you can decide where on the page you want the image to appear, either with number values or position keywords.

See also>>

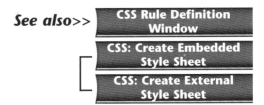

CSS Rule Definition Window

CSS: Create Embedded Style Sheet

CSS: Create External Style Sheet

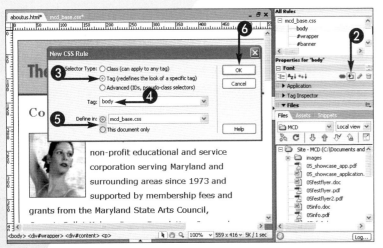

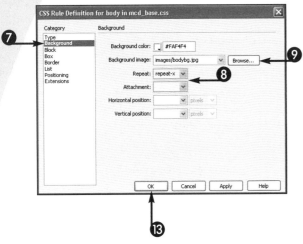

① Open the page in which you want to insert a background image.

② Click 🔁 in the CSS panel.

③ In the New CSS Rule dialog box that appears, click the Tag option (○ changes to ⊙).

④ Type **body** next to the Tag option under the Selector Type option

⑤ Click to select a Define in option (○ changes to ⊙).

⑥ Click OK.

The CSS Rule Definition dialog box appears.

⑦ Select Background.

⑧ Click here and select a Repeat option and an Attachment option.

Repeat and scroll are the default options.

Unless you specify values for Horizontal and Vertical positions, your image is inserted at the top-left edge of the page.

⑨ Click Browse.

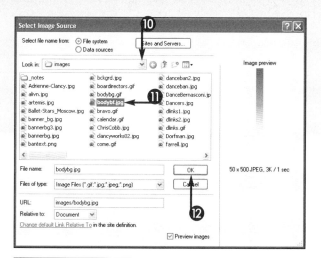

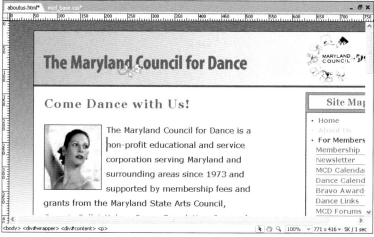

The Select Image Source dialog box appears.

⑩ Click here and navigate to your image folder.

⑪ Select the image.

⑫ Click OK to close the dialog box.

⑬ In the CSS Rule Definition dialog box, click OK.

Dreamweaver inserts the image on the page with the attributes that you specify.

Did You Know?

Macromedia Fireworks and Adobe Photoshop are two popular graphics programs that make it easy to create gradient backgrounds. You can use them to create a thin gradient image that tiles on the X- or Y-axis.

Try This!

Create an image that is the same color as the background color of your Web page. Draw a rectangle over it, and add your gradient, with one end color being the same as the background color. If you end the gradient about 10 pixels before the bottom of the background, you avoid a distracting line where your gradient image ends and the background color of the page begins. If the image repeats horizontally, then crop its height; if it repeats vertically, then crop its width.

BEHAVIORS:
Apply to Web Page Events

You can easily add behaviors to your pages by selecting a tag in the Tag Selector and selecting the appropriate behavior in the Behaviors panel. Dreamweaver provides dialog boxes for visually setting up, customizing, and managing its preset behaviors. After you apply a behavior, you can also easily edit its original parameters.

You can associate a behavior with the *event* that the user must execute to trigger the *action*. Examples of events are onMouseOver, which indicates that the user's mouse has hovered over

a link, and onClick, which indicates that the user's mouse has clicked a link.

Behaviors perform *actions* that can add interactivity to your pages, such as playing a sound or swapping in a new color when the mouse hovers over it. They can also initiate a task, such as validating a form or redirecting the visitor to an alternative Web address.

See also>>  Behaviors Panel

See also>> Tag Selector

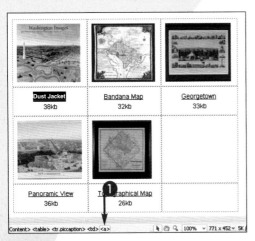

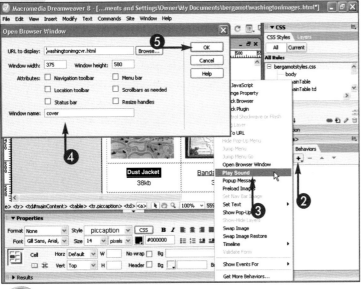

Apply Behaviors

① Select a tag in the Tag Selector to which you want to add an action.

② Click the Add button (⊞) in the Behaviors panel.

③ In the menu that appears, select a behavior.

④ In the dialog box that appears, type or click (☐ changes to ☑) to specify the options that you want for the behavior.

⑤ Click OK.

Dreamweaver applies the behavior.

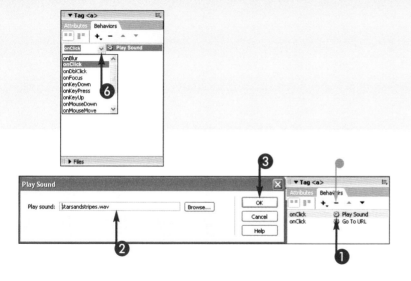

⑥ In the Behaviors tab, click here and select an event.

Dreamweaver applies the behavior to the specified event.

Manage and Modify Behaviors

① Double-click a behavior.

The dialog box for that behavior appears.

② Edit the behavior options.

③ Click OK.

Dreamweaver applies the new options.

● To remove a behavior, you can click the behavior, and then click the Delete button (⊟).

More Options!
When you have more than one behavior, the order in which they occur can be critical. You can select a behavior in the Behaviors panel and use the Move Behavior Up (▲) and Move Behavior Down (▼) arrows to change the order in which the behavior appears.

Caution!
To address security concerns, some users disable JavaScript in their browser preferences. Others may disable pop-up windows to prevent unsolicited advertising. You can use alternatives to JavaScript to accomplish some tasks. For example, you can create the effect of rollover images with CSS instead of using Dreamweaver's rollover behaviors. Also, keep in mind that the various browsers implement JavaScript differently. Although Dreamweaver writes behaviors that work in a broad range of browsers, it is a good idea to test them.

BEHAVIORS:
Check Browser

You can use the Check Browser behavior to send visitors to different pages, depending on which browser or browser version they are using. Your site may have features that do not work well on certain browsers, or that cause older browsers to crash. The Check Browser behavior allows you to keep most of your site's content accessible to everyone, while still allowing you to provide up-to-date features.

You can create a simple entry page and attach the Check Browser behavior to its body tag. The behavior automatically redirects visitors with current browsers to the full-featured site. Visitors with older browsers

or with JavaScript disabled stay on the entry page, where you can provide a choice of links to click. One link goes to the full-featured page, and the other link goes to a page for older browsers.

Dreamweaver also allows you to customize the Netscape and Internet browser versions that each link targets.

See also>>  Behaviors Panel

See also>> Tag Selector

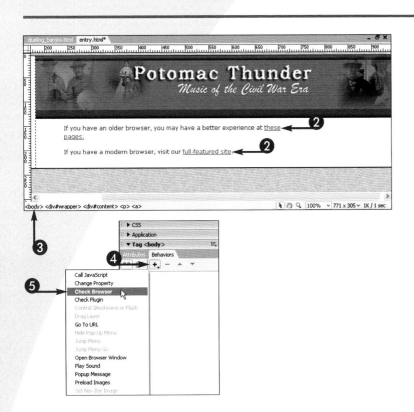

❶ Create a new page.

❷ Create a link to the page for older browsers, and a link to the page for current browsers.

If the visitor has disabled JavaScript, they can use these links to select the appropriate page.

❸ Click the <body> tag.

❹ Click ⊞ in the Behaviors panel.

❺ In the menu that appears, select Check Browser.

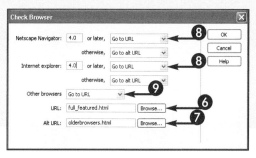

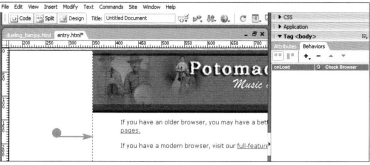

The Check Browser dialog box appears.

⑥ Click Browse next to the URL field, and navigate to your full-featured page.

⑦ Click Browse next to the Alt URL field, and navigate to your older browser page.

⑧ Click here and select Go to URL for later browsers.

⑨ Click here and select Go to URL if you are targeting current browsers.

● Dreamweaver adds the behavior to the `<body>` tag using the `onLoad` event.

Check It Out!

In addition to all of the different browsers, there are also many versions of each one. As a result, keeping track of the features that each browser supports can be difficult. There are good browser support charts for each platform at Web Monkey that you can print out. For example, the chart for Windows browser support is at webmonkey.wired.com/webmonkey/reference/browser_ chart/. The chart for Macintosh browser support is at webmonkey.wired.com/webmonkey/reference/browser_ chart/index_mac.html. These pages also link to charts for other platforms, such as Unix/Linux, WebTV, and OS/2.

More Options!

You may use Cascading Style Sheets on your pages while having to support older browsers that do not recognize them. You can use the Import Attach option (○ changes to ◉), which hides style sheets from older browsers, rather than set up the Check Browser behavior.

BEHAVIORS:
Go to URL

You can use the Go To URL behavior to open a new page or pages in the current window. While loading a new page is the default behavior for ordinary links, the Go To URL behavior lets you change the `onClick` event to a different event. For example, you can allow a new page to open in the browser window when the visitor's mouse hovers over an image or other object. This is the `onMouseOver` event.

You can use the Go To URL behavior to control how content loads into frames. For example, you can set the behavior so that when the user clicks or hovers over one link, two or more frames change

simultaneously. This behavior provides the user a smoother experience when viewing content in complex framesets.

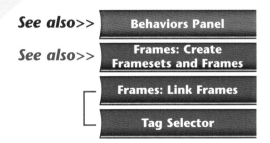

See also>> Behaviors Panel

See also>> Frames: Create Framesets and Frames

Frames: Link Frames

Tag Selector

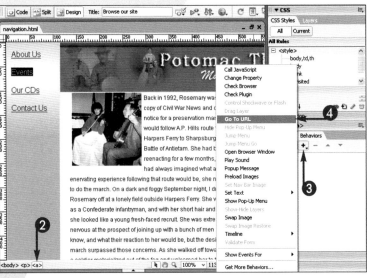

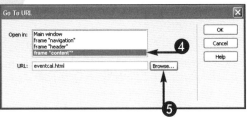

① Open a frameset page.

② Click the object or tag in the Tag Selector to which you want to apply the Go To URL behavior.

③ Click (🔲) in the Behaviors panel, and select the Go To URL behavior in the menu that appears.

The Go To URL dialog box appears.

④ Click the first frame in which you want to load a new link.

⑤ Click Browse and navigate to the first frame page.

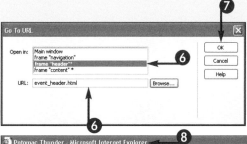

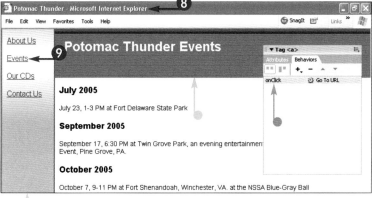

6 Repeat steps **3** to **5** for each frame in which you want to load a new link.

7 Click OK.

Dreamweaver adds the behavior to the Behaviors panel.

● The default event is `onClick`.

8 Preview your page in a browser.

9 Click the element to which you applied the Go To URL behavior.

● The browser swaps in new pages to each frame to which you applied the Go To URL behavior.

Check It Out!

You should always test your pages in as many browsers and on as many platforms as possible. Most browsers are free, and so you can download them to check your pages. You can find an archive of older browsers to download at Evolt: browsers.evolt.org/.

Check It Out!

As for testing on different platforms, you may only have a Mac or Windows computer. In this case, you can buy a cheap testing computer, ask friends or other Web designers to check your pages, or use a free or commercial service that allows you to test your pages. For example, you can test your pages in Apple's Safari browser using the free iCapture service at www.danvine.com/icapture/. Another free browser-checking service is at http://browsershots.org/.

BEHAVIORS:
Open Browser Window

You can use the Open Browser Window behavior to open a link in a new, customized window. You can specify the properties of the new window, including its size, attributes, and name.

Designers often use this behavior to make image galleries. They create a page with thumbnail images that each link to a full-sized image that opens in a new window. With the Open Browser Window behavior, you can type in a height and width for the new browser window to make it match the image's exact size. You can choose whether or not to include

such attributes as navigation toolbars, scroll bars, and a Status bar.

You can also use the Open Browser Window behavior to open small windows with help documents, PDFs, special alerts, and other information that you want to highlight. Placing these documents in a smaller window that does not cover the original enables visitors to easily refer to both pages simultaneously.

See also>> **Behaviors Panel**

See also>> **Tag Selector**

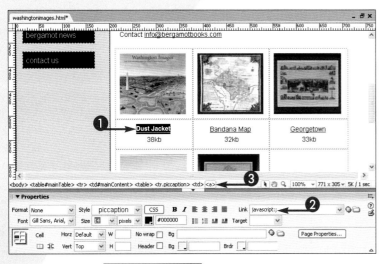

① Select the text or object to which you want to attach the Open Browser Window behavior.

② Type **javascript:;** as a dummy link in the Link field.

③ Select the <a> tag for the dummy link in the Tag Selector.

④ Click ⊞ in the Behaviors panel.

⑤ Select the Open Browser Window behavior in the menu that appears.

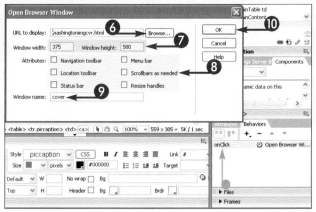

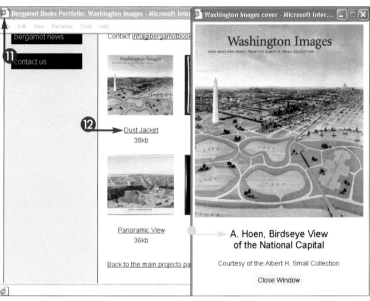

The Open Browser Window dialog box appears.

⑥ Click Browse to browse to the page that you want to open in a new window.

⑦ Type a width and height for the window.

⑧ Select the window attributes that you want to apply to the new window (☐ changes to ☑).

⑨ Type a name in the Window name field.

⑩ Click OK.

● Dreamweaver adds the behavior to the Behaviors panel with the `onClick` event.

⑪ Open your page in a browser.

⑫ Click the link that opens the new window.

● The new window opens with the attributes that you defined.

B

TIPS

Caution!

Visitors may be confused when a new window opens. As a result, many designers give visitors a visible warning so that the new window does not surprise them. Supplying a close window link is another courtesy that you can offer your visitors.

Important!

Sometimes you need to use a dummy link in order to get a behavior to work as expected. Dummy links allow your text or objects to function as links, but the links do not actually go anywhere. You can use one of two methods to create a dummy link. You can either type the number sign, which can sometimes cause the user's browser window to jump, or type **javascript:;** into the link field — a better choice.

BEHAVIORS:
Set Text of Layer

You can use the Set Text of Layer behavior to swap in new content based on the interactions of your visitor. For example, you can create a button that displays a submenu when visitors hover their mouse over it. You can add annotations to further clarify the text in a layer. You can also provide descriptions for images so that they appear when the visitor supplies a trigger such as the `onMouseOver` or `onClick` events. The Set Text of Layer behavior is a great way to give users more information without making them wait for a new page to load.

Dreamweaver displays a dialog box for you to enter your text and then writes the JavaScript when you apply the behavior. You can even add HTML formatting in the dialog box to enhance the text's appearance or add functionality, such as adding a link to the text.

See also>> **Behaviors Panel**

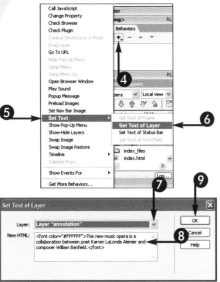

① Create and name a new layer in which you want to place the annotation or dynamic text.

② Click the object to which you want to add the annotation.

③ Type **javascript:;** in the Link field of the Properties inspector.

④ Click ⊞ in the Behaviors panel.

⑤ Click Set Text in the menu that appears.

⑥ Click Set Text of Layer.

The Set Text of Layer dialog box appears.

⑦ Click here and select the layer in which you want the text to appear.

⑧ Type the text in the New HTML field.

⑨ Click OK.

By default, Dreamweaver sets the event to `onMouseOver`.

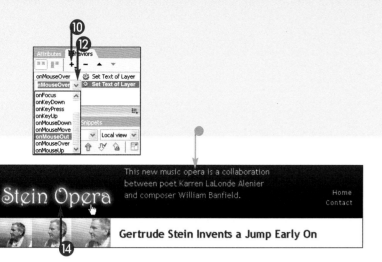

⑩ Repeat steps **4** to **6**.

⑪ Repeat steps **7** to **9**, selecting the same layer to which you applied the original Set Text of Layer behavior, but this time leaving the New HTML field empty.

⑫ Click here and select the onMouseOut event.

⑬ Open the page in a browser.

⑭ Hover your mouse over the object to which you applied the annotation text.

● Dreamweaver displays the annotation text.

When you move the mouse away from the object, the annotation text disappears.

Try This!

Even if you do not know HTML, you can still add links to your text in the Set Text of Layer dialog box. Open a blank Dreamweaver document and use the Properties inspector to create your link. Select the link, click Split, copy the link code, and paste it into your Set Text of Layer dialog box.

Try This!

You can also use the Properties inspector to format your text. If you use CSS, then Dreamweaver creates a new style. You must first copy and paste the HTML code and text into the Set Text of Layer dialog box. You then need to copy the style that is in the head of the first document into the head of the second document.

BEHAVIORS:
Show and Hide Layers

You can use the Show and Hide Layers behavior to manage the visibility of layers. This action is useful when you want to show and hide layers as the user interacts with content on the page. For example, you can use this behavior to show submenus when the user's mouse hovers over a button.

Photo galleries are another popular use of the Show and Hide Layers behavior. For example, you can place a row of thumbnails on a page, and then insert larger layers beneath the thumbnails to hold the full-sized image for each thumbnail. Each of these layers occupies the same area of the page, but its

Visibility setting will show or hide depending on which thumbnail image the user clicks.

See also>> Behaviors Panel

Layers

Layers Panel

See also>> Behaviors: Apply to Web Page Events

Images: Insert in Documents

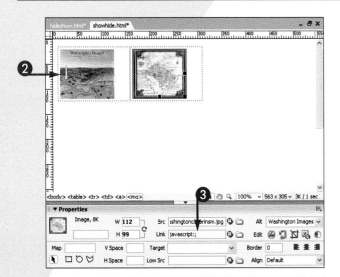

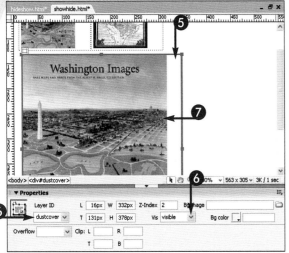

① Insert a thumbnail image in the page.

② Select the thumbnail.

③ Type **javascript:;** in the image's Link field in the Properties inspector.

④ Repeat steps **1** to **3** for each image.

⑤ Insert the layer that will hold the larger version of an image.

⑥ Type a Layer ID and select a visibility setting for the layer.

You may want to set the layer for the first image to Visible so that a large image displays when the page loads.

⑦ Insert the full-sized image in the layer.

⑧ Repeat steps **5** to **7** for each thumbnail image.

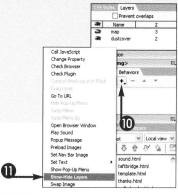

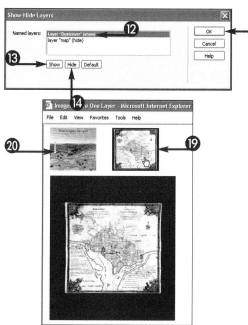

⑨ Click the first thumbnail image.

⑩ Click ⊞ in the Behaviors panel.

⑪ Click the Show-Hide Layers behavior.

⑫ In the Show-Hide Layers dialog box, click the layer that you want to display when the user clicks a thumbnail.

⑬ Click Show.

⑭ Repeat step **12**, but click Hide instead of Show for step **13**.

⑮ Repeat step **14** for each layer on which you want to set visibility.

⑯ Click OK.

By default, Dreamweaver applies the onClick event.

⑰ Repeat steps **9** to **16** for each thumbnail image.

⑱ Preview your page in a browser.

⑲ Click an image.

Dreamweaver shows the larger version of the image in the shared layer space.

⑳ Click each thumbnail to show the layer with its larger version, while hiding the other images.

TIPS

More Options!

As you add layers for larger images, it can become difficult to work with all of the overlapping layers. You can turn off visibility for all layers except the one with which you are working. You can select each layer in the Layers panel and click its open-eye icon (👁) to change it to a closed-eye icon (👁), which indicates that the layer is now invisible.

Did You Know?

Dreamweaver automatically assigns a Z-index to each layer that you insert. The Z-index controls the stacking order of layers, or their order from front to back when they overlap the same space on the page. However, only one layer in the photo gallery displays at a time, and so its Z-index does not matter very much.

B

171

BORDERS:
Set Properties in HTML

You can quickly add a border to an image using the Border field in the Properties inspector. Dreamweaver adds a solid border to all sides of the image. Although you can control the pixel width for the border, its color relies on the visitor's browser. Some browsers give borders the same color as text, while others, like Internet Explorer 6, draw a black border. If your image is also a link, then its borders adopt the colors that you specify for page links.

You can also use the Properties inspector to add borders and border colors to tables. When you add a border to a table, it also adds borders between cells.

If you want to have complete control over borders, as well as the ability to add them to elements other than images and tables, then you can use Cascading Style Sheets.

See also>> **Properties Inspector: Tables**

See also>> **Borders: Style with CSS**

Images: Insert in Documents

Tables: Using for Page Layouts

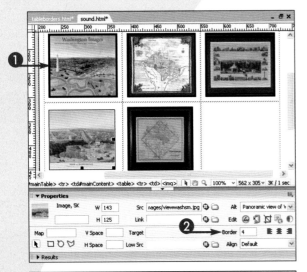

Adding Borders to Images

1. Select an image.

2. Type a number in the Border field in the Properties inspector.

3. Press Enter.

4. Repeat steps **1** to **3** for each image to which you want to add a border.

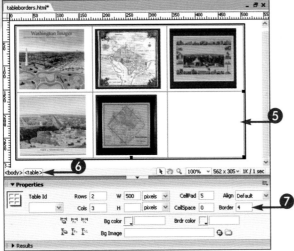

Dreamweaver applies a border to your images.

5. Click your cursor in a table.

6. Click the table's tag in the Tag Selector.

7. Type a number in the Border field of the Properties inspector.

Dreamweaver uses pixels for the unit of measurement.

8 Click the Brdr color box (⬛).

9 Click a color.

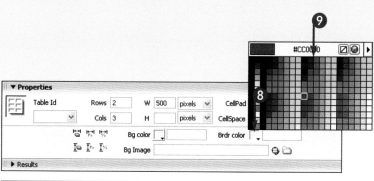

#CC0000

▼ Properties

	Table Id	Rows	2	W	500	pixels ✓	CellPad
		Cols	3	H		pixels ✓	CellSpace
		Bg color		Brdr color	
		Bg Image			⊕ 📁

▶ Results

● Dreamweaver adds the border to your table.

B

TIPS

Caution!

Even if you leave the Border field empty for your image in the Properties inspector, it does not necessarily mean that the table will not have a border. For example, if you use your image as a link, then it automatically takes on a border with the colors that you specify for text links. To avoid this, you must type **0** in the Border field.

Did You Know?

Before Cascading Style Sheets, Web designers used to nest one table inside another to create the effect of borders between rows and cells. The nesting often went several tables deep, and so reading this code slowed down the loading of the page.

BORDERS:
Style with CSS

You can use CSS to add a wide variety of borders to almost any HTML element. You can choose from border styles such as solid, dotted, dashed, grooved, and inset. You can set a unique width and color on each side of the element. You can even choose to have borders on only one, two, or three sides of the element.

CSS borders allow you to add creative design effects. For example, you can add a dotted border to only the bottom of a heading. You can add a thick border to the left, and a thinner border on the bottom of a paragraph to give it emphasis. You can also add

borders around lists and forms — the possibilities are endless.

See also>> CSS Rule Definition Window

See also>> CSS: Create Embedded Style Sheet

CSS: Create External Style Sheet

Images: Insert in Documents

Tables: Using for Page Layouts

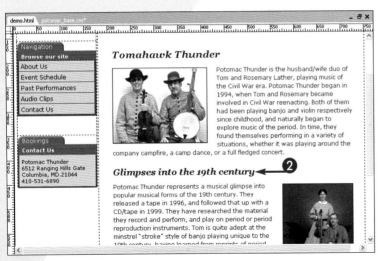

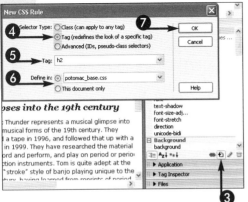

① Open a page with elements to which you want to add borders.

② Make a note of the element that you want to style.

③ Click the New CSS Rule button (🗐) in the CSS panel.

④ In the New CSS Rule dialog box, click the Selector Type that you want to style (○ changes to ◉).

⑤ Type in the Name, Tag, or Selector field, depending on your Selector Type.

⑥ Click a Define in option (○ changes to ◉).

⑦ Click OK.

174

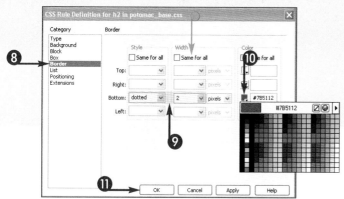

8 In the CSS Rule Definition dialog box, click Border.

9 Click here and select both a border style and a width.

● If you want to apply the border to selected sides, you can deselect the Same for all option (☑ changes to ☐).

10 Click the Color box (▣), and select a color.

You can also type the hexadecimal code for a color, or sample a color from the desktop.

11 Click OK.

● Dreamweaver applies the border to the target element.

B

TIP

Caution!

You must be careful about math when adding CSS borders or padding to elements in precise layouts. Although most current browsers follow a standard *box model*, Internet Explorer 5 and 5.5 use an aberrant box model. For example, if you allow 200 pixels for a div, or section, and add 2-pixel borders and 5 pixels of padding on each side, then a standards-compliant browser adds all properties and sees the total width as 214 pixels. Internet Explorer 5 and 5.5 subtract the borders and padding from 200 and allow a content area of only 186 pixels. Read about this critical problem and how to fix it in *The Box Model Problem* at www.communitymx.com/content/article.cfm?cid=E0989953B6F20B41.

CHANGE LINKS SITEWIDE:
Using the Site Command

You can use the Change Link Sitewide command in the Site menu to change a link throughout your site. When you change a filename, Dreamweaver automatically offers to update all pages that reference the file. Sometimes you may need to change a link that is referenced in many pages in your site. If your pages are not based on a template, or the link is not in a non-editable region, then you must change each link manually.

The Sitewide command is useful for several purposes. For example, you may have to update your e-mail address information, or you may link to an external

site that has changed its address. Dreamweaver allows you to update all pages that use the link by typing your original and new links in a dialog box. It then presents a list of all files that use the original link and offers to update them.

See also>>

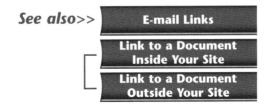

E-mail Links

Link to a Document Inside Your Site

Link to a Document Outside Your Site

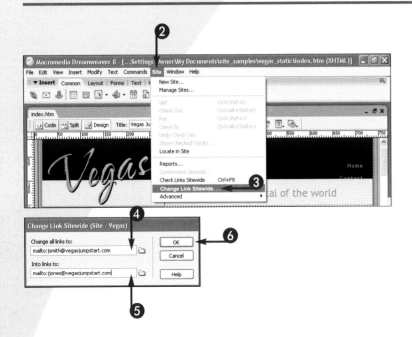

① Open a page in the site.

If you are changing an e-mail, FTP, null, or script link, then you do not need to select a file.

② Click Site.

③ Click Change Link Sitewide.

The Change Link Sitewide dialog box appears.

④ Type the link that you want to change.

⑤ Type the link to which you want to change.

For steps **4** and **5**, if the link is within your site, then you can browse for the file by clicking 🗀.

⑥ Click OK.

- The Update Files dialog box appears, displaying a list of pages on which it will change links.

7 Click Update.

- Dreamweaver updates the links in all of the files in the Update Files list.

TIPS

Attention!
You may notice the forward slash that Dreamweaver places in front of the filename in the Update Files dialog box and think it is trying to make your files root-relative, even if you have them set to document-relative in your Site Definition dialog box. This is just Dreamweaver's way of identifying your pages; it does not affect how you link your pages together.

Check It Out!
You may need to change a filename for your link, and your users may have the old one bookmarked. In this case, you can create a redirect page that uses a metatag to switch the user to the new location:

```
<meta http-equiv="Refresh" content="5;
URL=http://www.yourdomain.com/page.
html">
```

Read more about how to create a redirect page at http://www.mcps.k12.md.us/departments/web/redirect/

CHECK IN AND CHECK OUT:
Setup and Options

You can use Dreamweaver's Check in and Check out feature to manage team projects. If you are working with others who have access to the remote server, then more than one person may need to download and edit the same file, which may result in team members overwriting each other's work.

Team members can enable the Check in and Check out feature in the Site Definition dialog box. They can provide a Check in name and E-mail address, and enable the option to check out automatically when they open a file in the Local files view. Dreamweaver makes files that are checked out by a team member

read-only, and marks them with a red checkmark on the server until the team member checks them back in. Dreamweaver also provides a dialog box that allows you to see who checked a file out and supplies an e-mail link so that you can contact that person.

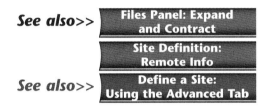

See also>> Files Panel: Expand and Contract

Site Definition: Remote Info

See also>> Define a Site: Using the Advanced Tab

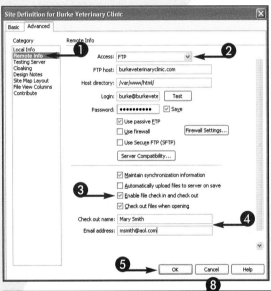

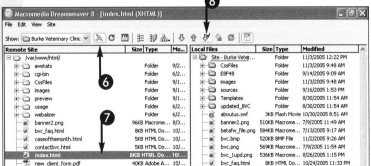

1 In the Advanced tab of the Site Definition dialog box for your site, click the Remote Info category.

2 Click here and select an Access option.

You can only enable Check in/Check out if you define the remote server.

3 Click the "Enable file check in and check out" option (☐ changes to ☑).

4 Type the Check out name and E-mail address.

5 Click OK.

6 Click the Connect button (⬛).

Using the Expanded Files view allows you to see both the Remote and Local views simultaneously.

7 Click a file that you want to edit.

8 Click the Check Out Files button (⬛).

If you enabled the "Check out files when opening" option (☐ changes to ☑), you can open the file in Local files view to examine it.

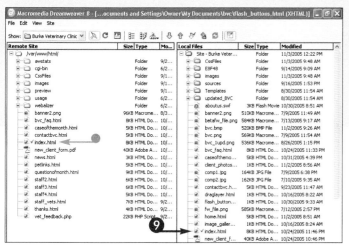

- Dreamweaver downloads the file to your Local Files.
- ⑨ Double-click to open the file.
- ⑩ Edit the file.

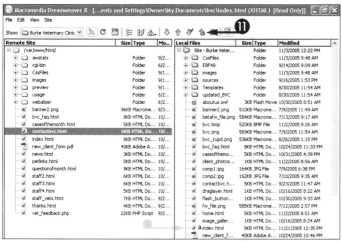

- ⑪ Click the Check in button (🔒).

  Dreamweaver uploads the updated page to the remote server.

- Dreamweaver places a Lock icon (🔒) next to the file on the local server.

TIPS

Caution!
The Check in and Check out system only works if other team members are using Dreamweaver or Contribute. If team members use another FTP program, then they can download and overwrite files.

More Options!
You can right-click (Ctrl-click) a file that another team member has checked out and select the Show checked out by command. Dreamweaver opens a dialog box and displays the name of the person who checked out the file. If the person provided an e-mail address in the Check in/Check out settings, then you can click the name to open your e-mail program with a preaddressed e-mail that you can send.

C

CLOAK FILES AND FOLDERS:
Hide from Site Operations

You can prevent Dreamweaver from including specific file types in site operations such as uploading to the remote server, generating reports, and synchronizing by cloaking the file types. You may have source files or images that you do not want on the server when you upload your entire site. Alternatively, you may have a folder of large MP3 files that you do not want to upload every time you upload the pages on which they are referenced.

You can exclude files from site operations based on file format, such as PNG and PSD, by configuring settings in the Site Definition dialog box. You can

also manage cloaking in the Files panel via a contextual menu. This menu has a cloaking submenu from which you can enable cloaking and access the Cloaking category of the Site Definition dialog box. You can also uncloak all previously cloaked files or cloak specific folders, but not individual files, from this menu.

See also>>

Files Panel

Site Definition: Cloaking

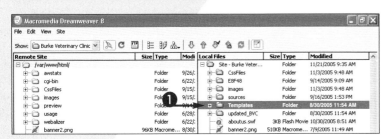

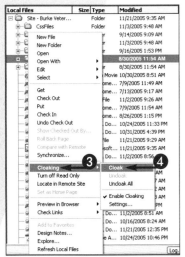

Cloak a File

① Select a folder in the Files panel that you want to cloak.

② Right-click (Ctrl-click) the file.

A contextual menu appears.

③ Click Cloaking.

④ Click Cloak.

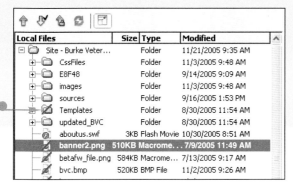

- Dreamweaver places a red slash through the folder () to indicate that it is cloaked.

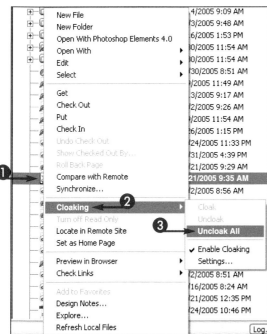

Uncloak a File

① Right-click a file.

② Click Cloaking.

③ Click Uncloak All.

Dreamweaver uncloaks all files and makes them available for site operations.

TIPS

Did You Know?

Although you can cloak only folders and not specific files from the contextual menu, you can use a feature in the Site Definition Cloaking dialog box to target a specific file. Although you usually type file extensions to exclude categories of files, the "Cloak files ending with" field recognizes full filenames.

Try This!

To cloak only one file with the .png extension and not all such files, type its full name and file extension, such as birmancat.png. Dreamweaver recreates the site cache and displays a ☒ to show that it is now cloaked.

COLOR PALETTES:
Create and Use

You can create a custom palette of colors that you can apply to text, backgrounds, borders, and other design elements. Whenever you use colors in your pages, Dreamweaver automatically adds them to the Colors category of the Assets panel. However, you may first want to create a palette of colors before adding your page elements. For example, a client or designer may give you a color scheme and expect you to exactly match its colors as you add elements to the page. You can use the Colors category in the Favorites section of the Assets panel to create your color scheme. Dreamweaver allows you to use its

Color Palette or your System Color Picker to add colors to the panel. You can even specify RGB values in the Color Picker to match an exact color.

See also>>

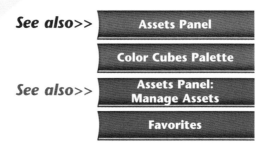

Assets Panel

Color Cubes Palette

See also>>

Assets Panel: Manage Assets

Favorites

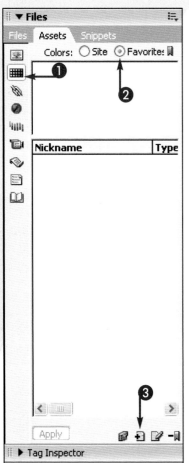

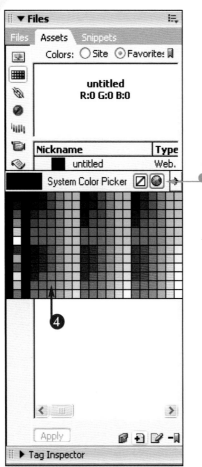

1 Click the Colors category icon (▦) in the Assets panel.

2 Click the Favorites option (○ changes to ◉).

3 Click the New Color icon (🔂).

The Color Palette appears.

4 Click a color.

● You can also click the System Color Picker icon (◉) to create custom colors.

182

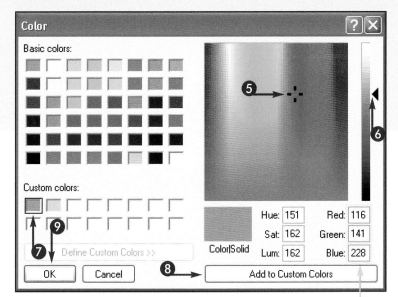

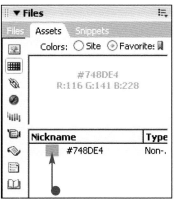

The Color dialog box appears.

5 Click a color range.

● If you know the RGB values of your color, then you can enter them in the Red, Green, and Blue fields.

6 Drag the color slider to the exact color that you want to use.

7 Click a well in the Custom colors section to store the color.

8 Click Add to Custom Colors.

9 Click OK.

● Dreamweaver adds the new color to the Color category of your Favorites panel.

COMMENTS:
Add to Documents

You can use the Comment icon in the Comment category of the Insert toolbar to add comments to the Code view of your documents. Comments do not appear in a browser window; their purpose is to provide additional information for those who maintain the pages. Designers often add comments to documents so that they can later remember what they were trying to accomplish in the page. They may add comments to the start and end of sections of the page to demarcate them. Comments also help team members to understand each other's work.

You can insert comments from either Design or Code view. When you are in Design view, Dreamweaver

displays a dialog box for you to type your comments. When you are in Code view, Dreamweaver places opening and closing comment delimiters within which you can type your comments.

See also>>
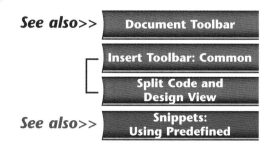

See also>>

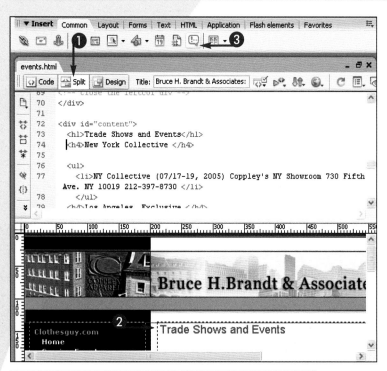

● Click the Split view button in the Document toolbar.

② In Design view, click your cursor in front of the element for which you want to provide a comment in Code view.

③ Click the Comment icon (🔲) in the Common category of the Insert toolbar.

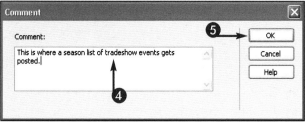

The Comment dialog box appears.

④ Type your comment.

⑤ Click OK.

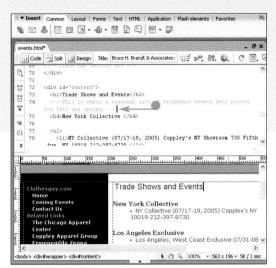

● Dreamweaver adds the comment before the element in Code view.

● You can also click your cursor directly in Code view where you want to add the comment.

⑥ Click 🖳.

Dreamweaver inserts the opening and closing delimiters of an HTML comment.

⑦ Type your comment between the delimiters.

Dreamweaver adds it to the document.

Caution!

Although your comments do not appear in the browser window, more savvy visitors know how to use the View Source command through the browser menu. When they look at your HTML source code, your comments are clearly visible.

More Options!

You can use a predefined snippet in the Snippets panel to add CSS comments. The Snippets panel has a Comments folder that contains comment snippets of various kinds, including one for CSS. CSS uses slashes and asterisks to enclose comments, like this: /* This is a CSS comment. */. Most experienced Web designers use comments extensively in their CSS documents to help them organize their code and keep track of how the CSS is structuring the page.

COMPARE FILES:
Using a Diff Utility

You can set up Dreamweaver's new File Compare preferences to use a third-party file compare program, or *Diff Utility*, to compare changes to files. You can compare files on your local computer, on the remote server, or on both the local and remote servers.

You may want to compare files if you are on a team and do not know if someone else has worked with the file. You may have previous versions of files and want to track the changes, or you may have forgotten the changes that you made since the last time you worked with a file.

When you use the File Compare command to compare local and remote files, Dreamweaver downloads a temporary copy of the remote file and launches your Diff Utility. The Diff Utility then loads the local version of the file in a pane on the right and the remote version in a pane on the left so that you can compare them. All files display as source code.

See also>> **Preferences: General**

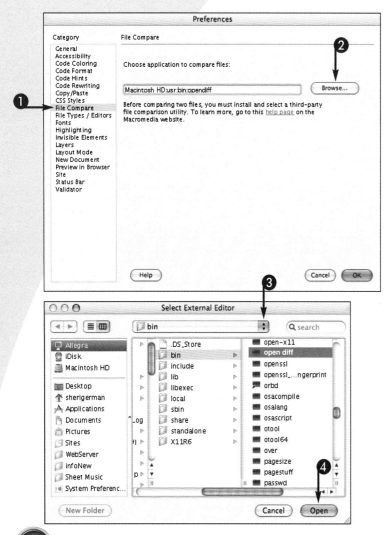

① Click the File Compare category in the Preferences dialog box.

② Click Browse.

The Select External Editor dialog box appears.

③ Navigate to your Diff Utility.

④ Click Open.

Dreamweaver inserts the path to your Diff Utility in the Choose application to compare files field.

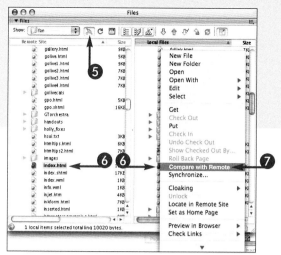

5 In the Expanded Files panel view, click the Connects to the Remote Server icon ().

6 Ctrl-click (⌘-click) to select both of the files on the remote and local servers that you want to compare.

7 Right-click (Ctrl-click) one of the files, and then click Compare with Remote in the contextual menu.

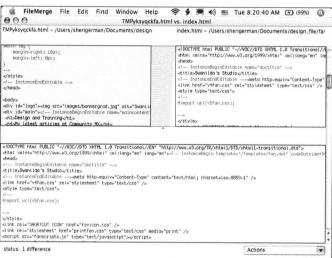

Dreamweaver launches your Diff Utility so that you can compare files and resolve differences.

TIPS

Attention!

Before comparing files, you must first install and configure a file compare tool such as the free WinMerge for Windows or Xcode for Mac OS X. Macromedia provides an article with complete directions on choosing, installing, and configuring Diff Utilities at its online Developer Center: www.macromedia.com/devnet/dreamweaver/articles/compare_utilities.html.

Apply It

File compare tools compare text files as opposed to binary code such as images; as a result, you can use them on CSS, PHP, ColdFusion, HTML, and other files that produce such code. You should explore the preferences and features of your Diff Utility. Many file comparison tools highlight the differences between files, allow you to merge differences into one version, offer code features such as line numbers, and display side-by-side comparison windows.

CONTRIBUTE:
Set Up and Administer

You can administer Contribute sites from within Dreamweaver after you enable Contribute compatibility in the Site Definition dialog box. Macromedia Contribute is a user-friendly program that allows the administrator to maintain control over the design, code, and standards of a site, while giving content editors and clients the ability to update their own pages, even if they know nothing about HTML.

When you enable Contribute compatibility, Dreamweaver displays a dialog box to warn you that it will enable Design Note options and the Check in/Check out system, both of which it uses to track the site. If you have not already done so,

Dreamweaver also asks you to provide your Check in and Check out contact information. Providing that you have Contribute installed on your computer, you can then launch Contribute from within Dreamweaver and set up users, create connection keys, and perform other administration tasks for your Contribute site.

See also>> **Design Notes**

See also>> **Check In and Check Out**

Define a Site: Using the Advanced Tab

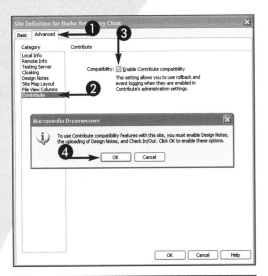

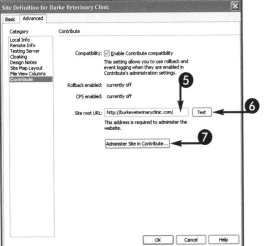

① Click the Advanced tab of the Site Definition dialog box for the targeted site.

② Click Contribute.

③ Click the Enable Contribute compatibility option (☐ changes to ☑).

The Macromedia Dreamweaver dialog box warns you that you need to enable other features.

④ Click OK.

Dreamweaver displays the Contribute options.

⑤ Type the site address.

⑥ Click here to test the connection.

⑦ Click Administer Site in Contribute.

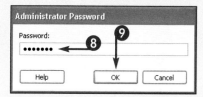

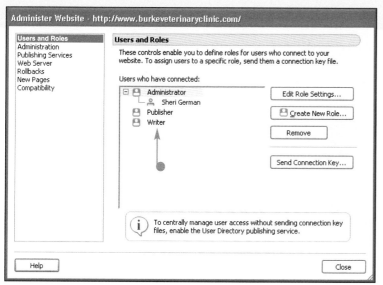

The Administrator Password dialog box appears.

⑧ Type the site's administrator password.

⑨ Click OK.

● Dreamweaver launches Contribute, and displays screens for your target site.

C

Apply It!

You can enable Contribute Publishing Server, or CPS, which is a collection of publishing applications and user management tools that allow you to integrate Contribute with an organization's user directory service, such as Lightweight Directory Access Protocol, or LDAP, or Active Directory. When you enable Contribute in your Site Definition dialog box, Dreamweaver reads the site's administration settings when you connect to the remote server, and detects whether rollback or CPS is enabled.

Caution!

You cannot enable Contribute compatibility if you are connecting to your remote site with WebDAV or Microsoft Visual SourceSafe. These systems are not compatible with the Design Notes and Check in/Check out features that Dreamweaver needs to use with Contribute sites.

COPY AND PASTE:
Folders and Files in Site

You can copy and paste files into your current site from anywhere on your computer without having to close or minimize Dreamweaver and switch to your computer's hard drive. The Files panel includes a menu that allows you to access the desktop, My Documents or Documents folder, or even the Program Files folder. You can even access a networked drive to copy and paste files from it. You can also launch programs and open files from within the Files panel.

You may have a style sheet, image, or even a folder of files that you want to copy to your current site. Dreamweaver's integration with the Windows Explorer

and the Macintosh Finder gives you a convenient way to access, copy, and paste your files. Using Dreamweaver in this way rather than switching directly to folders and files on your computer helps you to maintain the integrity of your files and their paths.

See also>> Files Panel: Using Files In

See also>> Copy and Paste

Paste Special

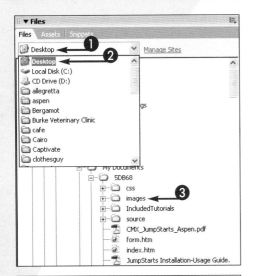

① Click the menu of sites.

② Click Desktop or the location on your computer that you want to access.

③ Navigate to the file that you want to copy.

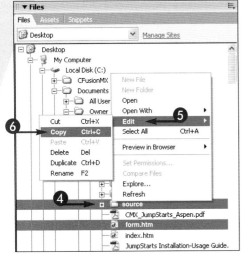

④ Select the files or folders that you want to copy.

⑤ Click Edit.

⑥ Click Copy.

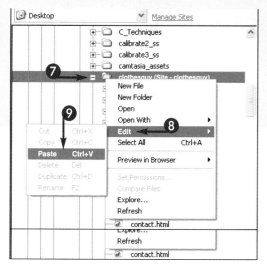

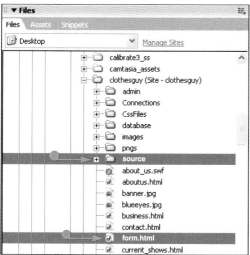

7 Click your original site folder.

You can navigate through its folders to target the exact location to which you want to copy.

8 Click Edit.

9 Click Paste.

● Dreamweaver pastes copies of your selected files and folders to the original site.

More Options!

While you are in a site within the Files panel, you can click the File Options button (▤) to access the Files menu. From there you can select Explore in Windows or Reveal in Finder in Mac OS X. You can navigate through files and perform file management without having to switch out of Dreamweaver.

Apply It!

Dreamweaver is full of hidden gems, and there is a little-known command in its File menu. If you are in one site, and you open a file from another site, then you can upload it to the current site by clicking File and then clicking Save to the Remote Server. This is another way to quickly manage files from anywhere on your computer or network.

COPY AND PASTE:
Objects

You can copy *objects* such as images, Flash movies, and MP3 files within the current site, from another site, or from anywhere on your computer without leaving Dreamweaver and without compromising the integrity of your file paths. Dreamweaver's integration with your computer makes it easy to manage, and copy and paste objects.

Sometimes you may have external images, MP3 files, Flash and QuickTime movies, and other objects that you want to copy to your current site. It is easy to insert these objects without ever having to leave Dreamweaver or the current site. You may also want

to copy or duplicate an object within the current site to create a backup, or to further manipulate the object in its native editing application.

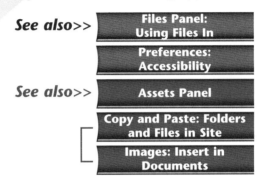

See also>> **Files Panel: Using Files In**

Preferences: Accessibility

See also>> **Assets Panel**

Copy and Paste: Folders and Files in Site

Images: Insert in Documents

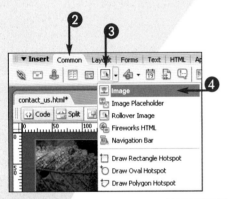

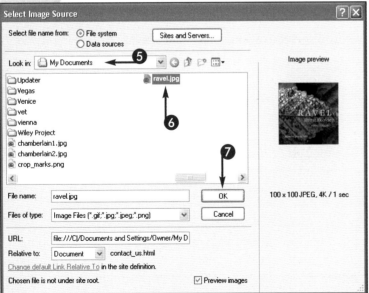

1 Click the cursor where you want to insert the object.

2 Click the Common category in the Insert toolbar.

3 Click the Image (⬛) or Media icon (⚫) to access its menu.

4 Click an object.

This example selects an image.

The Select Image Source dialog box appears.

5 Navigate to your image or other object that is not in your site's root folder.

6 Select the image.

7 Click OK.

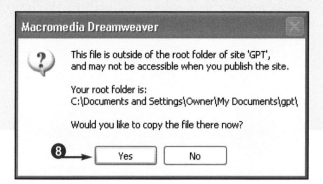

A Macromedia Dreamweaver dialog box appears, asking if you want to copy the object to the current site.

⑧ Click Yes.

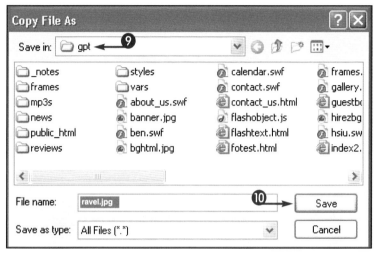

The Copy File As dialog box appears.

⑨ Navigate to your current site.

⑩ Click Save.

Dreamweaver copies the file to your site and inserts it in the page.

If you have accessibility turned on for images and other objects, then Dreamweaver displays the Accessibility dialog box before inserting the object.

More Options!

Dreamweaver provides many file management choices from its Edit menu in the Files panel. You can right-click (Ctrl-click) a file and select either Copy or Duplicate from its contextual menu. If you select Copy, then Dreamweaver allows you to paste the object into another location or application. If you select Duplicate, then Dreamweaver names the file "Copy of object name" in the same directory as the original.

Apply It

Another way that you can copy objects from other sites is through the Assets panel. You can use the Copy to Site command from the Assets panel option menu to copy assets from other sites.

CSS:
Create Embedded Style Sheet

You can embed your styles in the head of a document by using the This document only option in the New CSS Rule dialog box. Embedding styles creates an internal style sheet that affects only that one document.

You may have a page that you want to format differently than the rest of the site, such as a page with a data table. You may also use an external style sheet, but also have a few page-specific styles that you want to add. Because internal style sheets carry more weight than external style sheets, if you create different styles for the same selector, then the

embedded styles overwrite the external styles. You can also embed styles in template pages to keep content editors from changing the design of the page.

See also>> **CSS Rule Definition Window**

CSS Styles

See also>> **CSS: Create External Style Sheet**

CSS, Export Styles

Templates: Create a Template

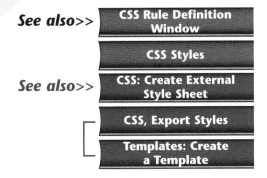

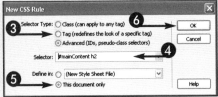

1 Open the page to which you want to add styles.

2 Click the New CSS Rule button (⊞) in the CSS Styles panel.

The New CSS Rule dialog box appears.

3 Click a Selector Type option (○ changes to ◉).

4 Type your selector.

5 Click the This document only option (○ changes to ◉).

6 Click OK.

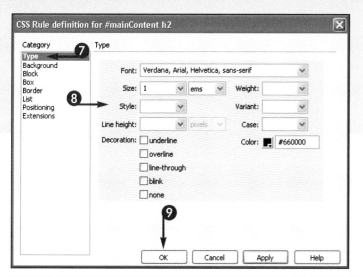

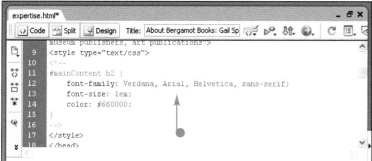

The CSS Rule definition for dialog box appears.

7 Click a category.

8 Type or select the properties that you want for your selector.

9 Click OK.

● Dreamweaver applies the style and inserts it in the head of the document using the style element.

TIPS

Apply It!

Many designers embed styles in a document while they are exploring layouts and designs for a new site. They then export the styles from the head and into an external style sheet after they complete the development process.

Did You Know?

The proper syntax for embedding styles is to enclose them in the head of the document within the style element. The styles themselves are usually surrounded by HTML comments to hide them from older browsers that do not understand them. You can examine how Dreamweaver writes the code into the head of the document after you insert your first embedded style. You can read all about embedding styles at www.w3schools.com/css/css_howto.asp.

CSS:
Create External Style Sheet

You can harness the power of Cascading Style Sheets, or CSS, by creating an external style sheet that you can add to as many documents as you like. An external style sheet puts your styles into a separate document with the .css extension. When you make changes to the style sheet, the sheet automatically updates all pages that are based on it. Using one external style sheet on multiple documents ensures that you maintain design consistency throughout your site as well as saving you many hours.

Dreamweaver allows you to begin your external style sheet by creating a new CSS rule in the CSS panel. It

then prompts you to save the style sheet in your site's root folder and links the style sheet in the head of your document. After you create your style sheet, you can add styles through the CSS panel.

See also>> CSS Styles

See also>> Attach and Detach

CSS: Create Embedded Style Sheet

CSS: Create External Style Sheet

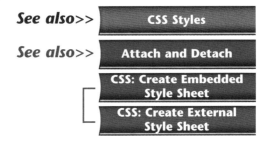

① Open the page to which you want to add an external style sheet.

② Click the New CSS Rule icon (⬚) in the CSS panel.

The New CSS Rule dialog box appears.

③ Click the Selector Type that you want to style (○ changes to ◉).

④ Type the Name, Tag, or Selector field, depending on your Selector Type.

⑤ Click here (○ changes to ◉) and select New Style Sheet File for the Define in option.

⑥ Click OK.

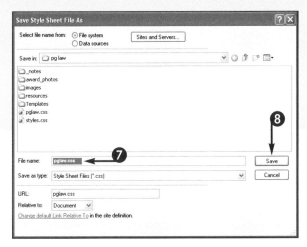

The Save Style Sheet File As dialog box appears.

⑦ Type a filename.

⑧ Click Save.

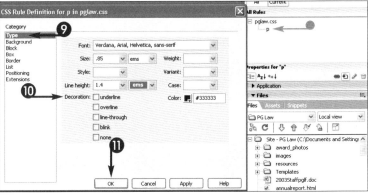

⑨ In the CSS Rule Definition for dialog box that appears, click a category.

⑩ Type or select the formatting for your new style.

⑪ Click OK.

● Dreamweaver applies the style and displays the new style sheet name in the CSS panel.

Try This!

You can also use the New Document dialog box to add an external style sheet document to your page. A CSS document is one of the Basic Page offerings in the General category. Dreamweaver creates a page in Code view that has a CSS comment at the top of the page (/* CSS Document */). If you know how to manually code CSS, then you can create an external style sheet this way and attach it with the Attach icon (⊜) at the bottom of the CSS panel. Once you attach the style sheet, you can add to it by using the CSS panel.

CSS, EDIT RULES:
From the CSS Panel

After you create your styles for a page or site, you can go back and edit them if you change your mind. You can edit both embedded styles and external style sheets. When you edit a style from an external style sheet, Dreamweaver reflects the change in every page that uses the style sheet.

Dreamweaver offers you several flexible options from which to select. You can use the CSS Styles panel to reopen the original CSS Rule Definition dialog box. You can also open the dialog box via the Edit Style icon at the bottom of the CSS Styles

panel. If you want to make quick edits, you can expand the categories in the Properties for panel for your selected rule, and access menus and fields to make direct changes that Dreamweaver instantly applies.

See also>> **CSS Styles Panel**

CSS Styles

See also>> **Panels: View and Resize**

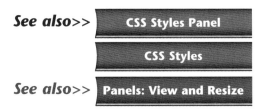

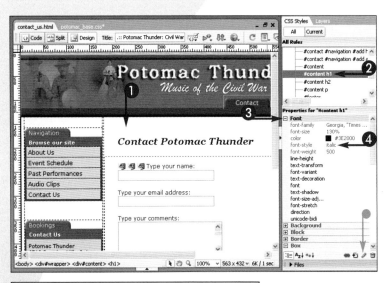

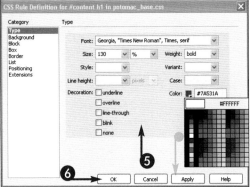

① Open a page in the site.

② Click the rule that you want to edit in the CSS panel.

③ Click the plus sign (⊞) for the category that you want to edit.

The ⊞ changes to ⊟.

● You can also click the Edit icon (🖉) or double-click the selected rule.

④ Edit the properties and values that appear.

Dreamweaver applies the styles.

The CSS Rule Definition dialog box appears.

⑤ Edit the categories and properties for your selector.

● You can click Apply to view your changes before you exit the dialog box.

⑥ Click OK.

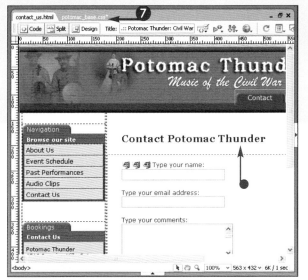

● Dreamweaver applies the edited style to your page.

⑦ Click the tab for your style sheet.

Dreamweaver brings the tab to the front of the Document Window.

⑧ Click File.

⑨ Click Save.

Dreamweaver saves your changes.

Apply It!

If you know how to manually code CSS styles, then you can also edit them by opening your external CSS document. You can type directly in the document, and as you begin typing, Dreamweaver displays a menu of code hints. Using code hints to select properties and attributes expedites the process and helps prevent typographical errors.

More Options

If you do not want Dreamweaver to open the CSS document and prompt you to save it whenever you edit your styles, then you can change this in the CSS Styles preferences. You can click to deselect the "Open CSS files when modified" option (☑ changes to ☐). The document will no longer open during edits, and Dreamweaver automatically saves your new properties.

CSS, EXPORT STYLES:
From the Document Head

You can use Dreamweaver's Export CSS Styles command to export embedded styles to an external style sheet. You may want to try out different layouts, colors, fonts, and styles on different pages while you develop the design for a site. After settling on the design that you want, you can take the embedded styles and convert them into an external style sheet that you can attach to other pages in your site. Before you exit the Attach External Style Sheet dialog box, you can even preview what the page will look like with the selected style sheet.

Unfortunately, you have to attach your external style sheet to one document at a time. To remedy this, you can create a template, and attach your external style sheet to it so that every page that you create based on the template automatically has the style sheet attached.

See also>> **CSS Styles Panel**

See also>> **CSS: Create Embedded Style Sheet**

CSS, Edit Rules

① Open a page with embedded styles that you want to export.

You can see the embedded styles listed within the style element in the CSS panel.

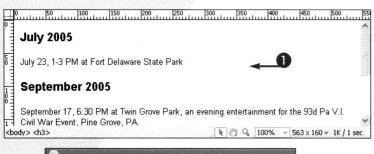

② Click File.
③ Click Export.
④ Click CSS Styles.

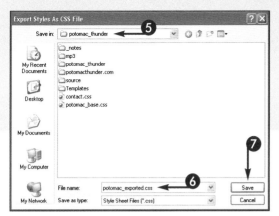

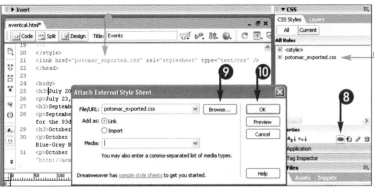

The Export Styles As CSS File dialog box appears.

⑤ Navigate to your site folder.

⑥ Type a name for your CSS document.

You must add the .css file extension.

⑦ Click Save.

Dreamweaver saves the exported style sheet to your site folder.

⑧ Click the Attach icon (▣) in the CSS panel.

⑨ In the Attach External Style Sheet dialog box, click Browse and navigate to your exported style sheet and click Open.

⑩ Click OK in the Attach External Style Sheet dialog box.

● Dreamweaver links the style sheet in the head of the document and adds it to the CSS panel where you can edit and add styles.

TIPS

Caution!

External style sheets are dependent files, just like images, Flash movies, and other objects that you insert into your pages. Only a reference to the files exists in the page, and not the actual objects themselves. Therefore, you must upload the files to the remote server, maintaining the same path and relationship, when you upload the pages to which you linked them.

Try This!

After you export styles from a document, you may want to attach the exported external style sheet to the same document. You can remove the original embedded styles by selecting the style element in the CSS panel and then clicking the Trash icon (🗑).

CSS, MEDIA TYPE STYLE SHEETS:
Create and Attach

You can use the Attach icon in the CSS panel to attach style sheets for different media types. Visitors no longer only view your Web pages on a computer screen. Some may use handheld devices like the Blackberry, visually impaired visitors may use screen readers, and visitors who want to print your content may need style sheets that optimize the page for printers.

There are ten media types, and you can attach style sheets for as many as your target audience warrants. Dreamweaver's Attach External Style Sheet dialog box includes a Media menu so that you can

select the appropriate media type for your style sheet. Dreamweaver then adds the correct link in the head of your document. After you create your media-dependent style sheet, you can see what your page looks like for that device by using the new Style Rendering toolbar.

See also>>

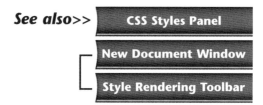

CSS Styles Panel

New Document Window

Style Rendering Toolbar

① Click File.

② Click New.

③ In the General tab of the New Document dialog box, click Basic page.

④ Click CSS.

⑤ Click Create.

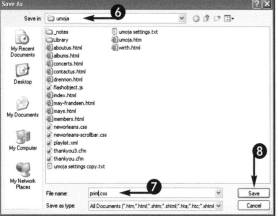

The Save As dialog box appears.

⑥ Navigate to your site folder.

⑦ Type a name for the style sheet.

⑧ Click Save.

Dreamweaver saves your blank style sheet.

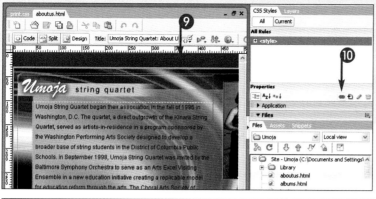

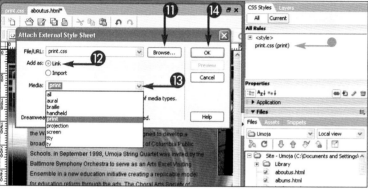

⑨ Open the page to which you want to attach the style sheet.

⑩ Click the Attach Style Sheet icon (▣) in the CSS panel.

The Attach External Style Sheet dialog box appears.

⑪ Click Browse to navigate to your style sheet.

⑫ Click the Link option (◯ changes to ◉) in the Add as section.

⑬ Click here and select a media type from the Media menu.

⑭ Click OK.

● Dreamweaver adds the style sheet to the CSS panel where you can begin adding styles to it.

More Options

If you only have a few styles that you want to create for an alternative device, then you can add them to your main style sheet by using the `@mediarule`. For example, you may want to add a few styles that optimize your content for visitors who want to print it out. You can change your font unit of measurement to points, and change sans serif fonts to serif, which are both standards for printed material. You can add this rule to your main style sheet, as follows:

```
@media print {
body { font: 11pt/130% Times New Roman, serif; }
}
```

Did You Know?

You can read more about media types at www.communitymx.com/abstract.cfm?cid=096A1.

CSS, INLINE STYLES:
Create

When you activate a contextual menu and use Dreamweaver's code hinting feature, you can add inline styles to your document. Inline styles are styles that you add inside the tag within the source code of the document. You can add CSS to tags by using the `style` attribute. For example, you can add a black border and 14-pixel Arial font to a specific paragraph in your page, as follows:

```
<p style="border: solid 1px #000000; font:
14px Arial">
```

You can then use the tag to display code hints, and then another list of code hints, this time with CSS properties. You can select a hint, and if there are any further attributes for the property, Dreamweaver continues to display new code hint lists.

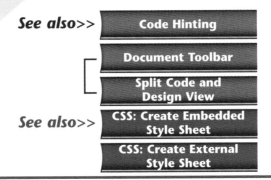

See also>> Code Hinting

Document Toolbar

Split Code and Design View

See also>> CSS: Create Embedded Style Sheet

CSS: Create External Style Sheet

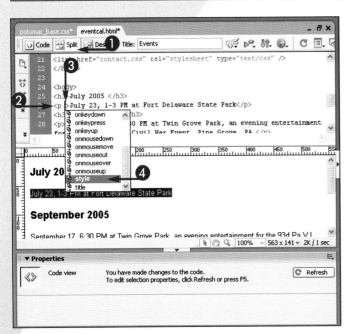

❶ Click the Split view button in the Document toolbar.

Dreamweaver displays the document in Code and Design view.

❷ Click inside the tag to which you want to add the inline style.

❸ Press the space bar to insert one space after the tag.

Dreamweaver displays code hints.

❹ Double-click style.

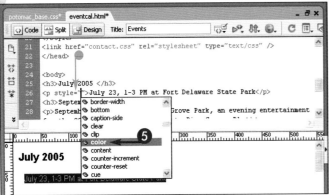

● Dreamweaver adds the `style` attribute to the tag, along with empty quotes.

Dreamweaver places your cursor between the quotes, and displays code hints again.

❺ Click a property or attribute.

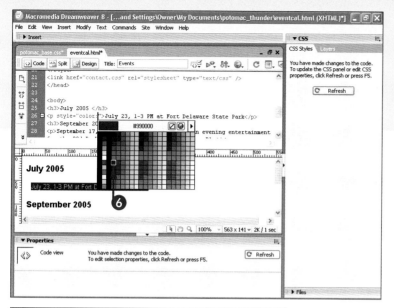

Dreamweaver continues to display code hints.

Because color was selected in this example, a Color Palette appears.

6 Click a color swatch.

● Dreamweaver completes the inline style.

7 Click your cursor in Design view.

Dreamweaver displays your inline style.

TIPS

Try This!

When you use the `style` attribute, you can add multiple properties and values within the tag if you type a semicolon (;) after each property value pair. If you press the space bar after the semicolon, then Dreamweaver again displays a list of code hints from which you can select.

Attention!

In the cascade, inline styles carry the most weight. An inline style overrides an embedded one, and an embedded style overrides a style in an external style sheet. Inline styles give you a very specific style for just one element. However, when you use inline styles, you lose much of the power of CSS; you should use them sparingly, if at all.

C

CSS, POSITIONING:
Overview

You can use the Positioning category of the CSS panel to design your pages without using tables. The markup for tables was originally conceived to display tabular data. Designers discovered that they could usurp table code and use cells and rows to control and align objects. Positioning techniques have evolved to replace tables for laying out pages so that they are more *semantic,* or used for their intended purpose in the markup.

The different positioning types — absolute, static, fixed, and relative — as well as the use of floats for positioning, cover most layout situations. Although you can apply positioning to almost any element, you will often wrap a DIV around a group of elements, using it as a container. You can then apply the positioning to the DIV, thus affecting all elements within.

See also>> **CSS Rule Definition Window**

See also>> **CSS, Positioning: Using Absolute Positioning**

CSS, Positioning: Using Relative Positioning

CSS, Positioning: Using Static Positioning

DIV Tags

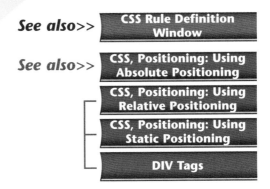

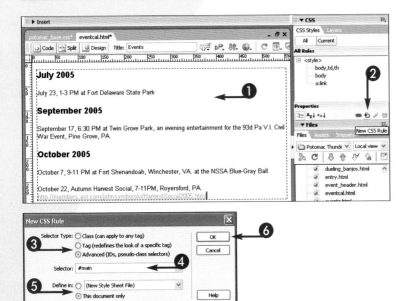

1 Open a page in which you want to add positioning to an element.

2 Click the New CSS Rule icon (⊞).

The New CSS Rule dialog box appears.

3 Click a Selector Type, such as Advanced, to position a DIV (○ changes to ◉).

4 Type a Selector, such as a DIV name.

5 Click a Define in option (○ changes to ◉).

6 Click OK.

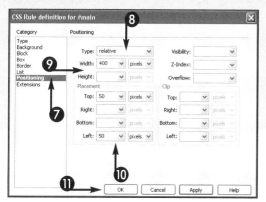

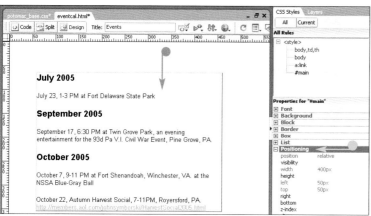

Dreamweaver opens the CSS Rule definition dialog box.

Note: *If you are starting a new external style sheet, the Save Style Sheet File As dialog box appears; save your style sheet and continue.*

7 Click the Positioning category.

8 Click here and select a positioning Type.

9 Type a width or height if the element requires it.

10 Type placement values.

11 Click OK.

● Dreamweaver applies the positioning to your target element.

● Dreamweaver displays the positioning properties in the Properties for panel.

Check It Out!

You will probably not use the `visibility`, `z-index`, `overflow`, and `clip` properties in basic page layout. If you want to know more about these advanced topics, then you can read about the use of positioning properties at www.w3schools.com/css/css_positioning.asp.

Apply It!

When you add any value to your positioned object, such as for its width or X- and Y-coordinates, you will notice that there are a number of units of measurement from which you can select. The Dreamweaver default is pixels, a unit of measurement that is familiar to most users. You may also want to learn about ems, percentages, and keywords, all of which invite much debate in the world of CSS. You can read more at www.webmonkey.com/webmonkey/reference/stylesheet_guide/units.html.

CSS, POSITIONING:
Using Absolute Positioning

You can use *absolute positioning* in the Positioning category of the CSS Styles panel to place objects on the page at precise X- and Y-coordinates. When you draw a Dreamweaver layer on the page, you are creating a DIV with absolute positioning. You can apply absolute positioning to other elements such as a *skip link* that allows visually impaired visitors to skip to the main content of the page.

Designers are so accustomed to using table grids to design their pages that they forget that HTML provides a natural flow that conforms to the browser window, or *viewport*. Designers place objects at the top left of the page, and continue to flow them in a

natural order. Absolutely positioned elements are no longer in the natural flow of the document, and so other objects on the page no longer recognize them.

See also>> CSS Rule Definition Window

Layers: Drawing

See also>> CSS, Positioning: Overview

CSS, Positioning: Using Relative Positioning

DIV Tags

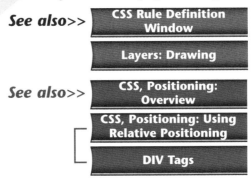

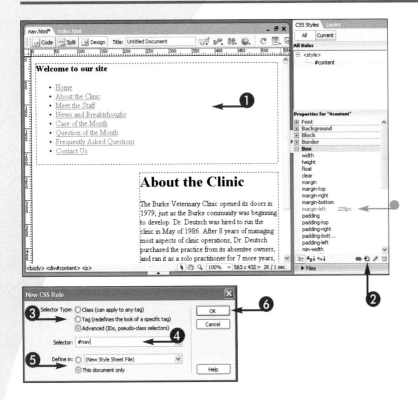

1 Open a page to which you want to add an absolutely positioned element.

● You may have two DIVs, one for navigation and one for content.

   For example, you can give the content DIV a margin-left of 225 to leave room for a 200-pixel-wide navigation area.

2 Click the New CSS Rule icon (🗐).

   The New CSS Rule dialog box appears.

3 Click a Selector Type, such as Advanced, to position a DIV (○ changes to ◉).

4 Type a Selector, such as a DIV name.

5 Click a Define in option (○ changes to ◉).

6 Click OK.

208

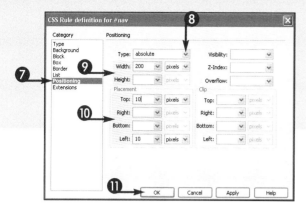

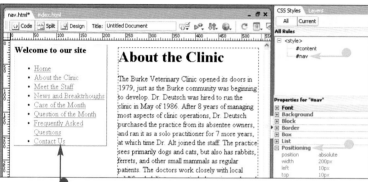

The CSS Rule definition dialog box appears.

Note: If you are starting a new external style sheet, the Save Style Sheet File As dialog box appears; save your style sheet and continue.

7 Click the Positioning category.

8 Click here and select the absolute positioning type.

9 Type a width or height if the element requires it.

10 Type placement values.

11 Click OK.

● Dreamweaver moves your element to the absolutely positioned coordinates that you specify.

In this example, because the left margin has a value of 225, the two DIVs do not overlap.

● Dreamweaver takes the element out of the flow, and moves the content after it to its vacated place.

TIPS

Caution!
While there are good uses for absolutely positioned elements, you should avoid laying out entire pages that way. For example, if you have two absolutely positioned layers next to each other, because they are at set coordinates, when a visitor increases text size, one layer may overlap the other. Still, absolutely positioned elements can be beneficial when you use them judiciously. You can optimize pages for search engines because you can put absolutely positioned elements anywhere in the source code.

Did You Know?
You can also use absolutely positioned elements for elements that you want to appear off-screen, such as skip links for screen readers. Read more about the pros and cons of absolutely positioned elements at www.macromedia.com/devnet/ dreamweaver/articles/css_concepts_pt6_03.html. Read about skip links at www.communitymx.com/ abstract.cfm?cid=B96B1.

CSS, POSITIONING:
Using Floats for Positioning

You can use the Float property in the CSS Box category to position elements on the page. While you often use floats to align text and images, you can also use them to create multicolumn layouts. For example, you may have a content area on the page that has a left margin of 225 pixels. You may then have a 200-pixel-wide navigation area that you want to float to its left. If you place the navigation area in front of the content area in your code, then you can use the Float property to create the two columns.

You can also create two columns with absolutely positioned elements, but for absolutely positioned columns, the navigation column must always be

shorter than the content column when there is more content below the columns. This restriction does not apply to floated columns.

See also>> CSS Styles Panel

See also>> Align Images: To Text with CSS

CSS Positioning: Using Absolute Positioning

DIV Tags

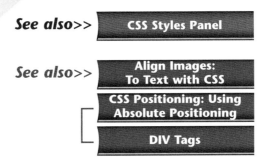

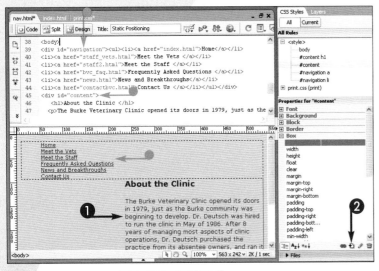

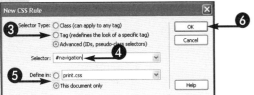

1 Open a page in which you want to float an element.

● The element that you want to float must come before non-floating elements in Code view.

2 Click the New CSS Rule icon (⊡).

The New CSS Rule dialog box appears.

3 Click a Selector Type, such as Advanced, to float a DIV (○ changes to ◉).

4 Type a Selector, such as a DIV name.

5 Click a Define in option (○ changes to ◉).

6 Click OK.

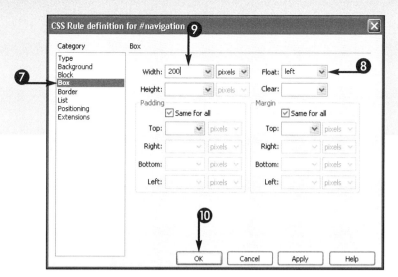

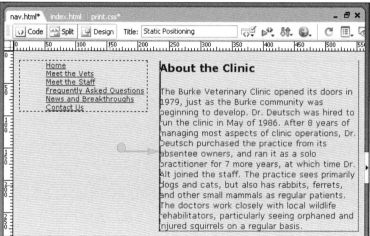

The CSS Rule definition dialog box appears.

Note: *If you are starting a new external style sheet, then the Save Style Sheet File As dialog box appears. Save your style sheet and continue.*

⑦ Click the Box category.

⑧ Click here and select either right or left.

You can also add margins to the float if you want.

⑨ Type a width for the floated column to prevent unpredictable behavior.

⑩ Click OK.

● Dreamweaver displays your element in the float direction that you select.

You can click each rule in the CSS panel and then read its properties in the Properties for panel.

Check It Out!

The Web Standards Group provides a whole series of tutorials, including tutorials on using floats to create equal-height two- and three-column layouts with headers and footers. You can find more information at css.maxdesign.com.au/floatutorial/.

Apply It!

If you place a footer or any other content beneath your multicolumn layout, then you must clear that element to prevent the content in the columns from bleeding into it. The float tutorial on the Web Standards Group Web site shows you how to clear footers at this page: css.maxdesign.com.au/floatutorial/tutorial0811.htm. You can also read about some sophisticated techniques for clearing elements at Position Is Everything, the official site of Web gurus John Gallant and Holly Bergevin: positioniseverything.net/easyclearing.html.

CSS, POSITIONING:
Using Relative Positioning

You can use *relative positioning* in the Positioning category of the CSS Styles panel to keep objects in the flow of the document. Although relative positioning is similar to the default behavior of the page, it allows you to give elements offset values for the top, right, bottom, or left coordinates relative to the parent container. For example, if the body of the page is the parent container for a relatively positioned DIV, then the offset is relative to the page margins.

Absolutely positioned layouts, or those that you can create by using Dreamweaver's Draw Layer feature, produce rigid layouts that invariably break when confronted with different browser and computer configurations. Relatively positioned layouts adjust to the browser window; they affect, and are affected by, other flowed elements on the page.

See also>> | CSS Styles Panel

See also>> | CSS, Positioning: Overview

CSS, Positioning: Using Absolute Positioning

DIV Tags

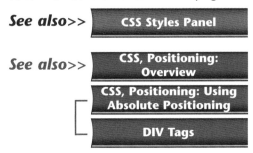

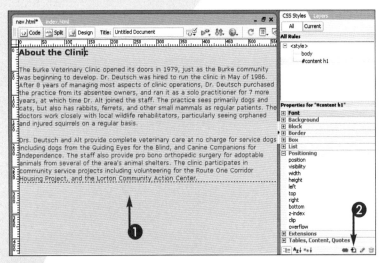

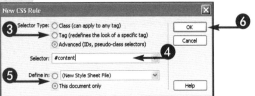

① Open a page to which you want to add a relatively positioned element.

② Click the New CSS Rule icon (▣).

The New CSS Rule dialog box appears.

③ Click a Selector Type, such as Advanced, to position a DIV (◯ changes to ◉).

④ Type a Selector, such as a DIV name.

⑤ Click a Define in option (◯ changes to ◉).

⑥ Click OK.

Note: *If you are starting a new external style sheet, the Save Style Sheet File As dialog box appears; save your style sheet and continue.*

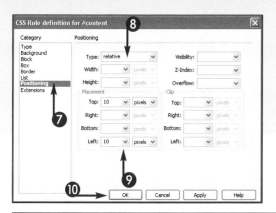

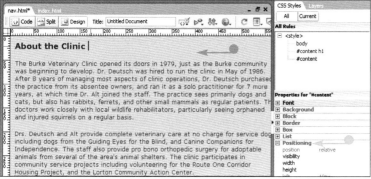

The CSS Rule definition dialog box appears.

⑦ Click the Positioning category.

⑧ Click here and select the relative type.

⑨ Type your placement values.

⑩ Click OK.

● Dreamweaver applies relative positioning to your target element.

● Dreamweaver displays the positioning properties in the Properties for panel.

TIPS

Caution!
If you offset your absolutely positioned element with top and left coordinates, then you should generally stay away from using right and bottom values, as they fight each other. However, you can also apply negative values to your coordinates for interesting effects.

Apply It!
You can combine relative and absolute positioning to have more control while retaining flexibility. By default, when you place an absolutely positioned element on the page, its coordinates take their starting position from the browser window. However, when you nest an absolutely positioned DIV inside a relatively positioned one, the absolutely positioned element's coordinates use the relatively positioned DIV as the starting point. The absolute and relatively positioned DIVs also move together.

CSS, POSITIONING:
Using Static Positioning

You can use the Positioning category of the CSS panel to assign a position of static to an element in your document. Static positioning is the page default; the elements flow one after the other, filling the browser window with block and inline elements. When you use static positioning on your elements, they do not respond to coordinate placement properties.

Because it is the default, you normally do not need to assign static positioning to an element. It can become useful when you need to reset elements that have another kind of positioning applied to them. For example, printers can have trouble with pages that

have any kind of positioning; only one page may emerge from the printer, or elements may be cut off. You can create a print style sheet that resets positioned elements to static so that they print properly.

See also>> **CSS Styles Panel**

See also>> **CSS, Media Type Style Sheets**

CSS, Positioning: Overview

Design-Time Style Sheets

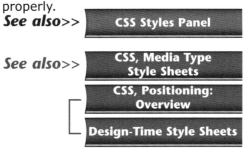

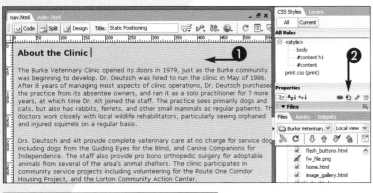

① Open a page in which you want to add static positioning to an element.

You can also create a new print style sheet and use it to reset an element from another position to static.

② Click the New CSS Rule icon (⊞).

The New CSS Rule dialog box appears.

③ Click a Selector Type, such as Advanced, to position a DIV (○ changes to ◉).

④ Type a Selector, such as a DIV name.

⑤ Click a Define in option (○ changes to ◉).

If you have created a print style sheet, then you can select it from the menu.

⑥ Click OK.

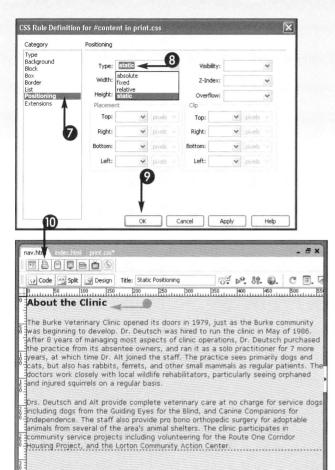

The CSS Rule Definition dialog box appears.

7 Click the Positioning category.

8 Click here and select the static positioning type.

9 Click OK.

● Dreamweaver applies static positioning to your target element.

If you applied the static type to an element in a print style sheet, then you can see it in Design view by clicking the Print icon (🖨) in the Style Rendering toolbar.

10 Click 🖨.

Dreamweaver shows how the page will look when the user prints it out.

Attention!

HTML provides a natural flow as you place objects starting at the top left of the page, and let them continue in order until you get to the bottom. There are two basic kinds of elements: inline and block. *Inline* elements follow one after the other horizontally in the flow of the page. *Block* elements, such as headings and paragraphs, are as wide as the browser window and stack vertically.

Apply It!

Although Dreamweaver 8 is much better at rendering your CSS layouts in its Design view, it still occasionally has trouble. You can reset positioned objects to static in a Design-time style sheet so that Dreamweaver can recognize them and allow you to more comfortably edit the page.

CSS STYLING:
Control Link Appearance

You can use pseudo-classes to control the appearance of your links, for example, to create a button look. Dreamweaver's Advanced menu in the New CSS Rule dialog box includes four pseudo-classes so that you can style the various states of links: a:link, which is the initial state of the link; a:visited, which is the state that reminds visitors that they have already visited a link; a:hover, which is the state that provides interactive feedback when visitors point the mouse over a link; and a:active, which is the state of the link when visitors press down on the link but have not yet released the mouse.

Some designers also use a:focus, a link state that creates a hover effect, instead of a:active; this state creates a hover effect when visitors use the keyboard instead of the mouse. Although Dreamweaver does not include the a:focus state in its Advanced menu, you can add it manually.

See also>>

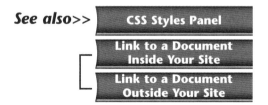

CSS Styles Panel

Link to a Document
Inside Your Site

Link to a Document
Outside Your Site

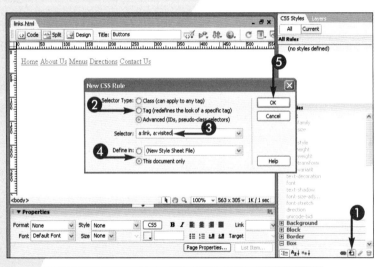

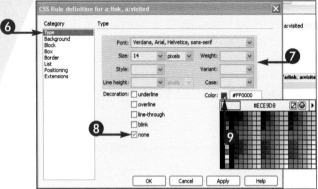

① With a page open that has a set of links that you want to style, click the New CSS Rule icon (🖻).

② In the New CSS Rule dialog box, click the Advanced option (○ changes to ◉).

③ Click here and select the pseudo-selector a:link.

You can also style a:visited to look the same way by grouping the selectors. Separate them with a comma, and then a space.

④ Click a Define in option (○ changes to ◉).

⑤ Click OK.

The CSS Rule definition for dialog box appears.

⑥ Click the Type category.

⑦ Specify your type options.

⑧ Click the Decoration: none option (☐ changes to ☑).

⑨ Click a text color.

C

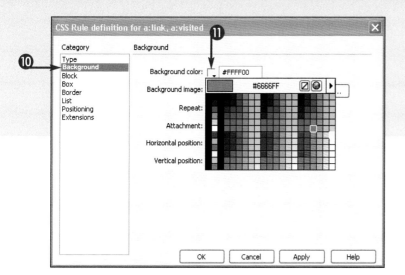

⑩ Click the Background category.

⑪ Click a background color ().

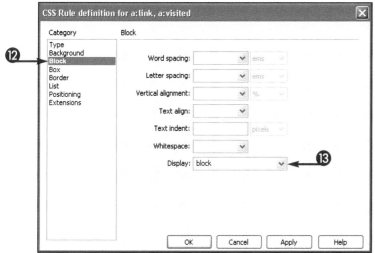

⑫ Click the Block category.

⑬ Click here and select block.

TIPS

Try This!

One of the benefits of using CSS, especially in external style sheets, is that it reduces the amount of bandwidth that your site requires. Each page in your site is smaller and downloads more quickly to the visitor's computer because most of the design code is in one central location.

Try This!

Another way to capitalize on the benefit of using CSS is to group selectors. If you want to use the same style on multiple selectors, then you can separate each selector by a comma and one space to style them all at once. For example, if you want your headings to have a 20-pixel left margin, then you can group them as h1, h2, h3, and h4 and apply the left margin to them.

CSS STYLING:
Control Link Appearance (Continued)

When you style your links, you must follow a prescribed sequence to ensure that they work properly in the browser: a:link, a:visited, a:hover, and a:active or a:focus. Many designers use a mnemonic device to remember the order: LVHA or LoVeHAte.

You can transform the default underlined, blue links into CSS buttons by using properties from various categories in the CSS Styles panel. You can remove the underline by using the Text Decoration property. You can turn them into block elements so that each button appears on its own line by using the Display

property. You can add borders and background colors to visually enhance the button appearance. You can add a width to the button, control the space between the edge of the button and the text within by adding padding, and use margins to add space around each button.

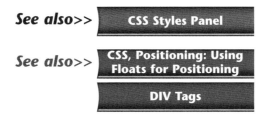

See also>> CSS Styles Panel

See also>> CSS, Positioning: Using Floats for Positioning

DIV Tags

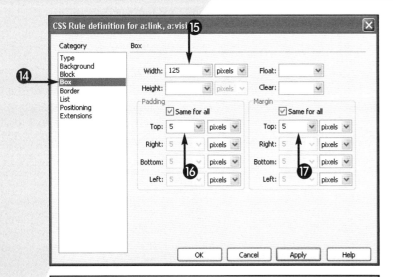

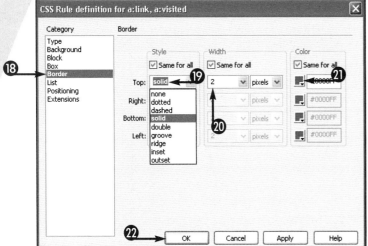

⓮ Click the Box category.

⓯ Type a width for the buttons.

⓰ Type a padding value if you want space between the borders of the button and the text.

⓱ Type a margin value if you want space around the buttons.

⓲ Click the Border category.

⓳ Click here and select a border style.

⓴ Type a value for border width.

㉑ Click a border color (⬛).

㉒ Click OK.

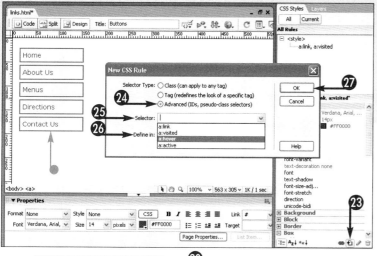

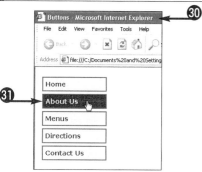

- Dreamweaver styles your links as buttons.

㉓ Click 🔁.

㉔ In the New CSS Rule dialog box, click Advanced (○ changes to ⊙).

㉕ Click here and select a:hover.

You can also type a comma, a space, and then a:focus to add it as a group selector.

㉖ Select a Define in option (○ changes to ⊙).

㉗ Click OK in the New CSS Rule dialog box.

㉘ In the CSS Rule Definition dialog box, repeat steps **9** to **11**.

㉙ Click OK in the CSS Rule Definition dialog box.

Dreamweaver applies the styles for the hover state.

㉚ Preview the buttons in your browser.

㉛ Point your mouse at a link.

The browser displays the hover state.

TIPS

Try This!
You can create a background image to apply behind each of your buttons. You can create an interesting texture or gradient, or even apply the image for only the a:hover state. Be sure to make the image bigger than the size of your buttons in case a visitor increases text size. Because you use only one image on all buttons, you still have the benefit of a small file size.

Apply It!
You can put your list of links in a DIV and give it an ID such as #navigation. You can then use the Float property to position the DIV to the left or right of your content. This creates a simple and elegant CSS layout.

CSS STYLING:
Control Text Appearance

You can use CSS styles to format the text in your Web pages. Web designers used to format text with tags and attributes such as font and align, which the World Wide Web Consortium has now deprecated. Although deprecated elements still work to provide backwards compatibility with older browsers, they will eventually become obsolete, and so you should learn to use CSS to format your text.

Dreamweaver helps by setting its General Preferences Editing options to use CSS instead of HTML tags as the default text formatting option. You can then use the Properties inspector to format your

text with CSS. However, a much more powerful way to format text is by using embedded styles or an external style sheet. That way, you can apply formatting to multiple elements and pages.

See also>> **CSS Styles Panel**

See also>> **CSS: Create Embedded Style Sheet**

CSS: Create External Style Sheet

CSS Styling: Style Heading Appearance

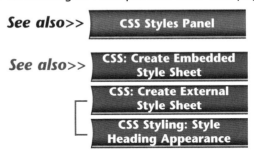

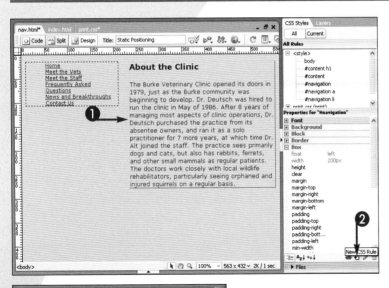

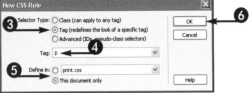

① Open a page in which you want to add text formatting.

② Click the New CSS Rule icon (🗔).

The New CSS Rule dialog box appears.

③ Click the Tag Selector Type.

④ Type <p> for the Selector, or click here and select p.

The p tag is the HTML tag for paragraph text.

⑤ Click a Define in option.

⑥ Click OK.

The CSS Rule definition dialog box appears.

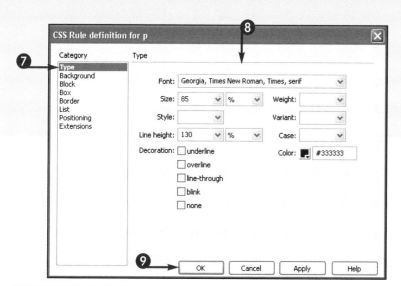

Note: If you define a new external style sheet, the Save Style Sheet File As dialog box appears; save your style sheet and continue.

⑦ Click the Type category.

⑧ Type or select your text options.

Dreamweaver allows you to select fonts, font-size, font style — such as italics — line-height, font-weight, small caps variation, case, and text color.

⑨ Click OK.

You can also experiment with background colors and borders by adding properties from those categories.

You can use the Box category to add margins or padding.

● Dreamweaver applies the type styles to your paragraph text.

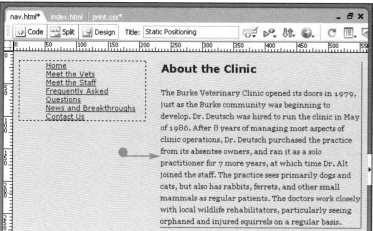

Try This!

You can add as many external style sheets to your document as you like. Many designers keep track of styles by modularizing their style sheets; for example, they put all text rules in one style sheet, and all positioning rules in another.

Apply It!

CSS includes more text formatting features than HTML. One such example is line-height, also known as leading in the print world. Print designers often use a two-point difference between font size and leading, such as 12-point type over 14 points of leading from baseline to baseline. Many Web designers feel that more generous space between lines, such as 18 pixels of line-height with 14-pixel text, makes it easier to read on a monitor screen.

CSS STYLING:
Style Forms

You can style your forms so that they look more attractive to your visitor. You can style the input tag, which includes Submit buttons and text fields, with a background image, a background color, and borders.

You can create an image with a gradient or a pattern that you can repeat on the X-axis until it fills the input form. The Repeat property allows the width of the image to be very thin, thus keeping the file size small. You can also set a background color on the input tag so that if the image height does not fill the text field, the background color matches the bottom

color of the image. For example, you can set the background color to white if you have a gradient that goes from blue at the top to white at the bottom.

See also>> **CSS Styles Panel**

See also>> **Forms: About Forms**

Forms: Insert Buttons

Forms: Insert Text Fields

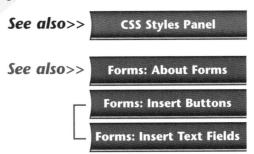

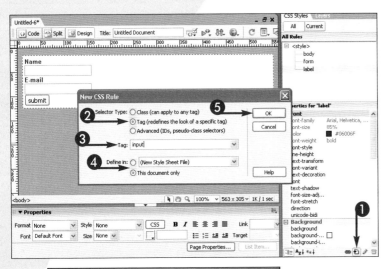

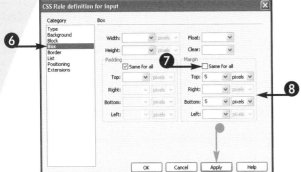

① In a page with a form that you want to style, click the New CSS Rule icon (⊞).

The New CSS Rule dialog box appears.

② Click the Tag Selector Type (○ changes to ◉).

③ Type **input** in the Tag field.

④ Select a Define in option (○ changes to ◉).

⑤ Click OK.

The CSS Rule definition dialog box appears.

⑥ Click the Box category.

⑦ Click to deselect the Same for all option (☑ changes to ☐).

⑧ Type values to add space between text boxes.

● You can click Apply to see the styles before exiting the dialog box.

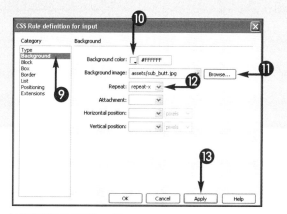

⑨ Click the Background category.

⑩ Click a Background color (▨).

⑪ Click Browse to locate your background image.

⑫ Click here and select repeat-x.

⑬ Click Apply.

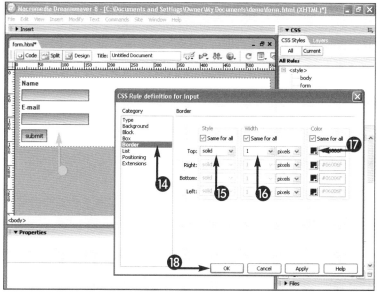

⑭ Click the Border category.

⑮ Click here and select a border style.

⑯ Type a border width.

⑰ Click a border color (▨).

⑱ Click OK.

● Dreamweaver styles the input tag.

Try This!

You can apply many of the same techniques to other form objects. Radio buttons and check boxes are additional form objects that fall into the input category. `Textarea` is the HTML tag for a multi-line text box that you can use for typing comments. The `select` tag is the HTML tag for lists and menus.

Check It Out!

You can add structure to your forms with a `fieldset` and its `legend`, or label. You can wrap the `fieldset` tag around a set of textfields that have a related purpose, such as name and e-mail address, to group them. By default, the `fieldset` tag places a border around the form objects that it encloses. Read more at www.quirksmode.org/oddsandends/fieldset.html.

CSS STYLING:
Style Heading Appearance

You can use CSS to style headings on the page to give them more visual appeal and to guide your visitors' eyes to important information. By default, headings have a weight of bold, and at least the first two of the six heading levels, h1 and h2, may seem too large for your layout. Similar to paragraph text, you can alter the fonts, font-size, and other type characteristics of your headings by using the Type category of the CSS Rule Definition dialog box.

You may want to use serif fonts on your headings to contrast with the sans serif fonts within paragraphs,

as many designers consider sans serif fonts to be easier to read on monitor screens. You can also experiment with borders, background colors and images, and margin and padding space to add creativity to your headings.

See also>> CSS Styles Panel

See also>> CSS Styling: Control Text Appearance

Headings

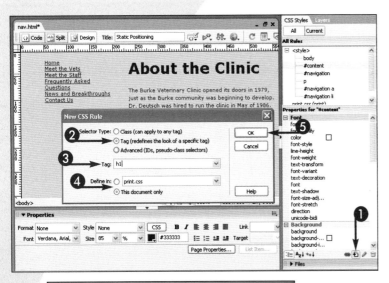

① In a page with headings that you want to style, click the New CSS Rule icon ().

The New CSS Rule dialog box appears.

② Click the Tag Selector Type (○ changes to ◉).

③ Type **h1** in the Tag field.

④ Select a Define in option (○ changes to ◉).

⑤ Click OK.

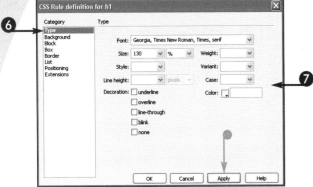

The CSS Rule definition dialog box appears.

⑥ Click the Type category.

⑦ Type or select the type options you want.

● You can click Apply to see the styles before exiting the dialog box.

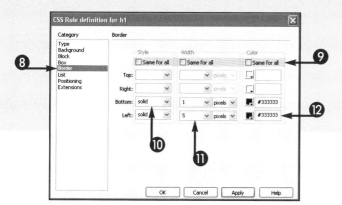

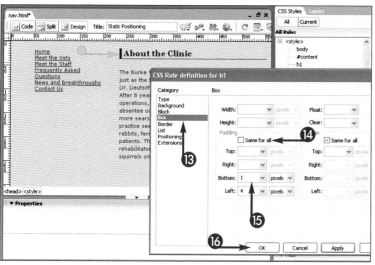

8 Click the Border category.

9 Click to deselect the Same for all options (☑ changes to ☐) for Style, Width, and Color.

10 Click here and select a border style.

11 Type a border width.

12 Click a border color.

13 Click the Box category.

14 Click to deselect the Same for all option (☑ changes to ☐).

15 Type the padding values that you want.

16 Click OK.

● Dreamweaver applies the heading style.

Try This!

Many designers use 100 percent for the universal font-size on the `<body>` tag, and then scale the size of other text elements from there. A 100-percent value represents whatever the visitor uses as the default size in their browser, usually 14 or 16 pixels. For example, if you set paragraph text to 85 percent, then it will be 85 percent of the visitor's browser default type size. This translates to about 12 to 14 pixels in most browsers. Some designers use 100.01 percent on the `<body>` tag to avoid unpredictable behavior in certain browsers that have trouble with a 100-percent value.

Apply It!

You can learn more about using CSS shorthand and other ways to make your CSS code more efficient by reading *Writing Efficient CSS* at www.communitymx.com/content/ article.cfm?cid=A43B828960590F55.

CSS STYLING:
Style List Objects

You can use the options in the List category of the CSS Styles panel to customize your lists. You can select a bullet type or numbering system for your ordered and unordered lists. You can also browse for a custom bullet image to use instead of the circle, square, and disc bullets in the Type menu.

Position is a property that you can specify when the text in a list item is longer than one line. When the bullet is set to outside, the text in the second line aligns with the text in the first line; the bullet is to the left of both lines. When the bullet is set to inside, the second line of text aligns with the bullet.

You can use this feature to group sets of related links into lists, a popular technique that Web designers use to enhance the accessibility of their pages.

See also>>

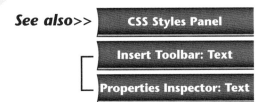

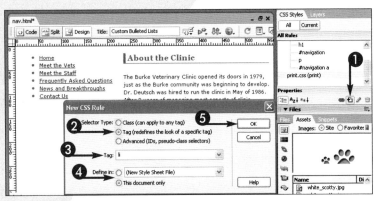

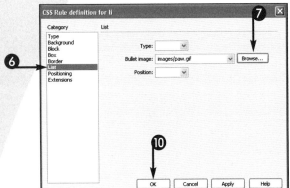

① In a page with a list that you want to style, click the New CSS Rule icon ([⊞]).

The New CSS Rule dialog box appears.

② Click the Tag option (◯ changes to ◉).

③ Type **li**.

④ Click a Define in option.

⑤ Click OK.

The CSS Rule definition for dialog box appears.

⑥ Click the List category.

⑦ Click Browse.

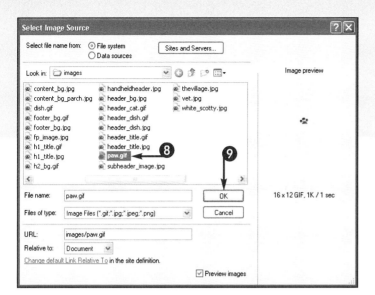

The Select Image Source dialog box appears.

⑧ Navigate to the custom bullet image.

⑨ Click OK.

Dreamweaver displays the name of the image.

⑩ In the CSS Rule definition for dialog box, click OK.

● Dreamweaver displays the custom bullets.

TIPS

Check It Out!

You can style all of the different list tags. For list items, the HTML code is `<li>`, for unordered lists it is `<ul>`, and for ordered lists it is `<ol>`. There is also markup for definition lists. You can read more about list tags at www.w3.org/TR/REC-html40/struct/lists.html.

Apply It!

Different browsers use different amounts of default margins or padding in lists. Some designers first *zero out* all unordered or ordered list margins and padding, which means that they specify a value of zero. This starts all browsers out on a level playing field. They can then add another CSS rule with a second value that will create the same margin and padding in all browsers.

CSS STYLING:
Tables and Cells

You can use the CSS Styles panel to style your tables, table rows, and cells. Most designers still create their layouts with tables. Using CSS positioning to create layouts is a recent technique that intimidates many designers. You can bridge the gap between CSS and tables by using a hybrid table–CSS technique. You can insert an unadorned table in the page that avoids using the Properties inspector to add HTML attributes. You can then use CSS to design the table.

By default, table rows and cells start their content at the left and vertical center of the container. If you

have two cells with an uneven amount of content, then they do not align at the top. You can use the CSS Block category to add a vertical alignment of top. You can use the Background category to add colors and background images to individual cells, rows, or tables.

See also>>

CSS Styles Panel

Properties Inspector: Tables

Tables: Using for Page Layouts

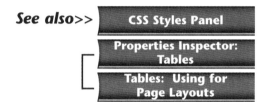

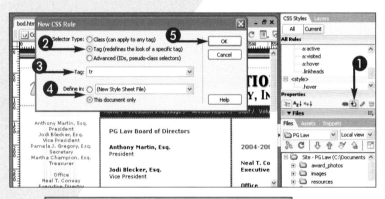

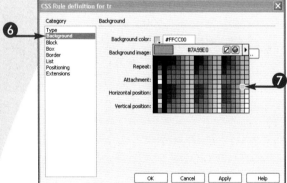

① In a page with a table that you want to style, click the New CSS Rule icon (▣).

The New CSS Rule dialog box appears.

② Click the Tag option.

③ Type **tr**.

You can also style the `td` tag or the entire table.

④ Click a Define in option.

⑤ Click OK.

The CSS Rule definition for dialog box appears.

⑥ Click the Background category.

⑦ Click a color swatch.

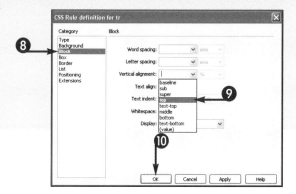

⑧ Click the Block category.

⑨ Click here and select top.

⑩ Click OK.

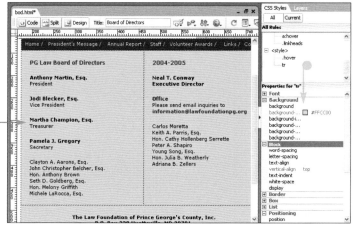

● Dreamweaver applies the table styles.

● The CSS Styles panel displays the table properties.

Check It Out!

You can view a hybrid CSS–table tutorial that includes exercise files by going to the Project VII Web site at www.projectseven.com/tutorials/css/ css_td/index.htm. The tutorial gently eases you into CSS, and even offers tips for creating layouts that accommodate older browsers such as Netscape 4.

Apply It!

You can apply almost any of the CSS style categories to tables and cells. For example, designers used to nest a slightly smaller table inside another table with a specific background color to achieve the illusion of borders. With CSS, not only can you apply borders directly to cells, rows, and tables, but you can also apply them to selected sides, such as the right, to create the appearance of columns.

CUSTOM CLASSES:
Create and Apply

You can create custom classes that you can then apply to selected text and objects on the page. For example, you may have a company name within a paragraph that you want to stand out whenever it appears. However, defining the paragraph tag is a global operation that affects all text in the paragraph. You can use the Class Selector Type option in the New CSS Rule dialog box to create a style that you can apply to specific elements.

Class names must begin with a period; however, if you forget to type it, then Dreamweaver adds it for you. After you select the properties and values that

you want to use in your custom style, you must still manually attach the style to selected objects. Dreamweaver lists all custom styles in the Style menu of the Properties inspector. When you select text and apply a class to it, Dreamweaver wraps it in a `span` tag.

See also>>

CSS Styles Panel

Preferences: CSS Styles

Properties Inspector: Text

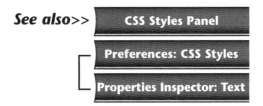

① In a page to which you want to add a custom class, click the New CSS Rule icon (🖹).

The New CSS Rule dialog box appears.

② Click the Class option.

③ Type a period and then the name of your class.

④ Click a Define in option.

⑤ Click OK.

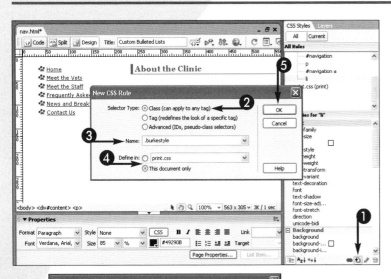

The CSS Rule definition for dialog box appears.

⑥ Click the category that you want to style.

⑦ Type or select the style options that you want.

⑧ Click OK.

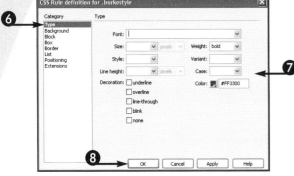

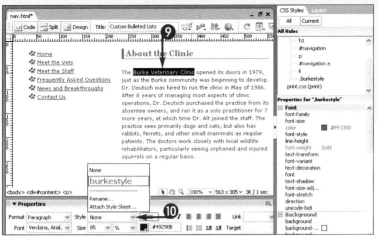

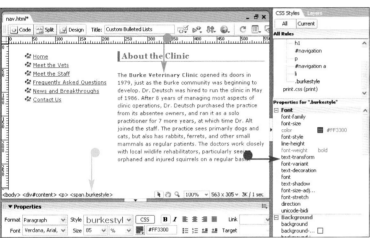

Dreamweaver returns to your page.

9 Select the text or object to which you want to apply the class.

10 Click here and select the class name.

● Dreamweaver displays the class style.

● Dreamweaver wraps your text in a `span` tag.

● Dreamweaver displays your class properties in the CSS Styles panel.

Check It Out!

You should understand the cascade in CSS. If there are two conflicting rules, then the rule with the most specificity wins out. Inline styles take precedence over embedded styles, and embedded styles take precedence over external style sheets. If you have two conflicting rules within one style sheet, the one with the highest specificity value wins out. You can read more about the cascade and specificity at www.w3.org/TR/CSS21/cascade.html.

Apply It!

You cannot apply classes to text that is not wrapped in a tag. For example, if you select your company name within a paragraph, then there may be no tags around it. In this case, Dreamweaver fixes the problem by adding a span around the text and then applying the class to the span.

DEFINE A SITE:
Using the Advanced Tab

You can use the Advanced tab in the Site Definition dialog box to define your site when you want to use advanced options that the Basic tab does not include. The Advanced tab contains additional screens to configure information for Cloaking, Design Notes, Site Map Layout, File View Columns, and Contribute administration setup.

If you work on a team, then you can create new columns that show additional information for each file when it is in the expanded Files panel view. For example, you can create a Design Note for each file, name it *Author*, and add the author name to the note.

You can then create a column that uses the author Design Note to add an author name to that column.

See also>>
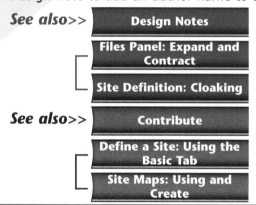
Design Notes

Files Panel: Expand and Contract

Site Definition: Cloaking

See also>>
Contribute

Define a Site: Using the Basic Tab

Site Maps: Using and Create

① Open the Site Definition dialog box.

   Note: *To open this dialog box, see the section "Define a Site: Using the Basic tab."*

② Click the Advanced tab.

③ Click the Cloaking category.

④ Click to select the Cloaking options that you want (☐ changes to ☑).

⑤ Click the Design Notes category.

⑥ Click the Design Notes options that you want (☐ changes to ☑).

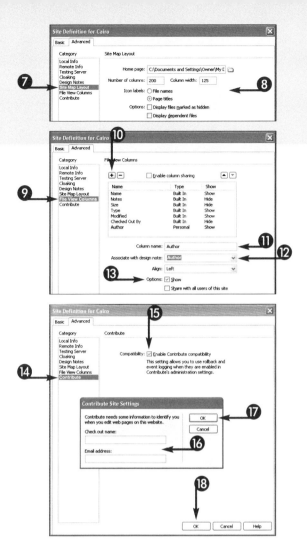

7 Click the Site Map Layout category.

8 Type or click the site map options that you want (☐ changes to ☑ or ◯ changes to ◉).

9 Click the File View Columns category.

10 Click the Add button (➕) to add a new column.

11 Type a column name.

12 Select the Design Note with which you want to associate the column.

13 Select or deselect the Show option to hide or show the column.

14 Click the Contribute category.

15 Click the Compatibility option (☐ changes to ☑).

16 In the Contribute Site dialog box that appears, type the Check out name and the Email address information.

17 Click OK.

18 Click OK to exit the Site Definition dialog box.

Dreamweaver configures all of your new site settings.

More Options!

Although you can use the Advanced tab to set up your initial site definitions, you can also use it to gain access to more site options after you first set up the basic site information through the Basic tab.

Apply It!

You can change the order of your columns by using the up (🔼) and down (🔽) arrows in the File View Columns screen. In order to share columns among team members, each member must select the Enable column sharing option (☐ changes to ☑) in the File View Columns category of the Advanced tab. If you want to share your custom columns with team members, then you must select the "Share with all users of this site" option (☐ changes to ☑).

DEFINE A SITE:
Using the Basic Tab

You can use the Site Definition dialog box to quickly set up your sites. Setting up a site definition is an essential first step that many new users skip. The Site Definition dialog box allows you to specify to Dreamweaver where you want to store your site's files, and how you want to connect to the remote server. This method also provides other critical information that Dreamweaver needs to perform many of the tasks that maintain the integrity of your site.

The dialog box displays two tabs — the Basic tab allows you to use a wizard, while the Advanced tab allows you more control and more options. Although

the Basic tab provides a wizard, it asks questions about server technologies for dynamic pages that may be too difficult for new users. However, if you are creating basic HTML pages, then you can safely leave most of the wizard's screens at their default settings.

See also>> Site Definition: Local Info

Site Definition: Remote Info

See also>> Appendix A

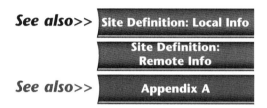

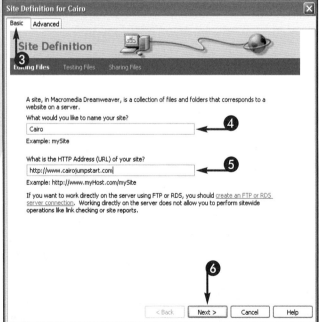

① Click Site.

② Click New Site.

The Site Definition dialog box appears.

③ Click the Basic tab.

The Basic tab appears by default in the Site Definition dialog box.

④ Type a name for your site.

⑤ Type the address for the site's location on the Internet.

You only need to do this if you plan to use the full Web address to link pages to each other within your site.

⑥ Click Next.

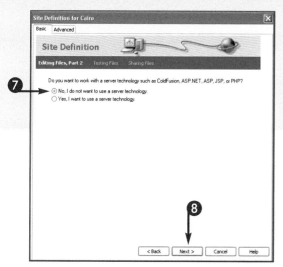

The Editing Files, Part 2 screen appears.

7 Click the "No, I do not want to use a server technology" option (○ changes to ◉).

You only need a server technology if you want to create dynamic pages.

8 Click Next.

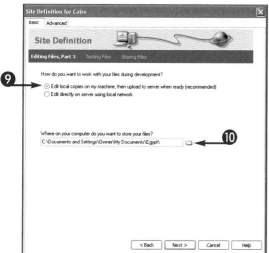

The Editing Files, Part 3 screen appears.

9 Click the "Edit local copies on my machine, then upload to server when ready (recommended)" option (○ changes to ◉).

10 Click the Folder button (🗐) to navigate to your site folder.

Caution!

You will probably want to avoid the "Edit directly on server using local network" option (○ changes to ◉). This is because when you work on live pages, a visitor can see your work in progress, errors and all. Working on your local computer also lets you revert to the original version if you encounter problems while editing the file, by downloading it again from the server.

Apply It!

When you create basic sites, you can store the local root folder almost anywhere on your computer, such as in the My Documents folder in Windows or the Documents folder in Mac OS. However, if you create dynamic sites, then you must store your files in specific locations so that the server can communicate with them.

DEFINE A SITE:
Using the Basic Tab (Continued)

You can use the Basic Site Definition Wizard to quickly set up your basic site structure and remote information. Creating a site definition makes it easier to ensure that your local site mirrors the one that you will upload to the remote server, thus preventing broken links, missing images, and other common impediments to getting your pages to work equally well online. Once a site is defined, Dreamweaver can carefully track your files, folders, and assets so that you can perform tasks such as site synchronization and link checking.

The Basic tab also allows you to enable the Check in and Check out features. If you want to set up other options like Cloaking, Design Notes, Site Map Layout, and Contribute, then you can tweak your site definition by using the Advanced tab.

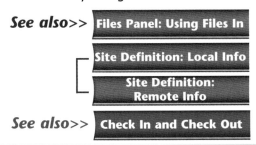

See also>> Files Panel: Using Files In

Site Definition: Local Info

Site Definition: Remote Info

See also>> Check In and Check Out

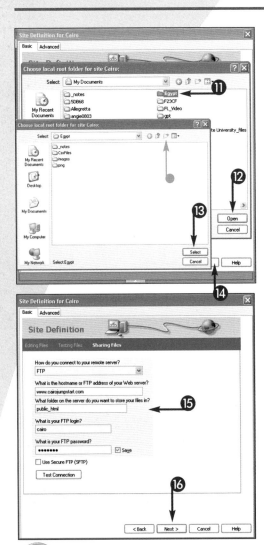

The Choose local root folder for site dialog box appears.

⑪ Navigate to the root folder that holds your site files.

● If you do not yet have a folder or files for your site, then you can click the New Folder icon (🗀) to create one.

⑫ Click Open (Choose).

A second Choose local root folder for site dialog box appears (Windows only).

⑬ Click Select to close the dialog box.

⑭ In the Site Definition dialog box, click Next.

The Sharing Files screen appears.

⑮ Type your remote server settings.

⑯ Click Next.

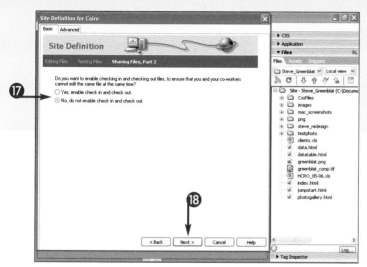

The Sharing Files, Part 2 screen appears.

⑰ Click a Check in and Check out option (○ changes to ◉).

If you work alone, then you will probably not need this feature.

⑱ Click Next.

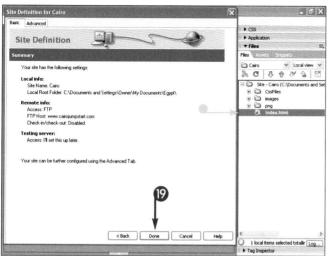

The Summary screen appears.

⑲ Click Done.

● Dreamweaver opens your new site in the Files panel.

TIPS

Apply It!
Give your site a descriptive name so that you can distinguish it from other sites as your list of sites grows. Dreamweaver lists names alphabetically, making it easy to locate individual sites.

More Options!
You can use an existing folder of files and add new ones within Dreamweaver. If you do not yet have site files, then you can create a new folder and add files to it from within the Files panel or the New Document window.

More Options!
If you need to modify information later, then you can do so by opening the Manage Sites dialog box, selecting a site name, and clicking Edit to reopen the Site Definition dialog box for that site.

DELETE FILES AND FOLDERS:
From a Site

You can clean up your site by deleting files and folders that you no longer need through the Edit menu in the Files panel.

You can select one file or multiple files. You can also select file and folder icons for deletion.

Dreamweaver displays one of two warning messages, depending on the file or folder status. If the file or folder is not linked to any other files in the site, then Dreamweaver displays a standard warning message. If the file or folder links to other files in the site, then Dreamweaver warns you of that fact and reminds

you that you can link the newly broken link to another file with the Change Links Site Wide command.

See also>> **Files Panel**

Orphaned Pages

See also>> **Change Links Site Wide**

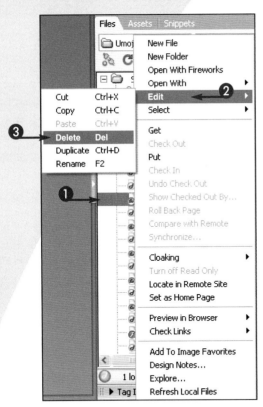

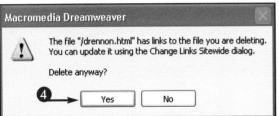

① Right-click a file or folder in the Files panel.

You can Shift-click to select a range of files, or Ctrl-click (⌘-click) to select multiple, non-contiguous files

② Click Edit.

③ Click Delete.

Instead of following steps **2** and **3**, you can also select file and folder icons and then press Delete or Backspace to delete them.

Dreamweaver displays one of two warning dialog boxes.

If the file or folder that you want to delete is linked to other files in the site, then Dreamweaver displays an appropriate warning.

④ Click Yes.

If the file or folder is not linked to other files, then Dreamweaver asks you to confirm that you want to delete the selected files or folders.

5 Click Yes.

Dreamweaver displays a Background File Activity window while it deletes the file.

D

Try This!
You can also use the Edit menu in the Files panel to rename, duplicate, cut, copy, and paste files and folders. You can move files and folders in the Files panel by dragging them to new directories.

More Options!
The warning message that displays when a file has links to other pages lists the first few files that use it. If you do not know whether a file links to other files in the site and want to see a list of these unreferenced files, then you can check for orphaned files using Dreamweaver's Link Checker in the Results panel. Dreamweaver only runs the Orphaned Files command for the entire site, not individual pages.

DESCENDENT SELECTORS:
Create and Use

You can use CSS rules called descendent selectors to make the same tags look visually different depending on their context. When you redefine the appearance of a specific tag, such as the h1 tag, it is a global operation that affects the style of all such headings, regardless of their context in the page.

You can vary the appearance of the same tag by creating a descendent selector. For example, you may have level-one headings in your page that you want to style with the color red and Arial font. You may also have h1 elements that you italicize, and in that context, you may want to style them with the color black and Georgia font.

See also>>

CSS Styles: Create a New Rule

CSS Rule Definition Window

See also>>

CSS: Create Embedded Style Sheet

CSS: Create External Style Sheet

CSS Styling: Style Heading Appearance

DIV Tags

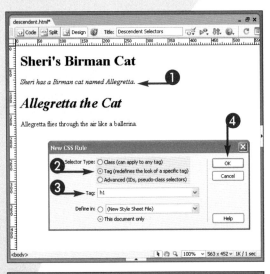

① Type your h1 heading text, then your emphasized text, and then text with both h1 and emphasized text, separating each style with a hard return.

Dreamweaver uses <em> for italics to follow the guidelines of the World Wide Web Consortium.

② Create a CSS rule that uses the Tag option (○ changes to ◉).

③ Type **h1** in the Tag text box.

④ Click OK.

You can now style your h1 heading in the CSS Rule Definition dialog box that appears.

● Dreamweaver applies the global h1 style to both h1-formatted text elements.

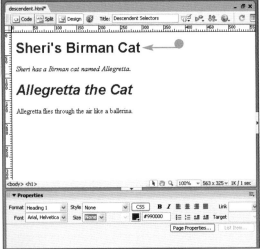

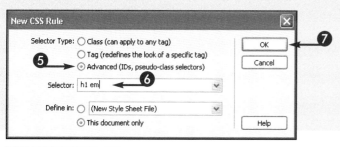

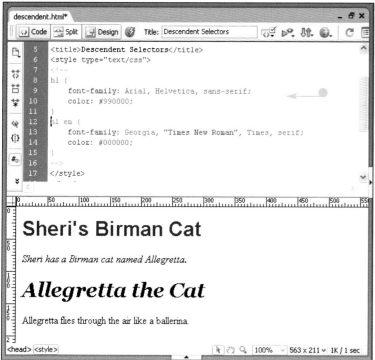

5 Create an advanced new CSS rule.

6 Type **h1 em**.

7 Click OK.

You can style your h1 em heading in the CSS Rule Definition dialog box that appears.

● Dreamweaver displays the styling from the descendent selector for any h1 text that also includes italics.

D

Apply It!

A common problem for designers is how to create different styles for links depending on where they occur. For example, one set of links may appear on a black background, while another set may appear on a white background, which means you need to make their link text colors different. For another example, you may want links in a content area to look like standard underlined links, and you may want links in a left column to look like buttons. You can do this by adding named DIVs to different areas of the page, such as #content or #sidebar. You can then style the links in context like this: #content a:link and #sidebar a:link. You can read more about how to do this at www.macromedia.com/devnet/dreamweaver/articles/css_concepts_05.html.

DESIGN-TIME STYLE SHEETS:
Create and Attach

You can use Design-Time style sheets to show or hide styles during the development of a page. Although Dreamweaver 8 renders CSS-based designs much better than previous versions, it still does not always display styles exactly as they will appear in Web standards-compliant browsers. This is not necessarily a problem unless Dreamweaver's rendering makes it difficult to edit the page. In this case, you can create a style sheet that compensates for Dreamweaver's limitations by modifying some of the styles that it does not understand, and show it as a Design-Time style sheet.

Design-Time style sheets only apply while you are working in Dreamweaver's Design view. When you display the page in the browser, only the styles that you have attached or embedded in the actual document appear. Dreamweaver uses Design Notes to associate a Design-Time style sheet with a page.

See also>> Design-Time Style Sheets

CSS Rule Definition Window

See also>> CSS: Create Embedded Style Sheet

CSS: Create External Style Sheet

CSS, Positioning: Using Static Positioning

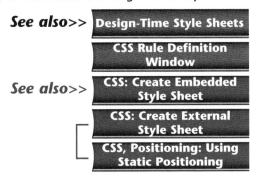

① Create a style sheet that will fix design-rendering problems in Dreamweaver.

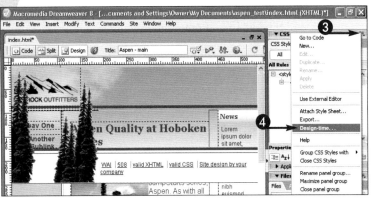

② Open the problem page.

③ Click the File Options button (▦) in the CSS panel.

④ Click Design-time.

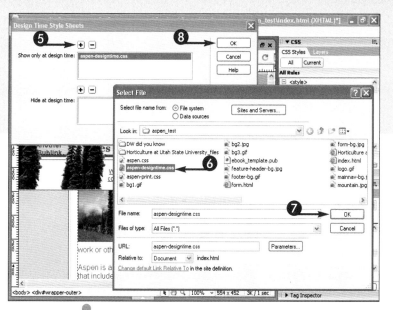

The Design Time Style Sheets dialog box appears.

⑤ Click ⊞ above Show only at design time.

The Select File dialog box appears.

⑥ Navigate to your Design-Time style sheet.

⑦ Click OK.

⑧ Click OK in the Design Time Style Sheets dialog box.

● Dreamweaver applies the style sheet only in Design view.

The browser still displays the page with the original style sheet.

Try This!

Although one solution does not work for all situations, changing a DIV's position to static in a Design-Time style sheet often solves Dreamweaver's CSS rendering problems. Keep in mind that you will have to try different solutions with positioning, margins, padding, and other CSS styles until you find a layout that allows you to easily edit your content in Design view.

More Options!

Sometimes you may have multiple style sheets on your page, and you may want to hide the styles of one or more of these style sheets at design time. You may also have one style sheet that you are linking and one that you are importing. The Design-Time Style Sheet feature allows you to hide one style sheet while you develop the other.

DIV TAGS:
Insert, Position, Name

You can use the Insert menu to insert DIVs in your page. DIV tags, or divisions, are empty elements that can serve as containers for other elements in your page. When you add position rules to DIVs, you can use them instead of tables to lay out your pages. Dreamweaver calls a DIV with a position of absolute a layer. You can also add a stacking order to overlapping DIVs to let the browser know which ones you want in the foreground.

Dreamweaver allows you to add DIVs at your insertion point or before or after specific tags. You can apply a pre-existing class or ID to a DIV, or you can name and then create a new CSS style rule by clicking the New CSS Style button.

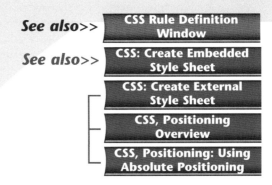

See also>> CSS Rule Definition Window

See also>> CSS: Create Embedded Style Sheet

CSS: Create External Style Sheet

CSS, Positioning Overview

CSS, Positioning: Using Absolute Positioning

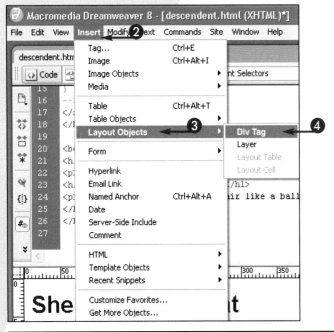

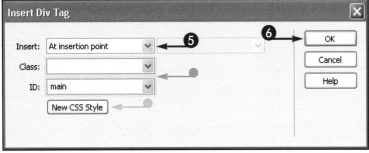

1 Click your cursor on the page where you want to add the DIV tag.

2 Click Insert.

3 Click Layout Objects.

4 Click DIV Tag.

The Insert DIV Tag dialog box appears.

5 Click here and select an Insert option.

● You can select a Class or ID name to use an existing style.

● You can also type a new Class or ID name and then create its style by clicking the New CSS Style button.

You can style the new DIV in the New CSS Rule dialog box that appears.

6 When you return to the Insert DIV Tag dialog box, click OK.

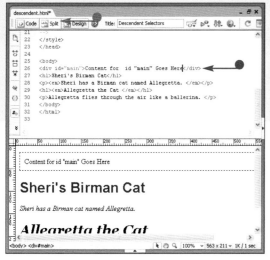

● Dreamweaver adds the DIV with placeholder content to the page.

● You can click the Split view button to see the DIV in both Design and Code views.

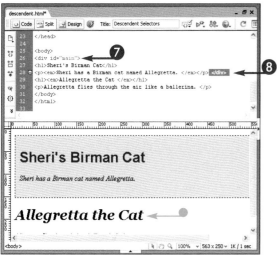

⑦ Replace the placeholder text with real content.

You can also move pre-existing content to the new DIV by moving the closing DIV tag to after the content that you want to include.

⑧ Select the closing DIV tag and drag the DIV tag to the end of the content that you want to include in the DIV.

● Dreamweaver displays the DIV with its content.

Did You Know?

DIV tags are block-level elements. This means that they are self-contained, with a break before and after the DIV. Block-level elements can include inline elements, which are elements that appear one after the other, without line breaks, in the natural flow of the document.

More Options!

Designers often give DIV tags descriptive ID names that reflect how they are using them in the page. For example, there can be header, content, sidebar, and footer DIVs that hold the appropriate elements in the layout. Each ID name can only be used for one DIV in a page. You can avoid problems, especially with scripts, by ensuring that each ID name is unique.

EDITORS:
Choose Application

You can launch external applications by double-clicking files in the Files panel. Dreamweaver natively opens documents with common Web extensions such as .html and .htm.

Dreamweaver also provides roundtrip editing for Flash and Fireworks documents; you can use an edit button in the Properties inspector to launch one of these applications, edit the document, and return directly to Dreamweaver with the edited file.

Double-clicking documents with other formats brings up an error message telling you that Dreamweaver cannot find a valid editor for that file extension.

However, you can add other extensions and designate an application to open them by modifying the File Types/Editors preferences. You can also add other editors for existing extensions and mark one as the primary application that you want to use when you double-click the file. The ability to launch applications directly from the Files panel saves you time and provides the convenience of not having to navigate for an application.

See also>>

Files Panel

Preferences: File Types and Editors

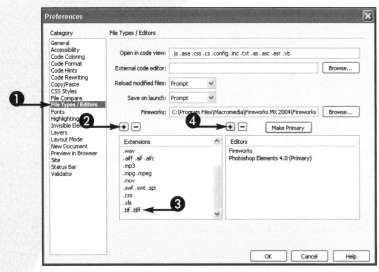

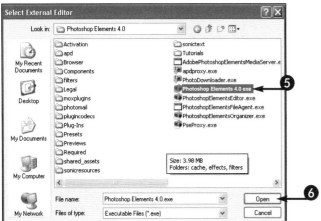

1. Select the File Types/Editors category in the Preferences dialog box.

2. Click the plus sign button (+) in the Extensions category.

   Dreamweaver creates a new field in which you can type extension names.

3. Type your extension names.

   You must type a period before each extension name and one space between each extension, and you cannot use commas.

4. Click + in the Editors category.

   The Select External Editor dialog box appears.

5. Navigate to the application.

6. Click Open.

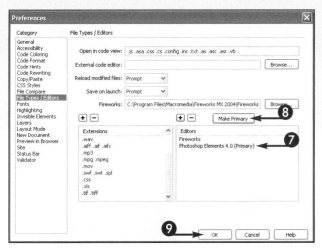

The Preferences dialog box reappears.

The name of the application displays in the Editors category.

⑦ Click the application name.

⑧ Click Make Primary.

⑨ Click OK to close the Preferences dialog box.

⑩ Double-click a file in the Files panel that is associated with the newly added application.

● Dreamweaver launches the appropriate application, and opens the file for editing.

Apply It!

You can set up more than one editor for a file, and access a different program from the primary editor. For example, you may list both Photoshop and Fireworks as file editors for graphics because you need the individual capabilities of each for different situations. If you do not want to use the primary editor for a file type, then you can control which application opens it by right-clicking (Ctrl-clicking) it in the Files panel. This brings up a contextual menu that displays a command for your primary editor as well as an Open with command that lists Dreamweaver, Fireworks, and a Browse button that allows you to navigate to another application.

E-MAIL LINKS:
Create

You can use Dreamweaver's Email Link command or the Email Link icon in the Common category of the Insert toolbar to easily add e-mail links to your Web pages. Dreamweaver inserts the necessary mailto: prefix in front of the e-mail address in the Link field of the Properties inspector. You can also use the Properties inspector to manually type e-mail links for selected text.

Many businesses have an e-mail link on their pages so that visitors can ask questions or request information. When the visitor clicks the link, it automatically opens their e-mail program with the

e-mail address added to the recipient field. You can even append a subject title to the e-mail link so that you can more easily recognize an e-mail as having come from your Web site.

See also>> Document Toolbar

Insert Toolbar: Common

Split Code and Design View

See also>> CSS Styling: Control Link Appearance

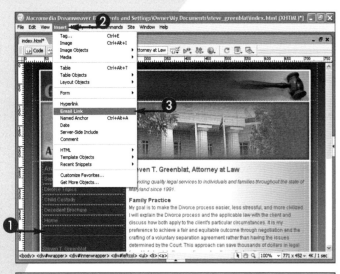

Using the Email Link Dialog Box

1. Click your cursor at the place on the page where you want to add the e-mail link.

2. Click Insert.

3. Click Email Link.

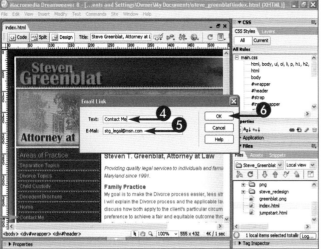

The Email Link dialog box appears.

4. Type the link text that you want to display in the Web page.

5. Type the e-mail address to which you want to link.

6. Click OK.

● Dreamweaver adds the link text to the page and the e-mail address to the code.

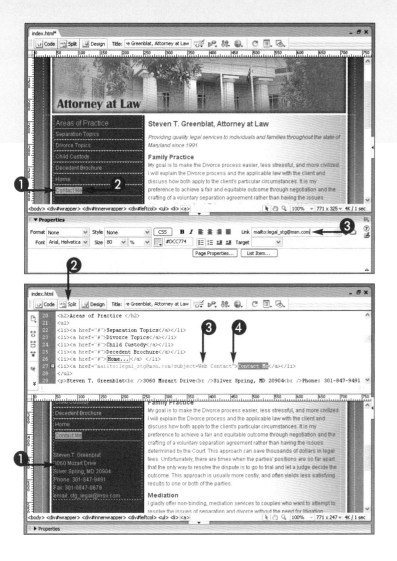

Manually Add an E-mail Link

① Type the text that you want to use directly on the page.

② Select the text.

③ Type the address in the Link text box, preceded by **mailto:** with no spaces. For example: **mailto:youraddress@web.com**.

④ Press Enter.

Dreamweaver places the link text on the page and the e-mail link in the code.

Manually Add the Subject Title to the E-mail Link

① Select your e-mail link text.

② Click Split in the Document toolbar.

Dreamweaver highlights the link in Code view to make it easy to find.

③ After the e-mail address in the link, type the following: **?subject=Subject Name"**.

④ Move the ending quote after the e-mail address to after the subject title.

Dreamweaver automatically adds the subject title to the e-mail link.

 TIPS

Check It Out!

You may get an increase in spam when you publish your e-mail address. Because many spam programs look for the @ symbol and extension information, you can obscure the e-mail address by typing **legal_stg at msn dot com**. You can also use JavaScript or encoders such as www.wbwip.com/wbw/emailencoder.html.

Caution!

E-mail links only work if visitors have an e-mail program available on their computers. However, if the visitor is at the library, they may not have access to an e-mail program. You can use the actual e-mail address as the text that appears on the page so that the visitor can write it down. You can also use a form that allows visitors to submit comments to you.

EXCEL DOCUMENTS:
Import

If you have Excel on your computer, you can import Excel spreadsheets into an existing or new page by using the Import Excel Document command. This saves you the time and effort involved in manually entering data into tables. Dreamweaver automatically imports your data into a borderless table with the correct number of rows and columns, unless you select the plain-text formatting option. Dreamweaver gives you four formatting options for the imported spreadsheet. In addition to plain text, you can import text with table, paragraph, and list structures, text with structure and basic formatting, and text and structure with full formatting.

If you import the spreadsheet with full formatting, then Dreamweaver adds Excel styles to both the Style menu in the Properties inspector and the Code view of your document. If you prefer to format the spreadsheet with your own Dreamweaver style sheet, then you may want to use the Text with structure option.

See also>> Split Code and Design View

See also>> Import Office Documents

Word Document

① Click your cursor where you want to import the Excel spreadsheet.

You can also create a new document.

② Click File.

③ Click Import.

④ Click Excel Document.

The Import Excel Document dialog box appears.

⑤ Navigate to your Excel document.

⑥ Click here to select a formatting option.

⑦ Click Open.

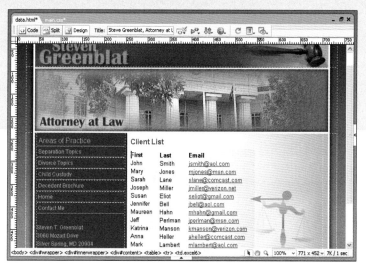

● Dreamweaver imports the data into a table.

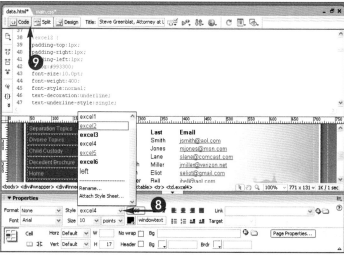

⑧ Click here and select a style.

If you selected the "Text, structure, full formatting" option in step **6**, then exported CSS styles display in the menu.

⑨ Click Split or Code in the Document toolbar.

You can view the exported CSS styles that Dreamweaver has added to the document.

Caution!
The Import Excel Document command is only available in the Windows version of Dreamweaver. If you are a Macintosh user, then you can export an Excel document as HTML by using Excel's Save as Web Page command. You can then open it in Dreamweaver and integrate it into the rest of your site. Alternatively, you can use the Import Tabular Data command on a spreadsheet that you convert to a tab-delimited text file using Excel's Save As option menu.

Apply It!
You can also provide a link to an Excel document so that your visitors can download it. When you drag the file to the page, Dreamweaver displays the Insert Document dialog box where you can select the Create a link option.

EXTENSIONS:
Install and Manage

You can use the Get More Commands menu command to take you directly to the Dreamweaver Exchange on the Macromedia Web site. You can browse hundreds of extensions and download the ones that you want.

Although you can freely browse extensions at the Dreamweaver Exchange, Macromedia requires that you set up an account if you want to download them. The registration process is quick and noninvasive. You only have to provide your name, an e-mail address — which also serves as your username — and a password.

After you download an extension, you can recognize it by its .mpx filename extension. When you double-click it, Dreamweaver opens the Extension Manager and installs the extension, adding it to the list of extensions. The Extension Manager also displays information about what the extension does and how to access it, such as through the Behaviors panel, as a command, or through the Insert menu. You must quit and relaunch Dreamweaver in order for the new extension to take effect.

See also>> **Preferences: Copy and Paste**

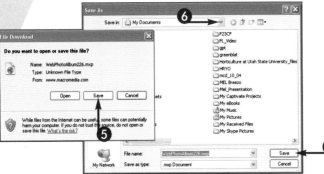

① In Dreamweaver, click Commands.

② Click Get More Commands.

Dreamweaver opens the Dreamweaver Exchange Web page.

③ Click here and select a category.

The Macromedia site displays relevant extensions that you can browse.

④ Click the Download link next to the extension that you want to download.

The File Download dialog box appears.

⑤ Click Save.

The Save As dialog box appears.

⑥ Navigate to where you want to save the extension.

⑦ Click Save.

The extension downloads to your computer.

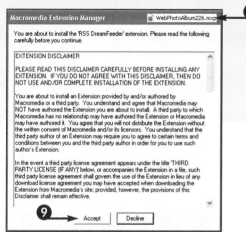

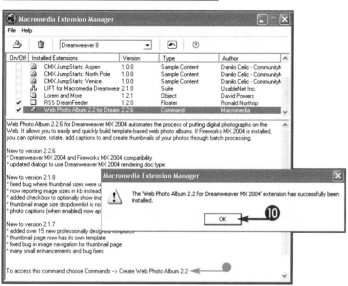

⑧ Double-click the extension.

The Macromedia Extension Manager window opens.

⑨ Click Accept to accept the licensing agreement.

A progress bar appears to show you that Dreamweaver is installing the extension.

Dreamweaver displays an alert message to let you know that it successfully installed the extension.

⑩ Click OK.

● Dreamweaver displays information about the extension and tells you how to access it within the Dreamweaver interface.

Check It Out!

The Macromedia Exchange interface allows you to click a category name to sort extensions by name, date, and Dreamweaver version number. To use it, you need to install a recent version of the Flash Player in your browser. You can download the latest version from www.macromedia.com/software/flashplayer/.

More Options!

The details page for each extension allows you to click a check box (☐ changes to ☑) to add it to your Favorites list. You can then click the Favorites link under Your Exchange to quickly navigate to a list of your favorite extensions. The details page also includes an option to add an extension to your Alert list. When the extension author updates the extension, Macromedia notifies you by e-mail.

FAVORITES:
Assign to Assets Panel

You can organize your frequently used images, colors, and other site assets by designating them as Favorites in the Assets panel. This feature is very useful if you have a large site with many different assets to track.

Every time you open a new site in Dreamweaver, all of the images, Flash movies, colors, and other assets in the site are catalogued and listed in the Assets panel. By assigning some assets as Favorites, you can more quickly locate and insert or apply those assets that you use frequently.

In addition to listing an asset as a Favorite, you can also add folders to organize your assets into related groups or give your assets nicknames to remind you of what they are for. For example, you may want to give a color asset a descriptive name that reminds you of how to use it in your site, or group all of your thumbnail images into one folder.

See also>> Assets Panel

See also>> Assets Panel: Insert Objects With

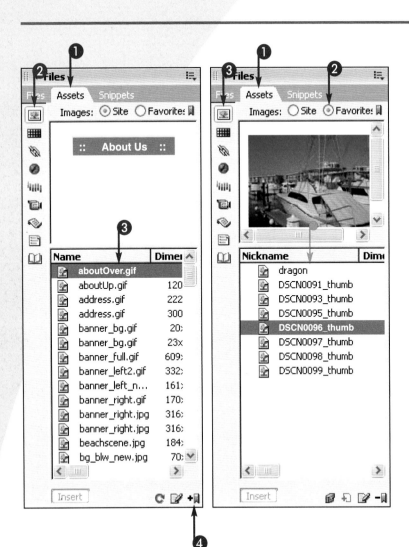

Designate Favorites

1 Click the Assets tab.

2 Click any category icon.

  You cannot add templates and Library items to Favorites.

3 Click a listed asset.

4 Click Add to Favorites (⊞).

  Dreamweaver adds the selected asset to the Favorites list.

View Favorites

1 Click the Assets tab.

2 Click the Favorites option (○ changes to ◉).

3 Click a category icon.

● Favorites display for the selected category.

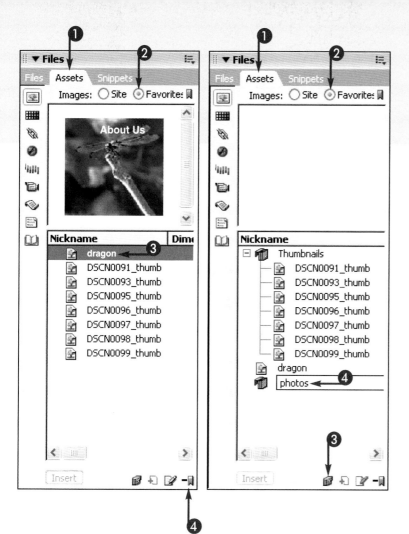

Remove an Asset from Favorites

❶ Click the Assets tab.

❷ Click the Favorites option
(○ changes to ◉).

❸ Click a listed Favorite.

❹ Click Remove from Favorites
(−▯).

Dreamweaver removes the
selected asset from the
Favorites list.

Add a Favorites Folder

❶ Click the Assets tab.

❷ Click the Favorites option
(○ changes to ◉).

❸ Click New Favorites Folder (▯).

❹ Type a name for the new folder.

You can drag assets into or out
of the folder to organize your
Favorites.

F

Did You Know?

Although Favorites are a
device that Dreamweaver uses
to help you organize your files
and settings, the assets are
not altered in any way by this
designation. If you remove a
Favorite, rename it, or organize
the asset into folders, the
actual file location, name, and
attributes assigned to the asset
remain unchanged.

More Options!

You can rename a Favorite by
right-clicking (Ctrl-clicking) it and
selecting Edit Nickname from the
contextual menu that appears.
As with other changes you make
in the Favorites panel, this
change does not alter the actual
filename or attribute value of the
asset.

FIND AND REPLACE:
Text and Code

You can locate and change text, code, links, tags, and other properties in individual documents or across an entire Web site. The Find and Replace feature in Dreamweaver is a very powerful tool that allows you to make fundamental changes to a single page or your entire site.

To begin the Find and Replace process, you select where you want the file command to run. You can run the command on a currently opened document, on all open documents, on an entire Web site, or only on selected files within a site. After you select which files to search, you can then determine what

kind of search you want to perform. You can search inside the source code, for text in the document, for strings of text with specific values, or for individual tags. In addition to these basic find-and-replace operations, you can also use advanced features such as regular expressions to perform sophisticated operations inside your files.

See also>> **Find and Replace**

See also>> **Links: Change Sitewide**

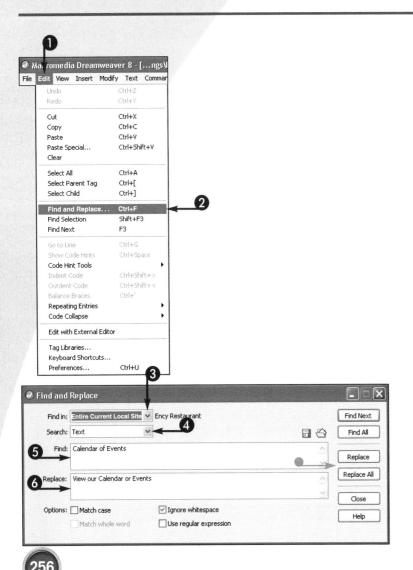

Find and Replace Text

① Click Edit.

② Click Find and Replace.

The Find and Replace dialog box appears.

③ Click here and select the location for the search.

④ Click here and select Text.

⑤ Type the text that you want to find.

⑥ Type the text to replace the found text.

● You can replace text one instance at a time, or replace all instances at once by clicking these buttons.

Dreamweaver replaces the text, based on the settings that you select, and provides a report in the Results panel.

Find and Replace Code

1 Click Edit.

2 Click Find and Replace.

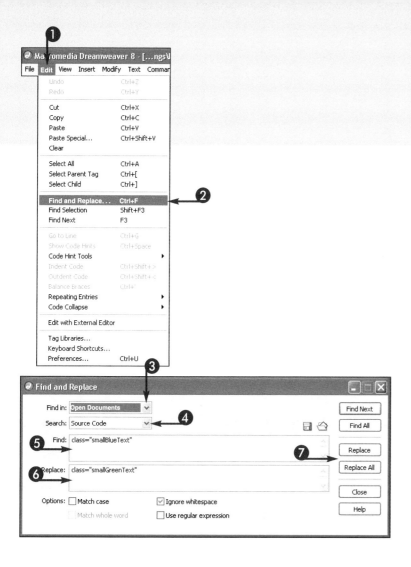

The Find and Replace dialog box appears.

3 Click here and select the location for the search.

4 Click here and select Source Code.

5 Type the code or code fragment that you want to find.

6 Type the code or code fragment that replaces the found code.

7 Click these buttons to replace code one instance at a time, or to replace all code instances.

Dreamweaver replaces the code in your document, based on the your settings, providing a report in the Results panel.

TIPS

Check It Out!

You can use the Find and Replace command to perform very sophisticated searches that include patterns of text, called regular expressions, rather than actual text strings. For example, to locate all of the text in a document that contains a numeral, you can search with the expression $\backslash d$, which finds any text or code containing a digit. You can read more about regular expressions and how they are used at www.regular-expressions.info.

Preview It!

To simply find all of the occurrences of text or code in your document and not replace them, you can use Find Next or Find All in the Find and Replace dialog box. When you select these options, Dreamweaver finds any text or code that you type and highlights it in the document.

F

FIREWORKS:
Edit Images

You can use a button in the Properties inspector to launch Macromedia Fireworks, edit the image as needed, and then use another button to save the image and return to Dreamweaver. Called *round-tripping*, this feature allows you to move from one application to the other when necessary. You must have Fireworks installed on your computer for this feature to work.

After launching Fireworks from the Dreamweaver environment, you are prompted to open the source Fireworks file that was used to create the image. Most Web designers who use Fireworks save their image files in the Fireworks PNG format and then export the image in the GIF or JPG format for use in their designs. This allows them to save information specific to the Fireworks program in case they need to perform additional edits in the future. It is best to use a PNG source file for your edits; working directly on a GIF or JPG file is a destructive process and you cannot undo it when you save the file.

See also>> **Properties Inspector: Images**

See also>> **Fireworks: Optimize Images**

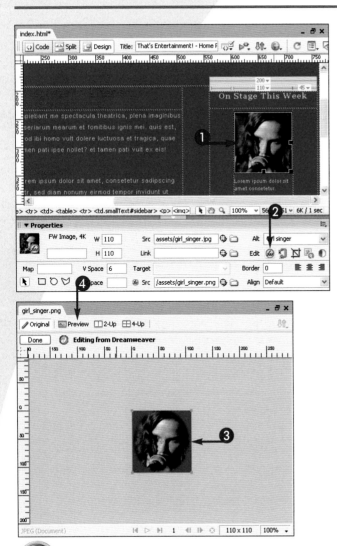

1 Click an image.

2 Click Edit in Fireworks (🖉).

Dreamweaver automatically tracks the source file if the image was initially created in Fireworks.

Note: If the image was not created in Fireworks, then you are prompted to locate the source file.

Fireworks opens the image file.

3 Perform the edits you want on the image.

4 Click Preview.

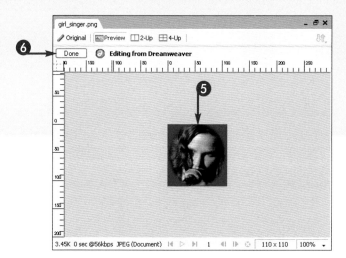

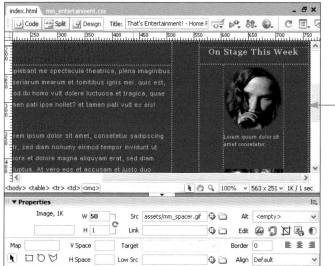

Fireworks opens the image in Preview mode.

⑤ Examine the image to see how it will appear in your Web document.

⑥ Click Done.

● Dreamweaver saves the edited image and displays the changes in the Design Window.

Did You Know?
You can perform any necessary edits to an image by round-tripping between Dreamweaver and Fireworks. You can resize, color, and apply effects to images, and change them in almost limitless ways. When you return to Dreamweaver, not only is the image that will appear in the document changed, but the source file is also altered, with all of your changes being automatically applied.

Remove It!
You can undo the edits that you make to an image by simply undoing the steps that you took to change it. Press Ctrl+Z (⌘+Z) until the image returns to the state it was in before you edited it in Fireworks. As you do this in Dreamweaver, the source image and the published image are both modified and saved.

F

FIREWORKS:
Optimize Images

You can modify the quality and color settings that you have applied to images to reduce their file size and improve their download time. Dreamweaver uses the file optimization utility in Fireworks to perform this operation.

Optimization is the process of finding the balance between smaller file sizes and an acceptable appearance. You can reduce the quality of an image slightly and have a dramatic impact on the file size. For example, a JPG image set to 100 percent quality may have a file size of 15KB, while reducing the quality to 80 percent changes the file size to

only 8KB. Small quality reductions do not usually lead to any discernible difference in the image's appearance. Web browsers can display images in one of two file formats — either GIF or JPG. Each format uses its own methods for controlling quality. In the GIF format, you can reduce file sizes by decreasing the number of colors that display. In the JPG format, you can adjust the quality setting to get smaller file sizes.

See also>> **Properties Inspector: Images**

See also>> **Fireworks: Edit Images**

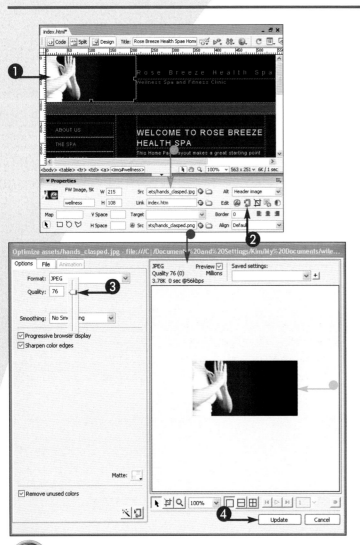

Optimize JPG Images

1 Click a JPG image.

● The image type is indicated by its file extension.

2 Click Optimize in Fireworks ().

3 In the Optimize dialog box, click and drag the slider to increase or decrease the Quality setting.

● The Preview window displays the updated image as you make changes.

● You can view the image size and download time to see the effect your changes have on the image.

4 Click Update.

Dreamweaver updates the image in your document.

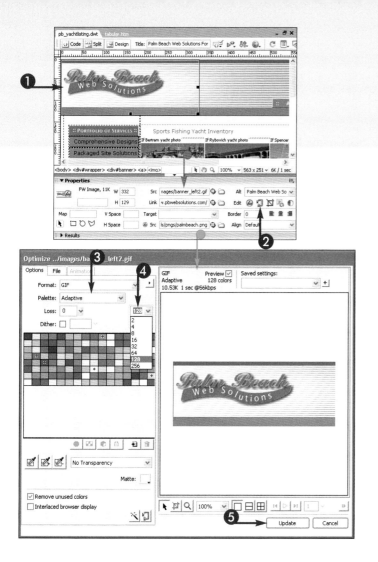

Optimize GIF Images

① Click a GIF image.

● The image type is indicated by its file extension.

② Click 🔲.

③ In the Optimize dialog box, click here and select a color palette to control the number of colors in the image.

④ Click here and select more or fewer colors to adjust quality and file size.

● You can view the file size and estimated download time as you make changes.

⑤ Click Update when you are done.

Dreamweaver updates the image in your document.

Check It Out!

The process of image optimization is a delicate compromise between reducing file size while maintaining visual quality. Because Dreamweaver uses the full-featured image optimization engine built into Fireworks, there are many different ways that you can optimize your images. To learn more and see some other tricks that you can use on your images, visit the All The Web site and read the article at www. pantos.org/atw/35273.html.

Remove It!

You can reverse the optimization settings that you apply by simply undoing them. Press Ctrl+Z (⌘+Z) or select Undo from the Edit menu to return the image to its original settings and appearance.

FIREWORKS HTML:
Create Interactive Images

You can create navigation bars, buttons, and other interactive images in Fireworks and insert the complete code for these objects directly in a Dreamweaver document. When you insert Fireworks HTML into a Web page, all the code necessary for the images to display and for assigned interactivity such as rollovers to work is copied directly into your document.

Fireworks offers a wide range of Web-specific features that make it the ideal image editor for working with Dreamweaver. You can create rollover images, navigation bars, pop-up menus, and disjointed rollover images in Fireworks, optimize the images for display on the Web, and then export all of

the images and the HTML to a file in your site. In Dreamweaver, you need only insert the HTML file that Fireworks generates to have a fully functional, interactive image in your page. To edit the images or make changes to the functionality of the object, you launch Fireworks to complete your edits; all of the changes are automatically applied when you return to Dreamweaver.

See also>> Insert Toolbar: Common

Properties Inspector: Images

See also>> Fireworks: Edit Images

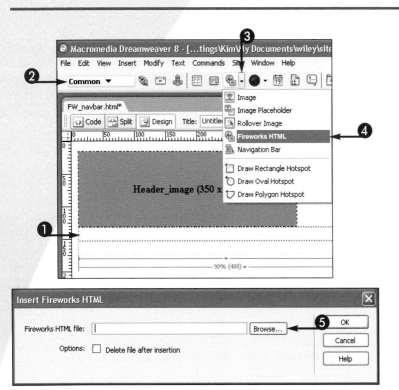

① Click in the page where you want to insert the Fireworks object.

② Click here and select Common.

③ Click the Image (🖳) arrow.

④ Click Fireworks HTML.

The Insert Fireworks HTML dialog box appears.

⑤ Click Browse.

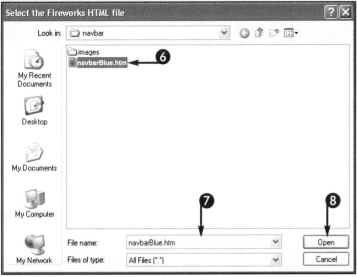

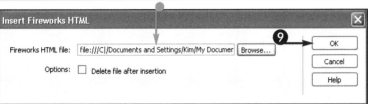

The Select the Fireworks HTML file dialog box appears.

⑥ Browse to the HTML file that was generated by Fireworks.

⑦ Select the file.

⑧ Click Open (Select).

● In the Insert Fireworks HTML dialog box, the path and name of the Fireworks HTML file display.

⑨ Click OK.

Dreamweaver inserts the Fireworks HTML file and all images into the page.

Important!

As you design interactive images in Fireworks, it is important to follow solid design principles. Pay close attention to the position and alignment of your objects, avoiding any gaps between them. By default, Fireworks creates tables to hold your images in place and to assign the necessary JavaScript for interactive elements. Images that are out of alignment, even by one or two pixels, will result in a very complex and difficult to edit table in Dreamweaver.

Did You Know?

When you edit a Fireworks HTML file, always select the table that contains the entire object before beginning your edits. The best method for this is using the Tag Selector. When you select the entire object, the Properties inspector displays a special editing button that launches Fireworks and completes your edits.

FLASH BUTTONS:
Create and Insert

You can create and insert navigation objects made with Flash to add buttons with visual rollover effects using the Flash button feature. Dreamweaver comes with this function built-in so you do not need to have Macromedia Flash installed to create your own Flash buttons.

When you insert a Flash button, Dreamweaver opens a complex dialog box where the parameters for the button are created. You can select from 44 different button styles ranging from buttons with simple rollover effects to others that include complicated animations. After you select the style of button you

want to use, you can further customize it by adding text, formatting the text, adding the link, and creating a background color.

Each button that you insert is saved as its own SWF file, which is the Flash movie format that displays Flash objects in browsers. All of the operations needed to create, insert, and save the file are in the single dialog box that Dreamweaver provides.

See also>>

| Insert Toolbar: Common |
| Properties Inspector: Flash |

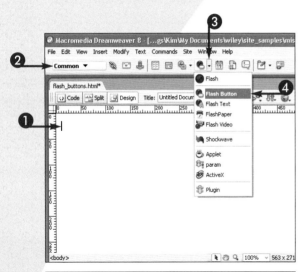

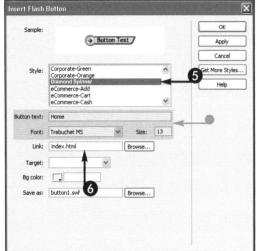

Insert a Flash Button

① Click in the page where you want to insert a Flash button.

② Click here and select Common.

③ Click the Media (⬤) arrow.

④ Click Flash Button.

⑤ In the Insert Flash Button dialog box, select the style of button that you want.

● You can type any text that you want to appear on the button and style the text using Font settings.

⑥ Type the filename for the link or click Browse to locate the file in your site.

You can type an absolute address in the Link field, such as www. mysite.com, to link to a page outside your site.

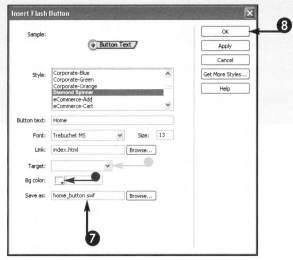

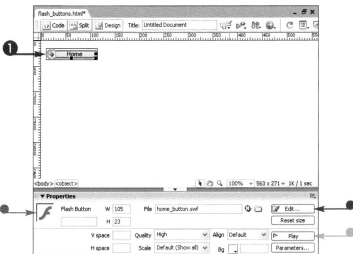

- You can open the linked file in a new page by clicking Target and selecting to _blank.

- You can click here (🔲) to select a background color to match your design's background.

⑦ Type a name for the SWF file or click Browse to select a location.

Note: If you use a relative link such as index.htm, you must save the SWF file in the same folder as the HTML page.

⑧ Click OK.

Dreamweaver inserts the Flash button into the page.

Preview and Edit a Flash Button

① Click a Flash button.

- The Properties inspector displays the properties of the button.

- You can click Play to preview the button.

- You can click Edit to display the Insert Flash Button dialog box to perform edits on the button.

Important!

Flash buttons are self-contained Flash movie files that have the links hard-coded into them. To change a link value, open and edit the button. In addition, you must be aware of the correct paths used in the button and to any files you link to. In cases where you use Flash buttons in different folders throughout your site, it is best to use absolute URLs for both the links and the SWF files.

Customize It!

You can download and install additional button styles from the Macromedia Exchange. Click Get More Styles in the Insert Flash Button dialog box to go to the Exchange where you can search for more Flash button styles.

F

FLASH MOVIES:
Insert and View

Macromedia Flash allows you to create and deliver rich media content that incorporates animation, sounds, interactivity, and video. Once you create a Flash file, you can insert it into a Dreamweaver document and provide formatting instructions so that the movie is positioned properly and plays back as you intend.

For Flash movies to play back in a Web browser, you must insert them into a standard Web page so the browser can use the Flash Player plug-in to render and play back the movie directly in the page. As with images and other objects, you must first determine where you want to position the movie on the page,

and then insert it at that location. Dreamweaver creates the necessary tags to allow any browser to play back the movie.

You publish Flash movies with the .swf file extension when you want to insert them into the page. Then, you can use the Properties inspector to view the movie directly in the Design Window and set the necessary parameters to control playback.

See also>>

Insert Toolbar: Common

Properties Inspector: Flash

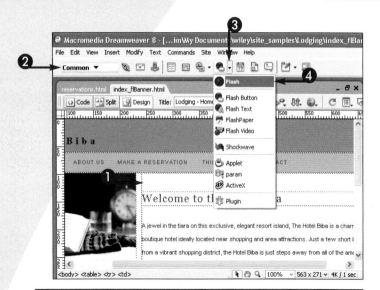

① Click in the page where you want to insert a Flash movie.

② Click here and select Common.

③ Click the ◉ arrow.

④ Click Flash.

The Select File dialog box appears.

⑤ Browse to the location of the SWF file.

⑥ Select the file.

⑦ Click OK.

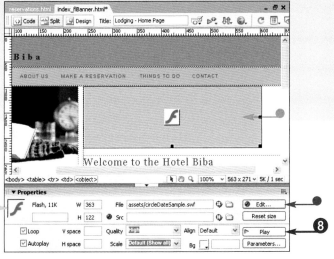

Dreamweaver inserts the SWF file in the page.

- The size and position of the movie file is indicated by a gray box with the Flash icon.

- The Properties inspector displays properties for the movie.

- You can click Edit to open Flash and make changes to the source file.

8 Click Play.

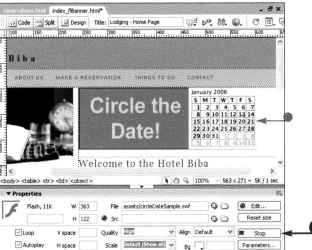

- The movie plays in the Document Window.

9 Click Stop to halt the movie playback.

Did You Know?

Working in Flash involves two very different file formats. When you author Flash content in the Flash program, you save the file with the .fla extension. You can only open FLA files in Flash and not in a browser. With the editing process complete, you must publish to the SWF file format. You then insert the published file into a Web page for playback within a browser window.

Check It Out!

Macromedia Flash is more than a tool to create animations or splash screens that display when a viewer enters a Web site. The Flash platform is a way to take advantage of a dynamic programming environment and its programming variant, called Macromedia Flex. You can learn more about the Flash platform at www.macromedia.com/platform.

FLASH TEXT:
Create and Insert

You can create interactive text objects with animated effects using the Flash text feature in Dreamweaver. This command builds Flash files directly in the Dreamweaver environment when you want to include text that has more visual impact than standard HTML text or simple images. You can also use Flash text for navigation objects by including a link to the text.

Dreamweaver provides a single dialog box where it creates all of the properties of the Flash text object. In this dialog box, you set and format the font for the text, insert the text, select to have a rollover

color displayed when the viewer's mouse moves over the text, and set any links that you want to apply to the text. When you finish defining the Flash text object, a file containing the Flash text is created and saved into the same site as the page. Each individual Flash text object that you create is saved as its own SWF file.

See also>>

| Insert Toolbar: Common |
| Properties Inspector: Flash |

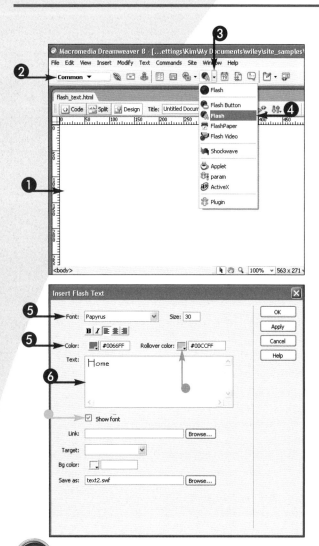

Insert Flash Text

① Click in the page where you want to insert a Flash text object.

② Click here and select Common.

③ Click the ● arrow.

④ Click Flash.

The Insert Flash Text dialog box appears.

⑤ Select the font type, size, and color that you want.

● You can select a rollover color by clicking the Color box (▦).

⑥ Type your text.

● You can select the Show font option to preview the text as you type.

268

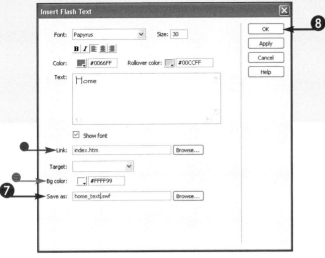

● You can specify link information if you want the text to function as a link.

● You can set a background color here.

7 Type a filename for the SWF file that Dreamweaver will generate.

You can click Browse to choose a location to save the file.

8 Click OK.

● Dreamweaver inserts the Flash text object into the page.

● The Properties inspector displays properties for the Flash text object.

● You can click Edit to display the Insert Flash Text dialog box to edit the text object.

TIPS

Did You Know?
Flash objects such as Flash text are considered active objects, so they always appear at the top of any elements in the page. If you have other items in your design that you want to appear above a Flash object, such as a drop-down menu, then you must set the wmode parameter to transparent in the Properties inspector.

Important!
One of the advantages of Flash text is the freedom that it allows the page designers to use any font they want in their designs. However, you should keep in mind that search engines cannot index pages properly without HTML text on the page.

FLASH VIDEO:
Create and Insert

Using a new feature in Dreamweaver 8, you can create all of the objects that you need to insert Flash video content into your Web pages entirely from within Dreamweaver. Because Flash video uses the Flash Player to control playback, the viewers of a page containing Flash video are not forced to select from competing formats such as QuickTime or the Windows Media Format.

When you insert a Flash video into a page, Dreamweaver creates a Flash playback object and links the video player to a Flash video file. Flash video files are compressed videos that have been converted to the FLV file format with a built-in

conversion utility or with another program such as Sorensen Squeeze. You must convert the file in your Flash video to the FLV format before inserting the Flash video object.

Dreamweaver provides you with numerous options for controlling your Flash video player's appearance. You can select the style of the player controls as well as set parameters for playback in the dialog box that Dreamweaver provides.

See also>>

Insert Toolbar:
Common

Properties Inspector:
Flash

---

① Click in the page where you want to insert a Flash video.

② Click here and select Common.

③ Click the ● arrow.

④ Click Flash Video.

The Insert Flash Video dialog box appears.

⑤ Click here and select Progressive Download Video for the video type.

You can use the Streaming Download video type if your video is hosted on a Flash Communication Server.

⑥ Type the URL of the Flash video file or browse to the FLV file in your site.

⑦ Click here and select a playback skin style.

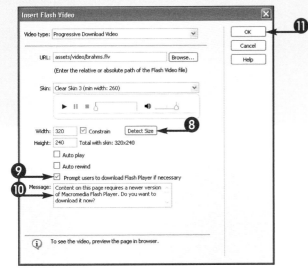

8 Click Detect Size to automatically size the player.

9 Click this option (☐ changes to ☑) to insert the Flash detection script into the page.

Note: Flash video inserted with Dreamweaver requires Flash Player version 8 or newer.

10 Type a message for viewers who do not have the required Flash Player version.

11 Click OK.

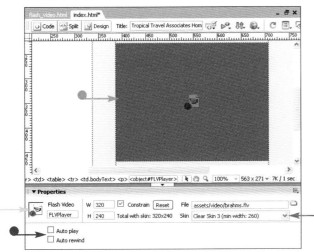

● Dreamweaver inserts the Flash video into the page.

● The Properties inspector displays properties for the Flash video.

● You can click to change basic playback options (☐ changes to ☑) and the player.

● You click here to select skins for the video player.

You must preview the page in a browser window in order to see the video playing.

Important!

When you insert a Flash video, a new Flash file is automatically created and placed in the same folder as the page where the video is inserted. This file has the same name as the selected video player skin. For example, the Clear Skin style is called Clear_Skin_3.swf. You must upload all the SWF files for the player and the FLV file for the video to your server in order for the video to play back correctly.

More Options!

You can change simple properties of Flash video files, such as the auto playback setting, without doing any additional work. To change the path to the file, the name of the file, or the download method, delete the file and insert the video again using the methods described here.

FONT LIST:
Create and Apply

You can create custom lists of fonts that are applied as a CSS style to control the appearance of the text in a document. When you create a custom font list, you have greater control over the appearance of your text and are no longer constrained by the HTML standard font lists. You create custom font lists in the CSS Rule definition for dialog box.

When you style text by creating a rule, you are normally constrained by the six font families common to all browsers. These families of fonts are created to ensure that the fonts the viewer of a page sees are

consistent with the fonts the viewer has on their computer. Because the viewer's browser can only use fonts that are installed on their computer, the number of fonts are limited to ensure the widest compatibility across the many millions of potential viewers of a page. Custom font lists allow you to add new font families that can use any font.

See also>> **Properties Inspector: Text**

See also>> **CSS Styling: Control Text Appearance**

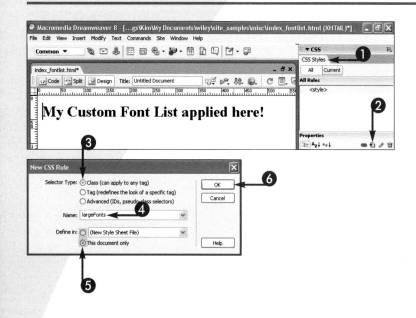

① Click CSS Styles.

② Click New CSS Rule (🖻).

■ The New CSS Rule dialog box appears.

③ Click the Class option (○ changes to ●).

④ Type a name for the new class.

⑤ Click either to create the new rule in the open document or in an external CSS style sheet. (○ changes to ●)

⑥ Click OK.

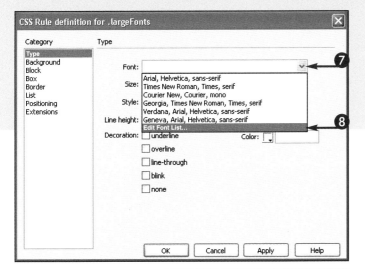

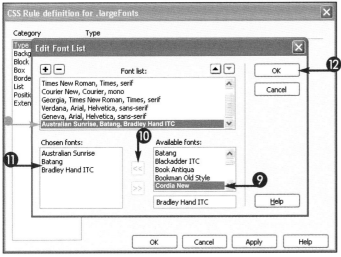

The CSS Rule definition for dialog box appears.

⑦ In the Type category, click the Font drop-down menu.

⑧ Click Edit Font List.

The Edit Font List dialog box appears.

⑨ Click the font that you want to add from the available list on the right.

⑩ Click the arrow (⟨⟨) to add the font to the list.

⑪ Repeat steps **9** and **10** until all of the fonts you want are listed.

● Selected fonts appear in the Font list.

⑫ Click OK.

TIPS

More Options!

The example shown here uses a custom class to apply a custom font to text. You can also redefine an HTML tag if you want the custom fonts to be applied automatically as you type text. For example, you can redefine the `<body>` tag to apply the `<custom>` tag to all of the text in the page, or redefine the `<h1>` tag to set the custom fonts on text formatted as a Heading 1.

More Options!

You can also store the styling information in an external style sheet to share among all of the documents in your site, rather than inserting the styling rule into the document as shown in this example.

FONT LIST:
Create and Apply (Continued)

You can use custom font lists as CSS classes, as redefined HTML tags, or with advanced selectors through element IDs or class selectors.

Although custom fonts provide you with a great deal of latitude in modifying the appearance of your fonts, this method has practical limitations. To maintain the overall design of a page, you must have fonts similar in overall size and weight on the page. Because fonts can have considerable differences in width and height even when they have the same size value, it is important that you select the fonts carefully. Also keep in mind that the fonts in the list are displayed

in order. When the browser reads the CSS rule, it tries to use the first font in the list. If that font is not present on the computer, it tries to display the second font and continues to try to show the subsequent fonts from the list until none are found. At that point, the default font for the browser displays.

See also>> Properties Inspector: Text

See also>> CSS Styling: Control Text Appearance

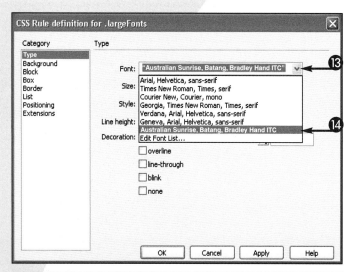

The new font list is created in the CSS Rule definition for dialog box.

⑬ Click the Font here.

⑭ Click the custom font list.

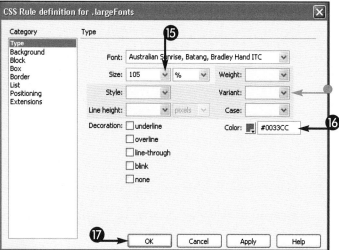

⑮ Click here and select the size of the font.

⑯ Click the Color box (▣) and select the color of the font.

● You can set additional options for weight, style, line height, and decoration.

⑰ Click OK.

Dreamweaver creates the new rule with the custom font list.

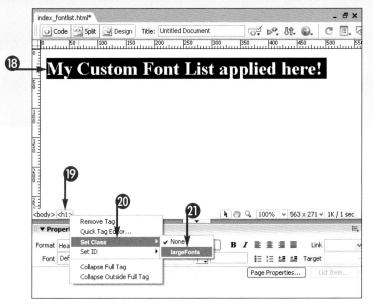

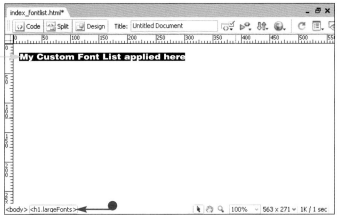

⑱ Select the item to which you want to have the custom font applied.

⑲ Right-click (Ctrl-click) the listing for the item in the Tag Selector.

⑳ Click Set Class.

㉑ Click the name of the class with the custom font.

● Dreamweaver applies the custom font to the selected text.

● The name of the custom class appears in the Tag Selector.

TIPS

Check It Out!

Typography is the study of fonts and text and the relationship between the fonts that you select and your text's readability. On the Web, typography plays a critical role in creating easy-to-read pages that convey the proper message. Designing Web pages for maximum impact means selecting the correct fonts, text colors, and page background colors, as well as the right space around different elements on the page, and the length of each line. For more about typography for Web design, visit www.wpdfd.com/wpdtypo.htm.

Remove It!

To remove a CSS class you have applied to text, right-click (Ctrl-click) the tag in the Tag Selector. Select None from the Set Class options; the custom class is removed from the tag.

FONTS:
Style with the Properties Inspector

You can use the Properties inspector to apply styling to the fonts in your document. When you create new styles for text, Dreamweaver creates a new CSS style in the head of the document and applies the styling rule to the selected text. As you create new style combinations, they are numbered sequentially, beginning with style1. Each new style appears in the Styles menu of the Properties inspector.

You can apply font styling that modifies the appearance of text by selecting a font combination from one of six available default lists. In order for a font to display, it must be present on the computer of the person who opens the document. Font families are designed to provide a consistent appearance to text by using similar fonts.

In addition to setting the font, you can also size text, select a font color, and set the text to bold or italic.

See also>> **Properties Inspector: Text**

See also>> **CSS Styling: Control Text Appearance**

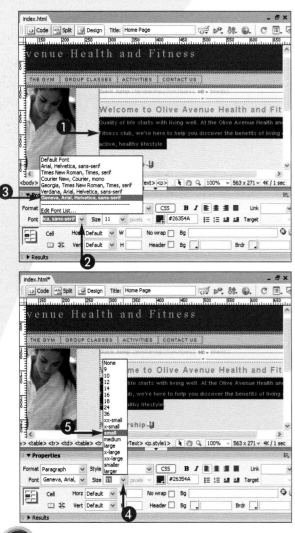

1. Select a block of text.
2. Click the Font drop-down arrow.
3. Click the font style that you want.

4. Click here.
5. Click the font size that you want.

You can type in values for font sizing based on percentages or em values.

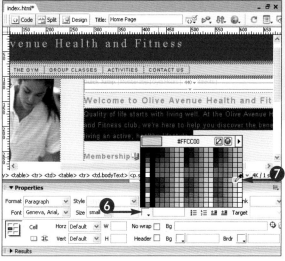

6 Click 🖼.

7 Click with the Eyedropper (🖋) to select a color from the Color Palette.

You can also move 🖋 onto the page to select a color from your design.

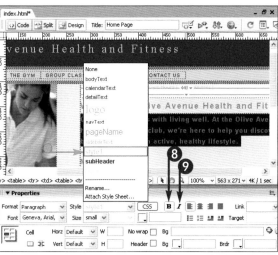

8 Click the Bold button (**B**) to apply a bold style to your text.

9 Click the Italic button (*I*) to apply italic styling.

● The new style is listed with a preview of your settings in the Style menu.

You can use the menu to apply the style to other text in your document.

Important!

Although applying font styles through the Properties inspector is a quick way to format your text, it is not the most efficient method. When you style text using the Properties inspector, you create a new style that is present only in the current document. The best method for using styles is to include them in an external style sheet that is linked to the document.

More Options!

You can edit the style that is created in the Properties inspector as you would any other CSS style. Use the CSS Styles panel to locate the style by its name and click the Edit Style button (🖉) to display the CSS Rule Definition dialog box where the style can be edited.

F

FORMS:
About Forms

You can collect information from visitors to your Web site using forms, which allow Web page viewers to interact with the site. Users enter information in menus and fields, and send the information back to the Web site owner.

Forms in HTML documents rely on and require `<form>` tags to create the basic actions needed for users to enter in and send back information to the Web server. Dreamweaver allows you to insert HTML `<form>` tags, `<form>` tags that rely on dynamic data, and `<form>` tags that support ASP.net form control methods. These tags define the method that collects

and processes the information that a visitor enters in the various form objects inside the form.

Dreamweaver form objects include text fields, hidden fields, buttons, check boxes, radio buttons, list menus, jump menus, file fields, and image fields. You insert form objects inside `<form>` tags to allow for the processing of the information that the viewer inputs.

See also>> | **Insert Toolbar: Forms**

See also>> | **Forms: Insert Buttons**

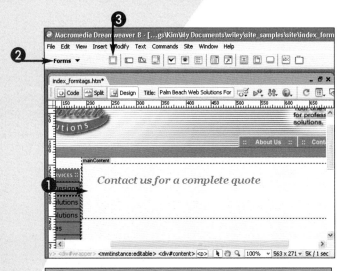

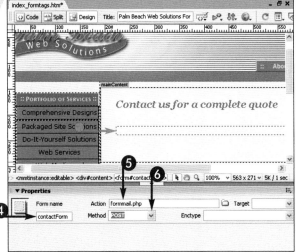

Insert a Blank Form Tag

① Click in the page where you want to insert a `<form>` tag.

② Click here and select Forms.

③ Click the Insert Form tag button ().

Dreamweaver inserts the form into the page.

● A red dashed line indicates a `<form>` tag.

④ Type a unique name for the form.

⑤ Type the name of the script that you want to be used to process the form.

⑥ Click here and select the processing method.

Note: *See Appendix A on Dynamic Design to learn more about form processing.*

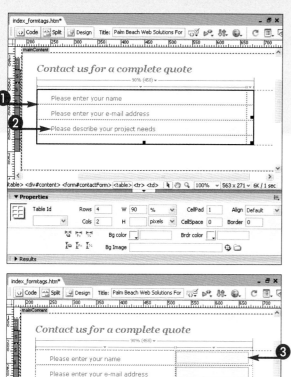

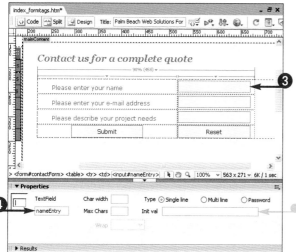

① Insert a table.

② Type in the labels for the form objects.

③ Insert the first form object.

This example inserts a textfield object.

Note: The Accessibility dialog box appears if you have preferences set to prompt for accessibility information.

④ Type a unique name for the form object.

● You can type a value that you want to appear in the text box here.

⑤ Repeat steps **3** and **4** to add and name additional form objects.

More Options!
You can organize the forms in your page in the same manner that you use with other objects that you insert into the page. It is a common practice to insert form objects into tables in order to organize the layout of the forms and present the viewer with a structured format. You can also apply CSS styling to form objects as you do with other elements to define borders, backgrounds, and sizing properties to meet your design goals.

Important!
You cannot insert one form tag into another form tag. If you attempt to insert a form tag inside an existing tag on the page, Dreamweaver simply ignores the insertion.

FORMS:
Create Accessible Forms

You can conform to visual and physical accessibility requirements and ensure that all of the visitors to your Web site can complete the forms that they find by inserting accessibility information into your forms. Accessibility settings address both of these potential issues by providing users with alternate methods for accessing your forms. You should enable accessibility prompts in the Preferences panel to assist you in creating accessible forms.

Because forms are visual, visually disabled people may use a screen reader program to read the contents of a Web page to them. These devices require a textual description of each form to function properly. In addition, some Web visitors may have physical limitations that prevent them from using a mouse and limit them to using a keyboard for text entry. For these people, a method is required that allows them to use keyboard commands or the Tab key to move through a form.

See also>> **Accessibility Preferences**

See also>> **Accessibility Reports**

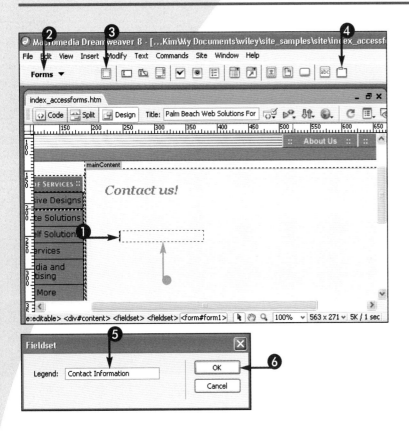

① Click in the page where you want to insert a form.

② Click here and select Forms.

③ Click 🔲.

● The form tag is indicated by a red dashed line.

④ Click Fieldset (🔲).

The Fieldset dialog box appears.

⑤ Type a legend for the fieldset.

Fieldsets help visitors who use screen readers to hear how a form is organized.

⑥ Click OK.

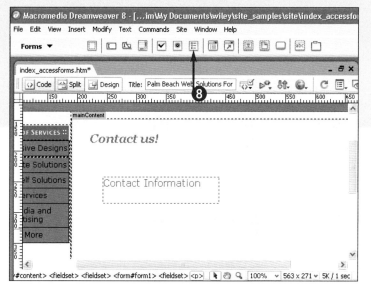

7 Press Enter.

8 Click these buttons to insert any form object.

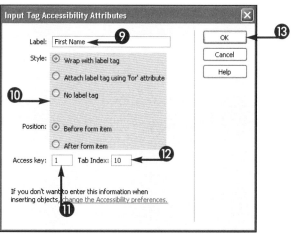

Note: The Accessibility Attributes dialog box appears for the form object that you selected.

9 Type a label for the form object.

10 Click these options (○ changes to ⊙) to set the label style and position.

11 Type the key to be pressed to activate the form object.

12 Type a number for the Tab Index.

13 Click OK.

The accessibility information is recorded in the form object tag.

Did You Know?

The Tab Index value represents the order that objects become active as a visitor presses the Tab key. The first active item has the lowest value in the page, the second item has the next highest value, and so forth. Many designers use multiples of ten as they enter the tab index so that they have additional numbers to select from in case they want to add a new indexed item later in the design process.

Check It Out!

Accessibility is a complex topic with many different options and methods for accomplishing the goal of making Web pages available to all viewers. Macromedia maintains a special section of their Developer's Center that deals with accessibility at www. macromedia.com/resources/ accessibility.

FORMS:
Insert Buttons

You can provide a method for viewers to submit and reset forms by inserting form button objects into your page. You can include a custom label for these buttons or use the default Submit and Reset labels.

The `</form>` tag on your Web page form determines how scripts process the form. Typically a script reads the data that a viewer inserts into the form, and transmits the data to a database for collection and storage. The buttons that you insert inside the `</form>` tag allow the script that submits the data to the Web server to run. Including a Reset button allows users to remove all of the information they have entered.

Although buttons have a default style applied through standard HTML, you can apply additional styling through CSS. For greater control of the appearance of your buttons, you can style buttons by defining a rule for the `<input>` tag.

See also>> **Insert Toolbar: Forms**

See also>> **CSS Styling: Style Forms**

Forms: About Forms

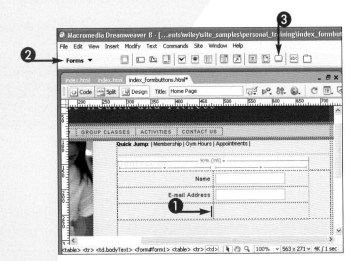

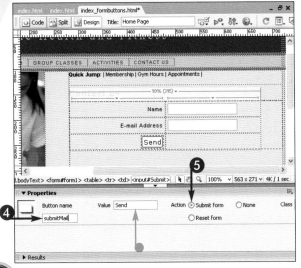

Insert a Submit Button

1 Click inside a form where you want to insert the button.

2 Click here and select Forms.

3 Click the Insert Button button (⬜).

Note: The Accessibility dialog box appears if you have preferences set to prompt for accessibility information.

Dreamweaver inserts the button into the page.

By default, the button is set as a Submit button.

4 Type a unique name for the form object.

● You can change the label on the button by typing a new one.

5 Click the Submit form option (○ changes to ◉) to have the button process the script for the form when it is clicked.

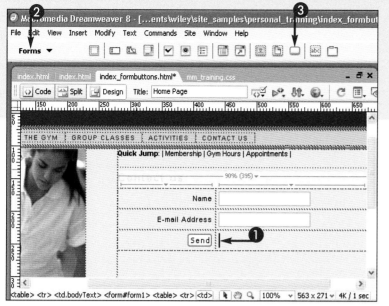

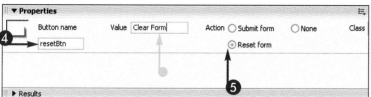

Insert a Reset Button

1 Click inside a form where you want to insert the button.

2 Click here and select Forms.

3 Click 🔲.

Dreamweaver inserts the button into the page.

Note: The Accessibility dialog box appears if you have preferences set to prompt for accessibility information.

4 Type a unique name for the form object.

● You can type a new label for the button in this field.

5 Click the Reset form option (○ changes to ◉).

A reset button is inserted into the page.

Important!

When you style buttons with CSS, be careful that the new style retains the form with which most people are familiar. While you can technically style buttons to no longer look like buttons, this defeats the purpose of this graphical object; if viewers must hunt through a form to find the button that submits information, then they may become frustrated and decide not to send it.

More Options!

In addition to standard HTML buttons, you can also use images to submit or reset forms. You insert form buttons that use images with the Image Field button. Once the image is in the document, you can use the Properties inspector to set the image to submit or reset the form information.

F

FORMS:
Insert Check Boxes and Radio Buttons

Check boxes and radio buttons provide users a simple method to select options in a form. You can insert these objects with the Insert toolbar and set their parameters in the Properties inspector.

Check boxes are the appropriate form to use when you want to allow a user to select from a number of options in a list. For example, if you have a question asking what kinds of ice cream a user enjoys, and you want them to select from a list, you insert a check box for chocolate, vanilla, strawberry, and other flavors.

Radio buttons provide an either/or interface that allows the viewer to make a single choice from a list of selections. For example, you can use a radio button to ask the viewer if they are male or female. Because there is only one correct answer to the question, a radio button is the appropriate form object to use.

See also>> Insert Toolbar: Forms

See also>> Forms: About Forms

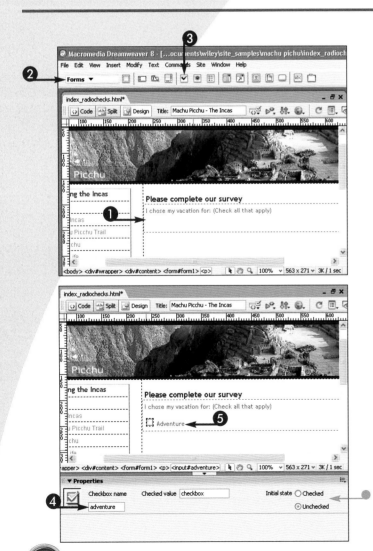

Insert a Check Box

① Click inside a form where you want to insert the check box.

② Click here and select Forms.

③ Click the Check Box button (☑).

Dreamweaver inserts the check box into the page.

Note: The Accessibility dialog box appears if you have preferences set to prompt for accessibility information.

④ Type a unique name for the form object.

Form object names may only contain numbers and letters; spaces and special characters are not allowed.

● You can specify whether the check box is checked when the page loads.

⑤ Add a descriptive label to the page.

⑥ Repeat these steps to continue adding check boxes.

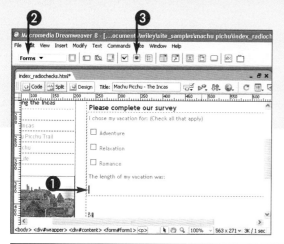

Insert a Radio Button

1. Click inside a form where you want to insert a radio button.

2. Click here and select Forms.

3. Click the Radio Button button (⊙).

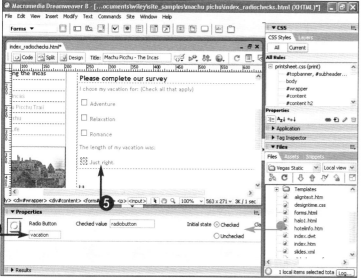

Dreamweaver inserts the radio button into the page.

4. Type a name for the form object.

   To make radio buttons in a group mutually exclusive, you must give all the form objects in the group the same name.

5. Type a descriptive name for the button.

   ● You click these options (○ changes to ◉) to set whether the radio button is selected when the page loads.

6. Repeat these steps to continue adding radio buttons.

More Options!

In addition to adding individual radio buttons, you can insert a Radio Group that allows you to insert a number of radio buttons at one time by entering values in a dialog box. Dreamweaver provides an interface that allows you to add, remove, and reorder all of the radio buttons in the group at one time to more quickly create a large group of radio buttons.

Check It Out!

Jakob Nielsen writes extensively on the best practices for Web page design and offers guidance on the best methods for user interface design. You can read his article about the use of radio buttons and check boxes, and the mistakes to avoid in their use, at www.useit. com/alertbox/20040927.html.

FORMS:
Insert File Fields

You can allow visitors to a Web site to locate and upload files from their computer to the Web server by providing a file field. A user can either manually enter the filename they want to upload to the server, or use the Browse button to locate and select their file.

File uploads depend on a script on your server to process the request to send the file, verify that the file is a permitted type for uploading, and determine where on the server to store the file. You can learn more about the kind of dynamic page processing required for file uploads in Appendix A at the back of this book. You can also consult the documentation

for the server technology for your site to get specific information on how the server processes a file upload request.

File uploads use the POST method for form processing to send the file to the address specified in the Action text box.

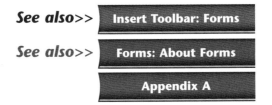

See also>>   **Insert Toolbar: Forms**

See also>>   **Forms: About Forms**

Appendix A

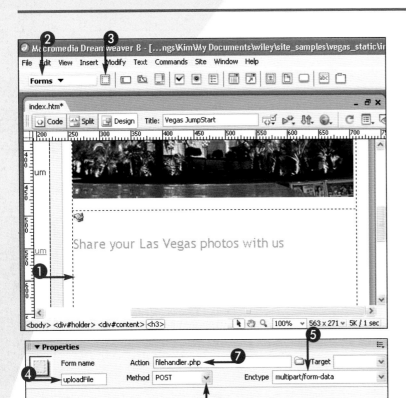

1. Click inside the page where you want to insert the form.

2. Click here and select Forms.

3. Click ▣.

   The Accessibility dialog box appears if you have preferences set to prompt for accessibility information.

   Dreamweaver inserts the form tag into the page.

4. Type a unique name for the form.

5. Click here and select the form type to multipart/form-data.

6. Click here and select the form method to POST.

7. Type the name of the server-side script that will process the file upload.

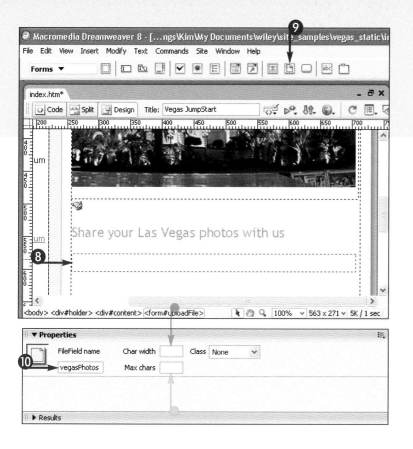

8 Click inside the form.

9 Click the File Field button ().

Dreamweaver inserts the file field into the page.

10 Type a name for the form object.

● You can set the maximum number of characters that will display in the Char width field.

● You can limit the number of characters that the user can input in the Max chars field.

You must add a button to the form to allow the user to submit their file or reset the form.

TIPS

Did You Know?

The real power behind file uploads lies in the server script that processes the form that is submitted by the viewer. You can set any number of parameters in the script to limit the size of the file that is being uploaded, the type of file that is permitted for uploads, and even create a message that displays to let the user know when the upload is complete.

Did You Know?

The methods for setting script parameters vary widely from one server technology to another, but all of the popular server programs such as ColdFusion, ASP.Net, and PHP provide a great deal of control over how file uploads are handled.

FORMS:
Insert Hidden Fields

You can pass information to a server when a user submits a form by including hidden fields in the form tag. You often use hidden fields to set parameters on the server that determine how to direct the form, or redirect the user to a URL after the form is processed.

Designers and developers can use hidden fields for many necessary functions. For example, a hidden field can check that the required fields in a form have data. When the form is processed, the server checks fields, and directs the user to an alternate page if the information is not present. Hidden fields can also

restrict the kinds of data that the user can insert into a form.

When a hidden field is entered into a page, Dreamweaver inserts a marker to let you know that the object is present. You can enter the value that you want to incorporate into the hidden field in the Properties inspector.

See also>> Insert Toolbar: Forms

See also>> Forms: About Forms

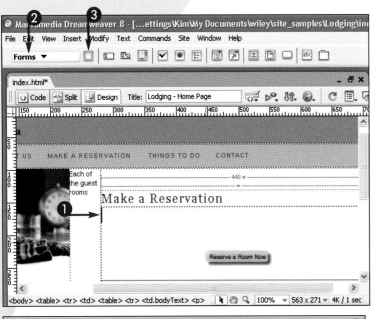

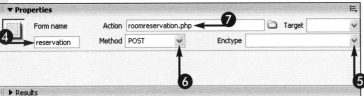

① Click inside the page where you want to insert the form.

② Click here and select Forms.

③ Click 🔲.

Dreamweaver inserts the form tag into the page.

④ Type a unique name for the form.

⑤ Click here and select the form type, if necessary.

⑥ Click here and select the required form method based on your script.

⑦ Type the name of the server-side script that will process the form.

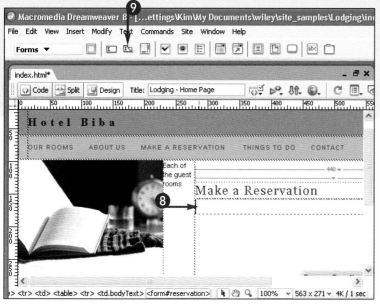

⑧ Click inside the form.

⑨ Click the Hidden Field button (🖾).

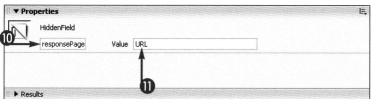

Dreamweaver inserts the hidden field into the page.

Note: The Accessibility dialog box appears if you have preferences set to prompt for accessibility information.

⑩ Type a name for the form object.

⑪ Type the value that you want to be passed to the server.

Dreamweaver inserts the hidden field into the form.

Check It Out!

Designers commonly use hidden fields with Common Gateway Interface, or CGI, scripts that allow users to interact with simple forms that require limited processing on the server. A CGI script can process form data and send it to an e-mail address that you specify in a hidden field. For more about this type of programming, visit the Wise-Women Web site at www.wise-women.org/tutorials/forms.

More Options!

You can hide or reveal hidden elements in your page with the Visual Aids button (🖾) in the Document toolbar. When you select the Invisible Elements option from the menu, all objects on the page that are represented by the standard yellow shield icon become visible. To hide all Invisible Elements, simply deselect that option.

FORMS:
Insert List and Menu Items

You can insert special form objects that allow your site visitors to select an option from a list of items. These form objects are useful when you have a large number of options for the user to select from, but a limited amount of space. They are also helpful when you want to ensure that the user inputs the correct information. Rather than use a text box where the viewer may type the information incorrectly, a menu gives them the values already in place.

You can create a drop-down menu by using the Menu option, or you can create a scrollable list of items by using the List option. Dreamweaver provides a single interface for inserting both lists and menus. The List Values dialog box allows you to create all of the labels and values that you want to include in your menus in one location. Once the information is in place, you finish setting the parameters for the form in the Properties inspector.

See also>> | **Insert Toolbar: Forms**

See also>> | **Forms: About Forms**

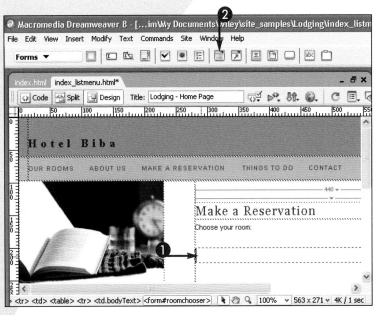

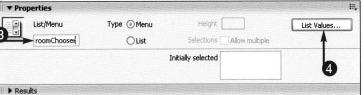

1 Click inside an existing form.

2 Click List/Menu (🗐).

Dreamweaver inserts the List/Menu object in the form.

Note: *The Accessibility dialog box appears if you have preferences set to prompt for accessibility information.*

3 Type a unique name for the form object.

4 Click List Values.

290

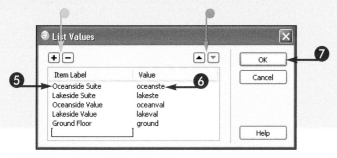

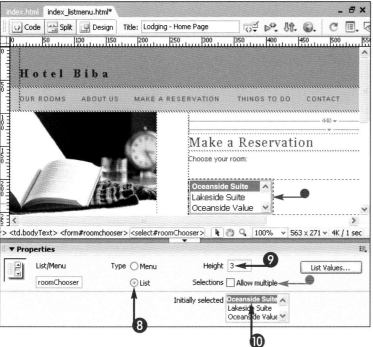

5 In the List Values dialog box, type a label for the menu.

6 Type the value that the processing script will pass to the server.

● You can click the plus (⊞) or minus (⊟) buttons to add new items or remove existing items.

● You can change the order of the list items with the Up (▲) and Down (▼) arrow buttons.

7 Click OK.

● The labels appear in the menu.

8 Click the List option (○ changes to ⊙).

9 Type the number of lines that you want in the menu.

● You can select the Allow multiple option (○ changes to ⊙) to allow multiple selections in the list.

10 Click here and select the item that you want selected when the page opens.

The list menu is prepared for use with the script that processes user entries.

TIPS

More Options!

To create a drop-down menu rather than a scrolling menu, select the Menu option (○ changes to ⊙) in the Properties inspector. Keep in mind that you cannot set the height of the menu or allow multiple selections if you select this option.

Did You Know?

You can use the Tag Selector to view and edit more of the attributes of a form object than those that display in the Properties inspector. For example, you can set the Access Key attribute, assign a class, select a language, and set a size and style for the tag that is inserted to create the menu. You may find that having all of the options presented in one panel is more efficient than working through the Properties inspector and a dialog box.

FORMS:
Insert Text Fields

You can insert text fields into a form that allow users to type information that is sent to your server for collection and processing. You can set text fields as single-line entries, multiple-line entries, or as password fields.

You insert text fields into a form with a single button in the Insert toolbar or through the Insert menu. You can then set the properties of the text field in the Properties inspector.

The Properties inspector controls the appearance and function of the text fields. You can set the maximum

number of allowable characters that a user can type in a text field, as well as set the number of characters that display in the field. Setting the character width value controls the width of the text field. Additional options allow you to set the height of a multiple-line text box and whether the entries in the field wrap inside the available space.

See also>>  Insert Toolbar: Forms

See also>> Forms: About Forms

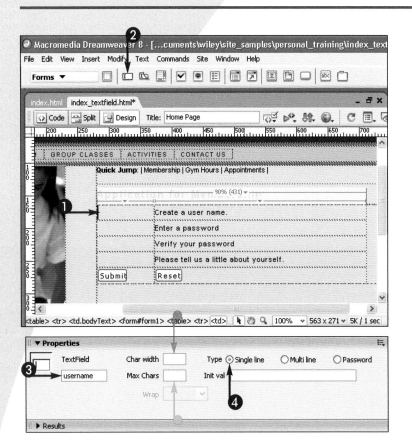

① Click inside an existing form.

② Click the Text Field button ([▭]).

Note: The Accessibility dialog box appears if you have preferences set to prompt for accessibility information.

Dreamweaver inserts the text field object in the form.

③ Type a unique name for the text field object.

④ Select the Single line option (○ changes to ⦿).

● You can set the maximum number of characters that display in this field, with the default setting being 20.

● You can limit the number of characters that the user can enter.

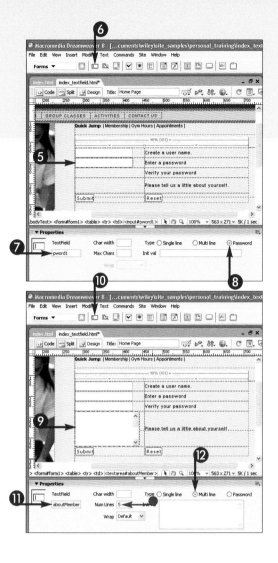

Dreamweaver creates a single-line text field in the form.

⑤ Click in the location for a password text field.

⑥ Click 🔲.

⑦ Type a unique name.

⑧ Click the Password option (◯ changes to ◉).

Dreamweaver creates a password text field.

⑨ Click in the location for a multiple-line text field.

⑩ Click 🔲.

⑪ Type a unique name.

⑫ Select the Multi line option (◯ changes to ◉).

● You can control the height of the text field by setting the number of lines that display.

Dreamweaver creates a multiple-line text field.

More Options!
You can control how text inserted into a multiple-line text field wraps inside the field by setting the Wrap options. You can set the text wrap option to off, to virtual, or to physical. When you set the word wrap to off, a scroll bar will appear when a line of text is inserted that is too wide for the text field. Virtual and physical will both cause text to wrap inside the text field. The virtual setting will unwrap the text when the form is submitted for processing.

Did You Know?
The default value for the width of all text fields is 20 characters. To increase or decrease the width of the text field, you can insert a value higher or lower than 20.

FRAMES:
Create Framesets and Frames

You can display multiple Web pages in a single browser by dividing the page into frames, a design that requires a document — called a frameset — to divide the page into different windows. The primary purpose of frames is to keep some areas of the design fixed while other parts of the design load with new content as the viewer navigates the site. A common frame-based design is one where the page header and navigation elements remain fixed, and a content frame loads new pages.

Pages that use frames and a frameset are really multiple pages that display in a single browser

window. Dreamweaver has several tools for creating and working with frame-based designs. You can start with a fresh page and divide it into the separate frames that appear by defining the frameset properties. You can then decide which documents you want to display inside the separate frames of the frameset to complete your design.

See also>>

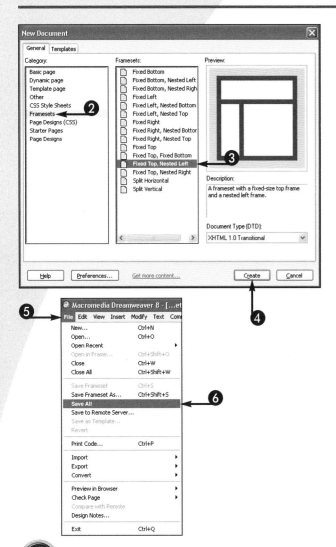

① Press Control+N (⌘+N).

The New Document dialog box appears.

② Click Framesets.

③ Click a frame layout.

④ Click Create.

Note: *If you have accessibility preferences for frames enabled, then a dialog box appears where each frame is named.*

Dreamweaver creates the frameset.

⑤ Click File.

⑥ Click Save All.

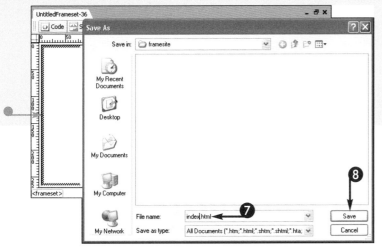

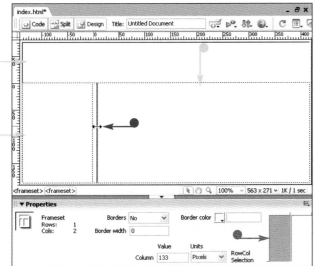

7 In the Save As dialog box, type **index.html** as the name for the frameset to save the file as the site's home page.

8 Click Save.

● The borders of the frameset display a hatched shading to show which file is being saved.

You must save a file for each of the frames in the frameset.

9 Continue saving the files until all frames are saved.

The frameset properties display in the Properties inspector.

● Each frame in the frameset is a separate HTML document.

● You can click and drag a border to adjust the size of frames.

● You can use the RowCol selection area to select different areas of the frameset.

TIPS

Did You Know?

Frame-based designs have fallen out of favor in recent years. Despite the fact that framed designs have some advantages in maintaining a consistent navigation through an entire site, the complex methods required to link documents in frames and the problems that frames cause users in printing and bookmarking pages have led most professional designers to abandon this format.

More Options!

You can use the Frames panel to gain greater control over how you select the documents that load into the frameset page. When you open this panel from the Window menu, Dreamweaver displays a graphical representation of the frameset. The Frames panel allows you to click the separate frames represented in the panel to select the corresponding frame in the Document Window.

F

FRAMES:
Link Frames

You can create links that load pages inside a design using frames by setting the Target property for the link.

When you create a frameset to define a page design, the frameset is divided into separate frames. Each frame loads a separate HTML document into the frameset, creating a design that is composed of multiple files. Linking inside a frame requires that you name the frame where the page should load. For example, if you have all of your navigation objects in one frame but want the pages containing your content to load into another frame, you must set the

name of the frame through the Target field. This ensures that the overall design of the frame-based page is maintained and that your content loads in the correct area of the design.

Linking inside a frame-based design can be confusing to even the most experienced Web designer. You can make the task easier by giving each frame in the frameset a descriptive name.

See also>>

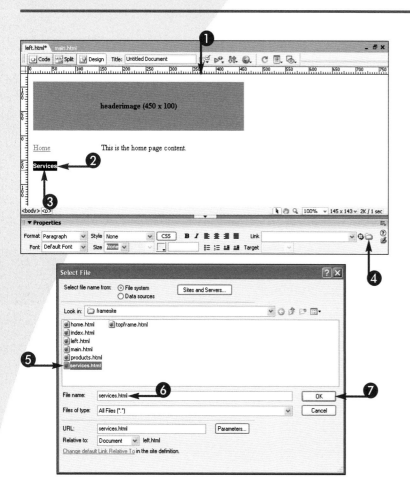

① Open a frameset page.

② Click inside the frame where you want to insert your links.

③ Type and select the text or image that you want to use as the link.

④ Click the Browse button (🗁).

The Select File dialog box appears.

⑤ Browse to the file that you want to load into the frameset.

⑥ Select the file.

⑦ Click OK.

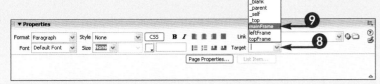

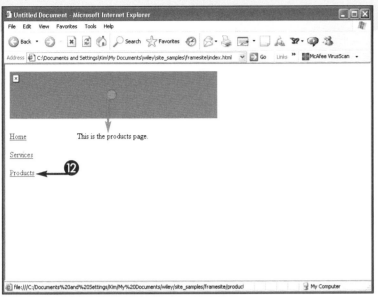

8 Click the Target drop-down arrow.

9 Select the name of the frame where you want the linked file to load.

10 Continue adding links to the pages in the site, targeting each link to the content frame.

11 Press F12.

The frameset opens in your default browser for testing.

12 Click a link.

● The content loads into the targeted frame.

F

TIPS

Important!

One of the keys to success in working with frame-based designs is to clearly name the different frames in the frameset. If you use simple names that have a relationship to their function, you have greater success in targeting your frames correctly. If your frames are named clearly, then you are less likely to target the frames incorrectly and have problems with your design.

More Options!

You can load pages into a frameset to see how the overall page design will appear to the viewer of the page. Click File and then click Open in Frame. Dreamweaver loads the page that you select in the frame where your cursor is located.

FTP:
Get and Put Files to a Web Server

You can transfer your files to a Web server using Dreamweaver's built-in File Transfer Protocol, or FTP, function. Dreamweaver allows you to copy files from your computer to the server with the Put command. To transfer files from the server to your computer, you can use the Get command.

To enable file transfers, you must enter the information that you receive from your Web host in the Remote Info category of the Site Definition dialog box. These settings include the address to the folder on the remote computer where your files are stored, as well as the username and password provided for you by your host.

You can perform file transfer operations on an entire site, on a folder, on a group of files that you select, or on a single file. Most file transfer operations are performed from the Files panel, but you can also get and put an open file using the buttons in the Document toolbar.

See also>> **File Transfer: Get and put**

See also>> **Files Panel**

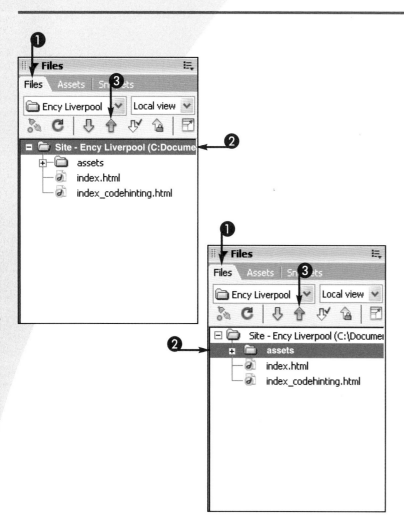

Put an Entire Site to a Server

1. Click the Files tab.
2. Click the root folder for the site.
3. Click the Put button (⬆).

   Dreamweaver displays a dialog box, asking if you want to put the entire site.

4. Click OK in the dialog box to confirm the file transfer.

Put a Folder to a Server

1. Click the Files tab.
2. Click a folder.
3. Click ⬆.

   Dreamweaver copies the selected folder to the Web server.

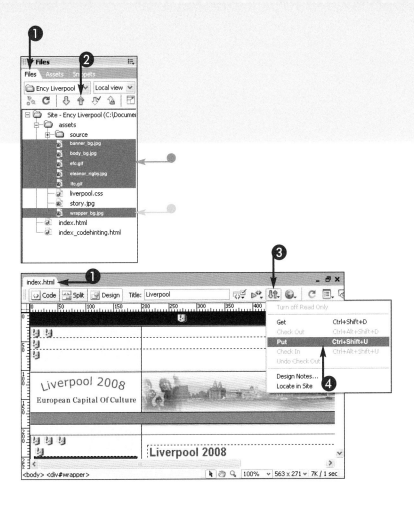

Put Selected Files to a Server

① Click the Files tab.

● You can press and hold Shift to select contiguous files.

● You can press and hold Ctrl (⌘) to select noncontiguous files.

② Click ⬆.

Dreamweaver copies the selected documents to the server.

Put an Open File to a Server

① Open a document.

② Press Ctrl+N (⌘+N) to save the document.

③ Click the File Management button (⬆).

④ Click Put.

Dreamweaver copies the file to the server.

More Options!

You can right-click (Ctrl-click) a document or a selection of documents and folders in the Files panel to Get or Put files. When the contextual menu appears, select the file operation that you want to perform.

Did You Know?

Dreamweaver can help with file transfers by automatically sending other files in the page along with the HTML document. These files are called *dependent files* because they are linked in the page and must be present on the server for the page to display correctly. Dreamweaver asks if you want to put or get dependent files when a page transfers. In most cases, you should accept the offer to handle those files so that your pages are up-to-date on the server as well as on your computer.

GRIDS:
Design Page Layouts

You can use Dreamweaver's grid feature to more easily design your pages with layers or layout tables. You can set an option that automatically snaps the layout objects to the grid's edges so you can quickly place them onto the page without worrying about layers or layout tables overlapping each other.

You can customize the appearance of the grid to match your design needs including the spacing between grid lines, grid color, or displaying the grid as a series of dots instead of solid lines.

As you drag a layout object onto the page, Dreamweaver expands or contracts the size of the object within five pixels of a grid line. Although snapping works whether the grid is visible or not,

it does not apply to images, Flash movies, and other objects you insert into the page. Grids appear only while you are working in Dreamweaver and are not visible when you publish the page.

See also>> | Grids |

| Insert Toolbar: Layout |

See also>> | Layout Block |

| Layout Table |

| Visual Aids |

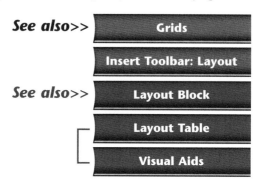

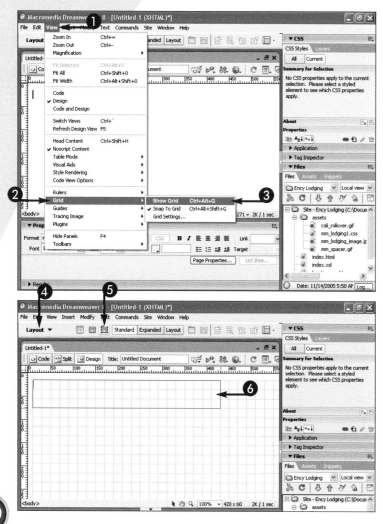

Lay Out Pages with Grids and Layers

1 Click View.

2 Click Grid.

3 Click Show Grid.

Dreamweaver displays the grid in the Design view window.

4 Click here and select Layout.

5 Click the Draw Layer button (▤).

6 Click and drag to draw a layer on the page.

Layers snap to the grid lines when you enable the Snap option.

Dreamweaver adds the code for new layers as you work on your document.

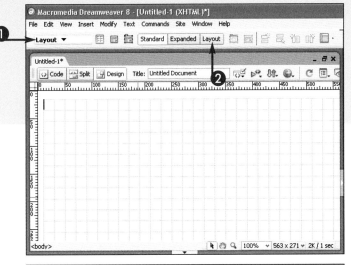

① Click here and select Layout.

② Click the Layout button.

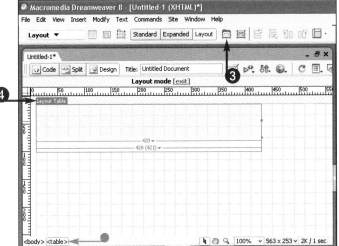

Dreamweaver switches to Layout mode.

③ Click the Layout Table button ().

④ Click and drag to add a layout table.

The table snaps to the grid lines when you enable the Snap option.

● Dreamweaver adds the code for the layout table to your document as you work.

TIPS

Caution!

The snap feature continues to operate even after you turn off the view of the grid. If your layout objects appear to be jumping around the page or do not go into the position that you want, then it is likely that you have left the snapping feature on, and the layer or table is still snapping to the now-invisible grid.

More Options!

Dreamweaver 8 has added an excellent tool for visualizing the position of layers on the page with the new CSS Layout Backgrounds feature. You can enable this feature through the View menu or the Visual Aids button ( ) in the Document toolbar to have an better idea of how the layers in a document are positioned.

GUIDES:
Place and Align Objects

You can use page guides, visible only when you work in Dreamweaver, to help you place objects on the page, to visualize where different items in a page design should go, and to simulate where the bottom of a page appears when seen at different resolutions.

Guides are lines that you create using the rulers on the top and left sides of the Design Window. You can also position an existing guide by double-clicking the guide and entering a pixel value. You can also place guides at the imaginary page fold that exists when a browser displays the page in different resolutions.

You can use guides for visualization as well as placement of objects. When you enable the snap feature that is available with guides, Dreamweaver moves layout elements, such as layers or layout tables, to the guide when they come within five pixels of the guide.

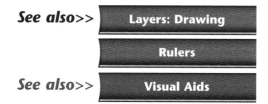

See also>> Layers: Drawing

Rulers

See also>> Visual Aids

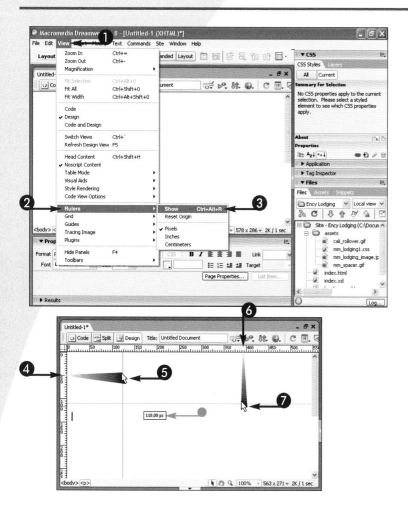

Creating Layout Guides

1 Click View.

2 Click Rulers.

3 Click Show.

Rulers appear on the top and left sides of the Design Window.

4 Place your mouse on top of the left ruler.

5 Click and drag to create a vertical guide.

6 Place your mouse on the top ruler.

7 Click and drag to create a horizontal guide.

● A tooltip appears as you create each guide to indicate its position.

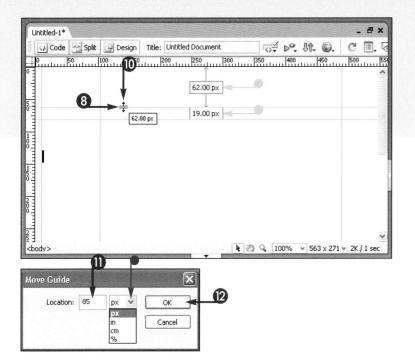

⑧ Place your cursor over a guide until a double arrow (⬍) appears.

⑨ Press the Control (⌘) key.

● The guide's distance from adjacent guides displays.

⑩ Double-click the guide while the double arrow is visible.

The Move Guide dialog box appears.

⑪ Type a value for the guide's location.

● You can set the guide's position in pixels, inches, centimeters, or a percentage of the page size using the drop-down menu.

⑫ Click OK.

The guide moves to its new location.

TIPS

Did You Know?

You can apply a number of additional options to guides using the commands in the View menu. In the Edit Guides window, you can change the color of the guide line, turn the snap option on or off, lock the guides on the page to prevent them from being moved, or clear all of the guides from the page.

Delete It!

To remove guides from the page, simply drag them back to the ruler area. You can also clear all of the guides from the page at one time by choosing that option from the View menu.

HEADINGS:
Apply to Text

You can use headings to create well-structured documents that viewers can more easily read and which search engines can accurately index. Many of today's modern search engines use heading tags to determine the importance of elements in a page.

You apply a heading tag to document text in a variety of ways, the most common being through the Properties inspector. You can also use the Text category of the Insert toolbar, or the Text menu item.

Applying headings in an HTML document is similar to the method for creating an outline. You should format the most important item in a document as Heading 1 and then style subcategories in descending levels of importance throughout the document. HTML allows you to format text as Heading 1 through Heading 6.

When you format text as a heading in HTML, Dreamweaver applies a default size to the text. You may consider using CSS to redefine the heading tags in your documents to give your viewers a more pleasing appearance.

See also>> Properties Inspector: Text

See also>> CSS Styling: Style Heading Appearance

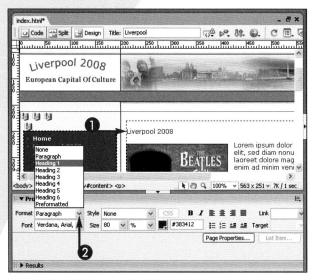

Apply a Heading Format with the Properties Inspector

① Click next to a line of text that you want to format as a heading.

You can also apply formatting to highlighted text.

② Click here and select a heading format that you want to apply.

This example selects Heading 1.

Dreamweaver applies the heading format that you specify to the text.

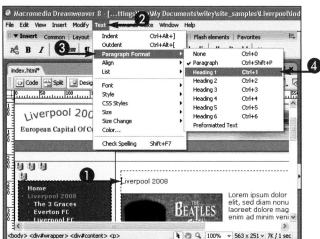

Apply a Heading Format with the Text Menu

① Click next to a line of text that you want to format as a heading.

② Click Text.

③ Click Paragraph Format.

④ Click a heading format that you want to apply.

This example selects Heading 1.

Dreamweaver applies the heading format to the text.

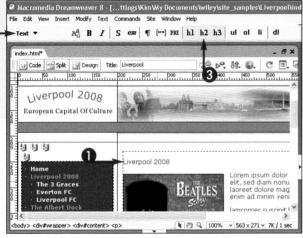

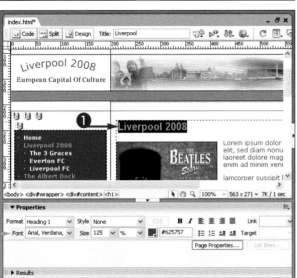

Apply a Heading Format with the Insert Toolbar

1 Click next to a line of text that you want to format as a heading.

2 Click here and select the Text category.

3 Click the heading button (`h1 h2 h3`) that corresponds to the heading format that you want to apply.

The Insert toolbar provides buttons only for Headings 1 to 3.

Dreamweaver applies the heading format to the text.

View Heading Styling Information

1 Select text that has been formatted as a heading.

● The Properties inspector displays CSS styling information for the font, size, and color of the heading text.

Note: It is best to use the CSS Styles panel to edit styling information for headings. Attempting to edit these values in the Properties inspector creates a new styling rule that may conflict with other rules that you have created.

Did You Know?

The use of headings to provide structure to a document is an important element in the movement towards creating pages that use *semantic markup*. A page that is structured *semantically* provides tags that describe the elements of a page in descending order of importance. For example, you format the most important element of the page as Heading 1, the second most important as Heading 2, and so forth.

Did You Know?

By including headings, you provide a structure that allows search engines to more easily determine what the essential elements of the page are and return results that are more relevant to viewers. When you use keywords in headings, you significantly improve the way that search engines index your pages.

HOME PAGE:
Designate for a Web Site

You can use the Site Map feature of Dreamweaver's expanded Files panel to more easily visualize your Web site's structure. In order to do this, you must designate a document as the top-level page in the site, or as a home page.

In most cases, the home page for a site uses the name *index* followed by the file extension. For example, you use index.htm for a static Web site, while you use index.cfm for a dynamic site that uses ColdFusion as its programming language. Dreamweaver automatically finds the page named

"index" in the site root folder and designates it as the site's home page.

If your site uses some other filename for the home page, such as default.htm, then you must manually select it as the home page before a site map can be built for the site. You can do this through the Site Definition dialog box for the site.

See also>> **Properties Inspector: Text**

See also>> **CSS Styling: Style Heading Appearance**

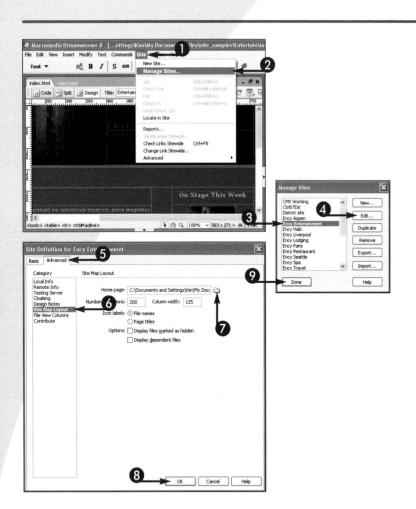

① Click Site.

② Click Manage Sites.

The Manage Sites dialog box appears.

③ Click the name of the site that you want to edit.

④ Click Edit.

The Site Definition dialog box appears.

⑤ Click the Advanced tab.

⑥ Click Site Map Layout.

⑦ Click the Folder icon (🗁) to locate the file that you want to designate as your site home page.

⑧ Click OK.

⑨ In the Manage Sites dialog box, click Done to complete the process.

HORIZONTAL RULES:
Insert and Style

You can separate objects on a Web page by inserting a horizontal rule. The horizontal rule contains default styling characteristics that you can modify to change its appearance.

When you insert a horizontal rule, it displays at two pixels in height and fills 100 percent of the width of the containing element. For example, if you insert a rule inside a table cell, it stretches from side to side in the table cell.

You can style the horizontal rule to change its height, to set a width as a percentage of the

containing tag, or to set a width based on a pixel dimension. You can also set an alignment value on the rule, aligning it to the default value of left, right, or center. You can choose whether the rule should appear with shading. In addition to these HTML attributes, horizontal rules can display in a color other than the default gray when you redefine the tag using CSS.

See also>>   **Insert Toolbar: HTML**

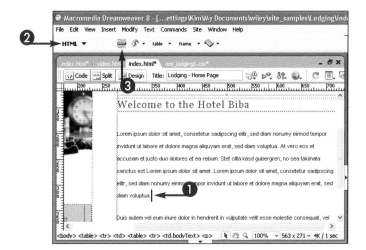

Inserting a Horizontal Rule

1. Place your cursor at the point in your document where you want the horizontal rule to appear.

2. Click here and select the HTML category.

3. Click the Insert Horizontal Rule button (▦).

   Dreamweaver inserts a horizontal rule into your document.

Editing a Horizontal Rule

1. Click the horizontal rule.

2. Type the width of the horizontal rule, and click to select a pixel or percentage value.

3. Type the height of the horizontal rule.

4. Click here and select the alignment of the horizontal rule.

5. Click to enable (☐ changes to ☑) or disable (☑ changes to ☐) shading for the horizontal rule.

   Dreamweaver applies your changes to the horizontal rule.

HOTSPOTS:
Create Interactive Images

You can make an image interactive by placing hotspots on top of the image and adding links to the hotspots. Thus, you can take a large image and include several interactive areas, which viewers can click to go to a new page or open a document.

You create hotspots by adding an image-map tag to the image that you define by its coordinates. You can create hotspots in rectangular, circular, or irregular shapes with the tools in the Properties inspector and Insert toolbar. Once drawn on the image, you can make the hotspot interactive by adding link information.

You can apply multiple hotspots to a single image; however, you should provide a unique name for each hotspot area. Hotspots also require an entry for an alternative to maintain accessibility to the image. Persons with disabilities who use alternative means of browsing your page are not able to navigate without a text description of the link.

See also>> **Insert Toolbar: Common**

Properties Inspector: Images

See also>> **Images: Insert in Documents**

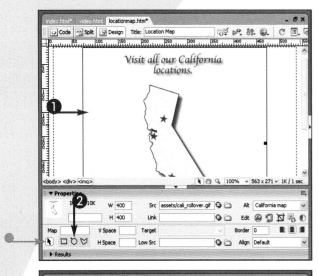

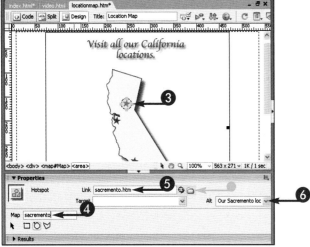

Inserting a Hotspot with the Properties Inspector

1 Click an image in your document.

2 Click to select the hotspot shape that you want to draw.

● You can click the arrow ([▶]) to return to Standard Selection mode.

3 Click and drag to draw a circular or rectangular hotspot; you can click and release to define the first point in a polygon hotspot, continuing until you complete the shape.

4 Type a unique name for the hotspot.

5 Type the link to open when a user clicks the hotspot.

● You can use these buttons to point to a file ([⊕]) or browse ([▢]) to a file in your site.

6 Type alternate text for the link.

Dreamweaver applies the formatting for the hotspot.

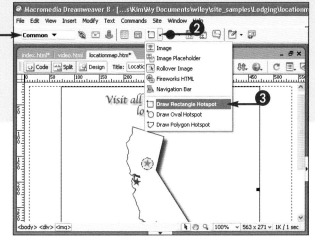

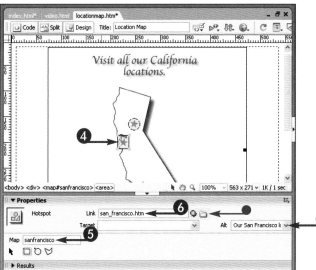

1 Click here and select the Common category.

2 Click the image object drop-down menu.

3 Click the hotspot shape that you want to draw.

4 Click and drag to draw a rectangular or circular hotspot. Click and release to define the first point in a polygon hotspot, continuing until the shape is complete.

5 Type a unique name for the hotspot.

6 Type the link that should open when a user clicks the hotspot.

● You can use these buttons to point to a file (⊕) or browse (📁) to a file in your site.

7 Type alternate text for the link.

Dreamweaver applies the formatting for the hotspot.

Did You Know?

You can use hotspot links in the same way that you use any link in a document. For example, you can apply a target in the Properties inspector to have the link open in a new window if you set the value to _blank. You can also use hotspots as page anchors, and to apply behaviors such as the Open Browser Window behavior by making the link value javascript; and then using the Behaviors panel to add the behavior.

Did You Know?

Hotspots are particularly useful when you have a large image that you want to make interactive. This may include a banner image at the top of the page, or a location map that provides viewers with links from a graphic that shows multiple locations for a company.

IMAGE PLACEHOLDERS:
Using for Page Layouts

You can insert an image placeholder into a page and use it for layout purposes during the initial design phase to simulate the size, placement, and position of an image. You can then work on prototype designs using different potential image sizes. Once your design is set, you can replace the image placeholder with the actual image.

Image placeholders are not actually images, but blocks of code that show an image's location on the page. When you insert the placeholder image, Dreamweaver displays a dialog box where you can set the size, name, and background color of the

image. If you preview the page in a browser, only the size and background color of the placeholder image display.

You can insert as many image placeholders as you need to create a prototype of your site. If you also have Fireworks installed, you can launch it through the Properties inspector and have it automatically set the canvas size to match the dimensions of the placeholder image.

See also>> | **Insert Toolbar: Common**

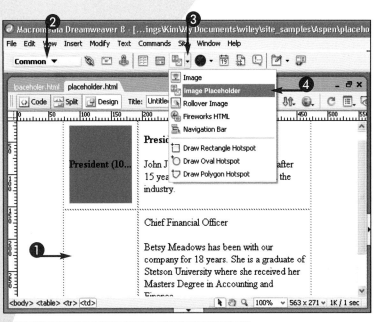

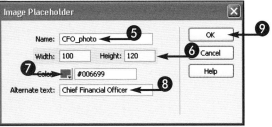

Insert an Image Placeholder

① Click in the page where you want to insert the image placeholder.

② Click here and select Common.

③ Click the Images button (🖬) arrow.

④ Click Image Placeholder.

The Image Placeholder dialog box appears.

⑤ Type a name for the placeholder.

Names cannot contain spaces.

⑥ Type the width and height of the placeholder.

⑦ Click the Color box (🖬) to select a color.

⑧ Type alternate text for the image.

⑨ Click OK.

Dreamweaver inserts the image placeholder in the page.

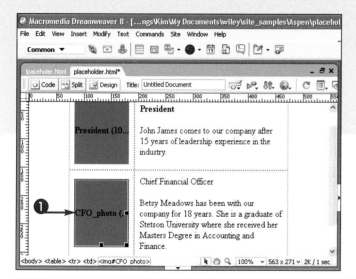

① Double-click the image placeholder.

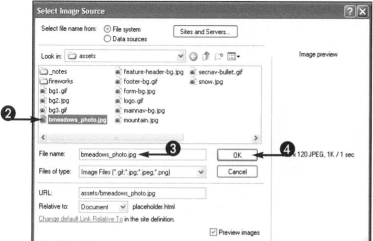

The Select Image Source dialog box appears.

② Browse to the file that you want to replace the placeholder image.

③ Select the file.

④ Click OK.

Dreamweaver replaces the image placeholder with the selected image.

TIPS

Caution!

When you replace an image placeholder, you should insert an image with the same dimensions as the placeholder. Because the image width and height are already established in your code, the replacement displays at those dimensions rather than the size of the image that you are inserting. If the width and height values are not the same, your new image may not display properly.

More Options!

If you do not have a replacement image prepared, you can launch Fireworks to create and insert a new image. Click Create in the Properties inspector to open Fireworks, where you can prepare your image and automatically insert it into the page.

IMAGES:
Edit with Dreamweaver

You can use the image-editing features built into Dreamweaver to modify images in your documents. Dreamweaver allows you to crop, resample, sharpen, and adjust the brightness and contrast of your images.

When you select an image in the Document Window, the Properties inspector displays properties and editing options for the image. Included in the Properties inspector are four buttons that allow you to perform basic editing operations to the selected image.

All of the editing operations that you perform in Dreamweaver permanently alter the image. While you can undo any steps that you make to edit an

image in this manner, once you close Dreamweaver, the edited image permanently changes.

To change the size of an image, you can crop the graphic to remove unwanted areas. You can also resize an image and then use the Resample button to adjust the image to match the new dimensions.

See also>>

Properties Inspector:
Images

See also>>

Fireworks: Edit Images

Fireworks:
Optimize Images

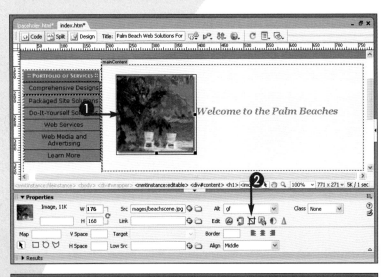

Crop Images

❶ Click an image.

❷ Click Crop (⬚).

A bounding box appears on the image.

❸ Drag the crop handles around the perimeter to change the size of the bounding box.

❹ Click and drag the four-headed arrow cursor (✛) to move the bounding box.

❺ Double-click inside the bounding box to accept the crop boundaries.

Dreamweaver removes the areas of the image outside of the bounding box.

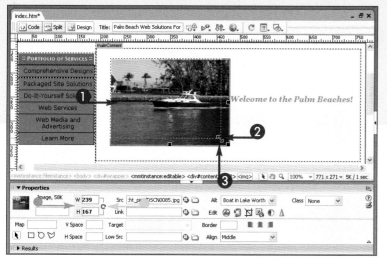

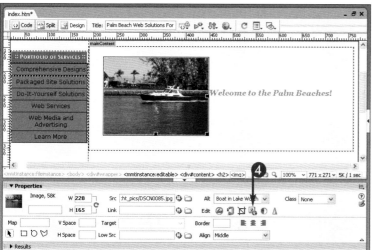

1. Click an image.

● The dimensions of the image display in the Properties inspector.

● You can click the Reset Size button (🔄) to return the image to its original size.

2. Click and drag the resize handles to change the image dimensions.

3. Release the mouse button when the image is at the dimensions that you want.

4. Click the Resample button (🖼).

Dreamweaver maintains the original appearance of the image by subtracting or adding pixels.

Did You Know?

When you resize an image with the resize handles, you are not changing the actual size of the image, but providing the browser with new dimensions at which it should be displayed. For example, if you insert a picture that is 300x300 pixels but resize it to 150x150 pixels, then the image that is downloaded is still 300x300 pixels. To improve download times for a resized image, always run the Resample command after you have reduced its physical size. Resampling also improves the quality of resized images, sometimes dramatically.

More Info!

You can maintain the proportions of the image when you hold down the Shift key while dragging the resize handle at the corner of the image.

IMAGES:
Edit with Dreamweaver (Continued)

In addition to resizing and cropping images, you can use the image-editing features in Dreamweaver to sharpen images and adjust their brightness and contrast.

When you adjust the brightness and contrast of an image, the picture elements, or *pixels*, that make up the image have their basic properties altered. When you adjust the contrast of an image, certain pixels are made brighter while others remain the same. This changes the highlights and shadows in the image.

When you adjust the brightness, all of the pixels in the image are altered at once. This is typically done to correct images that are too dark or too light.

Sharpening an image involves changing the pixels that are adjacent to each other to make the difference in colors and brightness more pronounced. Sharpening an image allows you to improve the appearance of details that may appear muddy or out of focus.

See also>> **Properties Inspector: Images**

See also>> **Fireworks: Edit Images**

Fireworks: Optimize Images

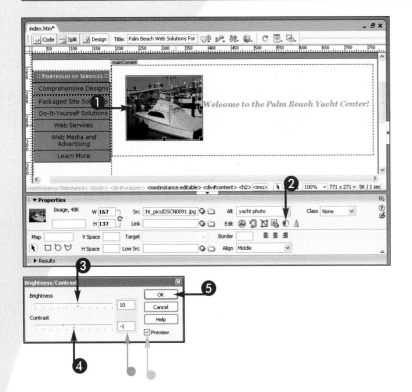

Adjust Brightness and Contrast

1 Click an image.

2 Click Brightness and Contrast (⬤).

3 In the Brightness/Contrast dialog box, drag the slider to increase values and make the image brighter, or decrease values to make it darker.

4 Drag the slider to increase values to increase image contrast, or to decrease values and the image contrast between pixels.

● You can type values in the text boxes instead of using the sliders.

● You can click the Preview option (☐ changes to ☑) to see your changes take place in the Design Window.

5 Click OK.

Dreamweaver applies the brightness and contrast settings to the image.

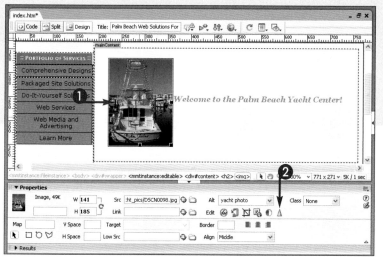

Adjust Sharpness

1 Click an image.

2 Click Sharpen (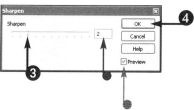).

The Sharpen dialog box appears.

3 Drag the slider to increase the sharpness of the image.

● You can type a sharpness value inside the text box instead of using the slider.

● You can click the Preview option (☐ changes to ☑) to see your changes take place in the Design Window.

4 Click OK.

Dreamweaver sharpens the image.

Caution!

Remember that modifying the sharpness, contrast, and brightness of an image in Dreamweaver permanently alters the image on the page. If you edit an original photograph, then you cannot undo the changes at a later date. Although the editing features in Dreamweaver are useful for making small edits to images, it is best to use an image editor such as Fireworks or Adobe Photoshop to modify a copy of the source image rather than the original.

More Info!

When you resize an image, it may sometimes appear blurry and slightly out of focus. Making small adjustments to the sharpness and contrast of a resized image often improves the appearance of the image.

IMAGES:
Insert in Documents

You can insert images in your Web pages using either the Insert toolbar or the Assets panel. Unlike a graphics or desktop publishing program, the image does not become part of the page. Instead, Dreamweaver inserts a block of code detailing the name, location, and size of the image, as well as information such as alternate text. The image and the Web page remain two separate documents. You must have both the Web page and any image files referenced in the page in a browser to display the page on the Web server.

Dreamweaver inserts the necessary code referencing the image file, and displays the image in the Design Window. You can use the Properties inspector to view and edit the properties of the image file's code and add other code such as a link or a hotspot.

See also>> Assets Panel: Organize and Manage Site Assets

Insert Toolbar: Common

Properties Inspector: Images

See also>> Images: Edit with Dreamweaver

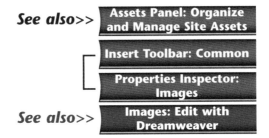

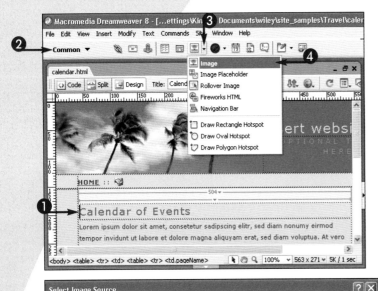

Insert Images with the Insert Toolbar

① Click in the page where you want to place the image.

② Click here and select Common.

③ Click the Image (🖭) arrow.

④ Click Image.

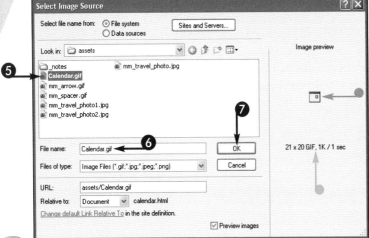

⑤ In the Select Image Source dialog box, browse to the image.

⑥ Select the image.

● A preview of the image appears.

● Dreamweaver displays the image dimensions, file size, and estimated download time.

⑦ Click OK.

Note: If you have the image accessibility prompt enabled in Preferences, then a dialog box for alternate text appears after you click OK.

The image appears in the Document Window.

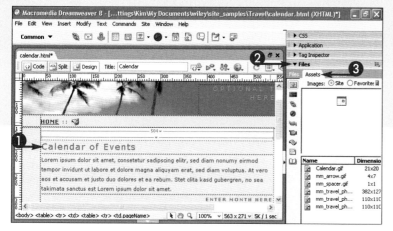

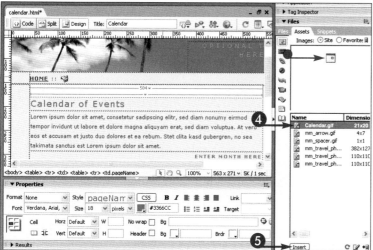

Insert Images with the Assets Panel

1 Click in the page where you want to insert the image.

2 Open the Files panel.

3 Click the Assets tab.

4 Click the image name.

● A preview of the image appears in the Preview pane.

5 Click Insert.

Dreamweaver inserts the image.

Note: If you have the image accessibility prompt enabled in Preferences, then a dialog box for alternate text appears after you click Insert.

Did You Know?

Images that you intend to display in a Web page must be in either the GIF or JPG file format. GIF files are useful for images that have a limited number of colors and are graphical in nature, such as buttons and logos. The JPG format is useful for images such as photographs where many different colors and shades are needed in order to display properly.

Did You Know?

Another format known as PNG is currently gaining favor among Web and graphic designers due to its superior ability to display images while maintaining small file sizes. However, because Internet Explorer does not support PNG files, you should be careful when using them.

IMAGES:
Set Spacing and Borders

You can insert vertical and horizontal spacing around an image to provide additional impact and to set it off from surrounding page elements as well as to add a border around it. Adding spacing or borders to an image does not modify the image itself, but rather adds new attributes to the code that references the image.

You enter spacing values in pixel dimensions for vertical and horizontal spacing. Any adjacent objects in the page are moved away from the image based on the values that you supply. This can be an effective way to force text away from an image so that it stands out and the text is more readable.

The value, in pixels, that you enter in the Properties inspector determines the image border's thickness. Borders you apply to images use the same color as the font color in the element that contains the image.

See also>> Properties Inspector: Images

See also>> Align Images: To Text with HTML

Images: Insert in Documents

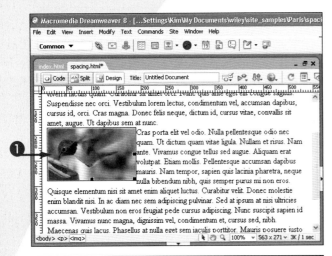

Set Spacing Properties

1 Click an image.

2 Type a value for vertical spacing, and press Enter.

3 Type a value for horizontal spacing, and press Enter.

● Dreamweaver applies vertical spacing to the top and bottom of the image.

● Dreamweaver applies horizontal spacing to the left and right of the image.

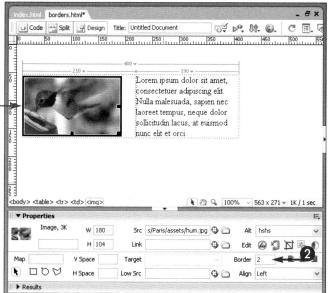

Set Border Properties

1 Click an image.

2 Type a value for the width of the border.

3 Press Enter.

● Dreamweaver sets a border around the image using the same color as the text in the containing element.

TIPS

More Info!

When you apply spacing and borders to images using the Properties inspector, you are adding new attributes to the image tag. This method is effective when you only need to add spacing or borders occasionally. If you intend to add spacing or borders regularly, then you should consider creating a custom CSS class that does the same thing. This allows you to add borders and spacing more quickly and consistently to all of the images in your site.

Remove It!

If you want to remove borders or spacing from an image, simply select the image and delete the values from the Properties inspector. When no values are in these areas, the spacing and border attributes are removed from the tag.

IMPORT OFFICE DOCUMENTS:
Insert Word and Excel Documents into a Page

You can import Microsoft Word and Excel documents directly into a Web page in the Windows version of Dreamweaver. This feature is not available in the Macintosh version of Dreamweaver or for Microsoft Office 97 or older.

When you import an Office document, Dreamweaver reads the contents of the file and applies the formatting options that you select. You can import the document as unformatted text, text that maintains the paragraph structure of the original, text that maintains the applied structure and the basic styles, or text with full structure and styling to match the source document. By default, Dreamweaver cleans up the HTML that Word and Excel generates to eliminate extraneous tags.

Dreamweaver does not permit you to import documents larger than 300KB. When you have a larger document to insert into a Web page, you can copy the text and insert it using the Paste Special command for Word, or using the Import Tabular Data command for Excel.

See also>>   **Clean Up Word HTML**

**Preferences:
Copy and Paste**

See also>>   **Import Tabular Data**

Import Word Documents

1. Click in the page where you want to insert the document.

2. Click File.

3. Click Import.

4. Click Word Document.

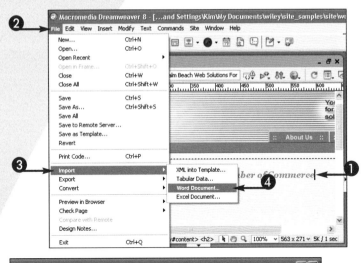

The Import Word Document dialog box appears.

5. Browse to the file that you want to import.

6. Select the file.

7. Click here and select the formatting options that you want.

8. Click Open.

Dreamweaver inserts the contents of the Word document into the page based on the formatting options that you chose.

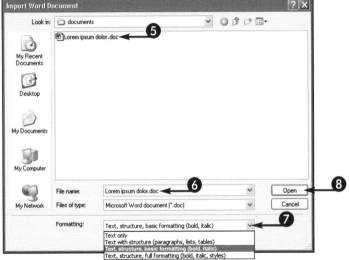

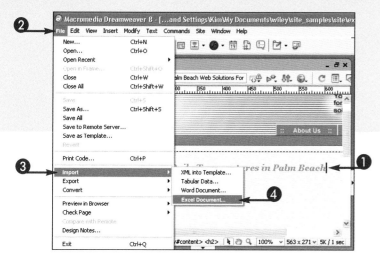

Import Excel Documents

1 Click in the page where you want to insert the document.

2 Click File.

3 Click Import.

4 Click Excel Document.

The Import Excel Document dialog box appears.

5 Browse to the file that you want to import.

6 Select the file.

7 Click here and select the formatting options that you want.

8 Click Open.

Dreamweaver inserts the contents of the Excel document into the page based on the formatting options that you chose.

Cross Platform!

Macintosh users cannot import Office documents directly into a page in Dreamweaver. To import text from Word, you can select and copy the text, and then use the Paste Special command to bring in the text with formatting intact. To import data from Excel, Macintosh users should either copy the data cells and use the Paste Special command or save the Excel sheet as a delimited text file and use the Import Tabular Data command.

More Options!

You can drag a Word or Excel document directly from the Files panel and drop it on the page in the Windows version of Dreamweaver. When you use this method, the Import dialog box for the appropriate file type appears, and you can enter your formatting preferences.

IMPORT TABULAR DATA:
Insert Delimited Files

You can import data, previously saved in a delimited format, directly into a Web page. Dreamweaver creates a table, applies the settings that you specify in a dialog box, and then imports the values in the file. This feature imports data that is stored in a spreadsheet or database program such as Microsoft Excel or Appleworks, and saved as delimited text.

Delimited files use a character to separate the different fields in the file. These characters, known as *delimiters*, allow plain-text files to be shared between programs. Although the most common character to use for delimited files is the tab character, Dreamweaver

can also read files that use commas, semicolons, colons, and even special characters as delimiters.

When you import tabular data, you set the delimiter type to match the one in your text file. Dreamweaver reads the contents of the text file and creates columns for each character set based on the existence of the text delimiters.

See also>>

Preferences:
Copy and Paste

Import Office
Documents

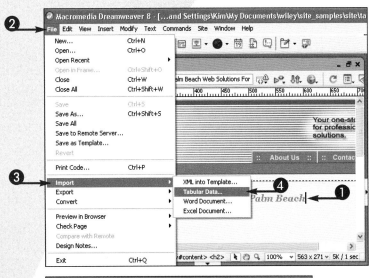

1 Click in the document where you want to insert the data.

2 Click File.

3 Click Import.

4 Click Tabular Data.

The Import Tabular Data dialog box appears.

5 Click Browse.

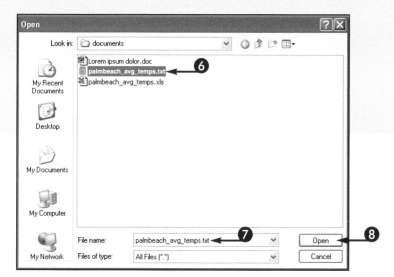

The Open dialog box appears.

6 Browse to the file that you want to import.

7 Select the file.

8 Click Open.

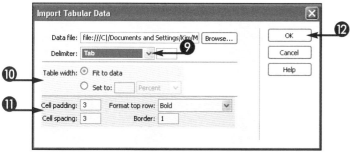

9 In the Import Tabular Data dialog box, click here and select the delimiter that matches the file.

10 Click the width options (○ changes to ◉) for the table that Dreamweaver creates.

11 Type more formatting options if you want.

12 Click OK.

Dreamweaver inserts the data into a new table in your document.

More Options!

In addition to importing tabular data into a document, you can also export data. When you select a table containing structured data in rows and columns, you can use the Export Table command to send the data to a delimited file. This allows you to save your data into a format that is readable by a spreadsheet or database program such as Microsoft Excel and Microsoft Access.

Change It!

If you do not provide values for the border properties of the new table, then it is likely that the table will use the default value of one. If you want to display the table without a border, set the border value to zero.

JAVASCRIPT:
Insert and Edit

You can add more functions, such as scrolling text messages and interactive objects, to your documents by inserting JavaScript into the page or by linking to a JavaScript file.

You use JavaScript to add interactivity and other functions to Web pages. You can find many free JavaScript resources to add functions that are not included in the Dreamweaver behaviors tool set. Although you can copy and paste JavaScript directly into your document in Code view, Dreamweaver also allows you to do this in Design view.

If you create your own JavaScript functions or want to use a script that you download from the Web, you must insert the JavaScript into your page manually. In Design view, you can use the Script dialog box to paste a copied script in place or to link to an external JavaScript file.

See also>> **Behaviors Panel**

See also>> **Behaviors: Apply to Web Page Events**

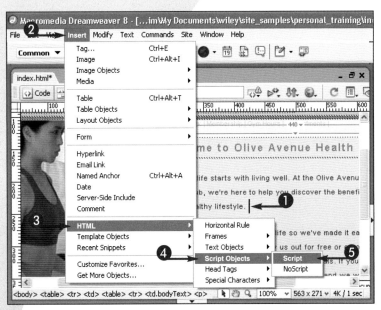

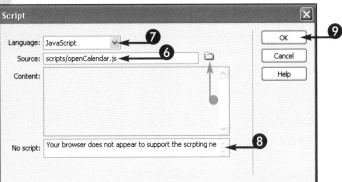

Link to an External JavaScript File

1 Click in the page where you want to add a script.

2 Click Insert.

3 Click HTML.

4 Click Script Objects.

5 Click Script.

6 In the Script dialog box, type the address of the external JavaScript file.

● You can click the Folder button () to locate the JavaScript file.

7 Click here to select the desired type of script; if you do not know what to select, select the generic JavaScript option.

8 Type a script or text that viewers see when they have JavaScript disabled in their browser.

9 Click OK.

Dreamweaver creates a link to the file that performs the requested function.

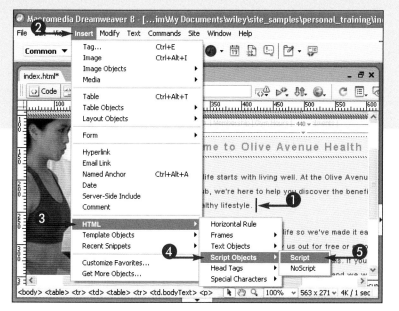

Paste JavaScript into a Page

① Click in the page where you want to add a script.

② Click Insert.

③ Click HTML.

④ Click Script Objects.

⑤ Click Script.

The Script dialog box appears.

⑥ Click inside the Content text box.

⑦ Press Ctrl+V (⌘+V) to paste in JavaScript that you have copied to the Clipboard.

⑧ Click OK.

Dreamweaver adds the script to the page.

More Options!

In addition to using the Menu bar to display the Insert Script dialog box, you can also insert scripts from the Insert toolbar. Switch to the HTML category in the Insert toolbar, and then click the Script button (⬙) to display the dialog box.

More Info!

Many JavaScript functions require that you insert part of the script into the head of the document and additional script into the body. Be sure to read the instructions that are included with the script to ensure that you insert the script blocks in the proper location.

J

JUMP MENUS:
Insert and Edit

You can create menus — called jump menus — in your pages so that users can go to pages within your site or elsewhere on the Web. Jump menus are useful when you have a numerous links to display, but cannot devote too much design space to them. Multiple jump menus, labeled with a description of the link, help viewers find which item to select on the drop-down menu. You can also simply include all your navigation elements in a single jump menu. You can also use jump menus with anchors on the page to allow the viewer to move within a long document.

There is no limit to the number of links that a jump menu form can contain. Dreamweaver provides a dialog box where you can add the jump menu items, label the links, and insert the address of the page or the name of the anchor to which the link will jump.

See also>> **Insert Toolbar: Forms**

See also>> **Forms: Create Accessible Forms**

Forms: Insert List and Menu Items

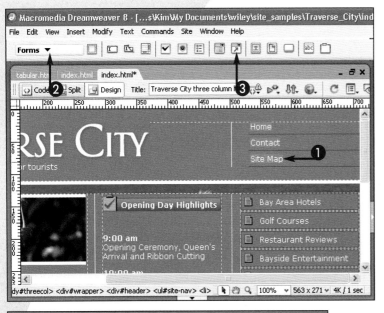

Insert a Jump Menu

① Click in the page where you want to insert the menu.

② Click here and select Forms.

③ Click Jump Menu (▣).

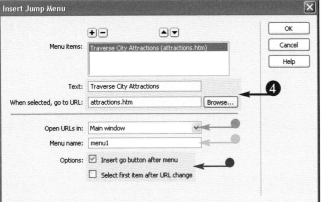

④ In the Insert Jump Menu dialog box, type a name for the first link and the URL where the link should take the viewer, or click Browse to locate the file.

● You can click here and select the window where the link appears if you designed the page with frames.

● You can type a name for the form or accept the default.

● You can select these option (☐ changes to ☑) if you want a button provided for the viewer to click or if you want the menu to go back to the first item in the list after users select a menu item.

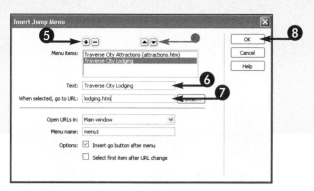

5 Click the Add (⊞) or Delete (⊟) button to add a new menu item or to remove an existing menu item.

● You can use the Up (▲) or Down (▼) arrow to change the order of the menu items.

6 Type the text for the second item.

7 Type the address for the second item.

You can repeat steps **6** to **8** until you have added all of the menu items and addresses.

8 Click OK.

Dreamweaver inserts the jump menu into the page.

Edit a Jump Menu

1 Click the jump menu.

2 Click the item that you want to appear first in the menu list.

3 Click List Values to display a dialog box where you can modify, arrange, add, or delete labels and addresses.

Changes made in the Properties inspector are applied immediately to the jump menu.

More Info!

If you do not include a Go button with your jump menu, the viewer of the page goes to the address that they select as soon as they click it. While some people appreciate the lack of an extra click, less experienced users may find the lack of a button confusing. As always, you should consider your target audience when designing navigation features.

Customize It!

You can use jump menus for e-mail links if you have a long list of contacts that you want to provide. To create an e-mail link, type the name of the individual in the Text field, and then add their e-mail address preceded by **mailto:**, for example, mailto:email@yoursite.com.

J

KEYBOARD SHORTCUT SETS:
Create and Modify

You can use the standard keyboard shortcut set that is included with Dreamweaver to perform common program operations such as copying and pasting, as well as those that are specific to Dreamweaver, such as previewing a page in a Web browser. You can also customize the keyboard shortcut set to create your own shortcut keys.

To create a custom keyboard shortcut set, you must first start by duplicating the standard set. When you duplicate the standard keyboard shortcuts, you can provide the new set with a unique name and save

the configuration file that stores information about your custom set.

Once you have duplicated the keyboard shortcut set, you can add, change, or remove keyboard shortcuts from your custom file. Dreamweaver displays a dialog box where you can access the same commands found in the various menu commands. Dreamweaver displays the current keyboard shortcuts that are assigned for menu commands and allows you to assign new shortcuts or to modify the existing key commands.

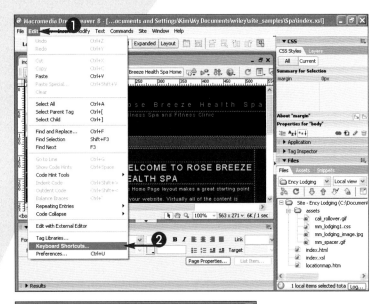

1 Click Edit.

2 Click Keyboard Shortcuts.

The Keyboard Shortcuts dialog box appears.

3 Click here and select a keyboard shortcut set to duplicate.

4 Click the Duplicate button (▣).

K

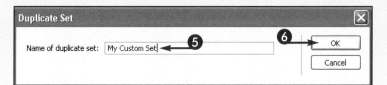

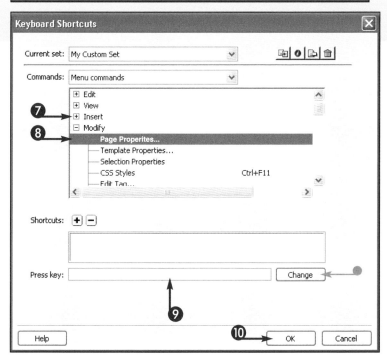

The Duplicate Set dialog box appears.

⑤ Type a name for your custom set.

⑥ Click OK.

The Duplicate Set dialog box closes.

⑦ Click the plus sign (⊞) to expand any menu listing.

⑧ Click the command to use as a keyboard shortcut.

⑨ Click here and press Ctrl plus at least one additional modifier.

If the shortcut is already assigned, a warning appears at the bottom of the dialog box.

● To change an existing keyboard shortcut, follow step **9**, but click Change.

⑩ Click OK.

Dreamweaver adds the new shortcut to your custom keyboard shortcut set.

More Options!
Dreamweaver installs with several keyboard shortcut sets to accommodate all sorts of users. You can switch from the default Macromedia Standard set to Dreamweaver MX 2004, to BBEdit, or to the Homesite set using the Keyboard Shortcut Editor. If you are used to working with these specific programs, then switching from the standard set to one that matches your particular workflow and habits may make you more efficient in Dreamweaver.

Did You Know?
Macromedia maintains a library of all of the keyboard sets they use in Dreamweaver. You can find the library on the Macromedia Web site at www.macromedia.com/support/documentation/en/dreamweaver. The site also offers Dreamweaver documentation, downloadable product manuals, and tutorials.

LANGUAGES:
Set Document Encoding

You can specify the language in which a page displays by setting the document encoding value. Doing so allows you to set the fonts to match the kind of language in which you are writing. For example, you can set the encoding of a page to display characters in Western European, Cyrillic, Japanese, Chinese, and other fonts. Dreamweaver lists a total of 32 different document encodings from which you can choose.

Dreamweaver allows you to set the default document encoding for all new pages that you create in the

Preferences panel. If you want to change document encoding to a new language after you create a page, then you can do so in the Page Properties dialog box. When you have modified the document encoding, you must also specify the fonts that display in the Fonts category of the Preferences panel.

See also>>  **Preferences: New Document**

See also>> **Fonts**

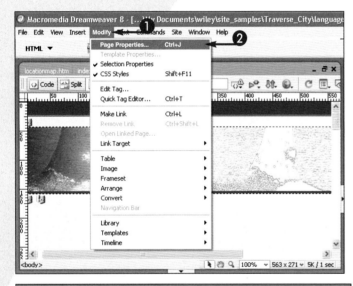

1 Click Modify.

2 Click Page Properties.

The Page Properties dialog box appears.

3 Click the Title/Encoding category.

4 Click here and select the document encoding that you want.

5 Click Reload.

6 Click OK.

Dreamweaver changes the document encoding language for the page.

To begin typing in the new language, you must set the font preferences to match the chosen language.

LAYOUT BLOCK:
Inserting DIV Tags for Layouts

You can create a relatively positioned container for your content in a page by inserting a layout block. A layout block is a DIV tag combined with CSS properties that define its location on the page. When you create layout blocks with relative positioning, you have greater freedom in your design to position elements based on their relationship to other DIV tags in the design.

You can set a number of properties for a DIV tag when you insert it into the page. You can insert the new DIV tag at the current cursor position, or place it inside other tags on the page. When you select the Before, Before End of, After, or After Start of Tag options, you must select the tag that appears to the right of the Insert menu. You can

also apply a CSS class to the new DIV tag and set an ID property for the tag when you insert it.

When you close the Insert Div Tag dialog box, Dreamweaver displays the new layout block in your document with placeholder text that indicates the name of the tag.

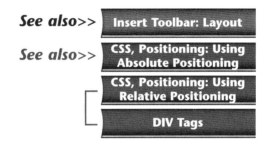

See also>> Insert Toolbar: Layout

See also>> CSS, Positioning: Using Absolute Positioning

CSS, Positioning: Using Relative Positioning

DIV Tags

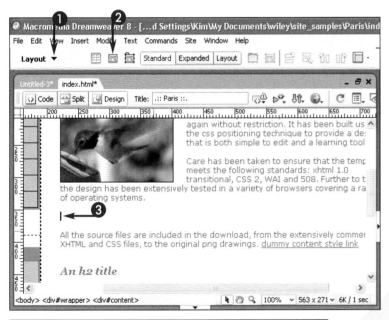

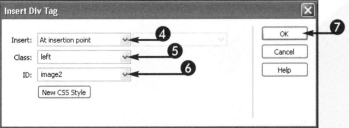

① Click here and select Layout.

You can click the Layout tab if you have changed the Insert toolbar to the tabbed view.

② Click the Insert Div Tag button (▣).

③ Click inside the document.

The Insert Div Tag dialog box appears.

④ Click here and select where to insert the key.

⑤ Click here and select a CSS class.

⑥ Type a unique ID for the new DIV tag.

⑦ Click OK.

Dreamweaver inserts a new DIV tag as a layout block in your document.

LAYOUT TABLES:
Design Page Layouts

You can draw a page layout in a document using layout tables and cells. With this feature of Dreamweaver, you draw all the various areas in your page before you insert the page content. For example, you can create a page with a header for a graphic, an area on the left for navigation, and a larger block on the right for the main content of the page.

While in Layout mode, you can insert most objects, with the exception of additional tables. You must also drag your cursor on the screen to draw new tables and cells.

You can create simple or complex layouts, and set the table's size to a pixel dimension, or set it to stretch automatically. When you set a layout table to autostretch, Dreamweaver prompts you to save a spacer image to maintain the integrity of the table.

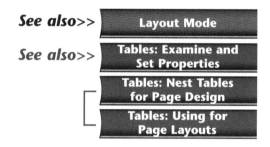

See also>> Layout Mode

See also>> Tables: Examine and Set Properties

Tables: Nest Tables for Page Design

Tables: Using for Page Layouts

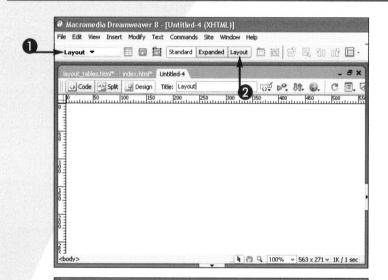

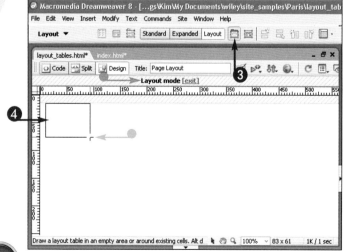

① Click here and select Layout.

You can click the Layout tab if you have changed the Insert toolbar to the tabbed view.

② Click Layout.

Dreamweaver switches to Layout mode.

● Dreamweaver displays a blue bar to indicate that you are in Layout mode and you can click the exit link to return to Standard mode.

③ Click the Layout Table button (▣).

● A crosshair cursor (+) appears to indicate where the new table will be located.

④ Click and drag to draw the layout table.

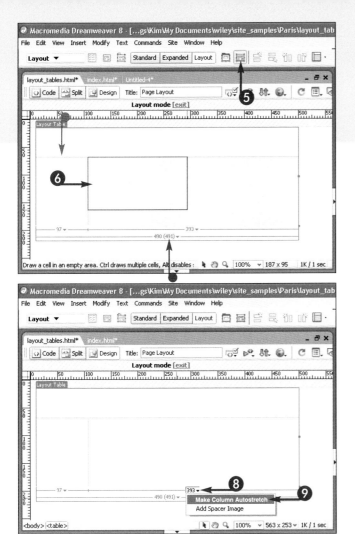

- Layout tables are outlined in green with a drop-down menu located at the center of the table.

5 Click the Layout Cell button (▤).

6 Click and drag inside the layout table to define your layout cell.

- Layout cells are outlined in blue.

7 Continue drawing layout cells until you complete your layout.

8 Click the table ▾.

9 Click Make Column Autostretch to change the width of a column to Autostretch.

Dreamweaver applies the properties for the layout table as you draw elements.

Important!
Layout tables and layout cells offer a quick and easy way to create the separate containers in a page for your content. However, they are not without their problems, especially when you need to add new cells, move or combine items, or change the basic structure of your document. Because these design devices are so easy to use, they can make it too easy to design sloppy pages and can lead to poor design practices. Also, because they use tables for page structure, they do not conform to the recommendations for modern Web page design as defined by the World Wide Web Consortium.

Remove It!
To return to Standard layout mode, you can click the exit link at the top of the page or click the Standard button in the Insert toolbar.

LIBRARY ITEMS:
Create and Insert

You can use Library items to automate the insertion and updating of assets within a site. You can create Library items from images, Flash movies, text, links, or any items that you normally insert into a page. This automatic updating feature is the main reason people use Library items in their designs.

When you insert a Library, Dreamweaver wraps the tag with special comments that allow the object to automatically update when you change the Library item. For example, if you create a Library item for a copyright, you can change the copyright when the year changes and have all of your pages updated at once.

When you create a Library item, Dreamweaver creates a new file in a special folder in your site named Library. This folder contains all of your Library items for each defined site. To edit a Library item, you can either open the file from the Library folder or use the options in the Assets panel.

See also>> **Library Items**

See also>> **Library Items: Edit and Update**

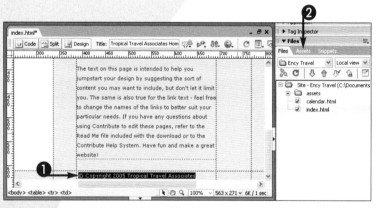

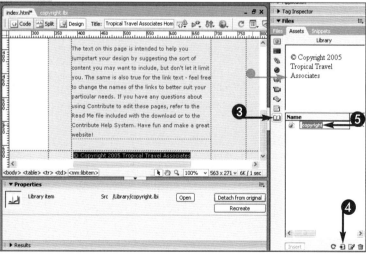

Create a Library Item

① Highlight text or select an item that you want to convert to a Library item.

② Click the Assets tab in the Files panel.

The assets display for the current site.

③ Click the Library category (📖) in the Assets panel.

④ Click the New Library Item button (🔲).

⑤ Type a name for the Library item.

● A preview of the Library item appears in the upper part of the Assets panel.

Dreamweaver stores the new Library item in the Library folder of the current site.

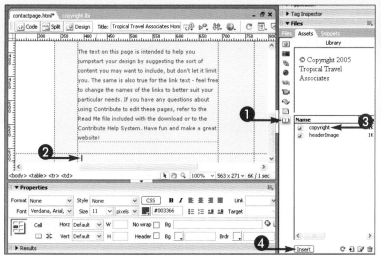

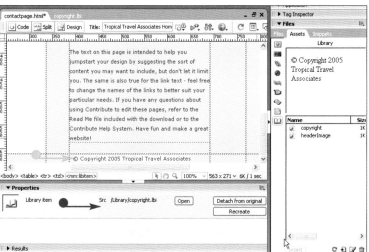

Insert a Library Item

1 Click 📖 in the Assets panel.

2 Place the insertion point where you want to insert the Library item.

3 Click the Library item that you want to insert.

4 Click Insert.

Dreamweaver inserts the Library item into the page.

● Library items are highlighted in yellow.

● The Properties inspector displays information about the Library item.

L

TIPS

Did You Know?
When you create a Library item, the object is actually removed from the page and replaced with a link to the Library folder where a file is created with the name that you provide. By linking to the object, Dreamweaver can update all instances of the Library item when you make a change to the original.

More Info!
Library items are a design-time feature of Dreamweaver and you do not need to upload them to your Web server for them to display correctly. However, if you are collaborating with others on a site, then you can share Library items by uploading them to your server and having your co-workers download them for their use.

LIBRARY ITEMS:
Edit and Update

You can update all Library items in a site, which means you can edit a Library item file and have Dreamweaver apply all of your changes automatically in every page that uses the item.

You edit Library items in the Design Window as you do any file. For example, if you have an image that has alternate text and you want to change the text, you can open the Library item from the Assets panel, and apply your changes. Once you edit the item, you can save the file like any other file.

A number of options are available for updating pages that contain Library items. When you edit a Library item and save the file, Dreamweaver prompts you to update all of the pages that contain the item and asks if you want to update the pages. You can also run an update manually by searching through an entire site, or by designating which files to update.

See also>>  Library Items

See also>> Library Items:
Create and Insert

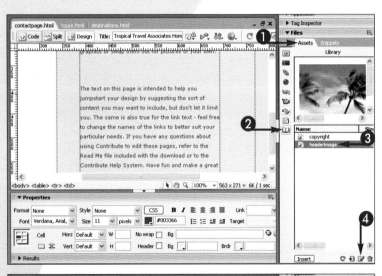

① Click the Assets tab in the Files panel.

② Click the Library category (▥).

③ Click a Library item that you want to edit.

④ Click the Edit button (▨).

The Library item opens in the Design Window.

⑤ Modify the Library item through the Properties inspector.

You can also edit the Library item directly in the Design Window or in Code view.

336

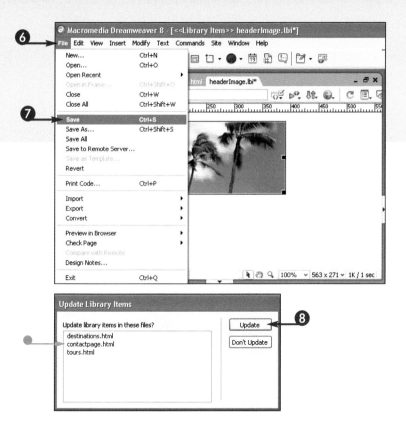

6 Click File.

7 Click Save.

The Update Library Items dialog box appears.

● Dreamweaver displays a list of all of the files it finds that contain the Library item.

8 Click Update.

Dreamweaver displays the Update Pages log with a record of the pages that have been changed.

TIPS

More Info!

You can manually update all of the pages in your site through the options in the Modify menu. When you select Library, you can update the current page or update all of the pages in the site. If you choose the Update Pages option, a dialog box appears allowing you to update the entire site, or to update pages by selecting a particular Library item.

Caution!

When Dreamweaver updates pages containing Library items, it automatically applies the update to the files and saves the changes. An exception to this occurs when files are already open. These files have the updates applied, but you must save them yourself.

LINKS:
Change Sitewide

You can change all of the links to a document inside your site using the Change Link Sitewide command. When you run this command, Dreamweaver compares the file that you have selected and rewrites the path to a different file that you specify.

The Change Links Sitewide command checks each relative link in your site and makes the necessary changes. You can use this command to change links that you have applied to text or images. For example, you may have a link that says "This month's events," with the link set to a file at the location events/september.html, and you need

to change the link to events/october.html. Using this command, you can change all of the links at one time when the month changes.

You can also use this command to change e-mail links. If you need to change an e-mail address, you must enter the entire e-mail link in the following format: mailto:name@websitename.com.

See also>> Link Checker

See also>> Links: Check Sitewide

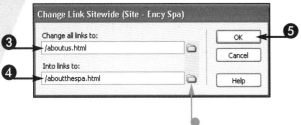

① Click Site.

② Click Change Link Sitewide.

The Change Link Sitewide dialog box appears.

③ Type the link that you want to change.

④ Type the new link value.

● You can click the Browse icon (📁) to browse to the file that you want to change or to the new file.

⑤ Click OK.

Dreamweaver updates all links in the current site to the new link value.

LINKS:
Check Sitewide

You can check links to documents within your site at one time to locate broken files or files that do not have links attached to them. This feature performs routine maintenance on your site and prevents failures in your pages and your links. For example, if you have files to which no other pages link — known as *orphaned* files — you can locate them and determine if you still need them. You can also check links to image files and other objects to ensure that the files are still in the location indicated in the path name. If you move files outside of Dreamweaver through Windows

Explorer or the Macintosh Finder, the path to the files may break and the image or other object may fail to display properly.

Dreamweaver only verifies links to documents within the site. Although Dreamweaver maintains a listing of links to Web addresses outside your site, it does not verify that the links are correct and that the pages exist.

See also>> **Link Checker**

See also>> **Links: Change Sitewide**

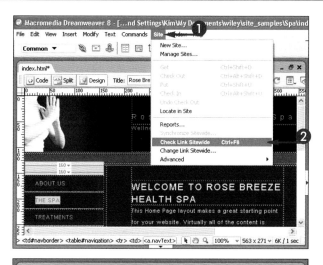

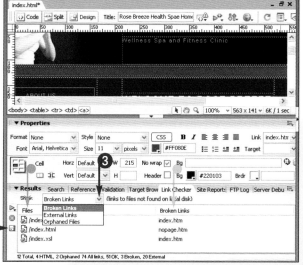

① Click Site.

② Click Check Link Sitewide.

Link reports display in the Results panel.

③ Click here and select the type of file report that you want to see.

● Dreamweaver lists the names of files that have broken or orphaned links.

● Dreamweaver lists the links that are broken or orphaned.

④ Click the Save icon (🖫) to save a text version of the link report.

339

LINK TO A DOCUMENT INSIDE YOUR SITE:
Create Relative Links by Browsing to a File

You can link pages together in your site using the Properties inspector as well as the Files panel. You can create these *relative* links, or links within your own site, in a number of ways. When you create a link in HTML, the object that you are linking uses the <a> tag to create the link, along with an attribute that specifies the path and name of the file. For example, when you link two pages together in the same folder, you need only supply the name of the file to create your link. When you have files located in different folders, you must provide the name of the folder as well as the name of the file.

Dreamweaver automatically writes the correct path and filename when you browse to the file or use the Point-to-File feature in the Properties inspector. This allows you to create your links more quickly and helps you to avoid problems that may occur when you manually type the file information.

See also>> Properties Inspector: Images

Properties Inspector: Text

See also>> Link to a Document Inside Your Site

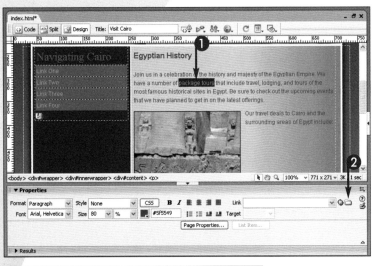

Create a Text Link

① Select the text where you want the link to appear.

② Click the Browse icon (📁).

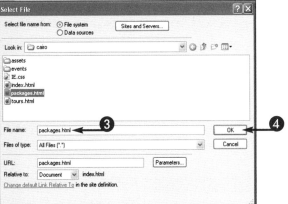

The Select File dialog box appears.

③ Browse to the file that you want to open when a viewer clicks the link.

④ Click OK.

Dreamweaver creates the link in your document.

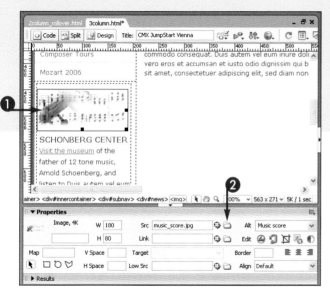

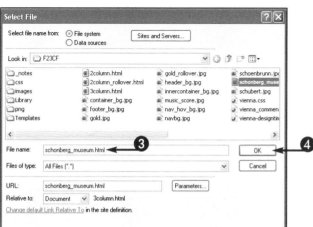

Create an Image Link

1 Select the image where you want to create the link.

2 Click 📁.

The Select File dialog box appears.

3 Browse to the file that you want to open when a viewer clicks the link.

4 Click OK.

Dreamweaver creates the link and makes the image clickable.

Caution!

The bottom of the Select File dialog box contains an option that allows you to set your links relative to a document or to your site. The default setting creates links relative to the document, and you should generally use that option. If you are working in an environment that includes both a testing server and a production server, the site administrator may direct you to make your links relative to the site. Otherwise, unless you receive specific instructions to change your links to site-relative, you should always leave this setting to the document-relative default.

Delete It!

To remove a link in your document, you can simply select the link and remove the path from the Link field in the Properties inspector.

LINK TO A DOCUMENT INSIDE YOUR SITE:
Create Relative Links by Pointing to a File

You can use the Point-to-File feature in Dreamweaver to quickly create a link by dragging from the icon in the Properties inspector to the Files panel. This method for creating links allows you to see exactly which file you are linking to and gives you a graphical way to create a link.

When you use the Point-to-File method of creating a link, Dreamweaver produces a document-relative link that writes the appropriate path to the file. In HTML you must specify not only the name of the file that you are linking to, but also the folder where it is located relative to the location of the page that

contains the link. Because this can be quite confusing, Dreamweaver creates the path for you and ensures that the file is linked correctly.

The Point-to-File icon is located in the Properties inspector next to the Link field.

See also>> Properties Inspector: Images

Properties Inspector: Text

See also>> Link to a Document Inside Your Site

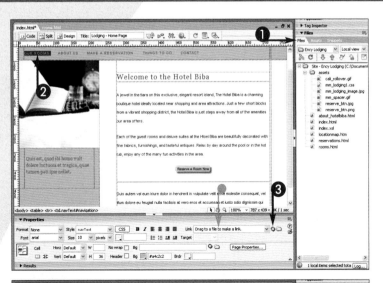

Create a Text Link

① Click the Files tab in the Files panel.

② Select the text where you want the link to appear.

③ Click and hold the Point-to-File icon (🔲).

● A message appears in the Link field.

④ Drag the cursor to the Files panel.

⑤ Place the cursor over the top of the filename.

⑥ Release the mouse button.

● The link appears in the Link field.

342

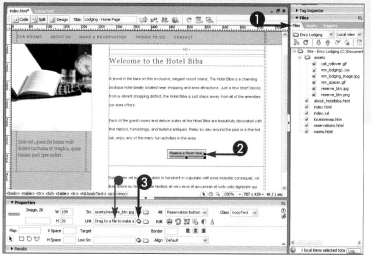

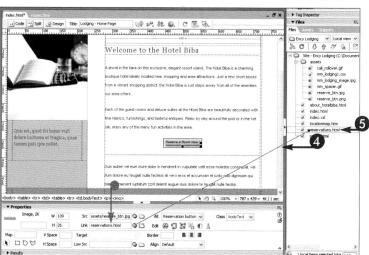

Create an Image Link

1 Click the Files tab in the Files panel.

2 Select the image where you want to create the link.

3 Click and hold the Point-to-File icon ⊕.

● A message appears in the Link field.

4 Drag the cursor to the Files panel.

5 Place the cursor over the top of the filename.

6 Release the mouse button.

● The link appears in the Link field.

TIPS

More Options!

You can create a link between two open documents by dragging the ⊕ from one document to another. This method only works when you do not have the documents maximized in the Design Window. You can also link to an anchor in the page by dragging the ⊕ to the anchor marker and releasing the mouse when ⊕ is over the anchor.

Did You Know?

Document-relative links like the ones you create with the Point-to-File icon allow for the greatest flexibility when working with your pages. If you need to move files within the Files panel, then Dreamweaver even updates the paths to your files for you and ensures that all of your links continue to function correctly.

LINK TO A DOCUMENT OUTSIDE YOUR SITE:
Create Absolute Links

You can create links to other pages and documents on the Web by inserting the complete URL in the Properties inspector. These kinds of links are called *absolute* links because they point to an address outside your own Web site.

An absolute link references the entire path to the file, including the method for retrieving the page. For example, to create a link to the publisher of this book, you set the link to www.wiley.com. Although commonly you type just the name of the site to visit in your browser, such as wiley.com, your link will fail if you do not also include the http:// reference.

The best method for ensuring that your absolute paths are correct is to visit the page in your browser, copy the path from the location or Address bar, and paste the value into the Link field in Dreamweaver. This method ensures that you are linking to the correct page and that the address has no misspellings.

See also>>

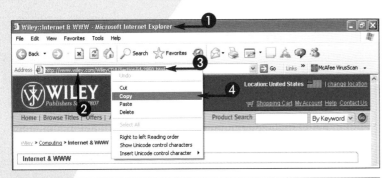

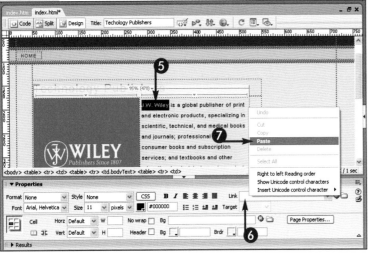

Create a Text Link to a Web Page

① Navigate to the page in your Web browser.

② Select the page address.

③ Right-click (Ctrl-click) the address.

④ Click Copy.

⑤ Select the text where you want to create the link.

⑥ Right-click inside the Link field of the Properties inspector.

⑦ Click Paste.

Dreamweaver creates the link on the selected text.

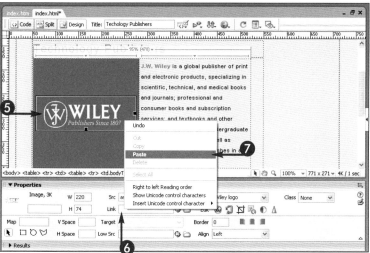

Create an Image Link to a Web Page

1 Navigate to the page in your Web browser.

2 Select the page address.

3 Right-click (Ctrl-click) the address.

4 Click Copy.

5 Select the image where you want to create the link.

6 Right-click (Ctrl-click) inside the Link field.

7 Click Paste.

Dreamweaver creates the link on the image.

TIPS

Important!
Links inside your own Web site should be created as relative links. This allows you to move the files on your hard drive or on your server, or even to change Web hosts or domain names without causing the links to fail.

More Info!
A link does not always have to be to a Web page. You can link to images, PDF files, Flash movies, and even documents created in Word, Excel, or another program. If you link to a file in a format that your browser cannot open, then either the link opens in a plug-in such as Acrobat Reader, or the viewer is prompted to select a program to open the file or to save it.

LINK WITHIN A PAGE:
Set Page Anchors

You can set markers in your page that allow a viewer to jump up or down in the document using a link. To add this function, you insert a page anchor and then link to the anchor in the Properties inspector.

First, you must give your anchor a name, and then, when it is in place, you highlight the text or select the image where you want the link. You then set the name of the anchor in the Link field of the Properties inspector. To link to the anchor, you enter the name of the anchor preceded by the pound sign. For example, if the name of the anchor is members, you type the link as **#members**.

You can also link to a named anchor using the Point-to-File icon in the Properties inspector. With this method, Dreamweaver enters the link information for you in the Properties inspector.

See also>>

Manually Link to an Anchor

① Place your cursor in the page where you want to create an anchor.

② Click here and select Common.

③ Click the Anchor button (🏷️).

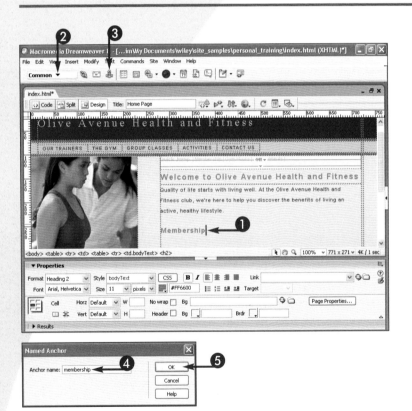

The Named Anchor dialog box appears.

④ Type a name for the page anchor.

⑤ Click OK.

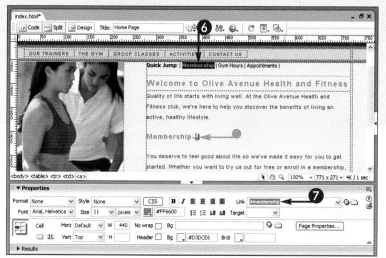

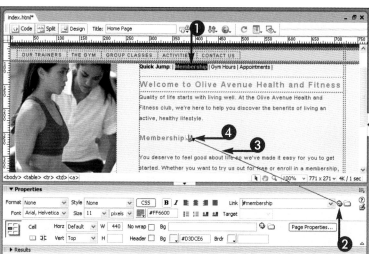

● The anchor icon appears in the page.

⑥ Select the text or image that you want to link to your anchor.

⑦ Type the name of the anchor preceded by the pound sign.

⑧ Press Enter.

Dreamweaver creates the link to the anchor.

Link to an Anchor with the Point-to-File Icon

① Select the text or image where you want to create the link.

② Click the Point-to-File icon (🔘).

③ Drag to the anchor icon in the page.

④ Release the mouse button when your cursor is on top of the anchor icon.

Dreamweaver creates the link to the anchor.

More Info!

You may find that the appearance of page anchor icons adversely affects your carefully constructed design. If you do not need to view the icons, then you can disable them by deselecting the "Invisible elements" option through the Visual Aids button (🖼️) in the Document toolbar or through the View menu.

Caution!

It is common to add an anchor at the top of a document to allow your viewers to jump back to the top of the page. You should avoid using the name *top* for that anchor because that name is reserved in HTML for other functions. You can use the name *pagetop* or a similar name to avoid problems with anchors at the top of the page.

LOCATE IN SITE:
Find and Select Files

You can automatically find and select a file on your local hard drive and on your remote site using the commands that Dreamweaver provides.

You can run the Locate in Site command from either the Site menu or the Files panel. When you run this command, Dreamweaver finds the file and highlights it in the Files panel. You can then quickly see its relationship to the files and folders in your site and perform file operations. For example, you can run this command to ensure that a document has been saved into the correct folder, or if you want to delete a file from the remote server.

To locate a file that is open in the Design Window on your local hard drive, you can run the Locate in Site command from the Site menu. You can run the Locate in Remote Site command from the contextual menu that appears when you right-click or Command-click a file in the Files panel.

See also>> Files Panel

See also>> Delete Files and Folders

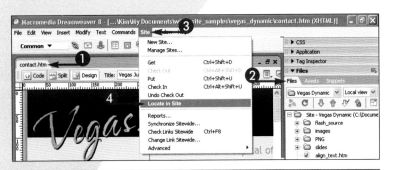

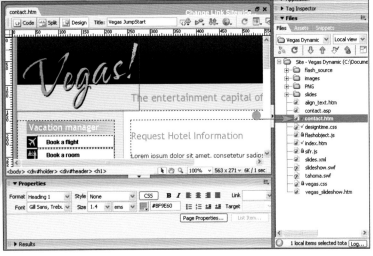

Locate an Open Document in Your Site

① Open a document.

② Open the Files panel.

③ Click Site.

④ Click Locate in Site.

● The open file is selected in the Files panel.

1. Open the Files panel.

2. Click here and select Local view.

3. Right-click (Ctrl-click) the file that you want to locate.

4. Click Locate in Remote Site.

● The Files panel switches to Remote view.

● Dreamweaver selects the file on the server.

TIPS

Check It Out!

Managing even a small Web site can be a daunting task. The number of HTML pages, images, CSS files, and other assets that make up a Web site can become overwhelming in a short period of time. Although Dreamweaver provides assistance with tools such as the Locate in Site feature, all Web developers should understand how to structure and build a site properly. You can learn more about site planning and how to properly structure your site at www.macromedia.com/go/tn_14029.

More Info!

You can refresh the listing of files and folders in your site by pressing the F5 key or by clicking the Refresh button in the Files panel.

L

MACROMEDIA EXCHANGE:
Get New Extensions

You can add new functions to Dreamweaver by downloading and installing extensions. The Macromedia Exchange provides a central location for third-party software developers to provide extensions that you can download and install.

From the start, Dreamweaver has been known for its *extensibility*, or the ability to include new source code that extends the software's capabilities. Over the years, many developers have created their own extensions for Dreamweaver and submitted them to Macromedia for inclusion at the Dreamweaver Exchange. Initially most extensions were offered for free, but as developers have created more complex

and full-featured extensions, the number of commercial extensions has increased. When you visit the Macromedia Exchange, they provide a summary, listing the functions that the extension performs and whether it is free or commercial.

To download free extensions from the Exchange, you must register at the Macromedia site. Free extensions are downloaded directly from Macromedia. When you choose a commercial extension, you are directed to the developer's Web site where you can complete your purchase and download the extension.

See also>> **Extension Manager**

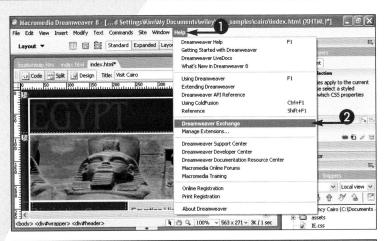

1. Click Help.
2. Click Dreamweaver Exchange.

Your default Web browser launches and takes you to the Dreamweaver Exchange site.

3. Click here and choose the category of extension that you want to download.

- Available extensions are listed with a summary of their function, the number of times downloaded, their rating, the product they extend, and the date approved.

- Free extensions are shown with a Download icon (⬇).

- You can click the Buy icon ($) to download a commercial extension from the developer's site.

4. Click Download.

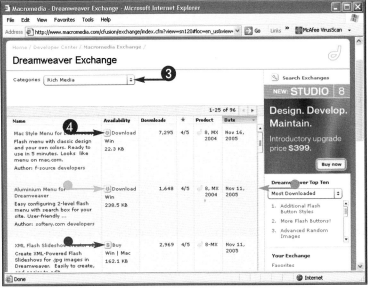

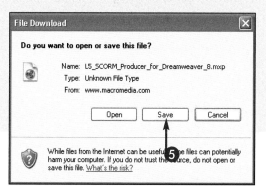

Your browser's File Download dialog box appears.

⑤ Click Save.

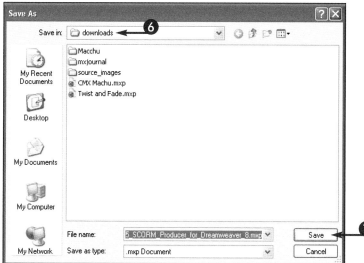

The Save As dialog box appears.

⑥ Navigate to the location where you want to save the file.

⑦ Click Save.

Dreamweaver saves the extension to your computer.

TIPS

Put It Together!

Locating and downloading an extension is just the first step in extending Dreamweaver. You must then install extensions that you download with the Extension Manager. The Extension Manager handles the installation and displays information on how to access the new features that the extension provides.

Remove It!

It can be tempting to install many extensions into Dreamweaver just to see what they do. However, you should know that with each extension that you add, you increase the time it takes Dreamweaver to start up. Some extensions may even conflict with one another and cause Dreamweaver to operate poorly. You can use the Extension Manager to disable or completely remove extensions if you no longer need them or find that they are causing problems.

METATAGS:
Insert into Documents

You can insert content into the head of a document that contains information hidden from the viewer of the page, but accessible to search engines and browsers. These MetaTags can include items that are common to most Web pages such as keywords or descriptions. You can also insert MetaTags that you create, such as the date the page was created, a document identifier, or the name of the page author.

Dreamweaver automatically creates some types of MetaTags, such as document type and character encoding. You can insert MetaTags, such as keywords and descriptions, using the Insert toolbar or the HTML category of the Insert menu. You must define custom MetaTags in the Meta dialog box, which is

where you select the attribute of the tag, set the value, and then create the content that you want to include.

MetaTags that are descriptive utilize the Name attribute and are used by the browser to perform operations such as refreshing the page using the HTTP-equivalent attribute.

See also>>

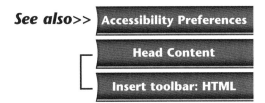

Accessibility Preferences

Head Content

Insert toolbar: HTML

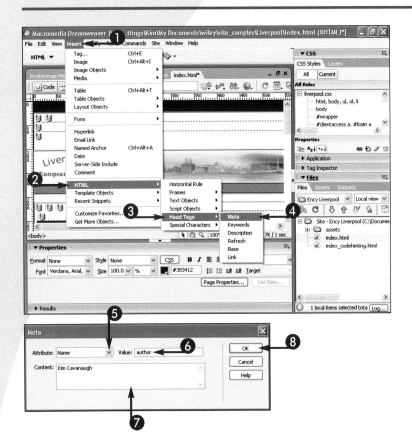

Using the Insert Menu

1 Click Insert.

2 Click HTML.

3 Click Head Tags.

4 Click Meta.

The Meta dialog box appears.

5 Click here and set the attribute to Name.

6 Type a custom MetaTag value.

7 Type the content to be inserted into the MetaTag.

8 Click OK.

Dreamweaver inserts MetaTag information into the head of your document.

Using the Insert Toolbar

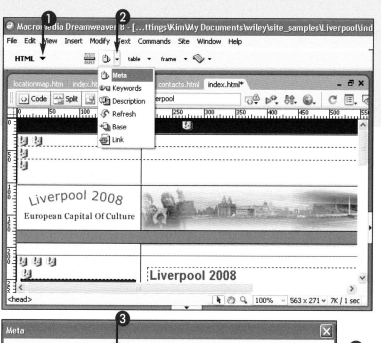

① Click here and select HTML.

You can click the HTML tab if you have the Insert toolbar set to tabbed view.

② Click here and select Meta.

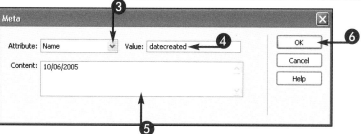

The Meta dialog box appears.

③ Click here and set the attribute to Name.

④ Type a custom MetaTag value.

⑤ Type the content you want to insert into the MetaTag.

⑥ Click OK.

Dreamweaver inserts the MetaTag information into the head of your document.

More Info!

MetaTags are often used as part of a navigation scheme, to make it easier to index pages, or for site maintenance. For example, by inserting an author's name as a MetaTag, you can add a site search feature that allows viewers to search for pages written by that author.

More Options!

You can use the View Head Content option to see all of the MetaTags that you have inserted into a page. When you enable this option from the View menu, a small toolbar appears above the document window listing all of the tags in the head of the document. You can then select the tag by its icon, and edit its properties in the Properties inspector.

NAVIGATION BAR:
Insert

You can use Dreamweaver's Navigation bar object to quickly add navigation with multiple button states. After you create the consistently sized graphics set for each link, the Navigation bar wizard allows you to assign them to four states: up, which is when the visitor's mouse is away from the button; over, which is when the visitor's mouse hovers over the button; down, which is when the visitor clicks the button; and over while down, which is when the visitor's mouse hovers over the button after they have clicked it.

Dreamweaver writes JavaScript that preloads all images so that there is no delay when the visitor interacts with them. You can select an image to initially display in its down state. The dialog box also gives you the default choice of organizing each button group into its own table cell, and it writes the code that inserts the table at your insertion point. You can select either a horizontal or vertical effect with your table.

See also>> Insert Toolbar: Common

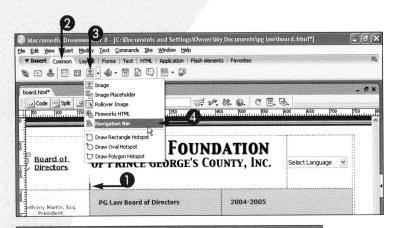

① Click the cursor where you want to add the Navigation bar.

② Click the Common tab in the Insert toolbar.

③ Click the Images button (▣).

④ Click Navigation Bar.

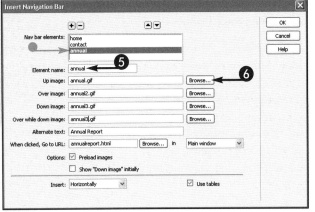

The Insert Navigation Bar dialog box appears.

⑤ Click in the Element name text box and type a unique name for the button set.

Do not use spaces or special characters.

● When you press Tab, Dreamweaver adds the name to the Nav bar elements field.

⑥ Click the Browse button next to the Up image text box.

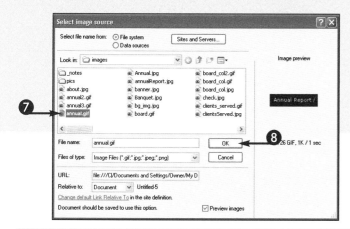

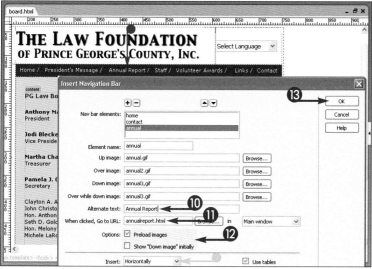

The Select image source dialog box appears.

⑦ Navigate to the first button state image.

⑧ Click OK to close the Select image source dialog box.

⑨ Repeat steps **6** to **8** for each button state image.

You do not have to use a unique image for each state.

⑩ Type a button set image description in the Alternate text box.

⑪ Browse to the file to which the button set links in the When clicked, Go to URL field.

⑫ Click to select the options you want.

● You can set table properties using the Insert options.

⑬ Click OK.

● Dreamweaver adds the Navigation bar at your insertion point.

Apply It!

Navigation bar objects are most useful when you use a frameset that includes a navigation frame and a content frame. You can use the content frame as the target for each link. When you select the Show "Down image" initially option (☐ changes to ☑), you can take advantage of the current page marker effect that the Down graphic provides for each link in your navigation frame.

Caution!

You can only add one Navigation bar object for each page. If you try to add another one, then Dreamweaver asks if you want to modify the current one. You can gain access to editing in this way, or you can edit your Navigation bar by using the command in the Modify menu.

NEW DOCUMENTS:
Create from Starter Pages

You can use Dreamweaver's professionally designed starter pages as the starting point for your Web pages. You can use the Start Page or the New Document dialog box to access a variety of design categories. Starter pages can help when you are new to Web design or to Dreamweaver, or when you need to create a page quickly.

Dreamweaver includes designs for dynamic pages, framesets, CSS-based designs, and table-based designs. The dialog box includes a Preview pane so that you can see each design before you select it. You can then assign a document type to the page.

After you select your design, Dreamweaver enables you to give it a name and save it to a site folder. Dreamweaver also copies all images and other dependent files to your site. You can then select page elements and modify them to make them uniquely your own.

See also>>

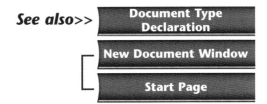

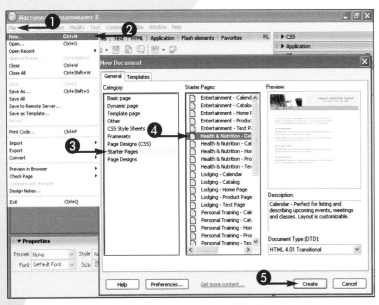

1. Click File.
2. Click New.

   The New Document dialog box appears.
3. Click Starter Pages.

   You can also access pre-built designs from other categories, such as Page Designs and Page Designs (CSS).

   The General tab displays by default; if you previously used the Templates tab, then Dreamweaver displays it instead.
4. Click a design from the Starter Pages category.

   You can preview designs in the Preview pane.
5. Click Create.

   The Save As dialog box appears.
6. Navigate to where you want to save the page.
7. Type a name for the file.
8. Click Save.

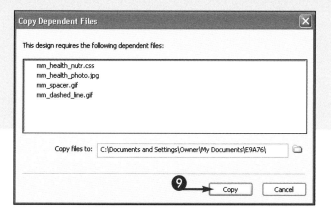

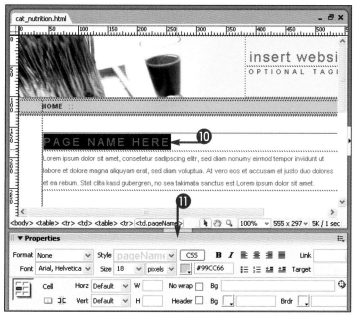

The Copy Dependent Files dialog box appears.

⑨ Click Copy.

Dreamweaver copies the list of files to your designated site folder.

Dreamweaver opens the page as the current document.

⑩ Select any elements that you want to modify.

⑪ Use the Properties inspector to modify colors, fonts, and other properties.

If you use a CSS based design; you can modify colors, fonts, and other elements in the design's style sheet.

Apply It!

It is easy to select text elements and replace them. However, there are other elements that you may want to carefully replace such as the document title. You can also replace the "dummy links" that Dreamweaver uses as placeholders until you add your own working links. When you select a link, javascript:; displays in the link field. You can browse for files or type filenames to link to real pages. Tables, DIVs, and images are a little more complex to customize.

Did You Know?

You can more easily retain the basic look of the starter page if you create graphics with the same dimensions as the sample ones. These elements will then leave the basic layout intact.

NEW DOCUMENTS:
Create from Templates

You can create new pages based on site templates by using the Templates tab in the New from Template dialog box. The Templates tab includes a list of all of your sites in the Templates for window. For those that include them, there is a list of all of the templates in the Site window.

Dreamweaver provides an image preview of each template, as well as a description if the template includes one. You can set the document type and select whether you want the child page to update when you update the parent template; this is the default setting and is usually what you want to do.

However, you may want to use the template as the basis of a new template in another site, and in this case you can deselect the update option.

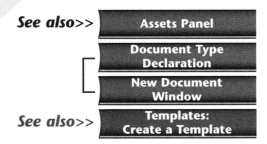

See also>> Assets Panel

Document Type Declaration

New Document Window

See also>> Templates: Create a Template

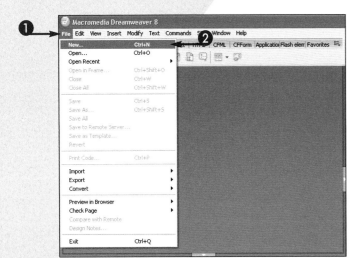

① Click File.

② Click New.

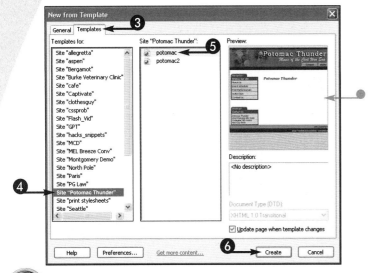

The New from Template dialog box appears.

③ Click the Templates tab.

④ Click the name of the site with the template that you want to use in the Templates for window.

⑤ Click the template that you want to use in the Site (template name) window.

● Dreamweaver displays a preview of the template in the Preview pane.

⑥ Click Create.

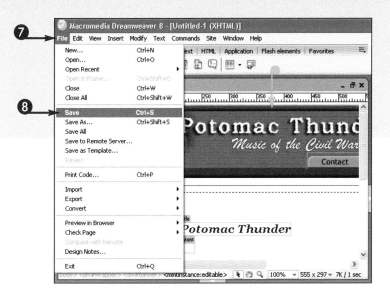

● Dreamweaver opens the page in the Document Window.

⑦ Click File.

⑧ Click Save.

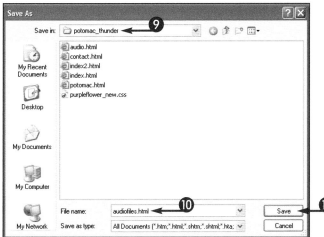

The Save As dialog box appears.

⑨ Navigate to the folder in which you want to save the page.

⑩ Type a page name.

⑪ Click Save.

You can now add unique content and customize the file.

More Options!

Creating a template-based page by using the New from Template dialog box means that you have to navigate to the appropriate site. This is a good method when you want to base pages, or even a new template in your new site on an existing template from another site. You can also quickly add template-based pages directly within a site folder using the Templates category in the Assets panel.

Apply It!

The New from Template dialog box also includes a Preferences button. Clicking it takes you to a preference screen that enables you to set global defaults for the document extension, document type, and default encoding of all your new documents.

PAGE PROPERTIES:
Set and Change

You can use the Page Properties button in the Properties inspector to set up basic styles for your page. After you complete the dialog box categories, Dreamweaver applies the styles to the page, and writes them into the head of the document.

The Appearance screen allows you to set a global font, size, and color for the page, add a background color and background image, and decide how you want the image to repeat. You can also set the page margins. The Links screen allows you to set a link's font, size, and underline style, as well as designate

the colors for each link state. The Headings category allows you to set a global font for headings, and to set individual sizes and colors for each heading level. The Title/Encoding category enables you to set the document type and language for the page.

See also>> Document Type Declaration

Page Properties

See also>> CSS, Export Styles

① Open a document.

② Click the Page Properties button in the Properties inspector.

The Page Properties dialog box appears for the default Appearance category.

③ Type or select the basic options that you want for the page.

This screen enables you to set global properties for the body of the document.

④ Click the Links category.

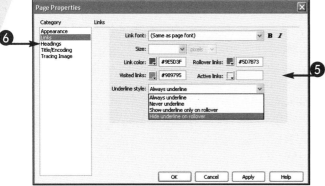

Dreamweaver displays the Links screen.

⑤ Type or select properties for the link states.

⑥ Click the Headings category.

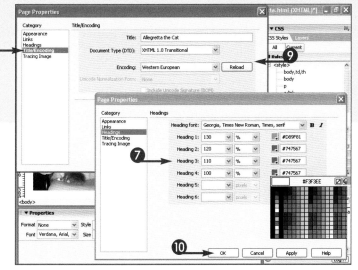

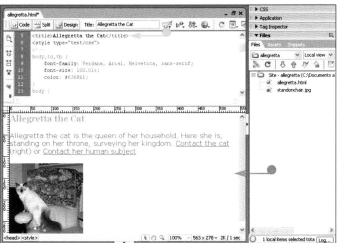

Dreamweaver displays the Headings screen.

⑦ Type or select the heading fonts, size, and colors.

⑧ Click the Title/Encoding category.

Dreamweaver displays the Title/Encoding screen.

⑨ Type or select your Document Type and Encoding.

⑩ Click OK to exit the Page Properties dialog box.

● Dreamweaver applies global styles based on your settings.

● Dreamweaver places the styles in the head of the document.

P

Apply It!

Once you set your starting styles, you have many options for adding new ones. You can use the CSS properties in the Properties inspector. You can also use the CSS panel to add more styles to the head of your document. If you want to apply the styles to multiple pages, then you can export them from the head and into an external style sheet.

More Options!

Browsers add default margins to Web pages similar to how word processors add default margins to text documents. Because browsers have variations in margin settings, many designers first zero out page margins. This way, each browser starts with the same margins, and ensures that the layout appears in the same starting pixel coordinates.

PANELS:
Organize and Modify

You can change how Dreamweaver groups panels together and put them into arrangements that are more convenient for specific projects and categories of Web development. For example, you may want to separate the Assets and Files panels so that you can see them both simultaneously when you are working in Design view. You can also create new panel groups and move selected panels to them.

After you modify how Dreamweaver groups panels together, you may prefer a name that is more descriptive of the new arrangement. You may also

want to give a descriptive name to a new panel group. You can use a panel group's Options button to rename a panel group. You can always return to the default panel arrangement at any time by using the Workspace Layout menu.

See also>> Panels

Workspace Layouts

See also>> Panels: View and Resize

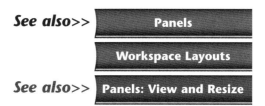

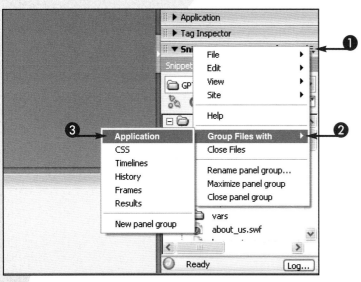

Add a Panel to an Existing Group

① Click the Options button (⧉) on a panel that you want to regroup.

② Click Group Files with, where *Files with* is the name of the panel you want to add to the group.

③ Click the Panel Group with which you want to group the panel.

● Dreamweaver adds the panel to the designated group.

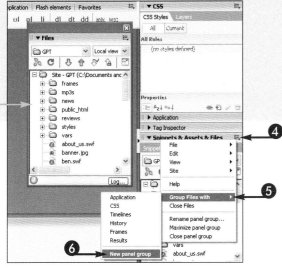

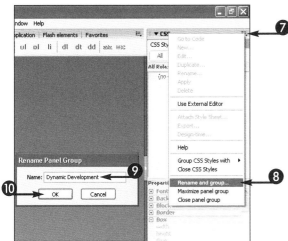

You can also put the panel in a new panel group.

④ Click 🖪 on a panel that you want to use to create a new group.

⑤ Click Group Files with where *Files with* is the name of the panel.

⑥ Click New panel group.

● Dreamweaver floats the panel.

You can group other panels with it, name it, and dock it on the right with the other panel groups.

Rename the Panel Group

⑦ Click 🖪 on the panel that you want to rename.

⑧ Click Rename and group.

The Rename Panel Group dialog box appears.

⑨ Type a name.

⑩ Click OK.

Dreamweaver renames the panel.

TIPS

Try This!

In Windows, you can use the Tab and arrow keys to navigate around panels. You can shift focus to the panels from your document by pressing Ctrl + Alt + Tab. Press this key combination again to shift focus to the next panel. Continue pressing the combination-key set until you reach the panel that you need.

Try This!

You can also press Ctrl + Alt + Shift + Tab to shift focus back to the previous panel. Once you are in the appropriate panel, you can use the Tab key to move through its options. If there are further choices within options, use the arrow keys to page through them, and use the Enter key to select one.

PANELS:
View and Resize

You can view, hide, and resize panel groups. For example, if you need more room to see your design, then you may want to temporarily hide panels. You can hide all panel groups using the arrow in the splitter bar to retrieve the panels. You can also use the Close option in a panel group's Options button to hide that specific panel group.

You can also widen or narrow panels. For example, if you want to see all of the columns of information in the Assets panel, then you can widen the panel group. If you undocked a panel and it is floating on

the screen, then you can resize it. To make a panel group longer, you can maximize it. The other open panels collapse to give the panel all of the available space.

See also>>

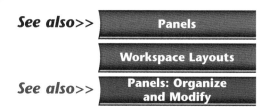

Panels

Workspace Layouts

See also>>

Panels: Organize and Modify

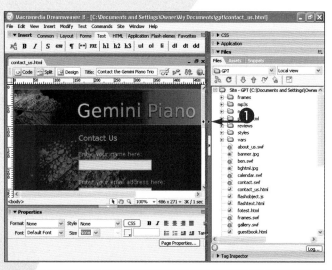

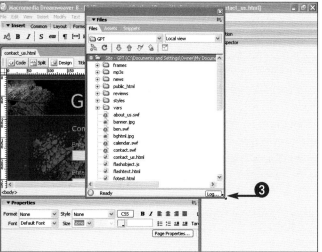

Resize Docked Panels

1 Hover your cursor over the splitter bar.

Your mouse turns into a double-sided arrow (↔).

2 Click and drag your mouse to resize docked panels.

Dreamweaver adjusts the width of the panel groups.

Resize Floating Panels

3 To resize floating panels, click and drag them by their resize handles.

Dreamweaver resizes the panels.

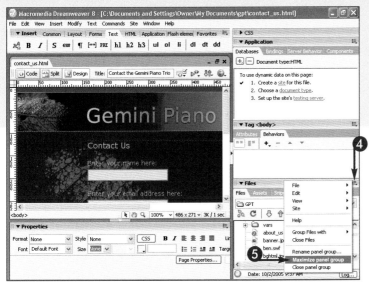

④ Click the Options button (📰) in a panel.

⑤ Click Maximize panel group.

● Dreamweaver closes other panels and maximizes the panel to fill the available space.

More Options!

Sometimes after you show, hide, and arrange panels, your Dreamweaver workspace becomes chaotic and you want to start fresh. You can quickly revert to the default panels by selecting the default Workspace Layout on Mac OS, or one of the preset Workspace Layouts on Windows.

Apply It!

After you work on documents for a while, a floating panel may disappear from view, even though the Window menu shows it as on the screen. You can use the Window menu's Arrange Panels command to clean up panel arrangements and bring missing panels back onscreen. You can also use the Window menu's Hide Panels command or the F4 function key to hide panels.

PASTE SPECIAL:
Using for Formatting Options

You can use the new Paste Special dialog box to control how text that you copy to the Clipboard is pasted into a destination document. When you paste text from another source such as e-mail, a Word document, or even another Web page, you do not always want to include the styles or structure from the original file. The Copy/Paste preferences set global formats for the Paste menu command. With the Paste Special dialog box, you can select options for each individual block of text that you copy and paste.

The Paste Special dialog box offers four options. The Text Only option strips out all formatting and pastes

a block of plain text. The Text with structure option pastes the text with original paragraphs, tables, and lists, but does not retain italics, bold, or any other formatting styles. The Text with structure plus basic formatting option retains the structure as well as basic formatting such as bold, italics, and underlines. The Text with structure plus full formatting option pastes text with structure, HTML, and CSS styles.

See also>> **Preferences:
Copy and Paste**

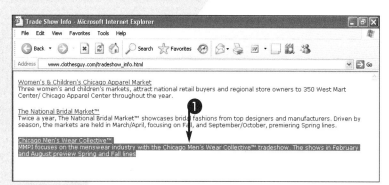

① Copy the text that you want to paste into your document.

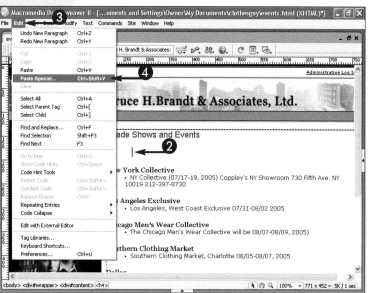

② Click your cursor in your document where you want to paste the text.

③ Click Edit.

④ Click Paste Special.

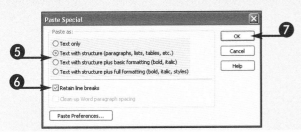

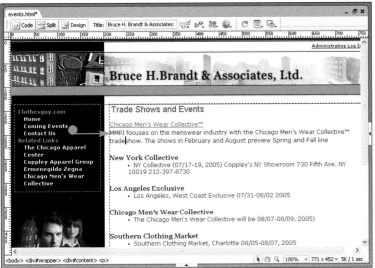

The Paste Special dialog box appears.

⑤ Click a Paste as option (○ changes to ◉).

⑥ Click to select the Retain line breaks option (☐ changes to ☑).

The Retain line breaks option (☐ changes to ☑) is not available with the Text only option (○ changes to ◉).

⑦ Click OK.

● Dreamweaver pastes the text with the formatting that you select.

Caution!
The Paste Special dialog box does not paste CSS styles that originate in an external style sheet. You may have to attach the style sheet or re-create the styles.

Try This!
You can click the Paste Preferences button in the Paste Special dialog box to open the Paste Preferences screen in preferences. You can set which of the pasting options you want to make the default when you press Ctrl+V (Cmd+V), or use the regular paste option.

More Options!
If you paste text from a Word document and select either the "Text with structure" or "Text with structure plus basic formatting" option (○ changes to ◉), you may want to select the "Clean up Word paragraph spacing" option (☐ changes to ☑) in the Paste Special dialog box. This option removes extra space between paragraphs when you paste your text.

REPORTS:
Using Workflow Reports

You can use Dreamweaver's Workflow Reports to help you keep track of your Web projects; they are especially useful if you are working in a team. You can run reports on the current document, the entire current local site, selected files in a site, or a folder.

You can run Workflow Reports on checked-out files, Design Notes, and recently modified files. With the Checked Out By option, you can enter a team member's name to view pages that they have checked out. The Design Notes option allows you to enter name and value pairs; it gives you a menu of

pattern-matching choices such as *is*, *is not*, and *contains*. The Recently Modified option allows you to search for files that have been modified within a range of dates, and displays the results both in the Results panel and as a table in your default browser. It also includes options for Contribute users.

See also>> **Design Notes**

See also>> **Check-In and Check-Out**

Contribute

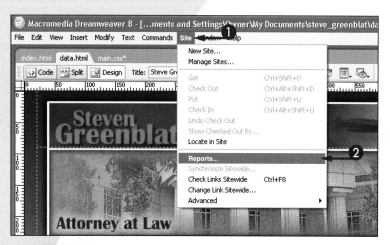

① Click Site.

② Click Reports.

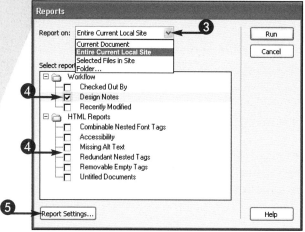

The Reports dialog box appears.

③ Click here and select a Report on option.

④ Click a Select report option (☐ changes to ☑).

This example selects the Design Notes option.

⑤ Click Report Settings.

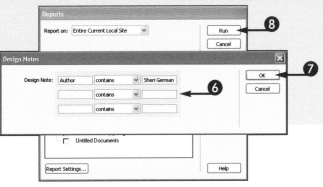

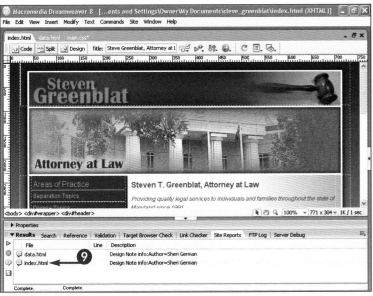

The Reports dialog box appears for the Report on option.

The Design Notes dialog box appears.

⑥ Select the options that you want.

⑦ Click OK to accept the options and to close the dialog box.

Repeat steps **4** to **7** for each Select report option that you want to run.

⑧ In the Reports dialog box, click Run.

Dreamweaver opens the Results panel with a list of results that match your criteria.

⑨ Double-click a result.

Dreamweaver opens the page in the Document Window.

R

More Options!
If you want to run reports on more than one workflow category, then you need to click Report Settings after selecting each option individually. After you enter settings for each, you can run the Workflow Report on all categories at one time.

Apply It!
You can save your reports to share them with other team members and keep a record of project development. When you click the Save Report icon (▣), Dreamweaver displays a Save As dialog box so that you can save your report in a preferred location. Dreamweaver saves your report as an Extensible Markup Language, or XML, document that you can open in Code view or a plain-text editor to examine later.

ROLLOVER IMAGES:
Create and Insert

You can use Dreamweaver's Rollover Image icon in the Common category of the Insert toolbar to quickly add simple rollover images to your page. Rollover images are images that change when the visitor moves the mouse over them. They are often used for navigation buttons; the new image that swaps in when the mouse hovers over the initial image gives the visitor interactive feedback that it is a clickable link.

Dreamweaver provides a visual dialog box so that you can easily insert rollover images. After you fill

out the fields, Dreamweaver writes the necessary JavaScript to make the rollovers work properly. It includes a default option to preload all rollover images when the page loads so that a visitor does not have to wait for the second image when he or she points the mouse over the original image.

See also>> **Behaviors Panel**

Insert Toolbar: Common

See also>> **Navigation Bar**

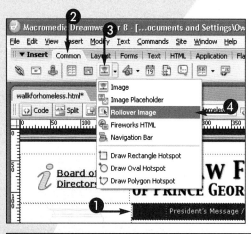

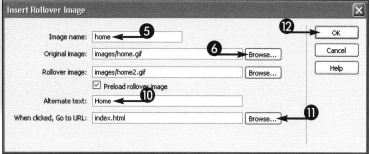

① Click the cursor where you want to add the rollover image.

② Click the Common tab in the Insert toolbar.

Dreamweaver displays the icons for the Common category.

③ Click the Image icon ().

④ Click Rollover Image.

The Insert Rollover Image dialog box appears.

⑤ Type a name for the rollover image.

⑥ Click Browse.

The Original Image dialog box appears.

370

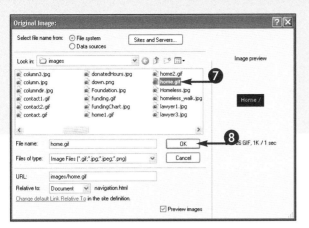

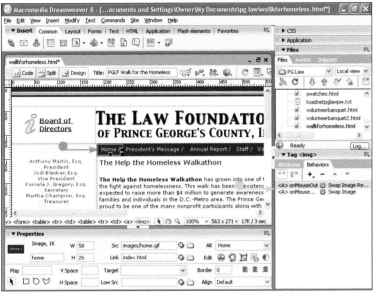

7 Navigate to the first image.

8 Click OK to close the Original Image dialog box.

9 In the Insert Rollover Image dialog box, repeat steps **6** to **8** for the rollover image.

10 Type text for the visually impaired in the Alternate text box.

11 Browse for or type the link address if the image will go to a link when clicked.

12 Click OK.

● Dreamweaver applies the rollover image to the page.

● You can see the behaviors that it applies in the Behaviors panel.

R

SERVER-SIDE INCLUDES (SSI):
Insert

You can use the Server-Side Include, or SSI, button in the Common category of the Insert toolbar to add a Server-Side Include to your document. Server-Side Includes are external files that contain content formatted in HTML, but that have no HTML head, or body tags.

You can save pages that include Server-Side Includes with an .shtml, .shtm, or .inc file extension. Dreamweaver inserts a reference to the SSI in these pages; the contents of an SSI file are not actually inserted into a document. The server processes and adds the content at runtime. However, with

Dreamweaver, you can preview the contents of a Server-Side Include in your document in Design view.

There are two types of SSIs: Virtual and File. If you use an Apache server, then you usually want to select Virtual. If you use a Windows server with Microsoft Internet Information Server, or IIS, then you usually want to select File.

See also>> Insert Toolbar: Common

New Document Window

Split Code and Design View

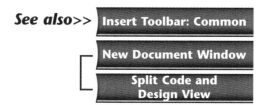

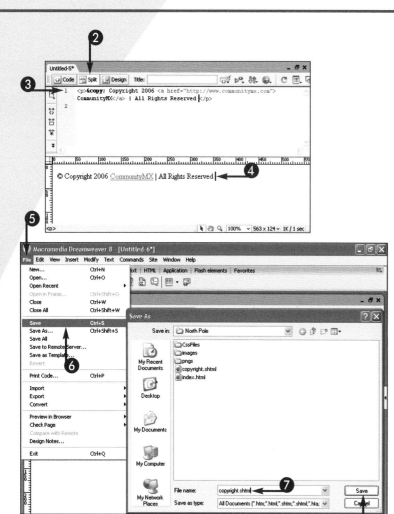

1 Create a new document.

2 Click Split in the Document toolbar.

3 Delete all HTML code until the Code view is blank.

4 Insert the content that you want in the Include.

5 Click File.

6 Click Save.

The Save As dialog box appears.

7 Type a filename and an .htm or .html extension.

8 Click Save.

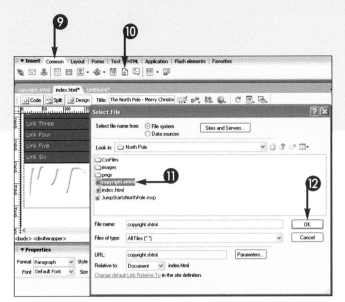

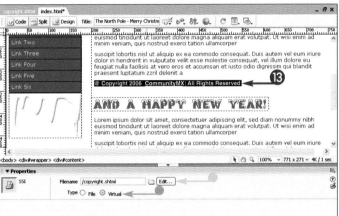

9 Click the Common tab in the Insert toolbar.

10 Click the Server-Side Include icon (⊞).

The Select File dialog box appears.

11 Navigate to the Include file.

12 Click OK.

You may need to use the .shtml, .shtm, or .inc extension on a page that has Server-Side Includes. You can ask the site administrator for the appropriate extension for your server.

Dreamweaver displays the Server-Side Include in Design view.

13 Click to select the Server-Side Include.

● You can change the Type option in the Properties inspector; Dreamweaver selects File by default.

● You can click Edit to open the Include page and modify it.

S

Apply It!
Server-Side Includes work like Library items in that you can add a reference to your pages for a frequently used bit of code like a copyright notice. However, unlike Library items, when you edit an SSI you only have to upload the new SSI file, and not the files that use it.

Caution!
Some servers are configured to examine all files to see if they contain SSIs. Other servers are configured to examine only files with the file extensions .shtml, .shtm, or .inc. If your SSI does not work properly, then you should ask your system administrator if you need to use a special extension in the name of the file that uses the SSI. Read more about configuring SSIs on a server at: www. ssi-developer.net/ssi/enabling-ssi.shtml.

SITE DEFINITION:
Export

You can export site definitions to the location of your choice by using the Export button in the Site Management dialog box. Saving site definition files allows you to move site definitions among computers, share them with other users, and provide a backup in case anything happens to the site.

A site definition allows Dreamweaver to organize and communicate with files in a target folder on your computer. It allows Dreamweaver to track and manage files, assets, links, and server information. When you export a site, Dreamweaver saves its site definition with the .ste file extension. There are two

export options: You can export with your username and password, or you can save the site to share with others without including this sensitive information.

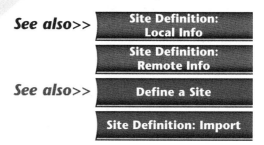

See also>> Site Definition: Local Info

Site Definition: Remote Info

See also>> Define a Site

Site Definition: Import

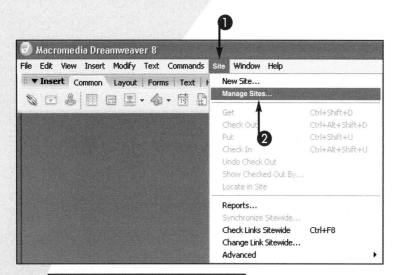

① Click Site.

② Click Manage Sites.

The Manage Sites dialog box appears.

③ Click the name of a site definition that you want to export.

④ Click Export.

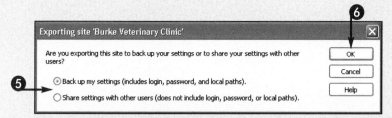

The Exporting site dialog box appears.

5 Click a settings option.

6 Click OK.

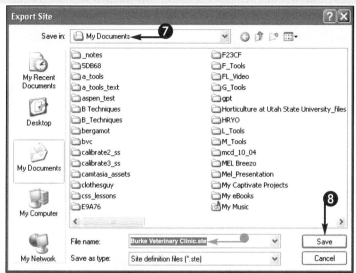

7 Navigate to where you want to save the exported site definition.

● Dreamweaver assigns the file a default name using the site name and the .ste file extension.

8 Click Save.

Dreamweaver saves your site definition.

TIPS

Caution!
If you export a site with the Back up my settings option (○ change ●) and need to import it to another computer, then you should keep the path to the local root folder on the new computer the same as the original. Otherwise, Dreamweaver cannot find the local root folder referenced in the site definition file, and asks you to select one on the new computer.

Attention!
While the import-and-export technique backs up your site definitions, it does not back up the local root folder on your computer that you use for each site. When you export site definitions, it is a good idea to back up the site files at the same time. These strategies keep your sites secure.

SITE DEFINITION:
Import

After you save an exported site definition to your computer or disk, you can import it into Dreamweaver on other computers, share it with team members, or use it if you need to reinstall Dreamweaver or transfer it to a new computer. If you want to use Dreamweaver's powerful site management features, then you must set up a site definition. Duplicating this effort for the same site on another computer wastes time and risks discrepancies.

You can import a site using the Import button in the Site Management dialog box and navigating to the exported site definition, which you can recognize by its .ste file extension. You can even import multiple sites at one time, or import a contiguous range of site names in the Import Site dialog box.

See also>>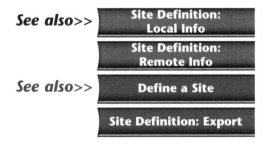

See also>>

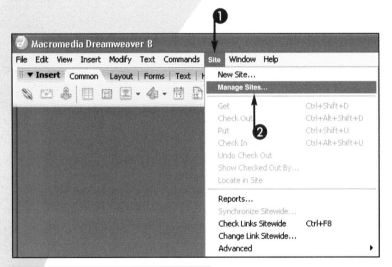

① Click Site.

② Click Manage Sites.

The Manage Sites dialog box appears.

③ Click Import.

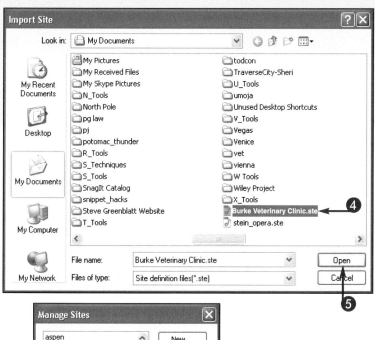

The Import Site dialog box appears.

④ Navigate to the exported site definition.

You can import multiple sites by Ctrl-clicking (⌘-clicking) the names of sites or by Shift-clicking a contiguous range of site names.

You can recognize the exparted site definition by the .ste file extension.

⑤ Click Open.

● Dreamweaver imports the site definition.

TIPS

Try This!

Dreamweaver exports site definitions as Extensible Markup Language, or XML, documents. If you click one, it opens in Dreamweaver's Code view. You can see all of the settings that you exported formatted as XML. To read more about XML, go to www.w3.org/XML.

Attention!

If you do not see the .ste file extension on your site definition files, you may need to display your file extensions. In Windows XP, double-click My Computer, then click Tools, and then click Folder Options. Click the View tab, and then deselect the "Hide extensions for known file types" option. In Mac OS X, click the Finder menu, and then click Preferences. Click the Advanced icon, and then select the "Show all file extensions" option (☐ changes to ☑).

SITE MAPS:
Create

You can view the local folder for a site as a visual site map represented by linked icons. You can use the site map to add new files and set up a site structure, or to add, modify, and remove links. The site map shows the site structure two levels deep, starting from the home page, which can be any file that you designate.

Dreamweaver uses color-coding to identify file status. Red text indicates a broken link. Blue text indicates external, e-mail, and script links. Green and red checkmarks indicate checked-in and checked-out files. A Lock icon indicates a read-only file.

You can set up Site Map options in the Site Definition dialog box. These options include the number of link columns and their pixel width, whether to display dependent files, what text you want to appear with an icon, and whether you want to display files marked as hidden.

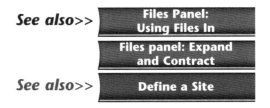

See also>> **Files Panel: Using Files In**

Files panel: Expand and Contract

See also>> **Define a Site**

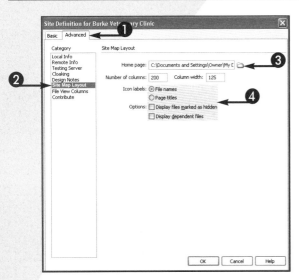

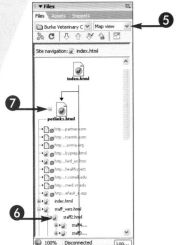

① Open the Site Definition dialog box for your site.

② Click the Site Map Layout category in the Advanced panel.

The Site Map Layout section appears.

③ Click the folder (▢) to navigate to the page that you want to use as the home page.

④ Click these options to set what you want (▢ changes to ☑ or ○ changes to ◉).

⑤ In the Files panel, click here and select Map view.

Dreamweaver displays your files in Map view.

⑥ Click a plus sign (⊞).

Dreamweaver displays linked files and changes the plus sign to a minus sign.

⑦ Click the minus sign (⊟).

Dreamweaver collapses the list of linked files (⊟ changes to ⊞).

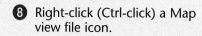

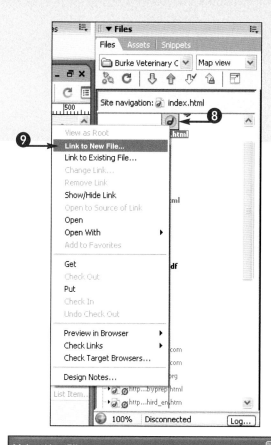

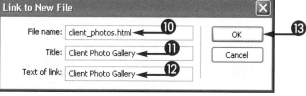

⑧ Right-click (Ctrl-click) a Map view file icon.

Dreamweaver displays map menu options.

⑨ Click a file option.

This example selects Link to New File to create a new, linked file in Map view.

Dreamweaver opens the Link to New File dialog box.

⑩ Type a filename.

⑪ Type a page title.

⑫ Type the link text that you want to display in the file from which you are linking the new file.

⑬ Click OK.

Dreamweaver adds the new file to your Files panel and to the Map view.

S

More Options!

You can click the File Options button (📄) in the Files panel to save an image of the site map. Click File, and then click Save Site Map. In the Save Site Map dialog box that appears, you can save the image in BMP or PNG format.

Apply It!

If you have multiple folders in a site, each with its own index page, then you should select the page title as the page icon label. This gives each page a unique, descriptive identifier.

Attention!

In this context, the home page is the starting point of the map. You can right-click (Ctrl-click) the file that you want to be the home page in Local view, and then click Set as Home Page.

SNIPPETS:
Create New

You can create your own custom snippets for frequently used code and text to streamline your workflow. You can then quickly add objects to your page in Code or Design view by selecting your snippet in the Snippets panel.

Dreamweaver offers two choices for snippets: You can either insert one block of code, or you can create two-part snippets that wrap around the beginning and end of a selected object. Depending on which option you choose, the new Snippet dialog box displays either one or two text entry fields.

You can create new folder categories for storing custom snippets. You must ensure that you select no other folder before you click the New Folder button, or the new folder nests inside the selected folder.

See also>>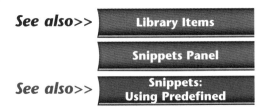

See also>>

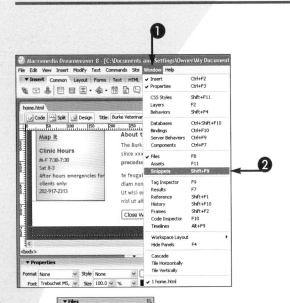

1 Click Window.

2 Click Snippets.

The Snippets panel opens.

3 Click the New Snippet Folder icon (▣).

● You can click the Name bar, if Dreamweaver has another folder selected, to deselect all folders.

This also changes the list to descending order; you can click Name again to revert to ascending order.

Dreamweaver adds an untitled folder.

4 Type a name and press Enter.

5 With your new folder selected, click the New Snippet icon (▣).

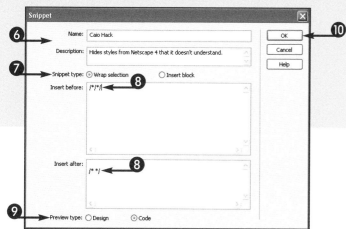

The Snippet dialog box appears.

6 Type a name and description.

7 Click a Snippet type option (○ changes to ⊙).

Dreamweaver displays one or two fields, depending on your selection.

8 Type your code.

9 Click a Preview option (○ changes to ⊙).

10 Click OK.

● Dreamweaver adds your new snippet to the selected folder.

TIPS

Share Snippets!

After you create a custom snippet, you may want to share it. Open the Dreamweaver 8 application folder at C:/Program Files (Windows), or C:/Application/Configuration/Snippet (Mac OS X). You can open the category folders to find individual snippets with the .csn file extension. You can then right-click (Ctrl-click) to save a copy of the snippet to the location of your choice.

Did You Know?

When you begin to lay out your pages with CSS positioning, you may encounter many differences in browser rendering. CSS experts create hacks to compensate, particularly for Internet Explorer. You can create snippets such as the Caio Hack that is used in the example on this page. Read more about hacks at www.positioniseverything.net.

SNIPPETS:
Using Predefined

You can use the Snippets panel to store frequently used pieces of code and text and add them to your pages with a single mouse-click. Snippets can be HTML, CSS, JavaScript, or almost any other code that you want to add. The Snippets panel also includes management options. For example, you can add, edit, remove, and organize snippets.

Dreamweaver 8 includes hundreds of ready-to-use snippets that you can insert into documents or use as a starting point for building your own custom snippets. For example, there is a predefined snippet to add a JavaScript Close Window button to your page.

You can insert snippets in Design or Code view. They can be inserted as one block of code, such as a CSS style rule, or you can wrap part of a snippet before and part of a snippet after a selected object in the page.

See also>> **Library Items**

Snippets Panel

See also>> **Snippets: Create New**

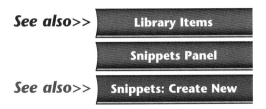

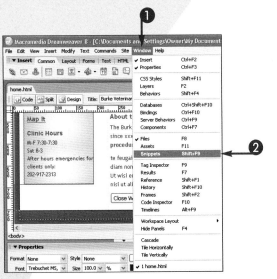

1 Click Window.

2 Click Snippets.

Dreamweaver opens the Snippets panel.

3 Click your cursor in Code or Design view where you want to insert the snippet.

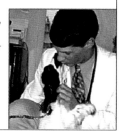

④ Click the plus sign (⊞) next to a folder.

The folder expands to reveal the snippets within (⊞ changes to ⊟).

⑤ Click the icon of the snippet that you want to use.

⑥ Click Insert.

● Dreamweaver inserts the snippet at your insertion point.

Rated among Washingtonian Magazine's Best Vets

Burke Veterinary Clinic was rated among Washingtonian magazine's best vets in Virginia. adipiscing elit, sed diam nonummy nibh euismod tincidunt ut laoreet dolore magna aliquam erat volutpat. Ut wisi enim ad minim veniam, quis nostrud exerci tation ullamcorper suscipit lobortis nisl ut aliquip ex ea

Washington Consumer Checkbook Magazine Top Rating For Quality Service

Burke Veterinary Clinic received Washington Consumer Checkbook Magazine's top rating for quality service. vulputate velit esse molestie consequat, vel illum dolore eu feugiat nulla facilisis at vero eros et accumsan et iusto odio dignissim qui blandit praesent luptatum zzril delenit augue duis dolore

Close Window

Attention!
If you want to add bits of code that automatically update when you make changes to one master file, then you should use Library items. Select the object that you want to save for reuse in the Document Window. Click Modify, then click Library, and then click Add Object to Library. Dreamweaver places the object in the Library category of the Assets panel, where you can name and manage the object.

Organize It!
You can organize your snippets and snippet folders by dragging and dropping them. If you inadvertently nest a folder inside another folder, drag it under the last folder in the panel. Dreamweaver places it alphabetically in the top level of the Snippets panel folders.

SOUND:
Insert Plug-ins

You can add sound to a Web page by inserting a generic plug-in object from the Media menu of the Common category in the Insert toolbar. Plug-ins are little pieces of software that give your browser enhanced functionality. However, visitors must have a particular plug-in if you insert files that are dependent on plug-ins. Most people do have some kind of plug-in that plays common sound formats like WAVeform, or WAV, in Windows, or Audio Interchange File Format, or AIFF, in Mac OS. Commonly installed plug-ins include Windows Media Player and QuickTime for the Mac.

After you insert your sound object, you must configure its properties by using the Parameters button to add values. You can also change Dreamweaver's default 32x32-pixel dimensions. If you know the download address for the plug-in, then you can enter it in the Plg URL field in the Properties inspector. If the visitor's browser does not have the required plug-in, then it automatically attempts to download it.

See also>> Insert Toolbar: Common

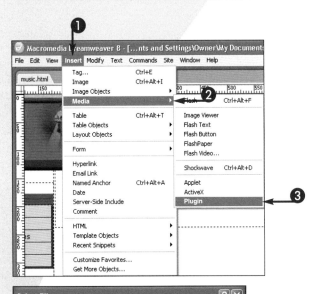

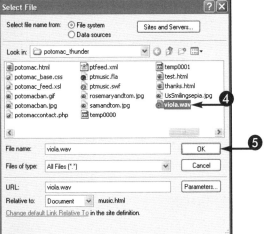

① Click Insert.

② Click Media.

③ Click Plugin.

You can also use the Media button (▣) in the Common category of the Insert toolbar to insert plug-ins.

The Select File dialog box appears.

④ Navigate to your sound file.

⑤ Click OK.

Dreamweaver displays the generic plug-in icon on the page.

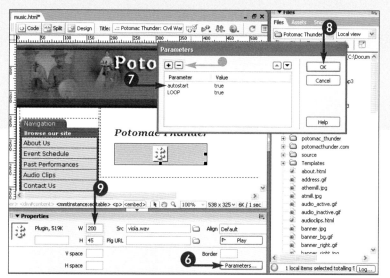

6 Click Parameters.

You can also click Parameters in the Select File dialog box before you insert the sound.

7 In the Parameters dialog box that appears, type a parameter and value pair.

● You can add and remove parameters using the Add (➕) and Delete (➖) buttons.

8 Click OK.

9 Type plug-in dimensions in the W and H fields.

● The browser displays the plug-in and plays the sound according to your parameter settings.

More Options!

You can add some common parameters to your plug-in. For example, if you want your sound to repeat, or loop, then you can set the parameter loop value to true. If you want your sound to automatically play when the page loads, then you can set the autoplay value to true. If you want to hide the sound controls, then you can type **hidden** in the parameter field.

Check It Out!

You can download Dreamweaver extensions that insert specific plug-ins. Look in the Rich Media category of the Macromedia Exchange to find the Insert a QuickTime Movie and Real Media Suite extensions. These extensions help Dreamweaver to write the correct code to ensure smooth plug-in performance. You can find them at the Macromedia Exchange: www.macromedia.com/cfusion/exchange/.

SPECIAL CHARACTERS:
Insert

You can use the Characters menu in the Text category of the Insert toolbar to insert special characters such as copyright symbols, diacritics, and nonbreaking spaces. You usually type on your keyboard to enter text in a page. However, there are special characters whose key combinations are not common knowledge or that require special font sets.

The Special Characters menu allows you to visually insert these characters and allows Dreamweaver to write the appropriate character entity into Code view. The Characters menu includes the most common special characters, such as the curly quote, em dash, and copyright, register, and trademark

symbols, while the Insert Other Character dialog box has an expanded list.

You can also use character icons to quickly insert line breaks and nonbreaking spaces. HTML does not recognize more than one tap of the spacebar. Nonbreaking spaces enable you to add more space between words. They also keep the browser from separating words that you do not want it to split apart.

See also>>

Insert Toolbar: Text

Page Properties

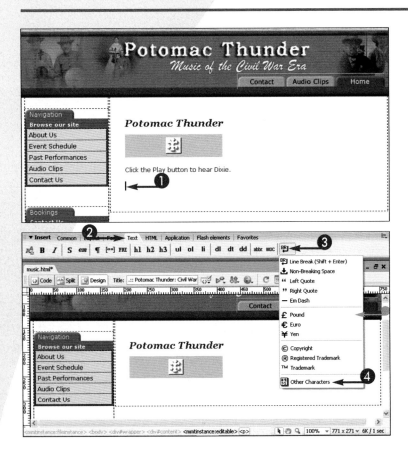

1 Click your cursor in the page where you want to insert a special character.

2 Click the Text tab in the Insert toolbar.

3 Click the Characters icon (🔤).

You can also click the Insert menu, then click HTML, and then click Special Characters.

● The most common special characters appear in the Special Characters menu.

4 Click Other Characters.

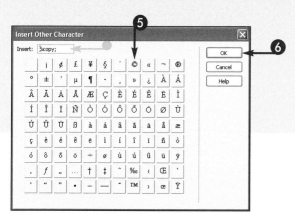

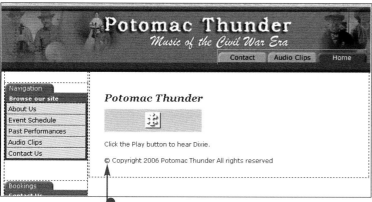

The Insert Other Character dialog box appears.

⑤ Click a character.

● The character code appears in the Insert field.

⑥ Click OK.

● Dreamweaver inserts the character into your document at the insertion point.

S

TIP

Caution!

There are two ways to represent special characters: as a named character or decimal code. For example, you can insert the copyright symbol as © or as ©. Dreamweaver adds the special characters to Code view in a combination of named characters and decimal code, depending on which is best supported by browsers.

Some browsers do not display character entities properly, or they require that you set your encoding to the Western ISO Latin-1 character set in the Page Properties window. Web Standards suggest that you encode your pages with Unicode, a universal standard that resolves conflicts among the different character sets. You can find a chart of special characters that have wide support in HTML 4 and Unicode at plato.stanford.edu/symbols/entities.html.

STYLE RENDERING TOOLBAR:
View Page

Depending on your audience, you may need to design your pages for more than the computer screen. You can preview how your Web pages look for different media types such as print or a mobile phone by using the new Style Rendering toolbar. For example, handheld devices and Web-enabled cell phones are proliferating rapidly, and different devices such as screen readers are making pages more accessible to the disabled. Optimizing pages for the best printing result is also a concern for sites that contain material that visitors need to print out.

As long as you create a media-dependent style sheet for a particular device, you can use the appropriate button in the Style Rendering toolbar to display how the page appears on that device. You can also turn off all style sheets to see how your page appears in older browsers or how a screen reader speaks its elements.

See also>> Style Rendering Toolbar

See also>> CSS, Media Type Style Sheets

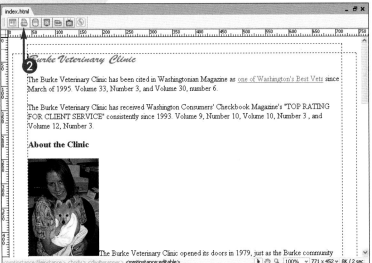

① Enable the Style Rendering toolbar.

Dreamweaver displays the page for the screen media type by default.

② Click the Render Print Media Type button () if you have a print style sheet attached to the page.

Dreamweaver renders the page as it would print out.

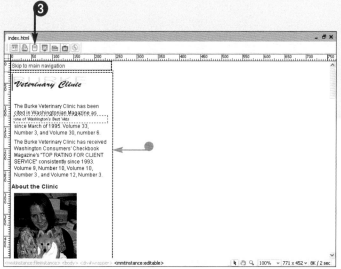

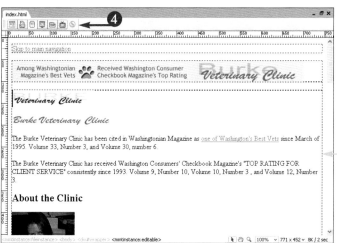

3 Click the Render Handheld Media Type button (image) if you have a handheld style sheet attached to the page.

● Dreamweaver renders the page as it would display on a handheld device.

You can continue to click buttons for every media type for which you attached a media-dependent style sheet to your page.

4 Click the Toggle button (image) for displaying the CSS styles to turn all style sheets on and off.

● Dreamweaver displays the unformatted page when you turn off style sheets.

Important!

If you lay out your pages with CSS positioning rather than tables, they may not print out as you expect. Printers have a hard time understanding CSS positioning, and only one page may emerge from the printer when a user prints your Web page. It is useful to include a print style sheet that optimizes your page with CSS rules that a printer understands.

Check It Out!

There are many good tutorials on the Web that teach you how to create style sheets for the various media types. Community MX has an article called Media Types and Their Uses at www. communitymx.com/content/article.cfm? cid=096A1. You can also find an article about creating print style sheets at CSS guru Eric Meyer's site: www. meyerweb.com/eric/articles/webrev/ 200001.html.

SWAP IMAGE BEHAVIOR:
Insert

You can swap one image for another in your page by using the Swap Image behavior. When you use the Swap Image behavior to create a simple two-state rollover button, Dreamweaver automatically applies three behaviors to the page: Swap Image to swap in a new image `onMouseOver`; Swap Image Restore to restore the original image `onMouseOut`; and Preload Images to ensure that the swapped-in image is downloaded with the rest of the page so that there is no delay when the visitor hovers their mouse over the initial image.

Dreamweaver writes the entire complex JavaScript that you need in both the head and body sections of Code view. The Swap Image dialog box automatically finds and displays all of the images in the current Web page to make it easy for you to select the image or images to which you want to apply the behavior.

See also>>

Behaviors Panel

Images: Insert in Documents

Rollover Images

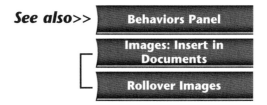

① Select the image to which you want to apply the Swap Image behavior.

② Click the Add button (➕) in the Behaviors panel.

③ Click Swap Image.

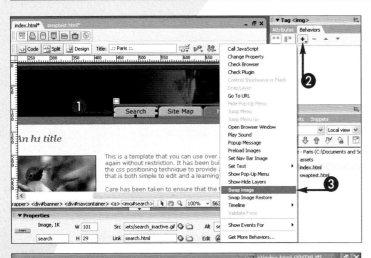

The Swap Image dialog box appears.

④ Select the image that you want to replace with another.

⑤ Click Browse.

⑥ In the Select Image Source dialog box, navigate to the image that you want to swap.

⑦ Click OK.

⑧ Click OK in the Swap Image dialog box.

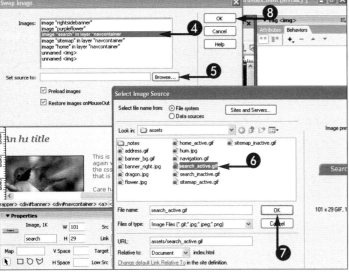

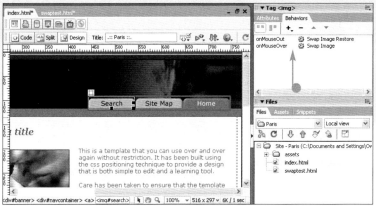

● Dreamweaver applies the Swap Image and Swap Image Restore behaviors to the image.

Dreamweaver also applies a Preload Images behavior to the body with the `onLoad` event.

⑨ Preview the Web page in a browser.

● Dreamweaver swaps in the replacement image `onMouseOver`.

Dreamweaver restores the original image `onMouseOut`.

TIPS

Caution!

It is helpful to give each image in a pair related names so that you can recognize them in the Swap Image dialog box. For example, you can name the original image "name_inactive," and the image that you want to swap in "name_active." You should also ensure that both states of the image are the same size. Otherwise, you will see a jumping motion `onMouseOver`.

Try This!

You can use the Swap Image behavior in many other ways. For example, you can type a list of slide names in one column, and provide the image for the first slide in a middle column. Then add the Swap Image behavior to each slide name to swap in its appropriate image.

SYNCHRONIZE:
Sites and Folders

You can use the Synchronize command to compare your files on the remote server with those on your local computer and transfer only the newest files in either direction. You can compare the entire site or only selected files, and choose the server, either local or remote, to which you want the newest files to flow. This saves you time after you modify many pages within multiple folders, as it searches out and uploads only changed files.

The Synchronize dialog box allows you to delete obsolete files. If the newest file transfer direction is from computer to server, Dreamweaver deletes files

from the server that are not in your local site. If the newest file transfer direction is from server to computer, Dreamweaver deletes files that are not on the server from your computer. Before you commit to synchronizing, you can preview files and select alternative actions.

See also>> **File Transfer: Get and Put**

Synchronize Files Command

See also>> **Compare Files**

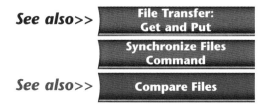

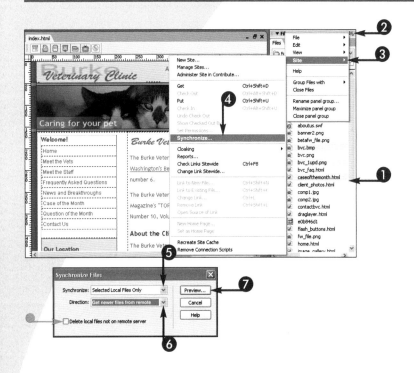

1. Select the files that you want to synchronize; if you plan to synchronize the entire site, then go to step **2**.

2. Click the File Options button (🔳) in the Files panel.

3. Click Site.

4. Click Synchronize.

   Dreamweaver connects to the site.

   The Synchronize Files dialog box appears.

5. Click here and select a Synchronize option.

6. Click here and select a Direction option.

   ● You can click the "Delete local files not on remote server" option (☐ changes to ☑) if you want to delete files that do not exist on the target server.

   If you synchronize Selected Local Files Only in step **5**, then Dreamweaver deletes local files that are not on the remote server.

7. Click Preview.

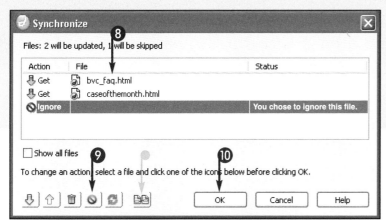

The Synchronize dialog box appears.

⑧ Select a file.

Note: You can ignore step 8 if you plan to use Dreamweaver's default actions.

⑨ Click an Action icon to change the file action.

● You can click this button (🔲) if you want to examine and compare the remote and local versions of the selected files. This feature only works if you specified a comparison tool for Dreamweaver.

⑩ Click OK.

The Background File Activity dialog box appears, displaying file transfer activity.

Dreamweaver puts and gets your files, synchronizing them according to the options that you set.

Caution!

Be very careful when you use the "delete local files not on remote server" option (☐ changes to ☑) to remove files on either the server or your computer. You cannot undo this action, and it is easy to confuse the side from which you are deleting files. In fact, whenever you perform an action that allows Dreamweaver to delete or overwrite files, it is a good idea to first make a complete backup of your site.

Attention!

If you are working with a team, then you may want to set up the Check in/ Check out system in your Site Definition dialog box. In this case, you do not need to use synchronization. You automatically put the newest version of the file on the server when you check a file in, and it matches the latest copy on your computer.

TABLES:
Examine and Set Properties

You can use the Properties inspector to examine the attributes that you have applied to a table and to edit its properties. This allows you to apply styling and structural changes to a table as needed. When you edit the properties of a table, Dreamweaver immediately modifies the underlying code that creates and defines the table in the document. You can examine the properties of a table and also change its fundamental attributes, using a series of text boxes, menus, and buttons, without having to edit the code directly.

The properties you can review include the number of rows and columns, and the table's width, height,

padding, spacing, and border properties. You can also view and edit the table's color values for borders and backgrounds and view or edit background image attributes. You can also modify the width and height values of the table or convert widths between pixels and percentages.

See also>> | Properties Inspector: Tables

See also>> | Import Office Documents

| Tables: Using for Page Layouts

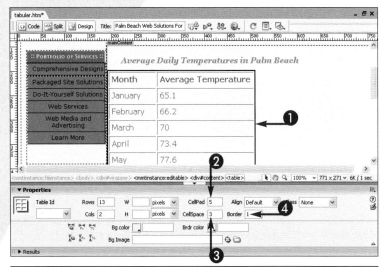

Set Padding, Spacing, and Borders

1 Select a table.

2 Type a value for cell padding to change the amount of empty space inside each cell.

3 Type a value for cell spacing to change the spacing between table cells.

4 Type a value for the borders to define the line around the outside of the table.

Spacing, padding, and border properties are applied as you type them.

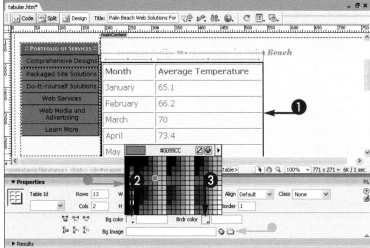

Set Color and Background Values

1 Select a table.

2 Click here and select a background color from the Color Palette.

3 Click here and select a border color from the Color Palette.

● You can type the name of an image to use for the table background.

● You can also point to the file in the Files panel or click the Browse icon ([📁]) to locate the file.

Color and background properties are applied as you select them.

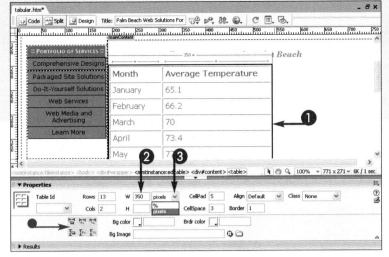

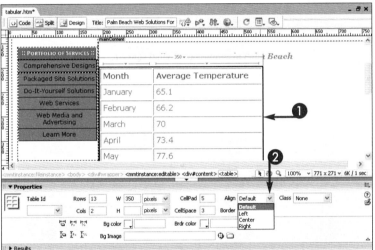

Set Width and Height Properties

① Select a table.

② Type a value for the width of the table.

③ Click here to select either percentage or pixel values for the table.

● You can use these buttons to convert table widths and heights.

Note: Most browsers ignore changes you make to table heights in the Properties inspector. Proper table design does not use the table height setting.

Table size properties are applied as you enter them.

Set Table Alignment

① Select a table.

② Click here and select an alignment for the table.

Tables are aligned relative to the tag that contains them.

Table alignment is set as you change values in the Properties inspector.

Remove It!
You can remove most values for table properties by deleting the listed value in the Properties inspector. For example, if you have a background color listed as #FFCCFF in the Bg Color text box, then simply delete that listing to remove the background color. Exceptions to this rule are the value for borders, padding, and spacing. Because browsers interpret these settings in different ways, you must enter a 0 (zero) for each setting if you want to have no padding, spacing, or border applied to the table.

Try This!
One of the easiest ways to select a table is to click in the page to the right of the table and drag your mouse to the left across the top of the table.

TABLES:
Nest Tables for Page Design

You can insert one table inside another table cell to control page layouts and separate functional areas of your design. When one table is inserted inside another, it is called a nested table.

Nesting tables allows you to use one table to control certain aspects of the design while using the nested table to hold unique content that is unaffected by changes to the outer table. For example, if you want to create a design that is centered on the page, then you can insert a table with a single table cell to use for alignment and for border and background properties of the design. You can then insert a second table inside this outer table to hold the actual content that you intend to put on the page.

This method allows you greater freedom for positioning and aligning your page elements. By nesting tables, you can create designs that make the best use of the available space on the page; you also have more options for formatting and styling.

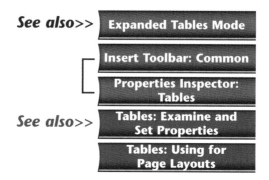

See also>> | Expanded Tables Mode
See also>> | Insert Toolbar: Common
| Properties Inspector: Tables
| Tables: Examine and Set Properties
| Tables: Using for Page Layouts

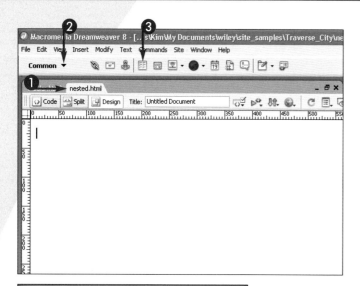

❶ Open an existing document or create a new blank document.

❷ Click here and select Common.

❸ Click the Table icon (▦).

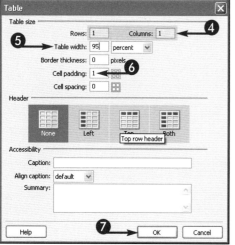

The Table dialog box appears.

❹ Type a value of 1 in the Rows and Columns fields.

❺ Click here and select a table width in pixel or percentage values.

❻ Set a value for cell padding.

❼ Click OK.

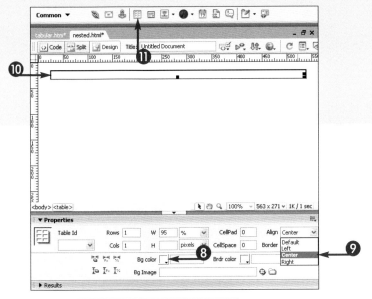

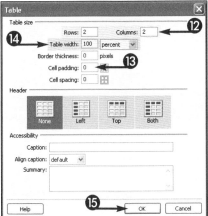

Dreamweaver inserts the table into the page.

⑧ Click here to specify a background color.

⑨ Click here and select a table alignment.

This example uses a center alignment.

⑩ Click inside the table cell.

⑪ Click 🗒.

The Table dialog box appears.

⑫ Type a value for the number of rows and columns.

⑬ Set a cell padding value.

⑭ Set the width of the table in pixels or percentage.

Dreamweaver uses the last values entered when you insert a new table.

⑮ Click OK.

The new table is nested inside the outer table. In this example the padding value creates a one-pixel border around the nested table.

Did You Know?

New users of Dreamweaver are often tempted to combine table rows and columns in order to create the containers they need for their page content. Using this method can lead to many design and maintenance problems later. Instead of spanning table columns and rows, the better method is to carefully consider your design and use nested tables to achieve the same results.

Apply It!

You can use Expanded Table mode to temporarily make the borders and padding in tables larger. This is particularly useful when using nested tables, as it can become difficult to see the position of your tables and select them when tables are nested inside one another.

TABLES:
Nest Tables for Page Design (Continued)

After you create the basic structure, you can continue your design by placing both the tables themselves and your content into the table cells. You should consider the values that you enter for cell alignment. In most cases you should change the default vertical alignment to top, which nests both the table and the content at the top of the table cell. If you do not specify alignment values, content is centered at the middle of the table cell. This default alignment may cause problems with your design if one cell contains more content than its neighboring cell in the same row.

While there is no particular rule for how many tables you can insert into another, try to keep the structure

of your page as simple as possible and use the least number of tables that allows you to achieve your design goals.

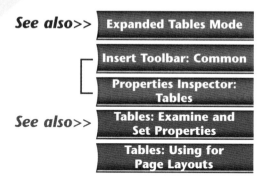

See also>> Expanded Tables Mode

Insert Toolbar: Common

Properties Inspector: Tables

See also>> Tables: Examine and Set Properties

Tables: Using for Page Layouts

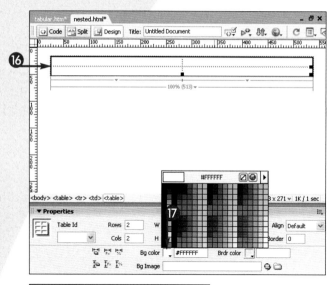

⑯ Select the new table.

⑰ Click here and select a contrasting background color for the new table.

⑱ Click Modify.

⑲ Click Page Properties.

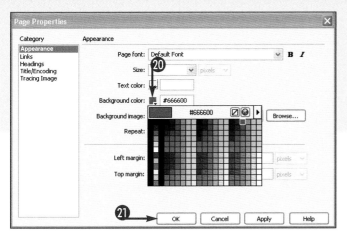

The Page Properties dialog box appears.

⑳ Click here and select a color for the page background.

㉑ Click OK.

Dreamweaver applies the page color.

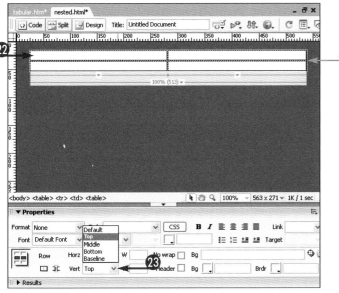

㉒ Click and drag from the top-left table cell to the bottom-right table cell.

● All of the cells are selected when a black border appears around the cell borders.

㉓ Click here and select a vertical alignment.

This example uses a top alignment.

Your table is now ready for you to add content.

Important!

Although creating page layouts with nested tables is perhaps the easiest way to accomplish a page design, this method is losing favor. Modern Web design separates the structure of the page from the design elements. In other words, when you design with modern methods, the structural elements of the page, such as tables, do not contain styling properties.

Check It Out!

Although creating standards-based designs with CSS methods may be more difficult than using nested tables, you may find that using modern methods has significant advantages when you need to make changes to your designs. You can read more about Web standards at www.webstandards.org.

TABLES:
Using for Page Layouts

You can divide your page design into different functional areas using tables to create containers for your page content. Dreamweaver's Layout mode assists you in drawing tables onto the page in preparation for adding your content. You can also work in Standard mode to insert tables and format their properties.

HTML is unlike traditional desktop publishing in that you must define the different areas of the page and control their position and size before adding content.

Using Layout mode allows you to quickly add the necessary tables and individual cells needed to

accomplish your design goals. Once you complete the initial layout, you can switch to Standard mode to insert content into your page.

See also>>

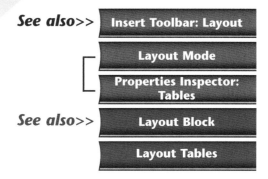

Insert Toolbar: Layout

Layout Mode

Properties Inspector: Tables

See also>>

Layout Block

Layout Tables

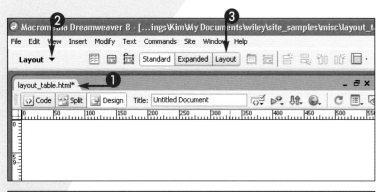

❶ Create a new page.

❷ Click here and select Layout.

❸ Click Layout.

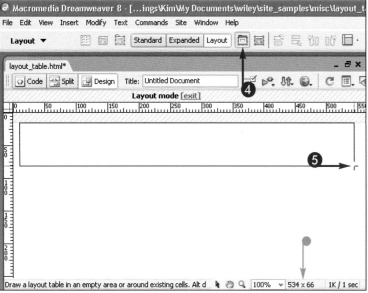

❹ Click the Layout Table icon (▢).

❺ Click and drag across the top of the page to create a page header.

● The dimensions of the layout table appear in the Status bar as you drag your cursor.

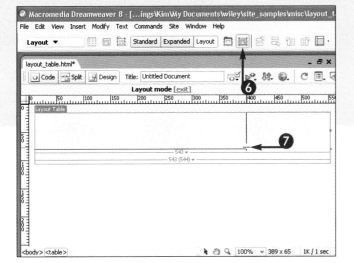

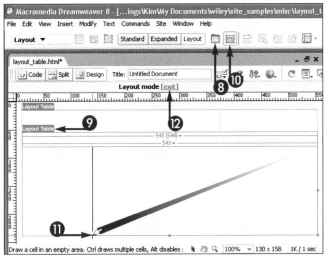

6 Click the Layout Cell icon (⊞).

7 Click and drag inside the layout table to create a layout cell.

Dreamweaver adds the layout cell inside the layout table.

8 Click 🗖.

9 Click and drag to create a new layout table below the header table.

10 Click ⊞.

11 Click and drag to add new layout cells in the content table.

To avoid alignment problems, you should completely fill layout tables with layout cells.

12 Click the exit link to return to Standard mode.

You can now style your tables and begin adding page content.

Try This!

If you cannot draw a layout object on the page, then try resizing the Document Window to give you more space to work. In Windows, you can collapse the panel groups; in Mac OS X, you can expand the Document Window.

Important!

You should only use Layout mode to design the blocks on the page where you want to place your content. Once you have the basic structure of the design laid out, you can return to Standard mode to insert the page content. Many of the standard insert commands are disabled while you are in Layout mode.

TAG SELECTOR:
Select and Edit Tags

You can quickly select elements on your page using the list of tags in the Status bar at the bottom of the Document Window. With the Tag Selector, you can select a tag so that you can view and edit its properties in the Properties inspector. You can also perform operations such as setting a class or ID, opening the Quick Tag Editor to make edits in the tag's code, or even removing the tag from the page.

The Tag Selector displays the tags in a page from left to right, based on their hierarchy. When you select a tag, the Tag Selector lists the tags in the order that

makes up that particular selection. For example, a table cell lists `<body> <table> <tr>` followed by the `<td>` tag. You can move any tag in the Tag Selector to move it up in the page's structure.

See also>>

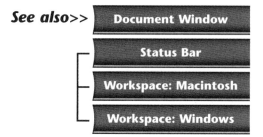

Document Window

Status Bar

Workspace: Macintosh

Workspace: Windows

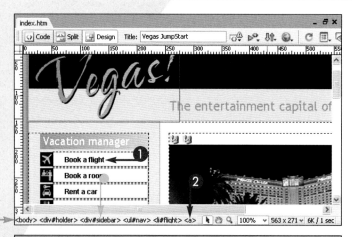

View and Select Tags

1. Click inside a page.

● The Tag Selector lists the order of the tags inside the selection.

● Tags with IDs applied are listed with the ID name preceded by a number sign.

2. Click a listed tag.

● The selected tag is highlighted in the page.

● The selected tag is highlighted in the Tag Selector.

● Properties for the selected tag are listed in the Properties inspector.

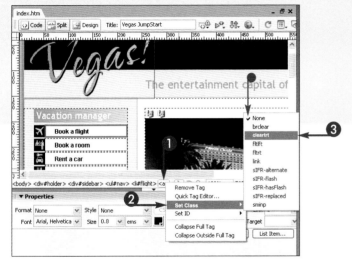

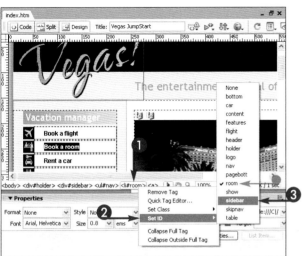

View and Change CSS Classes

① Right-click (Ctrl-click) a tag.

② Click Set Class.

● A checkmark (☑) appears next to the currently applied class.

③ Click a new class in the list.

Dreamweaver applies the new class.

View and Change Tag IDs

① Right-click (Ctrl-click) a tag.

② Click Set ID.

● A ☑ appears next to the current ID.

③ Click a new ID in the list.

Dreamweaver applies the new ID.

Did You Know?

The Tag Selector is one of the more indispensable tools found in Dreamweaver. With this one interface area, you can see how the tags on the page are structured, see the names of IDs and classes that have been applied to tags, select items more easily on the page, move your selection area up and down in the hierarchy of the page tags, and apply new settings directly to tags. Because of this, experienced Dreamweaver users probably turn to the Tag Selector more than any other interface.

Try This!

Use the Quick Tag Editor to add an ID to a tag that does not have one. This allows you to control the presentation of the tag more efficiently with CSS.

TARGET BROWSER CHECK:
Check Page Compatibility

Dreamweaver allows you to check the compatibility of your Web pages in different browsers and to view a report of any issues that it finds. You can test the HTML and CSS code in your page to ensure that the page displays correctly in all of the selected Web browsers.

By default, Dreamweaver checks the specified target browser each time you open a page. If it finds any errors on the page, an alert symbol displays on top of the Target Browser Check button in the Documents toolbar. This button gives options for viewing browser problems that Dreamweaver identifies.

Dreamweaver classifies target browser issues in three different categories. Errors are those issues that may cause serious problems in the page, such as an object disappearing from the page. Warnings are those errors that may cause an object to display incorrectly, but do not prevent it from being seen. Finally, code that is marked with an informational message may not be supported in some browsers, but does not cause display issues.

See also>>

Browsers

Results Panel: Using for
Target Browser Check

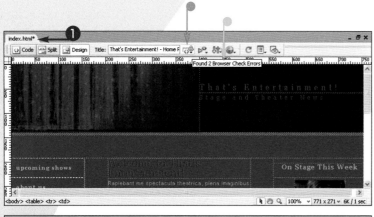

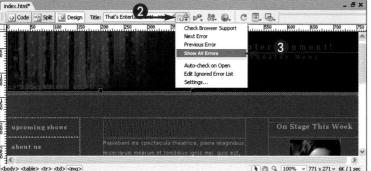

① Open a document.

● A Warning icon (🔲) appears when errors are found with the targeted browsers.

● When you hover your mouse over the icon, a tooltip displays the number of serious browser problems found.

Note: Although Dreamweaver checks pages when they are opened, it does not check your code as you edit the page.

To check documents after they have been changed, run the Check Browser Support command from the Target Browser Check button (🔲).

② Click 🔲.

③ Click Show All Errors.

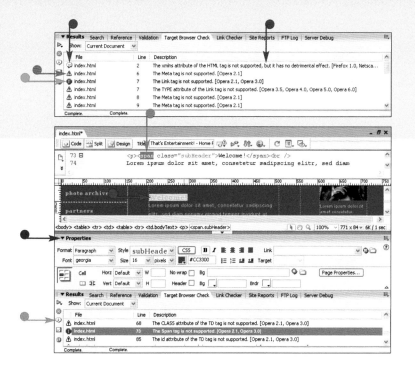

The Results panel opens.

● Informational errors are listed with a Talking Balloon icon (💬).

● Warnings are marked with ⚠.

● Critical errors are marked with a Stop Sign icon (🛑).

● A description appears of the error and the affected browser.

④ Double-click any error in the list.

Dreamweaver switches to Split view.

● The error in the code is highlighted in the code listing.

● The object containing the error is highlighted in the Design Window.

● The Properties inspector switches to the item that contains the error.

● You can click Info button (💬) to see additional details about the error.

Did You Know?
Identifying the browser errors in your pages is just the first step towards gaining browser compatibility. Dreamweaver only identifies the problems that it finds in your code; it does not change your code in any way. It is up to you to decide if you want to address the problem or ignore it.

More Options!
You can add or remove the browsers that are targeted when you check browser support by clicking the Target Browser Check button (🔍). Click Settings to display a dialog box that shows all of the currently targeted browsers. You can change the version of a particular browser, add a browser, or remove a browser in this dialog box.

TIPS

T

TARGET LINKS:
Open Pages in New Windows

You can cause a link to open in a new browser window using the target attribute in the Properties inspector. When the target of a link is set to _blank, a new browser window opens if the person viewing the page clicks the link.

You generally use link targets for pages that you build with frames and framesets. However, you may also use the _blank target value to open new browser windows from standard Web pages. This method opens a new full-size window, and takes the viewer to the linked document, which you can make a page on your own site, or a Web address that you

create by entering the URL to the Web page in the Link field of the Properties inspector. You can target a link that applies to text or an image.

For more control over how a new window is created when a user clicks a link, use the Open Browser Window behavior.

See also>>

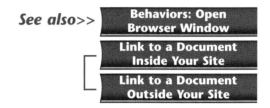

Behaviors: Open
Browser Window

Link to a Document
Inside Your Site

Link to a Document
Outside Your Site

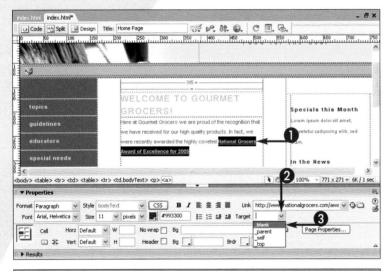

① Select a link in a document.

② Click the Target drop-down menu.

③ Click _blank.

● Dreamweaver sets the target to _blank in the Properties inspector.

TEMPLATES:
Apply to New Document

You can apply a template to a new document to quickly create a complete page design. You can incorporate the graphics, navigation objects, and page structure into pages that exist to maintain a consistent design throughout all of your pages.

Applying templates to new pages that do not yet contain content involves creating the page, and then using the Assets panel to locate the template that you want to apply to the new page. You can also apply templates to a page with the Modify menu.

In the Assets panel, you can view all the templates that you have created, and you can

preview a selected template before you apply it to the page. To apply a template to a page, you select the template that you want and activate the Apply button.

See also>> Assets Panel

New Document Window

Templates

See also>> New Documents:
Create from Templates

Templates:
Create a Template

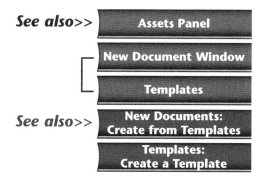

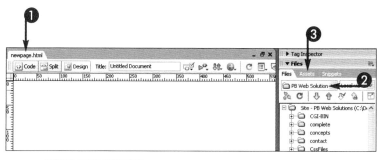

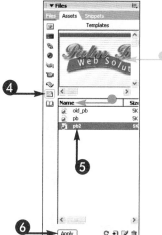

① Create a new blank document.

② Save the file in a site where you have created templates.

③ Click the Assets tab.

The Assets panel displays site assets.

④ Click the Templates icon (🖺).

● The Assets panel lists the available templates in the site.

⑤ Click a template name.

● The Preview pane displays the selected template.

⑥ Click Apply.

Dreamweaver applies the selected template to the page.

TEMPLATES:
Apply to Page with Content

You can apply a template to a document that contains text, images, or other page elements as you would to a new page. When a page contains existing content, you must determine how the existing content is placed into the editable regions of the page.

Dreamweaver tries to determine the correct editable region to place existing content when you apply a template to a document. If you are applying a revised template to a page that previously had a template attached, Dreamweaver may recognize editable regions and attach the template to the page without the need for additional work on your part.

In many cases where content exists in a page, you must respond in a dialog box where Dreamweaver displays a list of unresolved regions. Dreamweaver lists the content that it could not resolve when you applied the template, along with a list of the editable regions where the content can be placed.

See also>> **Assets Panel**

See also>> **Templates: Editable Regions**

Templates: Update Pages

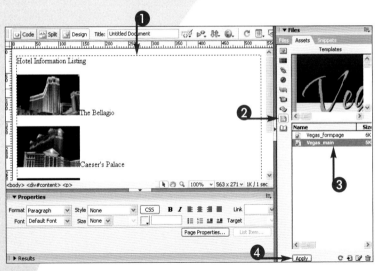

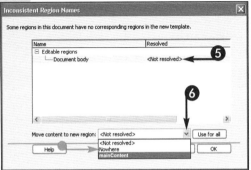

① Open a document that contains content.

② Click the Templates icon (🗔) in the Assets tab.

③ Click the template that you want to apply to the page.

④ Click Apply.

The Inconsistent Region Names dialog box appears.

⑤ Click a listed region.

⑥ Click here and select the editable region where the existing content should be placed.

● You can click Nowhere to remove the existing content from the page.

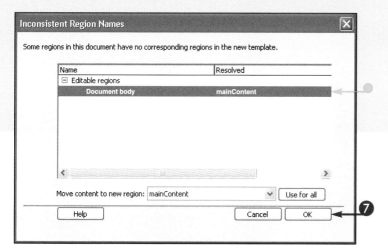

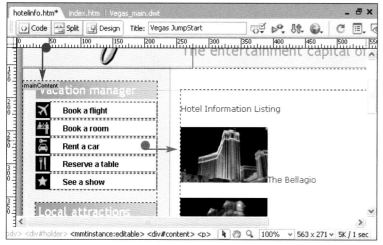

- The content appears next to the name of the region where Dreamweaver will place it.

⑦ Click OK.

- Dreamweaver applies the selected template to the page.

- Existing content moves into the editable region.

Delete It!

You can undo the application of a template to a page up until when you save the file and close Dreamweaver. Press Ctrl+Z (⌘+Z) to undo the application of the template and return to the original page design.

Caution!

Applying templates to pages with existing content can be difficult. If the structure of the existing page is vastly different from the template layout, then you may be better off creating a new blank page, applying the template, and then copying and pasting from the existing page to the new template-based version.

TEMPLATES:
Create a Template

With Dreamweaver templates, you can create a page design that you can quickly apply to all your site's pages. Templates define your site's structure, design, and navigation features, and allow you to automatically update these pages simply by modifying the template.

To create a template, you first complete a page design that contains all the elements that you want on every page, such as a header graphic, a navigation bar, and the separate containers to hold your page content. You then save the page as a template file with the extension .dwt, placing it into a folder named Templates in your site. You can then designate and name the editable regions in the

page where you intend to place new content. Finally, you can create new pages that start with the template or apply the template to existing pages.

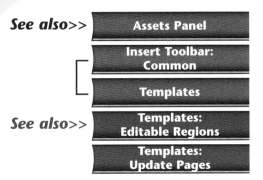

See also>> Assets Panel

See also>>
Insert Toolbar: Common
Templates

Templates: Editable Regions
Templates: Update Pages

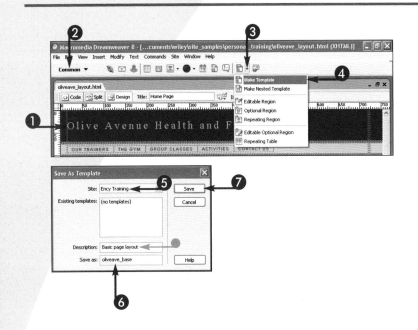

1. Open a document that contains a completed design.

2. Click here and select Common.

3. Click the Template (⬚) arrow.

4. Click Make Template.

The Save As Template dialog box appears.

5. Click here and select the site where you want to save the template.

● You can type a description here.

6. Type a name for the template file.

7. Click Save.

8. Click Yes when the Update links message appears.

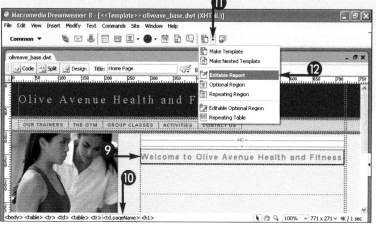

⑨ Click inside the first editable region that you want to create.

⑩ Click the containing tag in the Tag Selector.

⑪ Click the 🖹 arrow.

⑫ Click Editable Region.

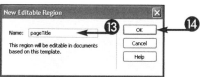

The New Editable Region dialog box appears.

⑬ Type a name for the editable region.

⑭ Click OK.

⑮ Save the file.

Dreamweaver creates the first editable region in the template.

Did You Know?

When you create a template, you can only place new content into, and modify the content of, editable regions in the page. Although every template must contain at least one editable region, it can contain as many as needed to meet your design goals. If you save a template without creating an editable region, then Dreamweaver displays a warning that says you cannot add new content until you designate an editable region in the template file.

Test It!

In order to function correctly, you must save all template files into the Templates folder at the root of the designated site. After you create a template for the first time in a site, you should open the Files panel and verify that Dreamweaver has created the Templates folder for you, and placed the template file inside.

TEMPLATES:
Delete from Site

You can delete template files from your Web site when you no longer need them. When you delete a template file, none of the pages that you have built from the template are affected. To remove the template markup from those pages and make them fully editable, you must detach the pages from the template.

It is a common practice to produce multiple templates when a Web site is in development. You may find that your clients request multiple changes to page designs that necessitate changes to your

templates. When you find that you no longer need a template, it is best to delete the file from your site to help you maintain your site files. You can run the Link Checker command and set it to check for orphaned files to locate templates that are not currently in use. Once those files are located, they can be safely removed from the site.

See also>> **Assets Panel**

See also>> **Templates: Detach from Document**

1 Click the Assets tab.

2 Click the Templates icon ([image]).

3 Click the template file that you want to delete.

4 Click the Trash icon ([image]).

A dialog box appears, asking you to confirm the file deletion.

5 Click Yes to confirm the file deletion.

Dreamweaver removes the template file from the site.

TEMPLATES:
Detach from Document

When you create a template, there are parts of the page that are locked, and others that you can edit. When you want to edit an area of a page that is outside an editable region in the template, you must first detach the file from the template.

Template files contain special coding, called *template markup*, which prevents you from making edits in a locked region. Locked regions are used to maintain the structure, design, and navigation elements that appear in all of the pages that you have created from the template and to allow for changes to be applied to those

pages that are built from the template. On occasion, you may need more freedom with a file to change its structure or to remove parts of the page. You can perform these edits after you have detached the template from the page.

When you detach a template from a page, Dreamweaver can no longer automatically update the page if you change the template file. In order to regain template updating, you must reattach the template file to the page.

See also>> **Templates: Update Pages**

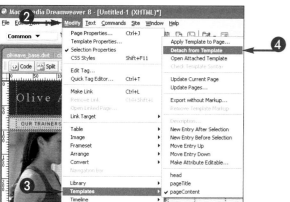

❶ Open a file that has a template attached to it.

● You cannot edit locked areas of the page, which have the "no" icon (⊘).

❷ Click Modify.

❸ Click Templates.

❹ Click Detach from Template.

Previously locked areas are now available for editing.

TEMPLATES:
Editable Regions

You can add new editable regions, remove existing editable regions, and change the name of the editable regions in a template file by using the Insert bar when you need to make modifications.

Editable regions in a template file allow you to add new content to a page that you build from a template. When you apply a template to a file, certain areas of the page are locked to maintain the integrity of your design and to allow Dreamweaver to perform updates when you change the template file. In the pages that you build from the template, called *child pages*, you can only add new content to the editable regions of the page.

When you must modify editable regions, you make all changes in the template file. When you save the template file, Dreamweaver applies all changes when the child pages are updated.

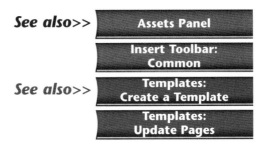

See also>> Assets Panel

Insert Toolbar: Common

See also>> Templates: Create a Template

Templates: Update Pages

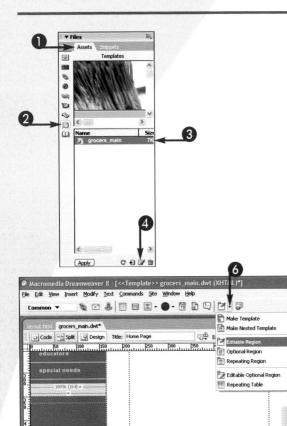

Open a Template for Editing

1 Click the Assets tab.

2 Click the Templates icon (⬛).

3 Click the template that you want to modify.

4 Click the Edit icon (✎).

Add a New Editable Region

5 Click the Tag Selector to select an empty `<table>`, `<td>`, or `<div>` tag.

6 Click the ⬛ arrow.

7 Click Editable Region.

8 In the dialog box that appears, type a name for the new editable region.

Dreamweaver creates the new editable region in the template file.

414

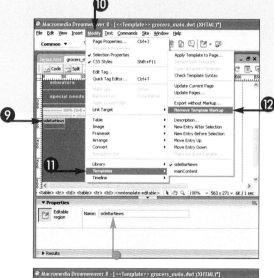

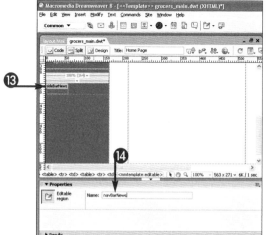

Delete an Editable Region

⑨ Click the tab in the upper-left corner of the editable region.

● The name of the editable region displays in the Properties inspector.

⑩ Click Modify.

⑪ Click Templates.

⑫ Click Remove Template Markup.

Dreamweaver removes the editable region from the template.

Rename an Editable Region

⑬ Click the tab in the upper-left corner of the editable region.

⑭ Type a new name in the Properties inspector.

⑮ Press Enter.

Dreamweaver changes the name of the editable region.

Important!

You must save the template file and update all of the child pages that use the template once you have made changes to editable regions. If you have renamed an editable region and a child page contains content in that region, then Dreamweaver displays a dialog box where you can select the editable region where you want to move the content.

Did You Know?

Updating templates only modifies the documents on your computer. In order to make the updates visible on the Web, you must upload the modified files to your Web server.

TEMPLATES:
Nested Templates

You can use a master template that contains the major elements of your design and then build sub-templates from the master to add more styling or structural objects.

Creating nested templates based on a master design allows you to plan for changes that may occur in the site design. If you change an object in the master template, then all of the nested templates that you have created from the master file are updated based on your changes to the master.

To create a nested template, you begin by creating a new file from a template. You then save the new file as a template, and you add new editable regions to

the nested template. Dreamweaver provides special color coding in the template files to show which editable regions are in the master file and which exist only in the nested template.

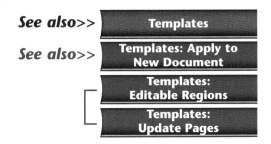

See also>> Templates

See also>> Templates: Apply to New Document

Templates: Editable Regions

Templates: Update Pages

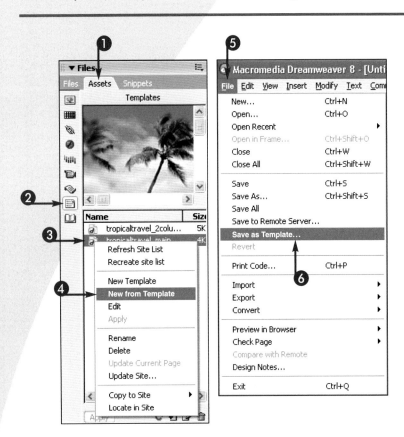

① Click the Assets tab.

② Click the Templates icon (▣).

③ Right-click (Ctrl-click) the template that you want to use as the master template.

④ Click New from Template.

The master template must have at least one editable region.

The new document opens with the master template applied.

⑤ Click File.

⑥ Click Save as Template.

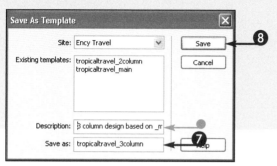

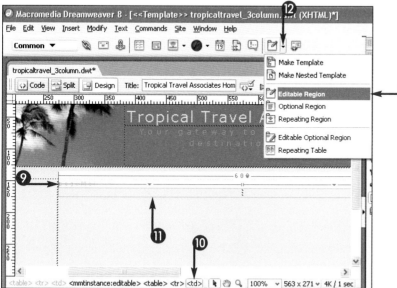

The Save As Template dialog box appears.

● You can add a description.

7 Type a name for the new template.

8 Click Save.

9 Click inside an editable region.

10 Add a table or page division for the new editable region.

11 Select the region that you want to be editable in the nested template.

12 Click the 🖹 arrow.

13 Select Editable Region.

Dreamweaver adds the new editable region in the nested template.

More Options!

You can prevent an editable region from passing through to nested templates by locking the code in the master template file. To do this, open the master template in Code view and type @@(" in front of the comments that open the editable region; then type ")@@ after the comment that closes the region.

Check It Out!

Many of the options for Dreamweaver templates were first introduced in Dreamweaver MX and are still relevant in the latest version. You can find a collection of tutorials that will help you understand how to make the most of Dreamweaver templates at www.dreamweavermx-templates.com. Although these tutorials were written for Dreamweaver MX, they still explain how to use many of the advanced features found in templates.

TEMPLATES:
Optional Regions

You can define certain areas of a template-based page that may or may not show based on input from someone working on the page. Optional regions are most often used in collaborative environments where one person is responsible for creating the templates for a site, and others prepare pages for publication. The Web developer can position all design elements and then share the file with others who decide on the final items to display.

Optional regions use a special, conditional statement in the code to determine whether to make the optional region visible. Once the optional regions are present in the page, you or a co-worker can decide whether

the element should appear. For example, if you have a series of photographs for products on sale, you can place all of the images into the page and then choose which image should display as you build new pages from the template.

See also>>

Templates: Apply to New Document
Templates: Editable Regions
Templates: Repeating Regions
Templates: Update Pages

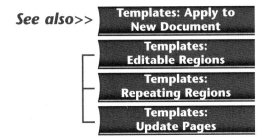

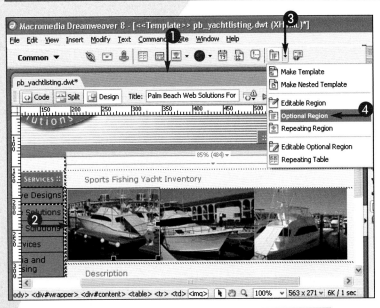

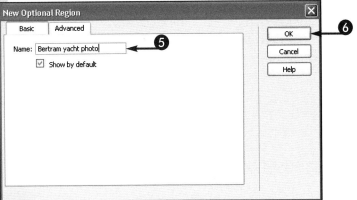

❶ Open a template file containing content that you want to include as optional regions.

❷ Select the object that you want to include as an optional region.

Your content must not be inside an editable region.

❸ Click the Template (🖾) drop-down arrow.

❹ Click Optional Region.

The New Optional Region dialog box appears.

❺ Type a name for the new optional region.

❻ Click OK.

❼ Repeat steps **2** to **6** for the remaining items.

❽ Save the template file.

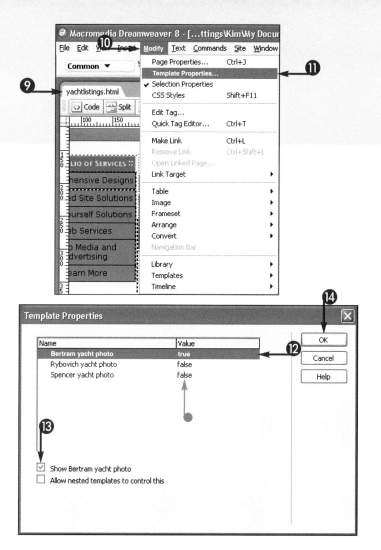

⑨ Create a new file from the template that contains optional regions.

⑩ Click Modify.

⑪ Click Template Properties.

The Template Properties dialog box appears.

⑫ Click the name of the region to appear in the page.

⑬ Click the option (☐ changes to ☑) for regions to appear in the page.

● Regions that are not set to show display a False value in the listing.

⑭ Click OK.

Only editable regions that are set to show in the page now appear.

TIPS

Put It Together!

Optional regions work well in a collaborative environment, particularly if the individuals responsible for adding new pages and creating content are not Web developers. In this case, you can design the templates and provide your content contributors with a copy of Macromedia Contribute. Contribute was designed with nontechnical Web authors in mind and has a simple interface that requires much less technical know-how than Dreamweaver.

More Info!

By using advanced template functions such as optional regions, you can maintain control over the presentation of a site while giving collaborators using Contribute of Dreamweaver the ability to make their own modifications.

TEMPLATES:
Repeating Regions

You can add elements to a template file that you can repeat, order, and delete on an as-needed basis. Repeating regions allow you to add new objects whenever they are needed without editing the templates.

As with optional regions, this feature is most often used when working in a collaborative environment. For example, if you have a product-listing page that another member of the design team needs, then you can design repeating regions into a template to allow them to create additional listings as new products are added. Although repeating regions are most often used with table rows, you can use them

with other structural objects such as paragraphs and page divisions.

In addition to creating the repeating regions, you must also add editable regions to the template.

See also>>

Templates: Apply to New Document
Templates: Editable Regions
Templates: Optional Regions
Templates: Update Pages

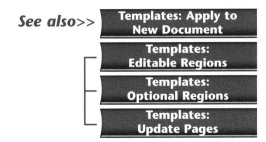

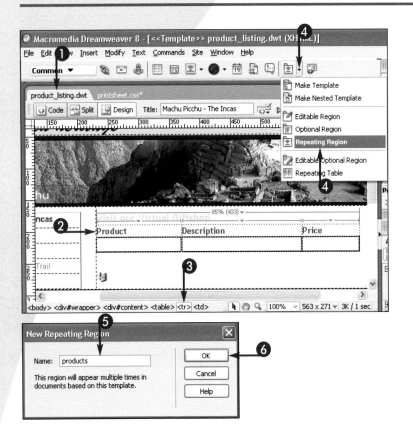

Create Repeating Regions

1 Open a template file where you want to add repeating regions.

2 Insert a table.

3 Select the bottom table row.

4 Click the 🖺 arrow and select Repeating Region.

The New Repeating Region dialog box appears.

5 Type a name for the repeating region.

6 Click OK.

7 Save the template file.

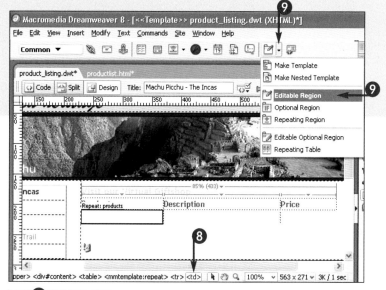

8 Select the first table cell to become an editable region.

9 Click the arrow and select Editable region.

10 In the dialog box that appears, type a name for the new editable region.

11 Click OK.

12 Repeat steps **9** to **11** for additional editable regions.

13 Save the template.

Working with Repeating Regions

1 Create a new page from a template that contains repeating regions.

2 Type content into the first row of the table.

● You can click the plus sign ([+]) to add a new region or the minus sign ([−]) to remove a region.

● You can use the Up and Down arrows ([▲] and [▼]) to move regions up or down in the listing.

More Options!

Dreamweaver allows you to create repeating tables as well as repeating regions. When you choose the repeating tables option, a dialog box appears where you design the table layout and provide basic information about the names of repeating and editable regions. Although this command is very similar to the Repeating Regions command, it does not allow you as many customization options.

Check It Out!

The Dreamweaver Developer Center has a number of tutorials and sample files from which you can learn about template options, including the use of repeating regions. You can find the Developer Center at www.macromedia.com/devnet/dreamweaver.

TEMPLATES:
Update Pages

You can update the pages that have been built from templates in a number of ways. Whenever you edit and save a template, Dreamweaver prompts you to update the pages that use the template. However, you can force an update of only those pages in your site that use a particular template, or perform a sitewide update that checks all files and all templates for changes.

When you update pages created from template files, Dreamweaver only looks for modifications to the locked areas of the template. For example, changing the graphic in the non-editable header of your template page changes every child page of the template.

Whenever you edit a template and save the file, you are prompted to update the child pages of the template. If you choose not to update those pages immediately, then you can run the Update command at a later time.

See also>>

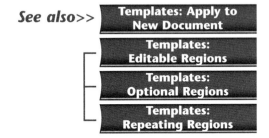

Automatic Updates

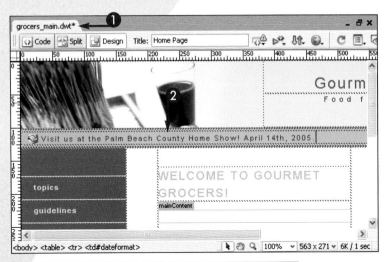

1 Open a template file.

2 Edit the template file by changing objects outside of editable regions.

3 Save the file.

The Update Template Files dialog box appears.

● Child pages of the template being saved are listed here.

4 Click Update.

Dreamweaver updates the files and provides a record of the files that have been modified.

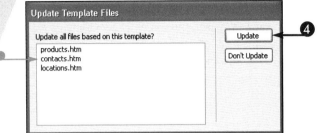

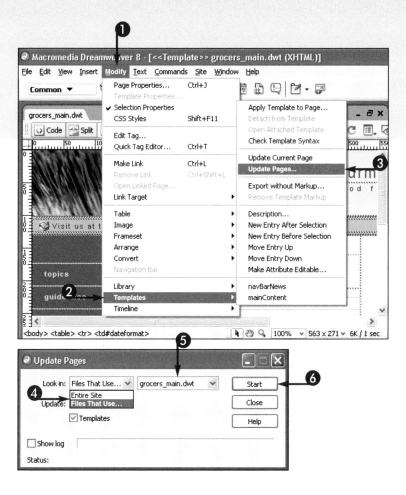

① Click Modify.

② Click Templates.

③ Click Update Pages.

The Update Pages dialog box appears.

④ Click to update pages that use a particular template or to update the entire site.

⑤ Click here to select the template file from the list.

⑥ Click Start.

Dreamweaver updates pages based on your selections, and provides a report on the files that are revised.

TIPS

Caution!

Dreamweaver's ability to update files that use templates depends on some very specific programming regarding the location of the template file within your site. All template files must be located in the folder named Templates at one level below the root folder for each site. You should never remove template files from the Templates folder or save other types of files into this folder. If a template file is moved from its proper folder, then Dreamweaver can no longer update the files that use the template.

Important!

Once you have performed an update on your site, you must put the modified files onto your Web server. Dreamweaver performs all of its operations on your computer. In order for others to see the updated files, these files must be put onto the server.

TEXT:
Create Lists

You can create lists in either a bulleted or numbered format by selecting the options available in the Properties inspector. When you create lists, Dreamweaver inserts an unordered list tag for bulleted lists or an ordered list tag for numbered lists.

The best method for creating lists is to simply type the text into your document and press the Enter key at the end of each line. Once you have inserted the text into the page, you can select the block of text and apply the formatting you want.

You can apply additional formatting to a list either through HTML attributes or through CSS rules. HTML attributes allow you to change the number style or starting number for numbered lists, and to change the bullet styles for bulleted lists. CSS styling allows you the greatest freedom in formatting your lists, including the ability to use images for bullets and lists as navigation objects.

See also>>

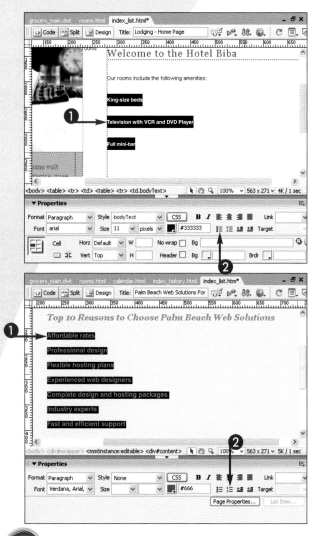

Create a Bulleted List

1 Select a block of text.

2 Click the Unordered List icon (▤).

Dreamweaver converts the selected text to a bulleted list.

Create a Numbered List

1 Select a block of text.

2 Click the Ordered List icon (▤).

Dreamweaver converts the selected text to a numbered list.

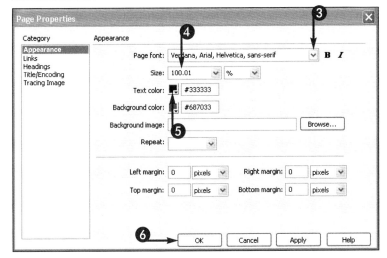

Create a Default Text Style

① Click Modify.

② Click Page Properties.

The Page Properties dialog box appears.

③ Click here and select the page font.

④ Click here and select the font size and unit of measurement.

⑤ Click here and select the font color.

⑥ Click OK.

Dreamweaver applies your default text styling information for the page.

TIPS

Did You Know?
While it may seem that you are editing the text in a document when you apply styles, you are actually changing the display characteristics of the tag that contains the text. For example, if you select a paragraph and create a new style, Dreamweaver applies the styling rule to the paragraph tag. Previously in Web design, the font tag was used to control the appearance of text. Because that method was difficult to maintain and edit, requiring that each block of text be styled independently, Dreamweaver now conforms to the recommendations of the World Wide Web Consortium and uses styles for all text styling.

Remove It!
You can remove all styling that is applied to text by setting the style to None in the Style menu of the Properties inspector.

TRACING IMAGES:
Using Images for Page Layouts

You can place an image into the Dreamweaver design environment to act as a guide as you create new site compositions. Tracing images allows you to use a graphical representation of your page design that you create in an image editor such as Fireworks or Photoshop to assist you in the creation of your page layouts. Tracing images display only while you work in Dreamweaver.

You can use a tracing image that has been saved in the GIF, JPG, or PNG format. Dreamweaver places these images into the background of the Document

Window so that you can see how the completed design appears, and can create the page elements that you need to meet your design goals. As you add objects to the page, you can change the transparency of the tracing image to make it less pronounced, or hide it entirely.

See also>>

See also>> Layout Mode

Page Properties

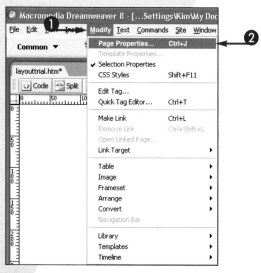

① Click Modify.

② Click Page Properties.

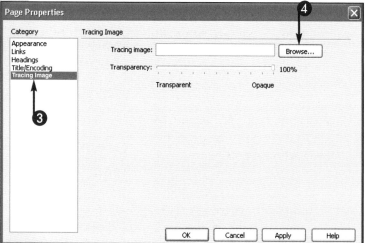

The Page Properties dialog box appears.

③ Click Tracing Image.

④ Click Browse.

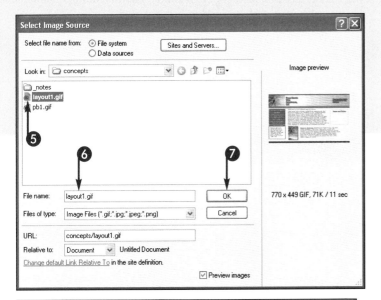

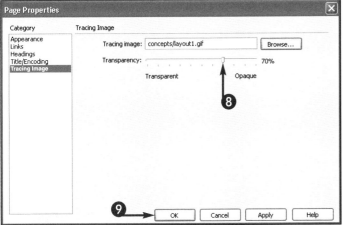

The Select Image Source dialog box appears.

5 Browse to the image that you want to use.

6 Select the image.

7 Click OK.

8 Move the slider to specify the transparency that you want for the tracing image.

9 Click OK.

Dreamweaver inserts the tracing image behind the Document Window.

You can add page layout elements directly on top of the tracing image to begin the design process.

TIPS

More Options!

You can use the View menu to adjust the appearance of the tracing image and change its position. When you select the Adjust Position command, you can specify the exact X- and Y-coordinates where the top-left corner of the tracing image should be set. You can also select an object on the page and reset the position of the tracing image to align with the object.

Try This!

If you create a color palette for a site, then you can save the palette as an image and set it as the tracing image for the page. Once the palette image is in place, you can then use the Eyedropper tool (⬚) in the Color Chooser to select colors for elements such as text and background colors.

VALIDATE FORMS:
Using Behavior To

You can use the Validate Form behavior to require your visitors to enter data into form text fields. You can also set options to check for the correct kind of data in a specific text field. For example, if you have a field that allows visitors to enter e-mail addresses, then you can have Dreamweaver check to ensure that the visitor enters the data in a valid e-mail format. If you have a phone number field, then Dreamweaver can check that the visitor enters numbers.

You can allow the Validate Form behavior to validate each text field as the visitor enters information, or you can select the entire form and allow

Dreamweaver to validate it when the visitor clicks the Submit button. In either case, if data is missing, the browser displays an error message and instructs the visitor to supply the information.

See also>>

Behaviors: Apply to Web Page Events
Forms: Insert Text Fields
Macromedia Exchange
Tag Selector

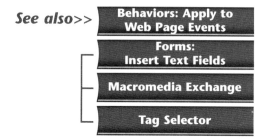

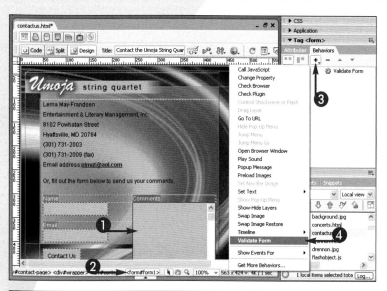

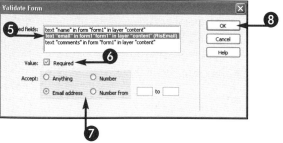

① Click inside your form.

② Click the form tag in the Tag Selector.

③ Click the Add button (⊞) in the Behaviors panel.

④ Click Validate Form.

The Validate Form dialog box appears.

⑤ Click the text form object that you want to validate.

⑥ Click the Value Required option (☐ changes to ☑).

⑦ Click an Accept option (◯ changes to ◉).

⑧ Click OK.

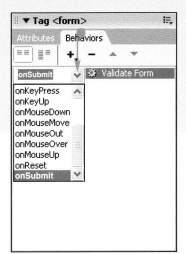

Dreamweaver adds the behavior to the Behaviors panel, and the JavaScript to your code.

● You can click here to select a different event if you want.

The browser displays an error message if the visitor omits a field or enters information incorrectly.

Check It Out!

The Validate Form behavior limits you to only text form objects, and its JavaScript for checking data types is fairly basic. You can perform more robust form validation by downloading and installing a dedicated extension such as the free Check Form extension, which is available at www.yaromat.com/dw/?t=Behavior&r=forms. This extension adds a behavior that checks text, radio buttons, menus, lists, and check-box form objects.

Check It Out!

The free Check Form extension also has very sophisticated scripts for checking and evaluating the kinds of data that visitors enter. It also enables you to replace the generic browser error message with custom error messages. You can look for other extensions that validate forms at the Macromedia Exchange by clicking Commands and then clicking Get More Commands.

VALIDATE HTML:
Using Command

You can use Dreamweaver's Check Page command to ensure that your code syntax is error-free. There are other kinds of validation tools on the Web, such as those for Cascading Style Sheets document accessibility. However, Dreamweaver's validation checks your markup according to the settings that you select in the Validation preferences. For example, you may have selected a specific version of XHTML or HTML. When you choose to validate your markup, Dreamweaver validates your page based on the World Wide Web Consortium's rules for the target markup languages.

Dreamweaver opens the Results panel and either displays a "No errors or warnings" message or, if there are possible problems, it lists page errors. You can double-click an error to get a description of its meaning. You can use the Browse Report icon to display a complete report in your browser. You can also use the Save Report icon to save the report as an XML file that opens in Dreamweaver.

See also>> Preferences: Validator

Results Panel:
Using for Validation

① Open the page that you want to validate.

② Click File.

③ Click Check Page.

④ Click Validate Markup.

The Results panel opens with the Validation tab displayed, performs a validation check on the page, and lists all errors based on your validation preferences.

⑤ Double-click an error.

● Dreamweaver opens to the problem location in Code or Design view.

⑥ Click the Info icon (🔲) to learn more about the error.

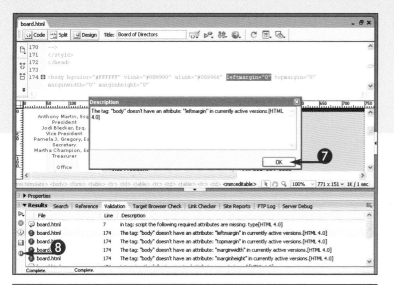

The Description dialog box appears, displaying information about the error.

⑦ Click OK when you are done.

⑧ Click the Browse Report icon (🖼).

Dreamweaver opens a full report in your browser so that you can read or save it.

Validator Results

Report date: November 07 2005

Report time: 11:27:53

Severity	File	Description	Line
Message	C:\Documents and Settings\Owner\My Documents\pg law\board.html	in tag: script the following required attributes are missing: type	7
Error	C:\Documents and Settings\Owner\My Documents\pg law\board.html	The tag: "body" doesn't have an attribute: "leftmargin" in currently active versions.	174
Error	C:\Documents and Settings\Owner\My Documents\pg law\board.html	The tag: "body" doesn't have an attribute: "topmargin" in currently active versions.	174
Error	C:\Documents and Settings\Owner\My Documents\pg law\board.html	The tag: "body" doesn't have an attribute: "marginwidth" in currently active versions.	174
Error	C:\Documents and Settings\Owner\My Documents\pg law\board.html	The tag: "body" doesn't have an attribute: "marginheight" in currently active versions.	174
Error	C:\Documents and Settings\Owner\My Documents\pg law\board.html	The tag: "table" doesn't have an attribute: "height" in currently active versions.	211

TIPS

Check It Out!

Many Web designers use a browser called Firefox and install its free Web developers' extension. When you download and install this extension, it places a Web Developer toolbar at the top of the Firefox window. The toolbar includes a menu of validation tools that direct your page to the CSS and HTML validation utilities at the World Wide Web Consortium, or W3C. These utilities check your pages and display warnings and errors so that you can fix them.

Did You Know?

You can find Firefox at www.mozilla.org/products/firefox/ and this page also includes a link to the extensions page where you can find the Web Developer's extension under the Developer's tools category.

VISUAL AIDS:
Show and Hide

You can show and hide the visual aids and invisible elements that Dreamweaver displays in Design view. Sometimes these elements get in the way and make it hard to adjust precise layouts. You can use the Visual Aids menu in the Document toolbar or Dreamweaver's View menu to hide these elements. You can hide all visual aids or you can target specific visual aids. After you hide all visual aids, you can toggle them back on to show previously enabled visual aids.

Dreamweaver provides several categories of visual tools. For example, there are visual aids that help

you troubleshoot your Cascading Style Sheets, and that help you work with tables and frames. Dreamweaver also displays symbols for HTML code that does not display on the page, such as named anchors. Invisible elements allow you to select and modify this code.

See also>>

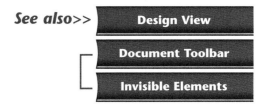

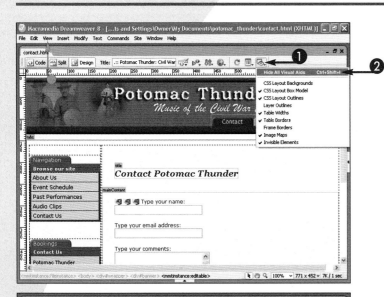

① Click the Visual Aids icon (🖼️) in the Document toolbar.

● You can also click View and then click Visual Aids.

② Click Hide All Visual Aids.

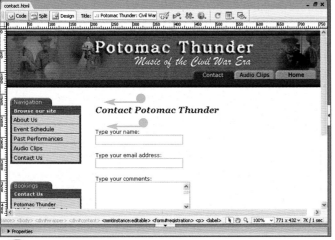

● Dreamweaver hides all visual aids and invisible elements.

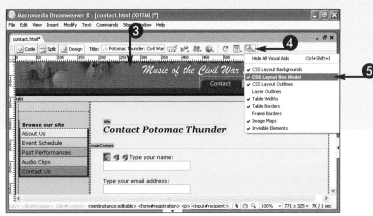

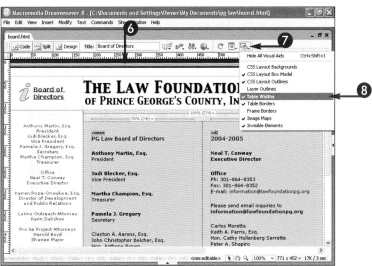

3 Open a document that includes the DIV tag.

4 Click 🔲.

5 Click a CSS option.

This example uses the CSS Layout Box Model option.

Dreamweaver applies the option.

6 Open a document that includes tables.

7 Click 🔲.

8 Click a table option that you want to show or hide.

Dreamweaver shows or hides the table element that you select.

Try This!

When you show and hide invisible elements from the View menu or the Visual Aids menu in the Document toolbar, it is a global operation. If you want to change the visibility of individual invisible elements, then you can do so in the Invisible Elements preferences. You can turn off symbols for default elements, and turn on symbols for other invisibles such as line breaks, comments, and scripts.

More Options!

You can also toggle visual aid options on and off by using the keyboard shortcut combination Ctrl+Shift+I. After you use the keyboard shortcut to hide visual aids, you can use the same keyboard combination to display those visual aids that you have previously enabled.

WEB PAGE PHOTO ALBUM:
Create

If you have Macromedia Fireworks on your computer, then you can use Dreamweaver's Create Web Photo Album command to automatically generate pages of thumbnail images that link to larger views of each image. This command launches Fireworks, which uses a script to create thumbnails and larger images from a target source folder and places them in your designated destination folder.

The Create Web Photo Album command processes any image in your source folder with the following extensions: .jpg, .jpeg, .png, .psd, .tif, or .tiff. You can select from among various GIF and JPEG quality options for the thumbnails and images that go into the gallery Web pages. You can also set the number of columns that you want to use to display thumbnails, select a thumbnail size, and select the option to display filenames under them. You can set the scale of the larger images to a percentage of the originals. You can also have Dreamweaver place each image in its own Web page, or you can link each thumbnail to only the larger image.

See also>> **Macromedia Exchange**

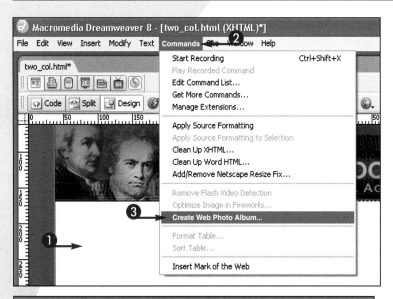

① Open any page in your site.

The Create Web Photo Album command is only available if a page is open.

② Click Commands.

③ Click Create Web Photo Album.

The Create Web Photo Album dialog box appears.

④ Type a Photo album title, subheading, and related information.

⑤ Select options for the thumbnail image display, as well as the thumbnail and image quality and scale.

⑥ Click Browse to navigate to your source images folder.

The source folder does not have to be in your local root folder.

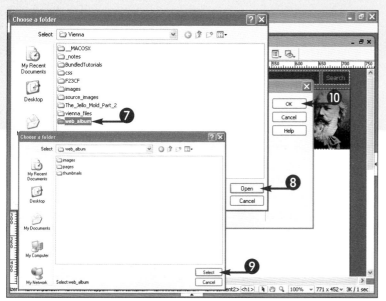

The Choose a folder dialog box appears.

7 Navigate to the folder that you want to use.

8 Click Open (Choose).

A new Choose a folder dialog box appears, displaying the folder contents (Windows only).

9 Click Select to return to the Create Web Photo Album dialog box.

Repeat steps **6** to **9** to select your destination folder.

This destination folder should go in your local root folder.

10 Click OK.

● Fireworks runs a script and displays an alert dialog box when it finishes creating your album.

● Dreamweaver opens the first page of the photo album.

Check It Out!

You can download the Create Photo Album 2.2 extension at the Macromedia Exchange. It has more options than the command in Dreamweaver, and does not require Fireworks if you select the "Create a photo album that includes only navigation pages" option (☐ changes ☑). You can create a custom theme or use one of the many pre-built themes. You can click to include or exclude individual files from multiple-source image folders. You can even customize the navigation style on generated pages.

Check It Out!

The Web Album 2.2 extension is at the Dreamweaver Exchange, which you can reach by clicking Commands, and then clicking Get More Commands. Although the name of the extension is Create Photo Album 2.2 for Dreamweaver MX 2004, it also works in Dreamweaver 8.

WORD DOCUMENT:
Import

You can import a complete Word document into an existing or new Web page. When you are in Design view, Dreamweaver's Import Word Document command converts your document to HTML with the formatting options that you select. It then inserts the converted HTML into your Web page. It includes images, tables, lists, and other objects, and you can import up to 300KB of HTML content from a converted document.

Dreamweaver includes four formatting options from which you can select. Text Only imports only unformatted text. Text with Structure imports basic paragraph, list, and table structure, but does not

retain basic formatting. Text with Structure Plus Basic Formatting imports the structure along with basic formatting such as bold and italics. This option also allows you to remove extra space between paragraphs. Text with Structure Plus Full Formatting imports text with all CSS styles and structure.

See also>>

Clean up Word HTML

Design View

See also>>

Excel Documents

Paste Special

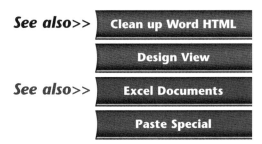

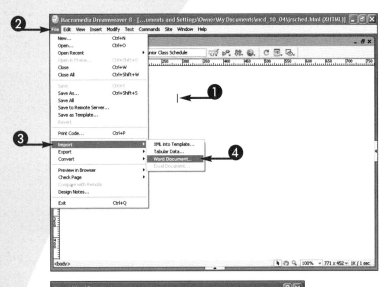

① Click your cursor in the page at the location where you want to import the Word document.

This command works in Design view.

② Click File.

③ Click Import.

④ Click Word Document.

The Import Word Document dialog box appears.

⑤ Navigate to your Word document.

⑥ Click here to select a formatting option.

⑦ Click Open.

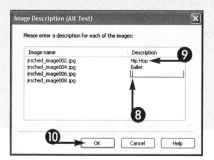

If your document includes images, then the Image Description (Alt Text) dialog box appears.

8 Click in a Description field.

9 Type a description.

10 Click OK.

Dreamweaver imports the Word document.

Try This!

If your Word documents are too large for the Import Word Document command, or you want to import only sections of a document, then you can use the new Paste Special command in the Edit menu. You have the same formatting options, but you can apply them to selected Word text that you copy and paste into your document.

Caution!

If your document uses the Track Changes feature in Word, then Dreamweaver shows deleted words. You can use the Reviewing toolbar in Word to accept or reject changes before importing into Dreamweaver. You can also save two versions of your document, one in which you keep version history, and one that you can use for importing into your Web page.

DYNAMIC WEB PAGES:
Make the Transition

Most of this book teaches you about the techniques you need to make static pages. Dreamweaver also includes many visual tools to help you make basic dynamic pages even if you don't know any programming languages. What exactly is a static or dynamic page, and why would you want to use one as opposed to the other?

Static versus Dynamic Pages

In the early days of the Web, it was common for all parts of a Web page — design and content — to exist within the Web document itself. HTML attributes provided the design for each element on the page. Designers typed or inserted content into the page, and the visitor's browser performed the task of parsing and presenting the page. The pages were *static*, meaning that everything was fixed on the page until the developer edited the page and re-uploaded it.

Dynamic Pages

There is another paradigm you can use that is more efficient for many kinds of Web pages. If you review any of this book's Cascading Style Sheet topics, especially those about external style sheets, you know that current "best practices" suggest that Web developers separate the presentation, or design, of a page from its content. All the design elements for the page go into a central document that Dreamweaver links in the head of each page. With dynamic pages, developers take this concept one step further. Not only is the design of the page not hard coded into the Web page, but most of the content itself is not on the page either. When the visitor arrives at a dynamic page, its scripts interact with a server and pull the content in at *runtime*, sometimes from a database, sometimes as output from a script, and sometimes as the result of interactions with the visitor. Now the HTML page only includes the *logic*, or the structure and code, that provide the directions

for bringing everything together when the visitor comes to a page.

Why Go Dynamic?

While using static pages is still a good choice for many sites, there are situations in which dynamic pages are the way to go. These may include some of the following:

- E-commerce
- Search engines
- Guestbooks
- Blogs
- Log in, or authentication systems
- Content Management systems

Most of these dynamic applications make use of databases. For example, a visitor might respond to a blog entry by typing a comment into a form. When the visitor clicks the Submit button, the comment then goes into a database on the server, and the server uses a script to pull the comment out of the database and translate it into a format that the browser understands. The blog content is fluid and continually changing; the entries and comments are not hard coded on the page, but reside in a database until a script pulls them out and presents them to the visitor.

Prepare to Go Dynamic

Dynamic pages in Dreamweaver require more preparation than static pages. While there are dialog boxes that let you visually set up basic dynamic pages, they do not work out-of-the-box. You must first configure your computer and/or the server as well as acquire some fundamental skills. You must also make some essential decisions before you begin:

- You must choose a server model
- You must choose a database system

Select a Server Model

Your browser only interprets markup, CSS, and some JavaScript. Dynamic pages require a *server model* that processes the dynamic code and outputs it into something your browser understands. Dreamweaver supports a number of popular server models, and the one you decide to use depends on what is available on your Web host's server:

- If you use a Linux or UNIX host with an Apache server, you can use PHP Hypertext Processor (PHP), an open-source technology.

- If you host your site on a Windows server that includes Internet Information Services (IIS), you can use Active Server Pages (ASP) or ASP.NET.

- If you have a Web host that provides it, you can use Macromedia's proprietary server technology, ColdFusion. ColdFusion is a tag-based technology that many designers find easier to grasp than scripting languages.

- If your Web host provides a Java-based server such as Tomcat or WebSphere, you can use Java Server Pages (JSP), a robust but more complex solution that may prove overwhelming to those new to dynamic pages.

Select a Database System

You also need to choose a database system, a decision you can make in tandem with your choice of server model. For example, most hosts who offer PHP provide MySQL as the database system that you can use with it. Some of the most common database systems are as follows:

- **Access:** The big advantage of Access is that many people already have the application on their computers. Access provides a file-based database, easily recognized by the .mdb extension. The disadvantage of Access is that it is not a good choice for serious Web applications or if you have more than 15 visitors using your database-driven page at one time.

- **MySQL:** A natural for working with PHP in Dreamweaver, it is an open-source database system that many Web hosts provide in their feature set. It is fast and robust, and lets you store large amounts of data.

- **Microsoft SQL Server:** A Microsoft database system that integrates with the Windows operating system, it is a good choice for developers who want to use ASP and .NET as their server models and need a database more robust than Access.

- **Oracle:** An enterprise-level database system that runs on multiple platforms, it is a good choice for large organizations and companies.

There are many other popular database systems such as FileMaker Pro and PostgreSQL that Dreamweaver doesn't natively support. No matter which database you decide to use, learning about the Structured Query Language (SQL) will make working with databases easier. You can take a free course, complete with online interpreter, at www.sqlcourse.com.

DYNAMIC WEB PAGES:
Create the Pages in Dreamweaver

After you make the decision of which server model and database combination you want to use, you must set up your computer and Dreamweaver. To use your computer as a testing server, you must configure it to understand your server model, define the dynamic Dreamweaver site, and let Dreamweaver connect to your database.

Set Up the Testing Server

You can develop your dynamic pages directly on the host's server, or you can develop and test them on your local computer as long as you set it up as a testing server. When you create a static site, you usually develop the pages on your own computer and then upload a mirror of the site to the live server. You can do the same with dynamic pages as long as your computer configuration supports the server technology that the Web host uses. For example, if your Web host offers you PHP, you must configure your computer to process PHP pages. There are advantages to developing your pages locally from the privacy of your computer, and many tutorials can help you configure the different server models. Depending on your platform, some server technologies work more seamlessly than others.

The Mac already has an Apache Web server built into its shipping installation. You can turn it on with the click of a button in the System preferences. PHP is also a part of the configuration, but you do have to enable it by typing some commands in the terminal. Finally, you have to install the MySQL database server. You can also set up a PC to test PHP dynamic pages. You can download visual installers at the following resources. Macromedia provides a free

developer version of ColdFusion that you can use for testing purposes on your own computer. Macromedia recently created a visual installer for the Macintosh and now fully supports ColdFusion on the Mac as well as the PC. For a complete listing of the various sites that can help you with setting up a test server, refer to the following tables.

If you have Windows 2000 or XP Professional, your computer may already have the IIS software it needs to develop ASP and ASP.NET pages. If you have Microsoft Office Professional, you already have the Access database application. You can learn more at the Macromedia Devnet ASP.NET topic center: www.macromedia.com/devnet/dotnet/.

PHP and MySQL on the Mac	
Web Site	*Description*
www.swanilda.com/unix4.html	Has complete configuration directions.
developer.apple.com/internet/opensource/php.htm	Includes information about PHP on the Mac.
www.entropy.ch/software/macosx/mysql	Has directions for installing MySQL.
www.serverlogistics.com/downloads.php	If you are squeamish about using the Terminal and typing commands, you can download visual installers here.
www.phpmyadmin.net/home_page/index.php	For a graphical user interface (GUI) for MySQL, you can download the free open-source application phpMyAdmin here.

PHP and MySQL on the PC	
Web Site	Description
httpd.apache.org/ download.cgi	Information on the Apache server
dev.mysql.com/downloads/	Information on MySQL
www.php.net/downloads. php	Information on PHP
www.communitymx.com/ content/article.cfm?cid= 59334	Complete directions for installing all the necessary pieces

ColdFusion on the Mac and PC	
Web Site	Description
www.communitymx.com/ abstract.cfm?cid=BFAE6	A complete guide for installing the developer edition of ColdFusion on the Macintosh. This article costs $3.00.
www.macromedia.com/ cfusion/tdrc/index.cfm? product=coldfusion	If your installer CD does not include the latest copy of the free ColdFusion Developer Edition, you can download it for Linux, Mac OS X, or Windows here.

Create the Site Definition

Before you can begin developing your dynamic pages, you need to create a Site Definition. You can use the Testing Server category of the Site Definition dialog box or page through the wizard screens in the Basic tab to set up your testing server so that you can develop the dynamic pages on your local computer. You can read about setting up your Testing Server on this Macromedia tech note page: /www.macromedia.com/cfusion/ knowledgebase/index.cfm?id=tn_14028.

Connect to the Database

To use a database in Dreamweaver, you must set up a connection to it. After you create the connection, Dreamweaver adds a Connections folder to your site. Inside this folder there is a page with the extension appropriate for your server model that includes a script with the necessary parameters to let Dreamweaver interact with your database. You create connections to the database by using the Databases panel that is part of the Application panel set.

The Application Panel Set

The Application panel set includes four panels that cover most of the basic dynamic tasks. You can access the panels by using the Window menu and then one of the four Application panel names: Databases, Bindings, Server Behaviors, or Components. This opens the entire panel group. There is also an Application category in the Insert bar, and there is an Application Objects menu in the Insert menu.

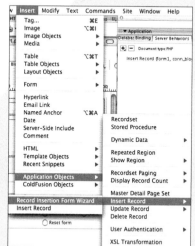

DYNAMIC WEB PAGES:
Create the Pages in Dreamweaver (Continued)

Bindings

This panel lets you define and edit sources of dynamic content, insert dynamic content in a page, and apply data formats to dynamic text. You can use this panel to define URL parameters, session variables, application variables for ASP and ColdFusion, and server variables. You can also cache content sources, change or delete content sources, copy a recordset from one page to another page, and make HTML attributes dynamic.

Database

The Databases panel lets you create connections to the database, to examine the content of your database tables, and to insert database-related code in your pages. With this panel, you can connect to a database and view your database within Dreamweaver.

Server Behaviors

You can access Dreamweaver's built-in server behaviors from the Server Behaviors panel, the Application category of the Insert bar, or the Application Objects menu in the Insert menu. Dreamweaver provides a visual interface for applying complex behaviors to the page. The Server Behaviors panel lets you accomplish the following:

- Define a recordset from a database to which you already made a connection.
- Use the Repeat Region behavior to display multiple records on a single page, specifying the number of records that you want to display per page.
- Create and insert a dynamic table into a page, and associate the table with a recordset.
- Insert a dynamic text object into a page and apply any of the Dreamweaver data formats to it.
- Create record navigation and status controls, master/detail pages, and forms for updating, inserting, and deleting information in a database.

You can also write your own Dreamweaver server behaviors or install server behaviors that other developers create.

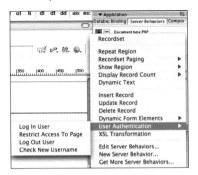

Components

You can use the Components panel to visually define a ColdFusion component and its functions. Dreamweaver creates a .cfc file and inserts the necessary CFML tags for you. After you click the Plus button on the Components panel, the Create Component dialog box opens for you to complete.

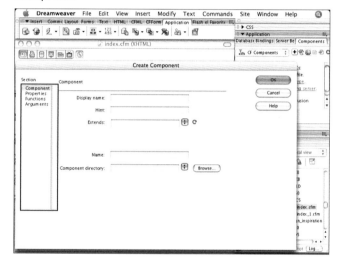

Where to Begin

Before you create dynamic pages, it helps to learn how to create forms and use form objects. This book includes many topics on this subject. You might also familiarize yourself with database design and the Structured Query Language (SQL). This makes designing your dynamic pages and working with databases easier. For more on the curriculum for a course that teaches students to create their first dynamic pages, visit: www.communitymx.com/content/article.cfm?cid=70A1A.

Café Townsend Dynamic Site

To create your first database-driven page, you can also start with the tutorial files for the Café Townsend Web site that Macromedia includes in the Dreamweaver application folder. You can find the folder on a PC at the following location: C:\Program Files\Macromedia\Dreamweaver 8\Tutorial_assets\cafe_townsend\. You can find the folder on the Macintosh in the following location: Macintosh HD/Applications/Macromedia Dreamweaver 8/Tutorial_assets/cafe_townsend.

You can follow along with the Café Townsend tutorial in the Dreamweaver Help files to learn how to define a recordset, display the database records, add dynamic fields to a table, create a repeated region, view your page with Live Data, and create a record insert form.

Dreamweaver Devnet

You can visit the Devnet pages to find tutorials and articles on creating dynamic pages. After you are comfortable with the basic Dreamweaver server application tools, you can make informed decisions about whether any given page will work best as a static or dynamic page.

Dreamweaver Devnet Sites	
Web Site	*Description*
www.macromedia.com/devnet/dreamweaver/	The Dreamweaver Development Center home page
www.macromedia.com/devnet/topics/databases.html	Dreamweaver and Databases
www.macromedia.com/devnet/dreamweaver/articles/going_dynamic.html	Going dynamic with Dreamweaver
www.macromedia.com/devnet/dreamweaver/articles/php_blog1.html	Creating a blog with Dreamweaver and PHP

CASCADING STYLE SHEETS:
A Guide to CSS Topics

With this guide to CSS, you can discover the "best practice" approach to your work. Using Cascading Style Sheets (CSS) is one of the most important modern technologies you can learn as you develop your Web design skills. This book strives to comprehensively cover all of Dreamweaver's features. In many cases, Dreamweaver gives you multiple ways to access tools and commands with different methods to accomplish the same task. In addition, the Web is evolving rapidly, and old-fashioned and modern techniques exist side by side. Dreamweaver includes some legacy methods, in large part to give you the opportunity to maintain older sites. When developing new sites, you should attempt to apply "best practices" whenever possible.

Working with Legacy Methods

Until recently, most developers mixed the design of the document with its content. They used HTML attributes such as `<align>` and tags such as `<font>`:

```
<div align="center"><font color="#FF0000"
size="3" face="Arial, Helvetica,
sans-serif">
The Old Fashioned Way</font> </div>
```

There were many problems with this method, not the least of which was that you had to apply this markup over and over to format each individual heading, span of text, and any other elements on the page. CSS provides a much better way.

The CSS Advantage

The advantages of CSS are so numerous and obvious that you will want to start learning to use it right away.

- Whether your CSS is embedded in the head of the document, or especially if it is in an external style sheet, the resulting lean and uncluttered pages load faster and exhibit fewer problems.
- You can quickly perform sitewide changes in one central file, saving you enormous time and ensuring consistency across all pages.
- The separation of content and design lets you use one HTML page for multiple browsing experiences; you can attach appropriate style sheets that change the look of the page depending on whether the visitor views the page with alternate devices such as a Blackberry or screen reader.
- Pages designed with CSS provide better accessibility for people with disabilities.
- Pages designed with CSS achieve better search engine optimization with their higher content ratio in the HTML document.
- You can validate your CSS at the World Wide Web Consortium's online validator at jigsaw. w3.org/css-validator/validator-uri.html to ensure that your code is error-free and thus more likely to display properly in browsers.

Even if these advantages do not matter to you, you can enjoy the benefits of greater typographical and design control that CSS provides. For example, there is no way in HTML to add space between your lines of text. CSS offers line-height so you can do just that. The additional CSS features give you many of the myriad options that until recently were only available to print designers.

Suggested Course of Study

To quickly understand CSS, you can approach the large number of CSS topics in this book in a codified manner. You must first make sure you have Dreamweaver's CSS features set up properly. You can do that by investigating the CSS Preferences, and then familiarizing yourself with the CSS panel group and dialog box.

After you decide what CSS method you want to use on your pages and site, you can proceed to the topics on the different kinds of selectors: tags, classes, and IDs and pseudo classes.

The last CSS topics you might explore are those dealing with positioning. You will probably some day want to wean yourself from using tables to lay out pages and use CSS positioning techniques instead. The book includes topics that cover all the positioning types Dreamweaver offers in the Positioning category of the CSS panel.

The following tables give a list of the various tools and techniques to review grouped in the suggested order of study.

CSS Preferences and CSS Panel Groups

Subject	Tool/Technique
CSS Preferences	PREFERENCES: CSS Styles (Tool)
	PREFERENCES: General (Tool)
CSS Panel Group	CSS STYLES PANEL: View Options (Tool)
	CSS STYLES: Create a New Rule (Tool)
	CSS RULE DEFINITION WINDOW: Create New Rules (Tool)
	ATTACH AND DETACH: Cascading Style Sheets (Technique)
	CSS: Create Embedded Style Sheet (Technique)
	CSS: Create External Style Sheet (Technique)
	CSS, INLINE STYLES: Create (Technique)
	CSS, EXPORT STYLES: From the Document Head (Technique)

Types of Selectors

Subject	Technique
Redefine Tags	CSS STYLING: Style Heading Appearance
	CSS STYLING: Style List Objects
	CSS STYLING: Style Forms
	CSS STYLING: Tables and Cells
	BORDERS: Style with CSS
CSS Classes	CUSTOM CLASSES: Create and Apply
	ALIGN IMAGES: To Text with CSS
Advanced IDs and Pseudo Classes	CSS STYLING: Control Link Appearance
	DESCENDENT SELECTORS: Create and Use
	DIV TAGS: Insert, Position, Name

Types of Selectors (continued)

Subject	Technique
Edit Styles	CSS, EDIT RULES: From the CSS Panel
Alternative Style Sheets for Media Types	CSS, MEDIA TYPE STYLE SHEETS: Create and Attach
	STYLE RENDERING TOOLBAR: View Page

CSS and Positioning

Subject	Technique
Positioning Objects	CSS, POSITIONING: Overview
Absolute Positioning	CSS, POSITIONING: Using Absolute Positioning
Floats	CSS, POSITIONING: Using Floats for Positioning
Relative Positioning	CSS, POSITIONING: Using Relative Positioning
Static Positioning	CSS, POSITIONING: Using Static Positioning

Your First CSS Layout

A gentle way to enter the world of CSS positioning is to use a CSS template such as the one Adrian Senior created for Community MX, an online tutorial site. This free CSS layout has two columns in a fixed-width, centered layout. There is a Fireworks source PNG that you can modify to brand with your own logos, graphics, and colors. The template comes bundled with a number of articles that fully explain the techniques Mr. Senior used to create the structure and design. You can download the package at www.communitymx.com/abstract.cfm?cid=D6D77.

Dreamweaver also provides CSS designs that you can access from its Start page. The book also has a Tool, "START PAGE: Using to Initiate Tasks," which describes the Start page.

CASCADING STYLE SHEETS:
A Guide to CSS Topics (Continued)

Hacks and Problems

CSS may seem like a dream come true, but you should be aware that the various browsers implement CSS in unique ways. This is particularly true for positioned pages. First, there are the "standards-compliant browsers" that try to follow the standards recommendations as closely as possible. There are still bugs and variations among them, but these are minor compared to the problems Internet Explorer presents.

Internet Explorer's bugs are too numerous and complex to list here, but you will overcome many of its rendering issues if you understand the box model. You can read a detailed article called *The Box Model Problem* at Community MX: www.communitymx.com/content/article.cfm?cid=20B41.

In summary, the box model problem occurs because Internet Explorer 5 and 5.5, as well as Internet Explore 6 when there is no Doctype on the page, interpret the box model differently than standards-compliant browsers. Blocks of content can have margins, padding, and borders around them. Most browsers add padding and border measurements to the dimensions you allocate for your content element. Internet Explorer, in the circumstances stated above, subtracts those measurements. For example, if you set a DIV to 400 pixels, and then add 10 pixels of padding and 2-pixel borders to both sides, a standards-compliant browser will read the total as 424 pixels. Internet Explorer, however, interprets the total as 376 pixels because it subtracts the padding and borders from the DIV width. (Margins are exempt from the box model problem.) If you have layouts that need to be pixel-precise, you will run into broken layouts.

Because of this and other browser rendering problems, creative Web developers have come up with ways to work around browser anomalies.

Box Model Fix

Many designers use what are called CSS hacks to work around browser anomalies. There is a well-known hack that you can use to fix box model problems in older versions of Internet Explorer. You can read a detailed explanation of this solution at the article mentioned earlier. You only need to modify the code by adding the element name you need to target and the measurements you want to adjust.

```
* html add your selector here {
width: new value; /* for IE 5*/
w\idth: original value; /* For IE 6 and IE
Mac */
}
```

Here are some good resources for learning about hacks and browser quirks. The second is for common coding problems with HTML and CSS:

- www.positioniseverything.net/
- www.communitymx.com/content/article.cfm?cid=A8E2DC392C467EEA

Provide a Doctype

As mentioned above, you should provide a proper doctype so that the browser can interpret your pages properly. The article, *Rendering Mode and Doctype Switching*, gives a thorough explanation of this topic. You can read the article at Community MX: www.communitymx.com/content/article.cfm?cid=E2F258C46D285FEE. You can also explore the following Tool from this book: DOCUMENT TYPE DECLARATION: Set and Modify Document Types.

Internet Explorer Conditional Comments

The plot thickens when Microsoft releases Internet Explorer 7, which will probably occur by the time you read this book. Microsoft is attempting to bring the latest version of its browser into better standards compliance. This means that it will no longer succumb to many of the current hacks that developers use to deal with its problems. Designers may need to deal with its remaining issues in another way. Fortunately, Microsoft addresses the problems of CSS rendering in Internet Explorer for Windows by offering something called Conditional Comments.

Starting with Internet Explorer 5, Microsoft created a way to use normal HTML comments and let IE browsers look inside and parse the code it finds there. Other browsers, including Internet Explorer 5 for Mac, do not read the styles inside the Conditional Comments, and completely ignore them. Thus, you can write CSS that only the versions of Internet Explorer you specify will parse. You can still use CSS hacks that fix older versions of Internet Explorer without harming the CSS you use for Internet Explorer 7. You can embed the styles in one page by using the style element, or you can create a link to an external style sheet where you can centralize all the styles you want to use just for Internet Explorer.

How to Write Conditional Comments

To target all versions of Internet Explorer, you can write your Conditional Comment like this:

```
<!--[if IE]>
<style>your styles here </style>
<![endif]-->
```

You can also insert a link to an Internet Explorer–only style sheet within Conditional Comments:

```
<!--[if IE]>
<link rel="stylesheet" type="text/css"
href="only-ie.css" />
<![endif]-->
```

You can also target individual versions of Internet Explorer, such as Internet Explorer 6:

```
!--[if IE 6]>
<style>your styles here </style>
<![endif]-->
```

You can use "greater than or equal to" if you want to target a group of versions within a specific range, such as 5.5 and above:

```
<!--[if gte IE 5.5 ]>
<style>your styles here</style>
<![endif]-->
```

You can learn more about Conditional Comments at these resources:

- Read all about Conditional Comments at the Microsoft Web site: msdn.microsoft.com/workshop/author/dhtml/overview/ccomment_ovw.asp.

- Read an article about preparing your sites for Internet Explorer 7: www.communitymx.com/content/article.cfm?page=1&cid=C6160.

Resources

The time you spend learning to use CSS will give you many rewards and will enrich the pages and sites you design. As you delve more deeply into the subject of CSS, you can explore these preeminent Web sites:

- Web site of CSS guru Eric Meyer: www.meyerweb.com/eric/css/.

- Web site of Web Standards evangelist, Jeffrey Zeldman: www.zeldman.com/.

- Web site of the Web Standards Group: www.webstandards.org/.

- Web site devoted to the "beauty of CSS," it features multiple designs for the same HTML document: www.csszengarden.com/.

You can also read about the curriculum for a course that teaches CSS within Dreamweaver at Community MX. The article name is *Teaching Dreamweaver the Web Standards Way* and you can find it at www.communitymx.com/content/article.cfm?cid=777DBwww.communitymx.com/content/article.cfm?cid=777DB.

Index

Symbols and Numbers

@ symbol, 249

A

<a> tag, 340
a:active state, 216
aberrant box model, 175
absolute links, 66, 344–345
absolute positioning
    absolutely positioned columns, 210
    absolutely positioned elements, 209, 213
    absolutely positioned layouts, 212
    overview, 208–209
Access Key attribute, 291
accessibility
    creating reports about, 136–137
    editing preferences, 2
    of forms, 45, 280–281
    guidelines, 75
    reports, 136–137
Accessibility Attributes dialog box, 45
Acrobat Reader, 345
Action text box, 286
actions, 160
Active Directory, 189
Active Server Pages (ASP), 441
add spacing attributes, 319
adding
    borders
        with CSS, 174–175
        to images, 172–173
    comments, to Code view, 184
    Excel styles to Style menu, 250
Address bar, 344
Adjust Position command, 429
Adobe Photoshop, 82, 159
Advanced menu, 216
advanced selectors, 274
Advanced tab, Site Definition dialog box,
    232, 236–237
a:focus state, 216
a:hover state, 216, 221
<align> tag, 446

aligning
    images to text
        with CSS (Cascading Style Sheets), 138–139
        with HTML, 142–143
    text within documents (HTML), 144–145
a:link state, 216
anchors, 343, 346–347
Apache Web server, 442
Appearance screen, 360
Appleworks, 322
Application category, Insert toolbar, 50, 443, 444
Application Objects menu, Insert menu, 443, 444
Application panel set, 443
Apply Source Formatting option, 77
Arrange Panels command, Window menu, 365
ASP (Active Server Pages), 441
ASP.net form control methods, 278
assets
    frequently used, storing, 33
    managing with Assets panel, 148–149
    organizing and managing, 3
Assets panel
    and applying templates to new pages, 407
    assigning Favorites to, 254–255
    Colors category, 182
    copying objects from other sites via, 193
    and editing of Library items, 334, 336
    Favorites section, 33
    inserting images with, 316
    inserting objects with, 146–147
    Library category, 65
    managing assets with, 148–149
    organizing and managing site assets, 3
    Templates category, 359
    viewing all columns of information in, 364
assigning
    Favorites to Assets panel, 254–255
    properties to columns, 16
Attach External Style Sheet dialog box, 150, 151,
    200, 202
Attach icon, 197
Attach Label Tag, 45
attributes
    Access Key attribute, 291
    Accessibility Attributes dialog box, 45
    add spacing attributes, 319

Index

Index

Index

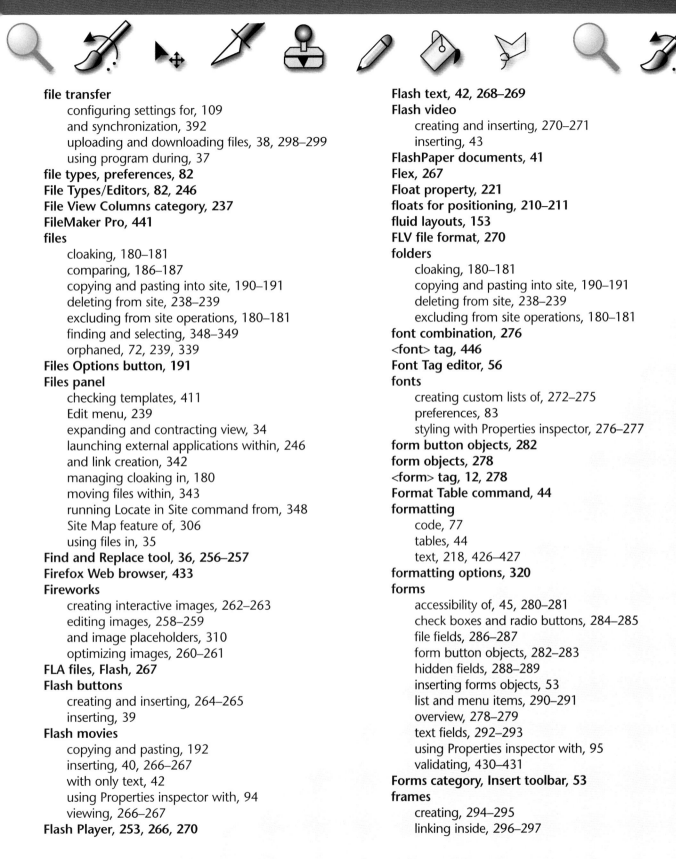

Index

Index

M

Macintosh Finder, 190

Macintosh workspace, 130

Macromedia ColdFusion
component, defining, 445
developer version of, 442
home page name, 306
overview, 441
references, 101

Macromedia Contribute, 188–189, 419

Macromedia Devnet ASP.NET topic center, 442

Macromedia Exchange, 253
getting button styles from, 265
getting extensions from, 39, 350–351, 385,
431, 437

Macromedia Fireworks. *See* Fireworks

Macromedia Flex, 267

Macromedia Homesite, 131

magnification, in document window, 67

Maintain Synchronization Information, 109

Manage Sites dialog box, 68, 235

Manage Workspace Layouts dialog box, 129

margin property, 145

master template file, 417

Match Case, 36

Match Whole Word, 36

MDI (Multiple Document Interface), 131

Media menu, 384

media type style sheets, 202–203

Menu bar, 325

menu commands, 328

menu items, on forms, 290–291

Menu option, 290, 291

menus
Advanced, 216
Application Objects, 443, 444
Characters, 386
Column Header, 152
contextual, 180, 204, 299, 348
Edit, 193, 239, 261
Insert, 443, 444
Insert Media, 41
jump, 326–327
Media, 384
Modify, 337, 355

Save As option, 251
Style, 230, 250, 426, 427
View, 112, 113, 301, 303, 353, 429, 434, 435
View Options, 124
Visual Aids, 434, 435
Window, 365
Workspace Layout, 129, 131, 362

Meta dialog box, 352

MetaTags, 48, 141, 352–353

Microsoft Excel documents, 250–251, 320–321

Microsoft Office Professional, 442

Microsoft SQL Server, 441

Microsoft Visual SourceSafe, 189

Microsoft Word documents
importing, 438–439
inserting, 320–321

MIME encoding format, 95

Modify menu, 337, 355

monitor resolution, 69, 92

Move Behavior Down, 161

Move Behavior Up, 161

movies. *See also* Flash movies
QuickTime, 192, 385

moving files, within Files panel, 343

MP3 files, 192

multi-line text box, 223

Multiple Document Interface (MDI), 131

multiple-line text field wraps, 293

multiple-source image folders, 437

MySQL, 441, 442

N

Name attribute, 352

Navigation bar, 354–355

navigation column, 210

navigation objects, 424

nested templates, 416–417

nesting, 173, 396

Netscape, 87, 151, 162

New CSS Rule dialog box, 194, 216, 230

New CSS Style button, 244

New Document dialog box, 197, 356

New Document window, 70, 113, 114, 235

Index

Index

Index

Index

Read Less–Learn More®

Visual®

There's a Visual book for every learning level...

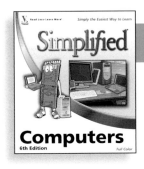

Simplified®

The place to start if you're new to computers. Full color.

- Computers
- Mac OS
- Office
- Windows

Teach Yourself VISUALLY™

Get beginning to intermediate-level training in a variety of topics. Full color.

- Computers
- Crocheting
- Digital Photography
- Dreamweaver
- Excel
- Guitar
- HTML
- Knitting
- Mac OS
- Office
- Photoshop
- Photoshop Elements
- PowerPoint
- Windows
- Word

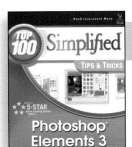

Top 100 Simplified® Tips & Tricks

Tips and techniques to take your skills beyond the basics. Full color.

- Digital Photography
- eBay
- Excel
- Google
- Internet
- Mac OS
- Photoshop
- Photoshop Elements
- PowerPoint
- Windows

Build It Yourself VISUALLY™

Do it yourself the visual way and without breaking the bank. Full color.

- Game PC
- Media Center PC

...all designed for visual learners—just like you!

Master VISUALLY®

Step up to intermediate-to-advanced technical knowledge.
Two-color interior.

- 3ds max
- Creating Web Pages
- Dreamweaver and Flash
- Excel VBA Programming
- iPod and iTunes
- Mac OS
- Optimizing PC Performance
- Photoshop Elements
- QuickBooks
- Quicken
- Windows Server
- Windows

Visual Blueprint™

Where to go for professional-level programming instruction.
Two-color interior.

- Excel Data Analysis
- Excel Programming
- HTML
- JavaScript
- PHP

Visual Encyclopedia™

Your A to Z reference of tools and techniques. Full color.

- Dreamweaver
- Photoshop
- Windows

For a complete listing of Visual books,
go to wiley.com/go/visualtech

Visual
An Imprint of WILEY
Now you know.